Table of Contents

Preface

Land reclamation encompasses remediation of industrial wasteland, improvement of infertile land for agricultural production, preservation of wetlands, and restoration of disturbed areas. Land reclamation is an integral part of sustainable development which aims to reconcile economic productivity with environmental preservation. During the 1980s, significant progress was achieved in the application of advanced technologies to sustainable development projects. The goal of this international symposium was to serve as a forum to review current research and state-of-the-art technology dealing with various aspects of land reclamation, and provide an opportunity for professional interaction and exchange of information in a multi-disciplinary setting.

The scope of the symposium was as broad as the topic itself. The keynote address by Professor John Cairns focused on a systems approach in land restoration projects and challenges facing scientists in global biotic impoverishment. Other topics discussed in ten technical sessions included development and applications of computer models, geographic information systems, remote sensing technology, salinity problems, surface and ground water monitoring, reclamation of mined areas, soil amendment methods and impacts, wetland restoration techniques, and land use planning for resource protection.

The symposium was sponsored by the American Society of Agricultural Engineers (SW263, SW264) and co-sponsored by 14 professional organizations and government agencies. Cooperating organizations and members of planning committees are listed on the following page. Their cooperation ensured the success of the symposium.

We would especially like to acknowledge the contribution of authors, from a dozen countries, who provided a worldwide view of reclamation projects and made the publication of these proceedings possible.

It is our hope that you will find these proceedings a valuable source of information for planning and implementation of reclamation projects as well as a good reference for future research.

Tamim Younos
Symposium Chairman
Department of Agricultural Engineering
Virginia Polytechnic Institute and State University
Blacksburg, VA 24061-0303 USA

Committees and Sponsors

Sponsored by:

The American Society of Agricultural Engineers
2950 Niles Rd.
St. Joseph, MI 49085-9659 USA
Phone: 616.429.0300

Cooperating Organizations:

American Society of Agronomy
American Society of Civil Engineers
American Water Resources Association
Association of Ground Water Scientists and Engineers
Land Improvement Contractors Association
National Association of Conservation Districts
Soil & Water Conservation Society of America
Soil Science Society of America
U. S. Bureau of Land Reclamation
U. S. Geological Survey
USDA Agricultural Research Service
USDA Soil Conservation Service
USDI Office of Surface Mining
Water Environment Federation

Symposium Planning Committee:

T. Younos, Symposium Chairman
W. F. Ritter, Program Chairman
M. R. Ice, Finances
W. L. Magette
K. M. Mancl
H. A. Elliott
R. A. Wiles

LAND RESTORATION: WHERE DO WE GO FROM HERE?

John Cairns, Jr.*

Natural ecosystems provide a variety of services essential to the survival of human society. Among these services are: micro- and macroclimate modification, production of oxygen, and transformation of societal wastes. If ecosystem services per capita are to be maintained at their present level while the human population grows to 10 billion sometime in the next century, ecosystem services must be expanded through ecological restoration. Although the ecological predictive capability is not as robust as it should be, and the outcome of restoration is less certain than we would like, we do not have the time for extensive research before undertaking restoration. We must learn by doing. Land restoration will prove to be an acid test of ecological understanding of ecosystem structure and function. Fortunately, restoration has proven surprisingly successful in that the result is almost always ecologically superior to the damaged condition. For the remainder of this century and certainly well into the next, a primary focus will be at the landscape level. That is, restoration projects must be undertaken not in isolation from each other but in a systems context. A notable feature will be the abandonment of fragmented environmental management (where each agency and discipline act as if they are the only flower facing the sun) and the implementation of integrated environmental management that takes into consideration aggregate effects and balances benefits in one sector against costs in another sector. Agronomists, foresters, horticulturalists, agricultural economists, soils specialists, and wildlife biologists must learn to work on interdisciplinary teams with engineers, ecologists, hydrologists, sociologists, and a number of other disciplines. One of the biggest challenges facing practitioners of ecologist restoration is global biotic impoverishment or reduction in biodiversity, which means that the genetic pool of species suitable for a wide variety of restoration projects is being dramatically and steadily reduced. This necessarily limits the options because the more species available for restoration projects, the more likely that precisely the right ones will be utilized.

ARE RESTORATION AND RECLAMATION SYNONYMOUS?

The term <u>restoration</u> is used in numerous regulations and public laws when what is meant is <u>reclamation</u>, <u>rehabilitation</u>, or <u>mitigation</u>. In 1937, the U.S. Congress enacted the Federal Aid

JOHN CAIRNS, JR., University Distinguished Professor of Environmental Biology, Department of Biology, and Director, University Center for Environmental and Hazardous Materials Studies, Virginia Polytechnic Institute and State University, Blacksburg, Virginia.

to Wildlife Restoration Act (P.L. 75-415), which was intended to aid wildlife restoration projects. However, in the statement of purpose, the terms restoration and rehabilitation are used interchangeably. Further, the bill deals only with "...improvement of areas of land or water adaptable as feeding, resting, or breeding places for wildlife..." More recently, a memorandum of agreement between the U.S. Army Corps of Engineers and the U.S. Environmental Protection Agency (1990) defines restoration as "measures undertaken to return the existing fish and wildlife habitat resources to a modern historic condition [emphasis mine]. Restoration then includes mitigation as well as some increments of enhancement." Mitigation as defined in Webster's Third New International Dictionary is simply the alleviating of any or all detrimental effects arising from a given action. Mitigation need not, and often does not, involve in-kind restoration or creation. The National Research Council [NRC](1991) defines restoration as the return of an ecosystem to a close approximation of its condition prior to its disturbance. Cairns (1991) states that "restoration might be defined as the resetting of an 'ecological clock'." However, should the clock be set to: (a) the time just before the disturbance occurred (i.e., a close approximation of ecological condition prior to disturbance) or (b) the present time, but an ecologically-superior condition compatible with the landscape in which the damaged patch, however large, occurs (i.e., a close approximation of the condition that natural succession would have produced had no damage occurred)? In either case, Cairns (1991) indicates that restoration means recreating both the structure and the function of the damaged ecosystem. Unfortunately, restoration is rarely perfect, and predisturbance condition frequently may not be a viable option (Cairns, 1989). It is important to remember that restoration is an intent (albeit possibly not achievable in full) to return and repair a damaged ecosystem to a former natural condition! The terms creation, reclamation, and rehabilitation imply putting a landscape to a new or altered use to serve a particular human societal purpose. Reclamation is a process designed to adapt a wild or natural resource to serve a utilitarian, human purpose. This means putting a natural resource to a new or altered use. It is often used to refer to processes that destroy native ecosystems and convert them to agricultural or urban uses. Rehabilitation, on the other hand, is used primarily to indicate improvements of a visual nature to a natural resource -- putting back into good condition or working order; in short, restoring ecological attributes of particular interest to human society but not all ecological attributes. Creation is a relatively new term in this regard and generally means bringing into being a new ecosystem that previously did not exist on a particular site. For example, a wetland might be created on a site that was formerly forested but then surface mined. This has been done in Florida where phosphate mining occurred (e.g., Pratt and Cairns, 1985). Preservation is the maintenance or protection of an existing ecosystem presumably in good condition or it would not be worth preserving.

Unfortunately, these terms are used in different contexts in different disciplines and professions and often are used as synonyms when they should not be. Regrettably, they are often used without being defined in the context in which they are used, leaving those outside of a particular specialty (and often even those within a particular specialty) to guess what is meant.

THREE FUTURE SCENARIOS FOR THE RELATIONSHIP BETWEEN
HUMAN SOCIETY AND NATURAL SYSTEMS

There are only three options to consider regarding the
relationship between human society and natural systems: (1)
continue destruction of natural systems at the present rate and
hope that the ecosystem services upon which human society depends
will continue; (2) restore natural systems at a rate equal to the
present rate of destruction to obtain a no-net-loss situation;
(3) restore natural systems at a rate in excess of damage, thus
building up ecological capital (Cairns, in press). The course of
continued destruction without restoration (option 1) appears
philosophically unacceptable to most human societies. A no-net-
loss situation (option 2) would mean that ecosystem services per
capita would be reduced as long as the human population keeps
growing. An extended discussion of ecosystem services is given
in Ehrlich and Ehrlich (1991). Briefly stated, illustrative
ecosystem services are maintaining the atmospheric gas balance,
improving water quality, regulating micro and macro climatic
effects, transforming societal wastes into less harmful
materials, etc. If ecosystem services per capita are to be
maintained at present levels (option 3) while the population
increases to 10 billion some time in the next century, the rate
of restoration of systems must exceed the rate of destruction by
a substantial margin (Cairns and Pratt, in press). Since
restoration ecology is a newly developing field, every
restoration project undertaken is partly and perhaps entirely
experimental. As a consequence, considerable flexibility will be
needed so that course corrections can be made as new information
develops both on a particular site and in the larger field of
ecological restoration. In short, prescriptive legislation would
be very unfortunate because the uncertainties and the lack of a
broad database do not ensure that a rigid approach will work. On
the other hand, a robust body of information indicates that
ecological improvement over the damaged condition has a high
probability of success in a wide variety of terrestrial and
aquatic ecosystems.

SELF MAINTENANCE VERSUS SOCIETAL SUBSIDIES

Botkin (1992) has an interesting commentary on the fact that
scientists once thought that terrestrial ecosystems, particularly
forests, reached a climax or steady state that was then
maintained. As he notes, the view now is that ecosystems are
continually dynamic as they respond to complex, multivariate, and
ever changing conditions. Nevertheless, integrity is maintained
despite these dynamic processes (e.g., Karr, 1991). In addition,
natural systems are capable of self-maintenance in the sense that
their integrity remains intact except during periods of mass
extinction occurring over geological times and, of course, severe
anthropogenic stresses. In an era of scarce societal resources,
it would be most helpful if a substantial portion of the
ecosystems that should be kept in a semi-natural state were self-
maintaining. In short, no management subsidy should be necessary
to maintain their integrity. Although diagnostic methodology for
determining whether an ecosystem is self-maintaining is simply
not available, some measurements might help in this regard.
Nevertheless, if self-maintenance is a goal, it should be clearly
stated because, until it is, the methodology and the funding to
develop the methodology will simply not be available.

The prospect for self-maintenance is markedly improved as the
size of the ecosystem increases. Scale effects have been

abundantly studied in ecosystems, and it is quite clear that small fragments do not maintain for any extended period the characteristics of an originally larger system. However, properly managed restoration from a small fragment of a terrestrial ecosystem to a much larger area can be quite successful (e.g., Janzen, 1988). The NRC (1991) book emphasizes the importance of integrating a restored area and the larger natural ecological landscape in which it occurs. The better the integration, the higher the probability of beneficial interactions with the surrounding areas, which will maintain the integrity of the restored system. The reverse is also true. That is, poor integration means ecological isolation, which reduces the probability of the system being self-maintaining. As a consequence, while restoration of the smallest area should not be denigrated, long-term sustainable use of this area without management costs will only be possible if the system is self-maintaining. Thus, large is better than small in this respect.

FINANCING LAND RESTORATION

Some damage to land by forestry or other practices (e.g., Cairns et al., 1992) can be financed by the organization causing the damage. This category could include surface mining activities, damage caused by highway construction, and derelict land such as abandoned farms, ancient mining sites, and the like. If the organization or individual causing the damage can be identified and located, ideally repairing the damage should be the responsibility of that entity. However, society will have to pay the major costs in a number of areas. In order to do this, a land restoration trust fund should be established nationally. At the same time, care should be taken that this fund is not charged with restoring recently damaged sites for which financial responsibility should fall on those responsible for the damage. To avoid the evasion of institutional and/or individual responsibility by declaring bankruptcy and other similar ploys, the potential for environmental damage should be bonded before permits to proceed with the activities are issued. This would then ensure that the type of evasion of responsibility currently practiced would be diminished, although it seems unlikely that it would be totally eliminated. In all the present cases of bonding for other purposes, a record of responsibility on the part of the applicant for the bond reduces the cost. "Unlimited" bonds are totally inappropriate because companies issuing bonds simply will not do so if the bond is not limited. In addition, applicants for bonds would not be willing or able to pay the price of such bonds even if an insurance company were willing to issue them. A limited bond is far better than none at all. Some financing recommendations for aquatic ecosystem restoration are given in the NRC (1991) publication; these are illustrations of what could be done for land restoration. One of the most important recommendations in financing is to use opportunity analysis rather than the traditional cost-benefit analysis.

ESTABLISHMENT OF NATIONAL RESTORATION GOALS

There are some national restoration goals in the NRC (1991) volume that apply to both aquatic and terrestrial systems, although, in some cases, slight modification is necessary for land. These follow.

(1) <u>A national restoration strategy should be directed toward broad-based and measurable goals</u>.

For aquatic systems, the book recommends restoring damaged wetlands at a rate to offset further losses with a goal of gaining 10 million wetland acres by the year 2010. This represents less than 10% of the approximately 117 million acres of wetlands that have been lost in the United States over the past 200 years. Another recommendation is that a total of 400,000 miles of streams and rivers be restored within the next 20 years, which represents approximately 12% of the 3.2 million miles of streams and rivers in the United States. Approximately 2 million acres of degraded lakes are recommended for restoration by 2010, about half over the next 10 years. No comparable recommendations are given for land restorations, but the first step would be establishing an inventory of damaged terrestrial ecosystem amenable to restoration. The NRC volume does not recommend attempts to restore prime agricultural lands, heavily urbanized areas, and other areas of critical importance to human society. Instead, many damaged ecosystems are suitable for repair, and these would not endanger agricultural or other economically valued activities and would, at the same time, be of societal benefit by making them more suitable for recreation and other purposes. Establishing an inventory of areas suitable for restoration and linking this information with the areas presently in good condition in a landscape context would help enormously in setting both area and time goals.

(2) <u>A national land restoration assessment project should be utilized to monitor the degree of realization of the nation's restoration goals</u>.

Establishing goals, such as no federal budget deficit by 1993, and realizing these goals are two quite distinct propositions. Therefore, realistic goals should be set, and failure to meet them should be cause for considerable concern!

ESTABLISHING PRINCIPLES FOR DECISION-MAKING AND PRIORITIES

(1) <u>All policies and programs for land restoration should emphasize a landscape perspective</u>.

Abundant evidence now shows that most ecological studies carried out in the past have inadequate temporal and spacial dimensions. Harte et al. (in press) examined 285 articles in four consecutive issues of <u>Ecology</u>, <u>American Naturalist</u>, <u>Oecologia</u>, and <u>Conservation Biology</u> during 1987-1988. They conclude "... that most research and ecology might just as well have been carried out on the planet Pluto -- climate and the chemical and physical properties of the soil, water, and atmosphere of Earth were irrelevant to the research. Even in the 22 percent of the articles that mentioned at least one of these factors, the reference was generally made as part of a site description and played no role in interpretation of results. In none of the papers surveyed were the interactions among these factors even mentioned." This indicates that, if these are representative articles and there is no reason to believe that they are not, not only are the spatial and temporal dimensions inadequate in most ecological studies but also the range of attributes that are synthesized is inadequate. The basic point of this recommendation is that successful restoration will be achieved only if consideration is given to the entire system within which all relevant interactions are occurring. Stated negatively, a fragment of the system, even if only a fragment is damaged, will not furnish an adequate quality or adequate quantity of information.

(2) <u>Land restoration projects should fully utilize principles of adaptive management and planning</u>.

White (1980) states "the sobering prospect is that most of the major public decisions about resource use and environmental management will be made in the face of large uncertainty deriving from ignorance of physical and biological systems involving techniques and social values." Adaptive planning and management involve a decision-making process based on trial, monitoring, and interactive feedback loops and may frequently require a course correction. Instead of developing a fixed goal and a prescriptive inflexible plan to achieve the goal, adaptive management assumes an imperfect knowledge of interdependencies existing within and among natural systems, which require plans to be modified as technical knowledge improves and social preferences change. In short, adaptive planning and management constitutes an approach that responds quickly and effectively to unique or changing conditions at a particular site rather than responding primarily to prescriptive legislation. It is a <u>sine qua non</u> that adaptive planning and management depend for their success on surveillance and monitoring of restoration policies, programs, and individual projects. These are the means of providing feedback loop information to effect an ongoing decision-making process. This requires informed professional judgment at all stages rather than at the planning stage only. Only information with a potential for influencing the decision-making process should be gathered. To state this negatively, monitoring or compliance to regulatory laws may be necessary but should only influence the decision-making process if the information is appropriate. In some cases, the information will be appropriate; in others, the information gathered will merely be for complying with a regulatory measure designed not for this particular system but for general use.

(3) <u>Opportunity costs rather than the traditional benefit-cost analysis should be used in the evaluation and ranking of restoration alternatives</u>.

In the opportunity cost framework, the correct answer to the question "how much restoration is enough?" is more likely to emerge than in the traditional cost-benefit analysis. Opportunity cost is even more likely to be productive when a number of restoration projects are possible but sufficient funds are not available to undertake all of them simultaneously. Opportunity cost analysis is substantively different from traditional cost-benefit analysis, and, as a consequence, its implementation may be organizationally complex. Opportunity cost analysis accepts a human oriented determination of values, but focuses on collective or integrative actions to define values achieved by restoration. It requires continual questioning of the value of restoration by determining whether an action is worth its cost, particularly relative to other courses of action. A more extended discussion of this is given in the NRC (1991) volume (particularly in the section beginning on page 358).

(1) <u>A uniform and consistent definition of restoration should be utilized in all federal agencies and in all appropriate legislation</u>.

Earlier in this discussion, some illustrative examples of conflicting uses of terminology are given. This illustrative list could easily be expanded by one or two orders of magnitude by perusing government documents. It is abundantly clear that no landscape level restoration project will achieve optimal results unless the activities of a number of government agencies cease being fragmented and become better integrated. For example, the U.S. Army Corps of Engineers spends a substantial amount of its annual budget dredging harbors, rivers, etc. A significant portion of the material dredged may result from various construction projects, including housing and highways, agriculture, urban runoff, elimination of wetlands that are effective sediment traps, other effective sediment traps, and the like. Additionally, any attempts to restore aquatic ecosystems is unlikely to succeed unless careful attention is given to the land management practices in the adjacent terrestrial system comprising the drainage or attachment basin. Cairns (1989) states that precise replication of predisturbance condition will not frequently be a viable option for a complex set of reasons -- the most persuasive is the frequent lack of detailed information about the ecological predisturbance condition of both the structural and functional attributes. Because restoration to predisturbance condition may often not be possible, care should be taken in the presentation of the project to the general public. When the idea of restoration to predisturbance condition is used as an aspiration, the general public should realize when such aspirations are realistic and when they are not. As a consequence, Cairns (1991) provides eight types of restoration, seven of which will probably not be self-maintaining.

(2) <u>Leadership for landscape restorations of national significance should be allocated to the federal government, and restoration programs of local or regional significance should rely on a combination of non-federal and federal agencies for coordination and implementation</u>.

Restoration at a landscape scale inevitably will cross at least small political boundaries, such as provinces, counties, etc. Since political and ecological areas are rarely identical, state boundaries, and even international boundaries, are likely to be crossed for some restoration projects. Even if the project is entirely within a political jurisdiction, it is at least possible that the sources of colonizing species may not be. Additionally, the establishment of federal reserves recommended by the NRC (1981) to serve as a source of test species for toxicological tests might be expanded so that these reserves could serve as a source of recolonizing species for damaged ecosystems. Janzen's (1988) restoration of Guanacaste dry forest in Central America is a good example of the involvement of both private and public sectors, as well as different levels of political organization. Ultimately, since the Guanacaste Forest once occupied an area the size of France on the western coast of Central America, it may be that national boundaries will be crossed in the restoration efforts on that once very large system.

7

(3) The federal government should espouse even stronger
interagency and intergovernment processes to develop a
coordinated integrated national strategy for wetland restoration.

Cairns and Crawford (1991) provide some illustrations of the
advantages of an integrated approach. At the same time, their
book provides illustrations of the dangers of a fragmented
approach. Leopold (1990) notes in his superb lecture that each
federal agency often acts as if it is the only flower facing the
sun. Also, he indicates that a commonly shared set of guiding
beliefs is essential to an effective policy.

(4) Establishment of a single "overview" environmental federal
organization to oversee all activities including restoration.

As Toffler (1991) notes, society is well into the information
age. Simultaneously, the age of mass production has advanced to
the production by industry of specialty items, sometimes with an
extraordinary short turnaround time to meet opportunities of
short duration. The Gulf War provided some good examples (also
some bad examples) of information flow coordination, integrated
action, and the like. Present bureaucratic structure is not
suitable for the information age because the flow of all the
information needed to make environmental decisions is too
fragmented and too compartmentalized. Worst yet, as a number of
examples show (of which the most notable is probably the Exxon
Valdez oil spill), the present system is incapable of a swift,
adaptive, appropriate response to an unanticipated episodic
event! As of the date that the final draft of this manuscript is
being completed (5 May 1992), the U.S. Congress has recognized
the need for an overview environmental agency, but not the
urgency.

(5) Present and proposed government programs should take
advantage of available opportunities for ecosystem restoration.

Mark T. Southerland (personal communication) of Dynamac
Corporation is involved with a U.S. Environmental Protection
Agency task force that is examining policy options the Agency
might pursue in the short term. The number of land and water
sites where restoration could be carried out effectively with
beneficial effects to the economy is numerous. Many need not
involve substantial expenditures of government funds. The NRC
(1991) volume has an example of aquatic restoration on the Rio
Blanco carried out virtually entirely with funds from the private
sector. Numerous examples are available of both terrestrial and
aquatic systems that have been cooperative ventures of public and
private sectors in restoration efforts. However, the citizens
and organizations involved would be encouraged if more robust
assurances were in place that their restoration efforts, if
successful, would not be negated by a governmental agency
following a different but legitimate (in the restricted context
of the agency mission) goal(s) of its own. Such assurances would
be more persuasive if all environmental information had to flow
to a single well empowered agency with the authorized ability to
override agencies with more limited missions.

DETERMINING SUCCESS AND FAILURE IN RESTORATION EFFORTS

No scientific component of restoration ecology deserves more
attention than the criteria for success or failure. Criteria for
ecosystem condition or health must be selected with considerable
professional judgment, and more functional criteria than are

presently available would be extremely helpful. Nevertheless, effective use is being made of criteria and methods already available!

Many restoration failures, however, may not be the result of inadequate methodology or science, but rather simple items that were neglected but are glaringly visible with 20/20 hindsight. A few illustrative examples follow.

(1) Failure to explicitly state specific goals.

Simply stating "return to predisturbance condition" without explicitly stating what characteristics or attributes should be used to diagnose whether the system is in good condition after restoration is an all too common practice. As Bradshaw (1983) notes "The acid test of our understanding is not whether we can take ecosystems to bits or pieces on paper, however scientifically, but whether we can put them together in practice and make them work." Statements of goals should include spatial, temporal, and level of detail dimensions.

(2) Intent to restore is not mitigation.

During summer, I often teach restoration ecology at Rocky Mountain Biological Laboratory on the western slopes of the Rocky Mountains near Crested Butte, Colorado. Just west of Gunnison, Colorado, on highway 50 is an area being restored to provide wintering grounds for elk; these are to replace those lost when Blue Mesa Reservoir flooded the elk wintering grounds. However, many years elapsed between the time the lost elk wintering grounds were covered with water and the initiation of restoration of the Beaver Creek area (formerly used for collecting and shipping cattle) that would serve as an elk wintering ground. I have been told by a number of persons knowledgeable about elk wintering grounds that the partially restored area, not too surprisingly, does not match the one lost. Similarly, a wetland lost through construction of an airport taxiway was to be replaced by constructed wetlands west of Gunnison, but these constructed wetland (years later) would not be classified as functioning wetlands by most wetlands ecologists. The essence of mitigation is to replace in kind -- not at some nebulous time in the future -- in order to keep the larger ecological landscape in which the damage occurs functioning as an integrated, interactive unit continuously! Mitigation at a too distant location may be replacement in kind, but it may not be appropriate in the landscape context unless it provides alternative ecosystem services within the system in which some services were lost.

(3) Making certain that appropriate expertise is available at critical times in the restoration effort.

The wetlands just described were not properly constructed since a hydrologist was not consulted to determine if the constructed wetlands were appropriately connected to the larger hydrological system in which they were located and no wetlands ecologists were present when the construction crews began to create the wetlands. As a consequence, a series of ponds were constructed rather than true wetlands. Even more regrettably, access roads damaged some adjacent natural wetlands since the contractors were more interested in the mitigative site than in the natural areas surrounding it. Finally, the depth was too great because the contractors underestimated the amount of gravel needed for the taxiway, and the deficiency was made up from the proposed wetlands site even though this made the depth too great. These are just two of the many instances when an intent toward mitigative restoration was expressed, but the implementation of the intent was not always in the hands of qualified people.

(4)   Failure to monitor restoration progress and to establish explicit course correction points.

The difficulty with the wetlands just described was identified by an ecologist affiliated with a local university. The difficulties should have been identified by an ongoing quality assurance or monitoring program. Furthermore, check points should have been established at crucial stages in the restoration project (e.g., completion of contouring, etc.) so that errors could be detected either before they occur or sufficiently quickly to make rapid error control course corrections. In this case, the project was carried to "completion" before serious errors in the mitigative effort were discerned, and the ecosystem services normally furnished by wetlands were not available to the larger ecological landscape to replace those that were destroyed.

Provision should be made for external peer review of all restoration projects at a minimum of four stages: (1) completion of project design; (2) completion of site preparation (contouring, etc.); (3) at one or more stages during the restoration process, especially for long-term restoration projects; (4) when all project goals have been met or substantive evidence is available to show why they cannot all be met.

Both of the projects mentioned as illustrations of troubles could have been more ecologically sound and completed sooner had deficiencies been identified at the project design stage. Outside review is appropriate in all scientific undertakings where considerable professional judgment is required. At the very least, properly carried out, reviews will force explicit statements of goals and all of the deficiencies already noted or to be noted. Additionally, the savings and loan scandal, the banking scandal, etc. have shown that regulators do not always regulate as well as they should. Restoration projects are often designed for long-term sustainable use and, therefore, deserve serious quality assurance measures. At the national level, major projects could be reviewed by the National Academy of Sciences in the United States, which would be one of the purposes that Abraham Lincoln intended to be served when he authorized the founding of that organization in 1863. Professional organizations such as the American Fisheries Society, the Society of Environmental Professionals, the Ecological Society of America, and the like could give the names of certified professionals to serve in this capability at local, regional, state, and national levels. Professional certification is extremely important because qualified professionals in that area of specialization would have examined the credentials of the review committee candidates. The National Research Council (the operating arm of the National Academy of Sciences and the National Academy of Engineering) has a particularly useful exercise in that, with the establishment of each committee, detailed and extensive conflict of interest statements must be formally prepared. In addition, at the first committee meeting, the committee chair and all members must make a verbal statement concerning conflicts of interest to all the other committee members, and each committee member may request additional information of any other committee member. Having such formal conflict of interest statements may be even more useful than professional certification, and, fortunately, there is no problem in requiring both.

(5) Access to all restoration sites must be available at all
times to the quality assurance committee, regulatory agencies,
and the like.

Of course, it would be unreasonable for anyone to demand access
to a restoration site at 3 a.m. on a holiday, especially if there
were no advance notice. Regrettably, access to restoration sites
has sometimes been denied even when people with appropriate
professional qualifications and a formal role to play in the
restoration projects gave ample advance notice. This does not
happen routinely, but it is sufficiently common to call for a
particular statement emphasizing this need.

(6) Adequate numbers of qualified personnel in all of the
categories mentioned above must be available at appropriate
times.

As Toffler (1980) notes, going from the era of mass production to
the information age is a difficult transition, and all too many
organizations forget the simple fact that resources must be
allocated to ensure that quality information is available and
integrated at appropriate time intervals. While this may be
costly, failure to have appropriate information when decisions
are made is orders of magnitude more expensive. Society,
particularly in environmental matters, has not given the same
attention to generation of information and information flow that
the military and many business organizations have. This
important matter deserves serious immediate attention.

(7) Cosmetic "restoration" is not a substitute for ecological
restoration!

One of the books in the environmental management series for which
I am a series co-editor (Cairns and Harrison, 1991) has a picture
of a gorgeous sunset just behind the Glomar Beaufort Sea drilling
platform located on Prudhoe Bay on the Arctic Ocean. This
particular book is not about restoration nor is there any attempt
to disguise a drilling platform. The point is that, taken at the
right moment, this picture had sufficient beauty to justify its
use on a book cover. Unfortunately, pictures taken of
restoration projects showing lots of green following lots of
brown and other colors may give the appearance of restoration
when in fact the green is a temporary monoculture not capable of
existing without management subsidies. Visual aids are important
in any evaluation, but they should not serve as a sole source of
information. There is nothing like an on-site visit by a well
qualified group, armed with explicit statements of goals and
objectives, to see whether the evidence corresponds closely with
the image provided by the visual aid.

CONCLUDING STATEMENT

A brief synopsis of "where do we go from here?" follows.

(1) Land restoration goals and objectives with temporal,
spatial, and level of detailed components must be established at
national, regional, and local levels.

(2) Project design must include a continuing systematic and
orderly determination of success or failure with appropriate
error control and feedback groups at all project stages.

(3)   The appropriate mix of qualified professionals must be identified and secured for design, implementation, and quality assurance activities associated with each project.

(4)   A national land restoration trust should be established, together with financial incentives for restoration in federal and state agencies, the private sector, and for private citizens. Opportunity analysis will probably be superior to the traditional cost-benefit analysis in making financial decisions.

(5)   Ecological preserves must be established to provide sources of colonizing species for restoration projects at the national, regional, and local levels. Quality assurance at all stages of restoration projects should be undertaken by qualified professionally certified scientists and engineers.

(6)   Society is in an information age, but neither the quality nor the flow of information in environmental decision-making is adequate for the information age.

(7)   All environmental activities including restoration would be best coordinated and facilitated by an "overview agency" (e.g., The National Institute) charged with this responsibility. This does not necessarily mean the elimination of present agencies with comparatively limited mission assignments, but rather that these fragmented assignments be integrated so that conflicting objectives and missions are identified before major action and expenditure of funds are undertaken. Beyond this, tremendous opportunities exist for facilitating beneficial or synergistic actions among and between federal and state agencies and other organizations.

REFERENCES

1.   Botkin, D. 1992. Essay: A natural myth. Nat. Conserv. May/June:38.

2.   Bradshaw, A.D. 1983. The reconstruction of ecosystems. J. Appl. Ecol. 20:1-17.

3.   Cairns, J., Jr. 1989. Restoring damaged ecosystems: Is predisturbance condition a viable option? Environ. Prof. 11:152-159.

4.   Cairns, J., Jr. 1991. The status of the theoretical and applied science of restoration ecology. Environ. Prof. 13(3):186-194.

5.   Cairns, J., Jr. In press. Commentary: Is restoration ecology practical? Restor. Ecol.

6.   Cairns, J., Jr. and T.V. Crawford. 1991. Integrated Environmental Management. Lewis Publishers, Inc., Chelsea, MI, 214.

7.   Cairns, J., Jr. and R.M. Harrison, series editors. Environmental Management Series. Sturges, W.T. 1991. Pollution of the Arctic Atmosphere. Elsevier Sciences Publishers, Ltd., Essex, 334.

8. Cairns, J., Jr. and J.R. Pratt. In press. Restoring the earth while the human population grows to 10 billion. In International Symposium on Aquatic Ecosystem Health, M. Munawar, ed. University of Waterloo, Ontario.

9. Cairns, J., Jr., B.R. Niederlehner and D.R. Orvos, eds. 1992. Predicting Ecosystem Risk. Princeton Scientific Publishing Co., Inc., Princeton, NJ.

10. Ehrlich, P.R. and A.H. Ehrlich. 1991. Healing the Planet. Addison-Wesley Publishing Co., New York, NY, 353.

11. Harte, J., M. Torn and D. Jensen. In press. The nature and consequences of indirect linkages between climate and biological diversity. In Global Warming and Biodiversity, R. Peters and T.E. Lovejoy, eds. Yale University Press, New Haven, CN.

12. Janzen, D.H. 1988. Guanacaste National Park: Tropical ecological and biocultural restoration. In Rehabilitating Damaged Ecosystems, Vol. II, J. Cairns, Jr., ed. CRC Press, Boca Raton, FL, 143-192.

13. Karr, J.R. 1991. Landscapes and ecosystem management. In Biodiversity and Landscapes: Human Challenges for Conservation in the Changing World, K.C. Kim and G.L. Storm, eds. Center for Biodiversity Research, Pennsylvania State University, University Park, PA.

14. Leopold, L.B. 1990. Ethos, equity and the water resource. First Abel Wolman Distinguished Lecture, National Research Council, National Academy of Sciences, Washington, DC.

15. National Research Council [NRC]. 1981. Testing for Effects of Chemicals on Ecosystems. National Academy Press, Washington, DC.

16. National Research Council [NRC]. 1991. Restoring Aquatic Ecosystems: Science, Technology, and Public Policy. National Academy Press, Washington, DC, 485.

17. Pratt, J.R. and J. Cairns, Jr. 1985. Determining microbial community equilibrium in disturbed wetland ecosystems. In Proceedings of the Twelfth Annual Conference on Wetland Restoration and Creation, F.J. Webb, ed. Hillsborough Community College, Tampa, FL, 201-209.

18. Toffler, A. 1980. The Third Wave. Morrow, New York, NY.

19. Toffler, A. 1991. Power Shift. Bantam Books, New York, NY.

20. U. S. Army Corps of Engineers and U. S. Environmental Protection Agency. 1990. Memorandum of agreement regarding mitigation for dredged or fill material disposal in wetlands. Feb. 6.

21. White, G.W. 1980. Environment. Science 209:183-190.

DECISION MODEL FOR SUCCESSFUL RECLAMATION OF DISTURBED LANDS

R.C. Sidle[*]   R.W. Brown[*]

Both shallow and deep-seated land disturbances present formidable problems for successful long-term reclamation. We can evaluate methods for reclamation of two general types of large-scale disturbances: (1) surface disturbances within the soil profile or soil moved from one site to another; and (2) deep-seated disturbances involving both soil and bedrock or soil and bedrock relocated from one site to another. Long-term reclamation plans must recognize the fundamental differences in rehabilitating these two types of disturbances.

Shallow disturbances are common in certain surface mining operations (e.g., sand and gravel pits), construction sites, oil and mineral exploration areas, and right-of-ways for roads and other transportation corridors. The direct effects on the site include removal of vegetation, disturbance of the soil profile, and compaction. These effects may cause increased surface erosion and sedimentation (Curtis, 1971; Gilley et al., 1977), changes in surface and groundwater chemistry (Babb et al., 1985; Garn, 1985), and reduced aesthetics at the site (Brotherton, 1989; Nieman and Meshako, 1990). Additionally, if slopes are steep (>25°), a hazard may exist for shallow landslide occurrence (Sidle et al., 1985).

Deep-seated disturbances result from open-pit mining (both hard- and soft-rock), mine tailings ponds, deep earth cuts for roads or hillslope development, and underground mines and tunnels where excavated soil and rock are relocated on the soil surface. The major reclamation limitations of these deep-seated disturbances are the high rock content, potential hydrologic changes, and weathering characteristics and chemistry of the disturbed material.

Physical properties of the deeply disturbed material (including rock) can reduce root penetration of vegetation (McSweeney and Jansen, 1984; Thompson et al., 1987), infiltration capacity (Schroeder, 1987), macroporosity and permeability (Potter et al., 1988), and available soil moisture (Hargis and Redente, 1984; Schuman et al., 1985). Groundwater flow in and around deep disturbances can be altered (Schwartz and Crowe, 1987). Additionally, geotechnical properties of surface materials, such as cohesion, angle of internal friction, and aggregate stability, may be modified. These physical alterations can lead to changes in surface erosion potential and sedimentation (Russell, 1977; Rogowski et al., 1990). In cases where slopes are steep or oversteepened by grading or cutting, changes in physical properties can increase the potential for mass wasting (Eyles et al., 1978; Sidle et al., 1985).

Weathering of disturbed substrate can increase the availability and movement of certain chemicals. Pyritic substrate produces acidic conditions and drainage when weathered (Nordstrom, 1982). Other acidic substrate can generate similar problems when exposed on the soil surface. Toxic metals are often associated with pyritic or highly acidic substrate (Johnson and Brown, 1979; Ramsey and Brannon, 1988; Sidle et al., 1991). In other deep disturbances, high salt levels may be a limiting factor (Hargis and Redente, 1984). These changes in chemical mobility in the environment brought about by the surface exposure or disturbance of deep regolith material, can adversely affect surface and groundwater quality (Moran and Wentz, 1974; McKnight and Bencala, 1990). Of course, both the physical and chemical changes resulting from deep-seated disturbances generally degrade site aesthetics.

---

[*]R.C. Sidle, Research Hydrologist, and R.W. Brown, Project Leader, Intermountain Research Station, 860 North 1200 East, Logan, Utah 84321.

In the case of both shallow and deep-seated disturbances, it is important to recognize the primary physical and chemical environmental problems and limitations of the modified site before developing a plan of reclamation. The objectives of the conceptual models presented for shallow and deep-seated disturbances are to provide a logical sequence of decisions concerning the physical and chemical attributes of the disturbed material, methods for ameliorating site limitations, and options for reclamation. Current reclamation practices often project a "desired end use" or condition of the site without accounting for the physical and chemical limitations of the disturbed matrix. In such cases, pollution of surface and groundwater may occur and long-term reclamation may be doomed to failure. In other cases, expensive reclamation practices may be used that are not necessary for successful reclamation.

CONCEPTUAL MODEL DEVELOPMENT

Surface Disturbance

Four initial questions concerning the nature of the surface disturbance must be answered to establish the physical and chemical constraints for the site. First, we must establish if extensive areas of soil have been disturbed or compacted and if these perturbations have adversely affected hydrologic conditions. Secondly, are slopes steep enough (usually >25°) that landslide potential is a concern? Third, is there a hazard of increased movement of undesirable chemicals into surface and groundwaters? Finally, is there a need to provide immediate stabilization of surface soils to prevent surface erosion? Answers to these initial questions will establish certain requirements of the reclamation plan that may affect later decisions and, thus, the final reclamation methodology. For example, if infiltration capacity has been significantly reduced by compaction, deep ripping may be recommended.

The conceptual model for reclamation of surface disturbances depicts decision steps (or questions) as "diamonds" on the flow diagram (Fig. 1) and necessary management actions or prescriptions as "rectangles". The management actions must be developed for regional and local environmental conditions such as precipitation distribution, temperature, wind, aspect, latitude,elevation, etc. Each management action requires detailed prescriptions that are beyond the scope of this paper.

Following the establishment of the initial conditions for reclamation (upper portion of Fig. 1) a management decision must be made as to the long-term sustainability of vegetation on the site. If the site will be intensively managed (i.e., vegetation not self-sustaining), then a detailed long-term reclamation plan is required. This will include scheduling fertilizer and lime applications, long-term planning for vegetation management, and topsoil and organic matter requirements needed to sustain nutrient cycling and desirable soil physical conditions. Of course, previous restrictions outlined in the initial conditions may limit the application of soluble chemicals and may require various site preparations.

If it is determined that the site will not be intensively managed (i.e., self-sustaining), then a series of additional questions need to be addressed to guide the reclamation plan. First, has topsoil been removed to the extent that reduced fertility and microbiology components will inhibit reclamation? Secondly, is organic matter significantly lower than in native soil and would these differences adversely affect microclimate, water-holding capacity, or long-term nutrient cycling? Finally, the desirability of native species needs to be established. Regional criteria related to the first two questions will establish guidelines for topsoiling and mulching or organic matter application if necessary (e.g., Schuman et al., 1985). If native species are selected, specific guidelines for revegetation should include: (1) integrating long-term native species establishment with short-term annuals (when a cover crop is necessary for erosion control); (2) seed availability and selection criteria; (3) inclusion of different lifeforms of species; (4) selecting species with low nutrient requirements to reduce fertilizer applications and promote long-term survival; and (5) special microclimate protection during the period of plant establishment (e.g., mulching to conserve soil moisture during an abnormally dry year).

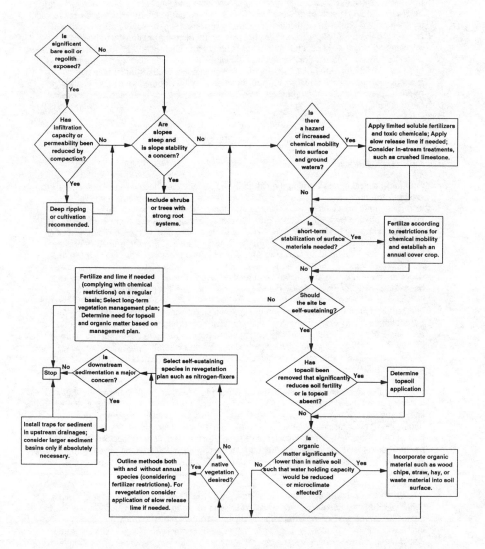

Fig. 1 Conceptual Model for Reclamation of Surface Disturbances.

16

As an alternative, a combination of adapted and native species may need to be considered.

Lastly, the need for off-site protection of streams and related habitat must be determined. With surface disturbances, the major concern is increased sediment transport and deposition in channels. If previously outlined erosion control measures are properly implemented, this may not be a problem. However, areas with extensive disturbances on either steep slopes or near channels may require remedial measures such as small check dams in upstream drainages or on slopes to prevent the transport of sediment off-site. Possibly, only temporary structures would be needed for the first few years following revegetation. Larger, more permanent, sediment retention basins should be used only if absolutely necessary, since they disrupt natural channel hydraulics and sediment movement and pose the risk of catastrophic releases of sediment during episodic events.

Deep-Seated Disturbance

The conceptual model for reclamation of deep-seated disturbances is more complex than the model for surface disturbances. This is due to the problems posed by the depth of the disturbance, changes in the physical and chemical nature of the exposed substrate, and the oversteepening of excavated or replaced slopes.

The first part of the reclamation model deals with physical restrictions of the disturbed material. If rock content is high (e.g., >30%) and if it in any way appears to limit reclamation, the following four questions should be addressed. (1) is infiltration capacity or permeability restricted by rock content or composition?; (2) is root penetration potentially limited by the physical matrix?; (3) is available soil moisture significantly decreased?; and (4) are significant changes in groundwater regime predicted? (Fig. 2). Reduced infiltration capacity and permeability should be related to either salt levels in the substrate or rock content and structure. Appropriate amelioration measures such as liming and leaching, ripping, or topsoiling can then be determined. Effects of deep-seated disturbances on groundwater recharge and piezometric levels should be evaluated. Depending on the impacts of the disturbance, hydrologic controls such as subsurface drainage, changes in over burden placement (including geometry), and rerouting of surface recharge may be necessary.

The second major question posed in the deep-seated disturbance reclamation model addresses the issue of slope stability, particularly in regard to slope oversteepening. If slopes are potentially unstable, then three basic questions must be asked: (1) will vegetation roots help stabilize the slope?; (2) is surface or subsurface drainage necessary to remove excess water from critical portions of the disturbed site?; and (3) are structural measures needed to insure stability of the site? (Fig.2). Answers to these questions will establish additional procedures that must be implemented in the reclamation plan before continuing. Deep disturbances into hillsides generate large quantities of spoil material that require regrading on terrain that may already be unstable. In these cases, restoration of disturbed land to approximately original contour may not be desirable because recompacted spoil may be less stable than natural slopes (Zipper et al., 1989). Also, the natural slope-regraded spoil interface may be an area for excess pore water pressures to develop (Sidle et al., 1985). Thus, any regrading on steep slopes must be carefully executed.

The third major step in the model examines the presence or absence of pyritic material or highly acidic substrate in the disturbance. The primary objective is to control acid drainage from the site. If acid drainage can potentially be controlled by topsoiling and revegetation and if topsoil is available, the successful long-term revegetation of the site may still be constrained by the acid conditions at the topsoil-pyrite interface. Topsoil can be applied and plans for revegetation can proceed if these restrictions can be ameliorated or if they are not present.

If these acidic restrictions cannot be ameliorated by liming, a reclamation approach must be implemented that parallels the actions needed when acid drainage cannot adequately be

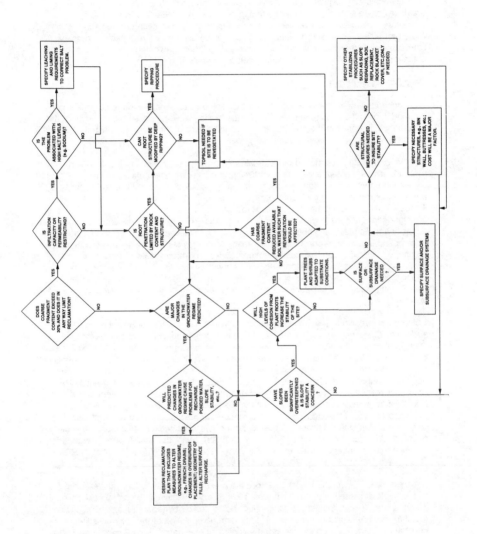

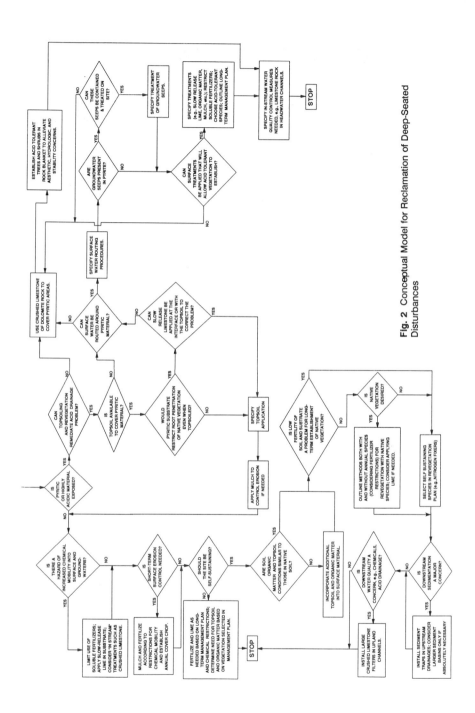

Fig. 2 Conceptual Model for Reclamation of Deep-Seated Disturbances

prevented by topsoiling and revegetation of pyrite. In this case, the disposition of surface water and groundwater seeps in the pyritic material must be evaluated. If, for some reason, excess surface water cannot be routed around the acidic material or if acid groundwater seeps cannot be contained and treated on-site, then critical disturbed areas should be covered with a "blanket" of limestone or dolomite rock. This rock "blanket" could be interplanted with acid-tolerant trees and shrubs to help stabilize and control water on the site, as well as for aesthetic concerns. If excess surface water can be routed around pyritic material and if groundwater seeps are either not present or can be contained or treated on-site, then we need to determine if any combination of surface treatments would promote the establishment of acid-tolerant vegetation. Assuming that this appears feasible, treatments such as slow-release lime and organic matter should be outlined for the long-term reclamation of the site. If the site is too acidic or if recommended treatments are not practical, the rock "blanket" cover treatment would be recommended. For either treatment (i.e., rock "blanket" or acid-tolerant vegetation establishment), in-stream water quality control measures, such as limestone rock filters or slow-release liming devices, should be installed in headwater drainages to curtail downstream movement of acid drainage and associated metals (Arnold et al., 1988).

If topsoil application appears beneficial for reclaiming pyritic substrate or if pyritic substrate does not exist, then we proceed to the final two steps for establishing initial reclamation conditions (Fig. 2). These steps involve the movement of chemicals into surface and groundwaters (not necessarily associated with pyrite) and the need for surface erosion control. These questions are answered in the same format as in the surface disturbance reclamation model.

Once the initial conditions of the deep-seated reclamation model have been satisfied, the remaining management decisions follow the same path as the surface disturbance reclamation model with two major exceptions. If it is determined that the site should be self-sustaining, then the fertility status of the substrate must be evaluated in terms of its ability to support long-term growth of native vegetation. Although land managers may wish to revegetate a deep-seated disturbance with native species, if the nutrient status of the disturbed site is dramatically different from that of native soil, such revegetation efforts may be doomed to failure in the long-term. The second exception involves adding a question at the end of the model relating to off-site water quality concerns (other than sediment). This is needed as a precautionary measure because of the potential release of undesirable chemicals into streams related to the weathering of the exposed substrate.

SUMMARY AND CONCLUSIONS

Large-scale disturbances associated with oil and mineral exploration, mining, road and right-of-way construction, residential development, and recreation activities are growing at a rapid pace. Prior planning of these disturbances and subsequent reclamation is essential to protect water quality, control soil erosion, maintain aesthetic aspects of disturbed sites, and manipulate modified landscapes to a desired end use (e.g., rangeland or crop production, native species establishment, wildlife habitat). Because of changes in physical and chemical properties of the disturbed material, some constraints may be introduced in the reclamation plan. Excellent examples of disturbed sites where reclamation methods with specific objectives have been implemented include: (1) strip mining of coal in the Great Plains (Ries and DePuit, 1984; Halverson et al., 1986) and Appalachia (Henry, 1983; Zipper et al., 1989); (2) mining disturbances in alpine rangelands (Brown et al., 1978; Brown and Chambers, 1990); (3) phosphate mines in the west (Farmer and Blue, 1978); and (4) sand and gravel borrow pits (Gaffney and Dickerson, 1987; Chambers et al., 1988). These recommendations focus on a desired "end product" such as revegetation with native species or a cover crop. However, in cases where substrate is unstable or has undesirable physical or chemical properties, it may be necessary to modify the end use of the landscape to insure protection of water quality, site stability and erosion, and hydrologic conditions. If the modifications, aimed at protecting the environment, are totally unacceptable, the disturbance project may need to be abandoned.

The two decision models presented in this paper outline a progressive sequence of reclamation steps necessary to insure protection of environmental resources for both shallow and deep-seated disturbances. The initial questions that are addressed in the models relate to the physical and chemical (also microbial) properties of the disturbed material and the restrictions these properties place on reclamation. Management must next address possible amelioration of these restrictions and then options for final reclamation (including desired "end use"). At sites where both deep and shallow disturbances occur, a combination of both decision models should be applied. In cases where specific portions of a disturbance pose a particular concern (e.g., exposed pyritic material), then different pathways of the same model should be applied to the respective problematic regions of the disturbed site. At a large scale, this could be facilitated by application of GIS systems. These decision models can be used as the basis for expert systems for reclamation.

ACKNOWLEDGEMENTS

Much of this research was conducted while the senior author was a Visiting Scientist with the Forestry and Forest Products Research Institute, Tsukuba Science City, Ibaraki, Japan, sponsored by Science and Technology Agency Fellowship No. 190056. The authors acknowledge Patricia Terry's contributions to flow chart design and graphics.

Key Words: surface disturbances, deep-seated disturbances, mining, water quality, erosion, native vegetation, self-sustaining reclamation.

REFERENCES

Arnold, D.E., W.D. Skinner and D.E. Spotts. 1988. Evaluation of three experimental low-technology approaches to acid mitigation in headwater streams. Water, Air, and Soil Pollution 41:385-406.

Babb, J.M., S.K. Enger and G.K. Pagenkopf. 1985. Chemical changes in a receiving stream due to oxygenation and dilution of mine tailings seep waters. Water, Air and Soil Pollution 26:219-224.

Brotherton, D.I. 1989. The evolution and implications of mineral planning in the national parks of England and Wales. Environment and Planning, A 21:1229-1240.

Brown, R.W. and J.C. Chambers. 1990. Reclamation practices in high-mountain ecosystems. In: Proc. symp. on whitebark pine ecosystems; ecology and management of a high-mountain resource, 329-334. Gen Tech. Rep. INT-270, USDA Forest Service, Ogden, Utah.

Brown, R. W., R.S. Johnston and D.A. Johnson. 1978. Rehabilitation of alpine tundra disturbances. J. Soil and Water Cons. 33:154-160.

Chambers, J.C., J.A. MacMahon and R.W. Brown. 1988. Seedling establishment in disturbed alpine ecosystems: implications for reclamation. In: High altitude revegetation workshop No. 8, Infor. Ser. 59, 173-191, Colo. State Univ., WRRI, Ft. Collins.

Curtis, W.R. 1971. Strip-mining, erosion and sedimentation. Transactions of the ASAE 14(3):434-436.

Eyles, R.J., M.J. Crozier and R.H. Wheeler. 1978. Landslips in Wellington City. New Zealand Geographer 34(2):58-74.

Farmer, E.E. and W.G. Blue. 1978. Reclamation of lands mined for phosphate. In: Reclamation of drastically disturbed lands, eds. Schaller and Sutton, 585-608. American Soc. of Agronomy, Madison, Wisc.

Gaffney, F.B. and J.A. Dickerson. 1987. Species selection for revegetating sand and gravel mines in the Northeast. J. Soil and Water Cons. 42(5):358-361.

Garn H.S. 1985. Point- and nonpoint-source trace elements in a wild and scenic river of northern New Mexico. J. Soil and Water Cons. 40(5):458-462.

Gilley, J.E., G.W. Gee, A. Bauer, W.O. Willis and R.A. Young. 1977. Runoff and erosion characteristics of surface-mined sites in western North Dakota. Transactions of the ASAE 20:697-700, 704.

Halverson, G.A., S.W. Melsted, S.A. Schroeder, C.M. Smith and M.W. Pole. 1986. Topsoil and subsoil thickness requirements for reclamation of a nonsodic mined-land. Soil Science Soc. Am. J. 50:419-422.

Hargis, N.E. and E.F. Redente. 1984. Soil handling for surface mine reclamation. J. Soil and Water Cons. 39(5):300-305.

Henry, D.S. 1983. Forage yield and quality on Kentucky surface mine spoils. J. Soil and Water Cons. 38(1):56-58.

Johnston, R.S. and R.W. Brown. 1979. Hydrologic aspects related to the management of alpine areas. In: Special management needs of alpine ecosystems, ed. D.A. Johnson, 65-75, Ser. 5, Soc. of Range Mgmt., Range Science, Denver, Colo.

McKnight, D.M. and K.E. Bencala. 1990. The chemistry of iron, aluminum, and dissolved organic material in three acidic, metal-enriched, mountain streams, as controlled by watershed and in-stream processes. Water Resour. Res. 26(12):3087-3100.

McSweeney, K. and I.J. Jansen. 1984. Soil structure and associated rooting behavior in minespoils. Soil Science Soc. Am. J. 48:607-612.

Moran, R.E. and D.A. Wentz. 1974. Effects of acid-mine drainage on water quality in selected areas in Colorado, 1972-73. Colorado Water Res. Circ. 25, Colorado Water Pollution Control Commission, Denver.

Nieman, T.J. and D. Meshako. 1990. The Star Fire mine reclamation experience. J. Soil and Water Cons. 45(5):529-532.

Nordstrom, D.K. 1982. Aqueous pyrite oxidation and the consequent formation of secondary iron minerals. In: Acid sulfate weathering, eds. Kittrick, Fanning and Hessner, 37-57. Soil Science Soc. Am., Madison, Wisc.

Potter, K.N., F.S. Carter and E.C. Doll. 1988. Physical properties of constructed and undisturbed soils. Soil Science Soc. Am. J. 52:1435-1438.

Ramsey, D.L. and D.G. Brannon. 1988. Predicted acid mine drainage impacts to the Buckhannon River, WV, U.S.A. Water, Air and Soil Pollution 39:1-14.

Ries, R.E. and E.J. DePuit. 1984. Perennial grasses for mined land. J. Soil and Water Cons. 39(1)26-29.

Rogowski, A.S., B.E. Weinrich and R.M. Khanbilvardi. 1990. A nonparametric approach to potential erosion on mined and reclaimed areas. J. Soil and Water Cons. 45(3):408-412.

Russell, M.J. 1979. Spoil-heap vegetation at open-cut coal mines in the Bowen Basin of Queensland, Australia. In: Ecology and Coal Resource Development (vol. 1), ed. M.K. Wali, 516-523, Pergamon, New York.

Schroeder, S.A. 1987. Slope gradient effect on erosion of reshaped spoil. Soil Science Soc. Am. J. 51:405-409.

Schuman, G.E., E.M. Taylor, F. Rauzi and B.A. Pinchak. 1985. Revegetation of mined land: influence of topsoil depth and mulching method. J. Soil and Water Cons. 40(2):249-252.

Schwartz, F.W. and A.S. Crowe. 1987. Model study of some factors influencing the resaturation of spoil following mining and reclamation. J. Hydrology 92:121-147.

Sidle, R.C., J.C. Chambers and M.C. Amacher. 1991. Fate of heavy metals in an abandoned lead-zinc tailings pond: II. sediment. J. Environ. Qual. 20(4): 752-758.

Sidle, R.C., A.J. Pearce and C.L. O'Loughlin. 1985. Hillslope Stability and Land Use. Water Resources Monograph 11, American Geophysical Union, Washington, D.C. 140p.

Thompson, P.J., I.J. Jansen and C.L. Hooks. 1987. Penetrometer resistance and bulk density as parameters for predicting root system performance in mine soils. Soil Science Soc. Am. J. 51:1288-1293.

Zipper, C.E., W.L. Daniels and J.C. Bell. 1989. Approximate original contour reclamation: an alternative in steep slope terrains. J. Soil and Water Cons. 44(4) 279-283.

SIMULATION MODEL OF SURFACE RUNOFF AND EROSION PROCESS (SMODERP)
APPLICATION AND VERIFICATION IN JAPAN

L. Jansky[*]
Member ASAE

J. Váška[**]

T. Furuya[***]

T. Okuyama[***]

B. Thoreson[****]
Member ASAE

The methods of mathematical modeling, based on basic physical processes in the environment, are becoming widely used in various studies on natural processes, such as surface runoff and soil erosion. The simulation model, presented here, is for determination of surface runoff and erosion. The model is part of a larger watershed model which is being developed in Czecho-Slovakia by the research team of the Department of Irrigation and Drainage, Faculty of Civil Engineering, Czech Technical University in Prague (Holý et al., 1989). Verification studies of the model are now being conducted in several countries, in addition to Czecho-Slovakia, recently also in Japan, in order to examine the model's accuracy under different environmental and management regimes. The present paper reports on the testing of the model in both laboratory and field plots and in natural fields in Japan.

INTRODUCTION TO THE SMODERP

The model determines rainfall-runoff relations on slopes. Its outputs provide data for the design of soil conservation measures. The model simulates surface runoff and erosion process from the rainfall of variable intensity within an area up to the size of 1 km^2. Different morphological, soil and vegetation conditions can be used in the model. The model can be utilized to determine:
- Characteristics of surface runoff (volume, peak flow rate, velocity, depth, tangential stress) in the chosen cross sections of the slope and time intervals from the beginning of the rainfall:
- Permissible slope length on the basis of the non-scouring tangential stress or non-scouring velocity;
- Soil loss rate.

The Concept of the Surface Runoff Model and Simulation Principle

The model of surface runoff is derived from the equation of continuity and the equation of motion on the basis of kinematic principles using experimental measurements on a tilting hydraulic flume in the laboratory and in field research plots. The results of field experiments carried out in Czecho-Slovakia and elsewhere as well as data published in literature (see references) were considered. The surface runoff model comprises the process of interception, soil

---

[*]L. JANSKÝ, Soil Conservation Specialist, National Centre of Soil and Water Engineering in Bratislava, Czecho-Slovakia; recently visiting scientist, National Research Institute of Agricultural Engineering (NRIAE), Tsukuba, Japan;[**]J. VÁŠKA, Associate Professor, Irrigation and Drainage Dept., Czech Technical University, Prague, Czecho-Slovakia;[***]T. FURUYA, Geotechnical Engineer and Head of Laboratory, and T. OKUYAMA, Soil Physicist, Lab. of Land Reclamation and Conservation, NRIAE, Tsukuba, Japan;[****]B. THORESON, Graduate Research Associate, Agricultural and Biosystems Engineering Dept., University of Arizona, Tucson, USA.

surface retention and infiltration of water into the soil.

In the model the slope is divided into homogenous segments with regard to morphological, soil and vegetation condition. Each segment is characterized by a uniform average slope gradient, a uniform soil type and specific crop and management. The maximum length and width of each slope is set to 1 000 m. The determination of the surface runoff characteristics is made for a representative design heavy rainfall (derived from a large set of rainfall data) or for a measured rainfall case. For prediction purposes and for design of soil conservation measures the use of design heavy rainfall is recommended.

In the first stage of a rainfall a process of interception occurs. Rainfall which is not intercepted by vegetation reaches the soil surface (net rainfall) and fills the retention volume of the surface. Water accumulating on the soil surface penetrates into the soil (downwards) depending on the soil infiltration characteristics. Surface runoff takes place at the moment when the water depth on the soil surface exceeds soil surface retention capacity. After the rainfall, surface runoff proceeds to the level of soil surface retention capacity and the remaining water infiltrates into the soil.

The actual simulation of rainfall-runoff relations is done stepwise from the beginning to the end of rainfall. The simulation step is 0.2 minutes. At the end of each simulation step the model balances the rainfall-runoff relations in all segments following each other downward in the direction of the slope gradient. For a more accurate analysis to be made, every segment in the model is automatically divided into elements and rainfall-runoff relations are solved in each simulation step for all elements.

Data of the heavy rainfall are the basic inputs for the modelling of the surface runoff. For the purposes of designing soil conservation measures, the decisive factor is heavy rainfall and its time-course.

The maximum quantity of water which may be intercepted by the leaves is given by potential interception which depends on the plant species and its growth stage. For the surface runoff model empirical mean values of relative leaf area and of potential interception are recommended for each crop and are given in the model documentation (Holý et al., 1989).

Soil surface has a specific value of retention capacity. After depletion of the soil surface retention capacity surface runoff takes place. On the basis of the experiments the value of 3 mm is recommended for agricultural soil surface retention capacity.

In order to express the roughness of vegetation cover and its effect on reducing the velocity of surface runoff, Manning's roughness coefficient for surface runoff was introduced. The recommended values of Manning's roughness coefficient for surface runoff for the soil and crop types are also a part of the model documentation.

As far as the infiltration of water into the soil is concerned, for calculation of infiltration rate the model uses the simplified relationship introduced by J.R.Philip (Kutílek, 1978; Morgan, 1976). Recommended values of coefficients of hydraulic conductivity and sorptivity for the basic soil types are also given in the model's manual. Soil sorptivity depends on the coefficient of hydraulic conductivity. The provided mean values of both parameters (in tabular form) are valid for medium wet soils where the ratio of actual moisture to the moisture of saturation is approximately 0.6. For higher saturation (ratio > 0.85), the soil sorptivity is equal to zero. If the actual values of coefficients of hydraulic conductivity and soil sorptivity are available from the investigated area it is recommended to use these data.

25

The Concept of the Erosion Process Model and Simulation Principle

The erosion process model proceeds from the dynamic concept of the erosion phenomenon: soil loss on the investigated slope is determined from the amount of detached soil particles by the kinetic energy of rainfall and surface runoff and its transport capacity. The simulation of the erosion process is based on the same principles as the simulation of surface runoff, i.e. on the division of the slope into homogenous segments (with a constant slope, homogenous soil and vegetation condition, etc.) which are further divided into elements, and the amount of detached soil particles and transport capacity of surface runoff are determined for each element. From the comparison of the movement of soil particles in the direction of the slope gradient and the sedimentation of soil particles it is determined whether the transport capacity of the surface runoff is less than the detachment by rainfall and surface runoff.

The simulation model contains also other subprograms:
- The subprogram for creation of rainfall data - enables creation, saving, displaying and printing rainfall data.
- The subprogram for creation of slope characteristics data - enables creation, display, printing and saving slope characteristics data or changes of input data. The program enables also to use the same data file created for determination of permissible slope length for simulation of surface runoff characteristics.
- The subprogram for determination of permissible slope length and for simulation of surface runoff characteristics and erosion process enables two types of simulation;
    - determination of permissible slope length,
    - simulation of time course of surface runoff characteristics and soil loss.
The program also includes choice of different forms of presentation of simulation results.
- The subprogram for checking contents of data files.

Input Data Necessary to Model

Input data which are necessary to the model basically consist of rainfall data, slope data and soil and vegetation data:
- Time from the rainfall beginning (minutes)
- Rainfall depth from the rainfall beginning (mm)
- Slope morphological data - length (m), average width (m), gradient (%)
- Soil type (sandy, sandy loam, loamy, clay loam, clay)
- Vegetation cover (bare soil, row crops, small grain crops, grass)
- Type of crops; plant ranking in the crop rotation
- Soil sorptivity ($cm \cdot min^{-0.5}$)
- Coefficient of hydraulic conductivity ($cm \cdot min^{-1}$)
- Manning's roughness coefficient for surface runoff
- Mean values of relative leaf area and potential interception for different types of crops.

COMPARISON OF COMPUTED AND MEASURED DATA

This is the first preliminary verification of the SMODERP model in Japan. The computed results of surface runoff and soil loss were compared with measured values from the following locations: 1) the sloping lysimeters of the National Research Institute of Agricultural Engineering in Tsukuba, 2) the test field plots of the Ibaraki Prefectural Pasture Experimental Station in Naka, 3) an elementary watershed, i.e. a newly reclaimed field in Central Honshu near Koriyama.

Sloping lysimeter

Measured data of surface runoff, soil loss and infiltration were obtained from experiments under simulated rainfalls made by Banzai (1990). The sloping lysimeters were 2.5 m wide and 10 m long, with a fixed slope of 12.3 percent. The lysimeters were filled with either loamy soil of volcanic ash (andisol) or sandy soil. The soils were also characterized by coefficients of hydraulic conductivity: sandy soil 0.072 cm.min⁻¹, andisol 1.430 cm.min⁻¹. Plots with bare slopes were chosen for analysis. Surface runoff and soil loss were measured data under a simulated rainfall of 150 mins. with an intensity of 1.3 mm.min⁻¹ and 0.67 mm.min⁻¹, respectively. The experimental data were compared with calculated data from SMODERP.

The measured coefficient of hydraulic conductivity for andisol was more than 10 times higher than the intensity of simulated rains. Despite this, the surface runoff occurred during the experiments. This confirmed the importance of soil structure on the infiltration properties of andisols: during rainfall their physical properties are changed and a thin, less permeable crust layer develops on the surface which decreases infiltration and initiates surface runoff. The hydrological module of SMODERP does not include this effect of surface crust development. Decreased soil infiltration was therefore substituted and simulated with the average value of hydraulic conductivity coefficient, 0.022 cm.min⁻¹ for the less-permeable sandy-loam soil according to Kutílek (1978). The results are shown in Table 1.

Table 1. COMPARISON OF MEASURED AND SIMULATED RESULTS ON SLOPING LYSIMETERS

	Sandy soil		Loamy soil (Andisol)	
Rain (150 minutes)	100 mm	195 mm	100 mm	195 mm
Total surface runoff (m³)				
- measured	1.18	2.12	0.68	1.68
- simulated	none	2.43	1.68	4.05
Maximum surface runoff (l.s⁻¹.m⁻¹)				
- measured	0.05	0.09	0.03	0.07
- simulated	none	0.02	0.02	0.04
Soil loss (kg.25m⁻²)				
- measured	68.0	196.0	25.0	99.0
- simulated	none	50.7	31.8	94.5

With parameters included for soil infiltration for erodibility, the SMODERP normally gives satisfactory results, corresponding fairy well with the measured data. However, the size of lysimeters used was not really suitable to test simulation models for applications in agriculture because the soils were quite different from cultivated fields; also, the slope length was too short to fully validate downhill runoff processes.

Field plots in Naka

The measured data of runoff and soil loss during natural rainfall were taken from experiment published by Asano and Aihara (1991). The size of the plots was 3 x 30 meters, with a slope gradient of 14 percent and soil type between loamy-sand and sandy-loam. The experimental plots were under corn cultivation, with compost mixed to the soil. For our verification we used data from the natural rainfalls of 8 Sept. 1988, with a heavy rain of 60 minutes, totaling 35 mm and with an average intensity of 0.58 mm.min⁻¹. The infiltration properties used were: average coefficient of hydraulic conductivity 0.058 cm.min⁻¹ and soil sorptivity 0.095 cm.min⁻⁰·⁵. The measured surface runoff from this field plot was 1.6 m³, the simulated value 2.0 m³; the measured soil loss was 170.0 kg but the simulated value only 44.0 kg.

Elementary watershed near Koriyama

The newly reclaimed field (in 1989) was 0.91 ha with a slope gradient of 3.5 percent. Only the runoff effect of an actual storm was measured. Surface runoff from this field was collected in a U-shape ditch collecting all surface runoff to a Parshall flume. The soil type was loamy sand - skeletal sandy loam. The infiltration characteristics were measured using the flooding method. The soil originated from land reclamation works, and was thus man-made soil known as "masa", i.e. weathered granite soil. Several authors have analyzed their physical properties, e.g. Okuyama et al. (1991). Ca. 65 percent of the area was covered by tobacco, the coefficient of hydraulic conductivity was 0.025 $cm.min^{-1}$ and soil sorptivity 0.065 $cm.min^{-0.5}$. The rest of the area was without vegetation, with a coefficient of hydraulic conductivity 0.022 $cm.min^{-1}$ and soil sorptivity 0.060 $cm.min^{-0.5}$. For verification, the watershed was modeled using a simplified characteristic profile. The heavy rain of 13 June 1991 measured 13.5 mm within 20 minutes, and had intensity of 0.68 $mm.min^{-1}$. The measured surface runoff was 8.266 m^3, slightly less than the simulated 13.800 m^3.

CONCLUSIONS

The results of measured and simulated data are quite satisfactory, being of the same order of magnitude. The differences seem to depend on differences in parameters of kinematic relationships in the hydrologic part of the model. Also, one validation problem with our data was the absence of typical heavy rainfalls in field plots and in the elementary watershed, as well as limited length of the runoff path on the sloping lysimeters. The slope in the Koriyama field seems to be not sufficient for surface runoff studies.

However, this was our first effort to elucidate the applicability of the SMODERP model in Japan. The results were encouraging, so that there are now plans to continue verification in more suitable areas and with more data from heavy rainfalls.

ACKNOWLEDGEMENTS

The authors highly appreciate a critical reviewing of the manuscript by Dr. Illka Havukkala and thank Prof. Miloš Holý, DrSc. of Czech Technical University in Prague and all members of the research team who were involved in developing the model for their support in verification studies conducted in Japan. This work was also supported by a Fellowship from Science and Technology Agency of Japan and by The Nomura Foundation in Tokyo.

REFERENCES

1. Asano, H.and Y. Aihara. 1991. Effect of the water erosion control on the sloped land of decomposed granite soil. Bull. of the Ibaraki Pref. Pasture Experimental Station 2:1-8. (In Japanese).

2. Banzai, K. 1990. The experimental study of the erosion from the slope of volcanic ash soil and sand. Technical developments for farm consolidation in sloping areas. Report No. 240. Tokyo, MAFF Publishing Bureau. (In Japanese).

3. Holý, M., K. Vrána and J. Váška. 1989. Simulation model of surface runoff and erosion process (SMODERP). Model documentation. Czech Technical University, Prague, 28.

4. Morgan, R.P.C. 1986. Soil erosion and conservation. Longman, Harlow.

5. Okuyama, T., T. Furuya and K. Kamimura. 1991. Change of soil consolidation properties due to weathering and organic matter mixing. Tech. Rep. of the Inst. Agric. Eng., Japan. 185:23-32. (In Japanese).

Literature Used for Developing of the SMODERP

Beasley, D.B., E.J. Monke and F.F. Huggins. 1981. ANSWERS: A model for watershed planning. Transactions, American Society of Agricultural Engineers. 23(4): 839-944.

Dýrova, E. and E. Soukalová. 1987. Protection and management of catchments (textbook). VUT, Brno. (In Czech).

Engman, E.T. 1986. Roughness coefficients for routing surface runoff. J. of Irrigation and Drainage. Division ASAE. 112 (1).

Holý, M. 1978. Soil erosion control. SNTL/ALFA, Praha. (In Czech).

Holý, M. et al. 1982. Procedures, numerical parameters and coefficients of the CREAMS model application and verification in Czechoslovakia. CP-82-23. IIASA, Laxenburg.

Holý, M., J. Váška, K. Vrána and J. Mls. 1982. Analysis of surface runoff. CP-82-33. IIASA, Laxenburg.

Holý, M. 1985. Relations between surface runoff and transport of nutrients in catchments of water supply reservoirs. Research report VÚ VI-4-15/01-03. ČVUT-FSv, Praha. (In Czech).

Holý, M. et al. 1986. The model of water management and agricultural production in catchments of water supply water courses. Vodohospodársky časopis, 43(1). (In Czech).

Knisel, W.G. (Ed.). 1980. CREAMS: A field scale model for chemicals, runoff and erosion from agricultural management systems. USDA Conservation Research Report No. 26, Washington D.C.

Kutílek, M. (1978). Water conservancy soil science. SNTL/ALFA, Praha. (In Czech).

Pasák, V., M. Janeček a M. Šabata. 1983. Soil conservation. Methodology No. 11. ÚVTIZ, Praha. (In Czech).

***

DRAINCALC Release 4.0

A COMPUTER MODEL FOR CULVERT AND OPEN CHANNEL DESIGN

Stephen J. Langlinais, P.E., P.L.S.
Member ASAE

INTRODUCTION

The design and engineering of any drainage system entails complex hydrological, hydraulic, geometrical and engineering computations. These computations can be greatly expedited through the use of **DRAINCALC Release 4.0,** a computer aided design tool which performs all the necessary design calculations without the need of cumbersome charts, tables, data sets and nomographs. All of the required data is incorporated into a set of data bases compiled within the program source code. A metric version is scheduled to be released in the fall of 1992.

DRAINCALC Release 4.0 was written to operate on any DOS 3.0 or higher operating system and requires an IBM PC, XT, AT, PS/2 or compatible with 384K of RAM and one disk drive. The program can also be permanently installed on the hard disk of any of the above IBM compatible computers.

DRAINAGE THEORIES USED IN SOFTWARE

Two of the most tedious and complex tasks involved in the design of any drainage system are 1) to **perform the drainage runoff calculations** and 2) to **perform the open channel, culvert or storm drainage design calculations.** Draincalc Release 4.0 was developed to accomplish the above two objectives.

Objective 1) above can be accomplished with Draincalc by using either of the two following methods: a) the *Soil Conservation Service (SCS) method* or b) the *Rational Method*. The *Soil Conservation Service (SCS) method* uses the following equation:

$$Q = C \times M^{5/6} \qquad (1)$$

where Q = required discharge rate (CFS) or
(m^3/sec)
C = Drainage runoff coefficient
M = Drainage area (square miles) or
(hectares)

In Draincalc, the "C" values are selected from menu prompts and the "M" value is entered through an input statement. SCS Runoff curves with varying "C" values have been adopted by SCS for each state of the U.S., and these values can be obtained from the respective curves.

Stephen J. Langlinais, P.E., P.L.S.; Associate Professor, Agricultural Engineering, University of Southwestern Louisiana, Lafayette, Louisiana.

The *Rational Method* is expressed as:

$$Q = C \times I \times A \qquad (2)$$

where Q = required discharge rate (CFS) or
(m^3/sec)
C = drainage runoff coefficient
I = rainfall intensity (inches/hr) or
(mm/hr)
A = drainage area (acres) or (hectares)

In Draincalc, both the "C" and "I" values are selected from menus, while the "A" value is entered through an input statement. Typical rainfall data may be obtained from the Department of Commerce and Weather Bureau statistical rainfall data for the state involved.

Either of the above two methods is selected at the discretion of the designer based upon standard engineering practice for the area being designed. The user merely selects the runoff method from a series of user friendly selection menus in the Draincalc Program.

Objective No. 2 above involves the determination of either the channel size, depth and width; culvert size, or bridge opening size. The determination of channel, culvert or bridge opening size needed to carry the adequate capacity for handling the discharge rate ($Q_{Req'd}$) through the structure as computed in Objective 1) above is computed from the *Continuity Equation* expressed as:

$$Q = A \times V \qquad (3)$$

where   Q = required discharge rate (CFS) or
(m^3/sec)
A = Cross sectional area of channel or
structure (sq ft) or (sq m)
V = Design Velocity (ft/sec) or (m/sec)

The Design Velocity (V) is computed by Manning's Equation:

$$V = \frac{1.49}{n} R^{2/3} S^{1/2} \qquad (4)$$

where   n = channel roughness coefficient
S = hydraulic gradient slope (ft/ft) or
(m/m)
R = hydraulic radius expressed as:

$$R = A/P \qquad (5)$$

where   A = cross section area (sq ft) or (sq M)
P = wetted perimeter (ft) or (m)

The trapezoidal shaped channel section as shown in Figure 1 is the most commonly used geometric section:

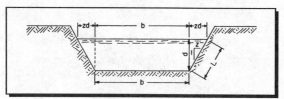

Figure 1. Design parameters for a typical trapezoidal open channel.

$$\text{where} \quad A = \frac{(b+2zd+b)}{2}(d) = (b + zd)(d) \quad (6)$$

$$P = (2)(L)+b = 2(d^2+(zd)^2)^{1/2} + b \quad (7)$$

When computing a rectangular shaped channel, the earth or concrete channel option may be used by entering a side slope (z) value of 0 (zero).

Four different options are available for computing "$Q_{req'd}$" for a trapezoidal channel. These are as follows:

1) input b, z, s, n and *compute "d"*
2) input d, z, s, n and *compute "b"*
3) *compute optimum "b"* and *"d"* using the hydraulic *critical depth method* (Chow, 1959)
4) *compute "b"* and *"d"* using the *permissible velocity method* (Chow, 1959)

The circular section as shown in Figure 2, is used for circular culverts flowing full in conjunction with Manning's equation.

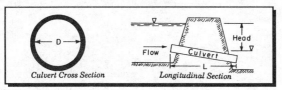

Figure 2. Design parameters for a typical culvert flowing full. Pipe types include concrete, corrugated metal and plastic.

$$\text{Where} \quad A = \pi (D^2/4) \quad (8)$$
$$\text{and} \quad P = \pi \times D \quad (9)$$
$$R = A/P = D/4 \quad (10)$$

For all circular pipes, the design values and standard diameter tables are included in the software. These tables include all commercially available 1) concrete, 2) corrugated metal, 3) corrugated plastic, 4) corrugated plastic with smooth lining, and 5) PVC pipes.

The values of the hydraulic properties for A, P, and R for (1) arch pipes, (2) horizontal elliptical pipes, and (3) vertical elliptical pipes are obtained from *"Concrete Culvert Design Manual"* published by the Americal Concrete Pipe Association and are used for concrete structures. The values for corrugated metal structures are obtained from *"National Engineering Handbook, Drainage"* published by the U.S. Soil Conservation Service. These published table values are all incorporated into the computer source code, and are used in computing the design discharge values for all the above culvert types. The options for adding design safety factors are available when designing and checking all culverts and storm drains.

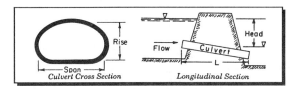

Figure 3. Design hydraulic properties for a typical arch pipe. In Draincalc Release 4.0, both values for reinforced concrete pipes (RCP) and corrugated metal (CMP) are readily available for selection through a tabular type menu system.

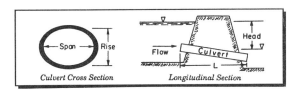

Figure 4. Design hydraulic properties for a typical horizontal elliptical pipe. In Draincalc Release 4.0, values for Reinforced Concrete Horizontal Ellipse (RCPHE) are available for selection through a tabular menu.

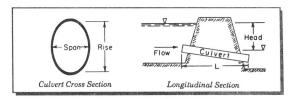

Figure 5. Design hydraulic properties for a typical vertical elliptical pipe. In Draincalc, values for Reinforced Concrete Vertical Ellipse (RCPVE) are available for selection through a tabular menu.

A second method available for calculating culvert design discharge capacities (Q_{design}) is the commonly known California Highway Curves Method (National Engineering Handbook, Drainage, 1961) expressed in general form as:

$$Q = C \times A \times (2gh)^{1/2} \qquad (11)$$

This is also commonly known as the general orifice flow equation
where A = culvert cross section area (sq ft) or
(sq m)
h = culvert operating head (ft) or (m)
g = 32.2 ft/sec/sec

For circular Corrugated Metal Pipes (CMP) flowing full:

$$C = 1/[(1+.16D^{.6}+(0.196L/D^{1.2}))^{1/2}] \qquad (12)$$

where D = culvert diameter (ft)
L = culvert length (ft)

For circular Reinforced Concrete Pipes (RCP) flowing full:

$$C = 1/[(1.1+(0.026L/D^{1.2})_{1/2}] \qquad (13)$$

where D = culvert diameter (ft)
L = culvert length (ft)

For Reinforced Concrete Arch Pipes (RCPA) and Reinforced Concrete
Boxes (RCB) flowing full:

$$C = 1/[(1.05+(.0045L/R^{1.25}))^{1/2}] \qquad (14)$$

where R = hydraulic radius or A/P
L = culvert length (ft)

The hydraulic properties for a Reinforced Concrete Box culvert
section, flowing full, are shown in Figure 6.

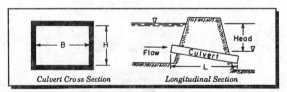

*Figure 6. The design hydraulic properties for a Reinforced
Concrete Box (RCB) structure.*

where A = B x H   (15)
P = 2B + 2H   (16)
R = A/P = (BxH)/2(B+H)   (17)

When computing culvert capacities, three different options are
available. Among these are:
1) input h, L, D and **compute Q** (CFS), (m³/sec)
2) input Q, L, D and **compute h** (ft), (m)
3) input Q, L, h and **compute D** (in), (mm)

Either the California Highway Curve (equation 11) or Manning's
Equation (equation 4) are solved for **Q**, **h**, or **D** depending upon
which of the 3 options above one selects.

When designing earth channels, a maximum permissible velocity (**Vpermissible**) may also be selected from a tabular menu or manually entered through an input prompt. Once each of the design routine options are selected and computed, the results are displayed on the monitor. You then have the opportunity to view the computed design parameters. When designing channels, the design Velocity (V) is generally checked for a maximum permissible value. If the design velocity is greater than the maximum permissible value, a warning will be displayed on the monitor.

The limiting minimum design velocity is generally above 2 ft./sec. (61 cm/sec) for storm drains in order to prevent siltation inside the culverts. The culvert head (h) or slope (s), where s = h/l, can be raised to increase the design velocity or lowered to decrease the design velocity. If the design velocity is less than 2 ft./sec., (61 cm/sec) or greater than 8 ft./sec. (244cm/sec) when designing culverts, a warning will also be displayed on the monitor.

Three different types of drainage structures are supported with Draincalc Release 4.0. These are 1) Earth Channels 2) Concrete Channels and 3) culverts. Ten different types of culverts including concrete, corrugated metal, and plastic pipes are supported which include the following:
1. Corrugated metal Pipes **(CMP)**
2. Reinforced Concrete Pipes **(RCP)**
3. Corrugated Wall Plastic **(CWP)**
4. Corrugated Smooth Plastic **(C/SP)**
5. Corrugated Metal Arch Pipe **(CMPA)**
6. Reinforced Concrete Arch **(RCPA)**
7. Concrete Vertical Ellipse **(RCPVE)**
8. Concrete Horizontal Ellipse **(RCPHE)**
9. Reinforced Concrete Box **(RCB)**
10. PolyVinyl Chloride Pipe **(PVC)**

All of the above culverts may be designed as flowing under 1) **Full Flow** conditions with submerged inlet and outlet (outlet control) or 2) **Partial Flow** conditions flowing partially full (inlet control) as shown in Figure 7. Under all conditions when designing channels or culverts, USER FRIENDLY graphic interface windows with dialogue boxes as shown in Figure 7 are displayed for ease of use in understanding the nomenclature of the program. This is particularly important for first time users and drastically shortens the learning curve. Figures 8, 9, 10, and 11 illustrate four additional GRAPHIC INTERFACE WINDOWS.

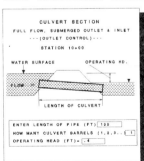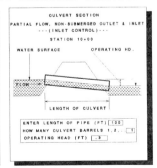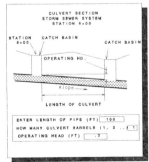

Figure 7. Typical USER-FRIENDLY GRAPHIC INTERFACE windows are displayed and dialogue boxes prompt the user for input data. Full, Partial flow and storm sewer surface profiles are depicted above.

35

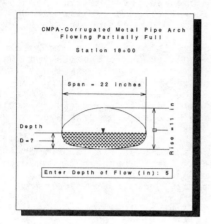

Figure 8.

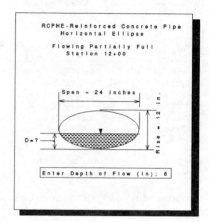

Figure 9.

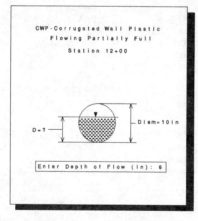

Figure 10.

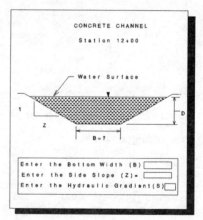

Figure 11.

DrainCalc Release 4.0

Typical USER FRIENDLY Graphic Interface
Windows displayed when prompted for input
data during channel & culvert design segments.
Prompts are displayed in dialogue boxes at
the bottom of each window.

Once the design parameters are displayed on the monitor, one can select the following options:

1) Satisfied or 2) Not Satisfied

If **Option 1**) Satisfied is selected, the computed data is dumped to the printer. If **Option 2**) Not Satisfied is selected, the user may then return to the beginning, input new design values, and display a new set of computed values, as many times as necessary, until the user is satisfied.

When using the Menu option to "**Check Existing Culvert**", and the existing culvert in the field is checked for adequate capacity, the "Q_{design}" is compared to the "$Q_{req'd}$". If the "$Q_{req'd}$" is greater than the "Q_{design}", the culvert is considered inadequate. Then additional computations are automatically executed to design several alternatives to:

1) **add** an additional culvert of the same type as the existing culvert; or

2) **replace** the existing culvert with:
   a) another culvert of same type and length as the existing culvert
   b) another **CMP** or **CMP** Arch
   c) another **RCP** or **RCP** Arch
   d) another **RC** Box
   e) another **RCP** Vertical Ellipse
   f) another **RCP** Horizontal Ellipse
   g) another **CWP** Plastic pipe
   h) another **PVC** plastic pipe

A typical Design Example Problem (Figure 12) along with the sample computer printout is shown for illustration purposes.

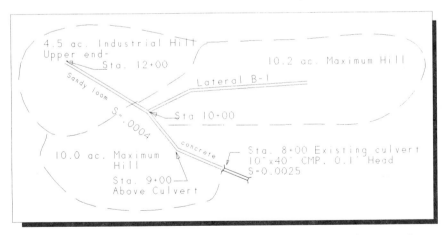

Figure 12. Design Example using DRAINCALC 4.0. In this example, the channel depth, width and culvert sizes are calculated, given the above design engineering input data.

The computer printout for the design example is shown in the Tabular printout below which was generated by the DRAINCALC 4.0 software. The printout below is shown with the printer in compressed mode using 140 character width. An option is also available to print out the data using a standard 80 character printer.

D R A I N A G E   A N A L Y S I S   D E S I G N

| OWNER : JOHN DOE | | | | | PROJECT DESCRIPTION: MORGAN CANAL | | | | | | METHOD: | RUN-OFF CURVES | |
| DESIGNED BY: STEVE LANGLINAIS | | | | | DATE | : 4-18-89 | | | | | | | |

STA. No.	Location	Drain Curve	Area Acres	Req'd cfs	S	N	A Sq.Ft	P ft	R ft	V ft/s	Des'nd cfs	Designed B(ft) D(ft) 1:z	S/S	Actual B(ft) D(ft)
12+00	Upper End	Ind. Hill	4.5	2.5	.00040	.045	5.5	7.6	0.7	0.5	2.9	4.0 1.0 1.5		4.0 1.0 Earth
	SAFETY FACTOR = 1.00	C = 156.00												
10+00	Lateral B-1	Max. Hill	10.2	6.7	.00040	.045	10.2	9.8	1.0	0.7	7.0	4.0 1.6 1.5		4.0 1.6 Earth
	SAFETY FACTOR = 1.00	C = 131.00												
9+00	Above Culvert	Max. Hill	10.0	10.8	.00040	.013	6.2	8.0	0.8	1.9	12.1	4.0 1.1 1.5		4.0 1.1 Concrete
	SAFETY FACTOR = 1.00	C = 131.00												
8+00	Culvert		10.0	10.8	.00250	.000	0.5	2.6	0.2	1.0	0.5	D= 10 in L= 40 Ft 1 - CMP		
	SAFETY FACTOR = 1.00	C = 131.00												

1 - (CMP) D= 10 (in) is inadequate since the design flow is Q= 0.5 (cfs) < 1 x 10.8 (cfs) = 10.8 (cfs) USING (CALIF.CURVES)

There are a few choices you may select from below:

ADD	: 1 - (CMP) D= 30 (in) which will carry 11.0 (cfs) under 0.1 (ft) of head													
	CULVERT DESIGN DATA		10.0	10.8	.00250	.000	4.9	7.9	0.6	2.2	11.0	D= 30 in. L= 40 ft. 1 - CMP		
	SAFETY FACTOR = 1.00	C = 131.00												

REPLACE	: 1 - (CMP) D= 36 (in) which will carry 11.5 (cfs) under 0.1 (ft) of head													
	CULVERT DESIGN DATA		10.0	10.8	.00250	.000	7.1	9.4	0.8	1.6	11.5	D= 36 in. L= 40 ft. 1 - CMP		
	SAFETY FACTOR = 1.00	C = 131.00												

REPLACE	: 1 - (RCP) D= 33 (in) which will carry 12.7 (cfs) under 0.1 (ft) of head													
	CULVERT DESIGN DATA		10.0	10.8	.00250	.000	5.9	8.6	0.7	2.1	12.7	D= 33 in. L= 40 ft. 1 - RCP		
	SAFETY FACTOR = 1.00	C = 131.00												

REPLACE	: 1 - (RCB) B= 3.2 (ft) D= 1.6 (ft) which will carry 10.8 (cfs) under 0.1 (ft) of head													
	CULVERT DESIGN DATA		10.0	10.8	.00250	.000	5.1	9.6	0.5	2.1	10.8	B= 3.2 ft. D= 1.6 ft. L= 40 ft. 1- RCB		
	SAFETY FACTOR = 1.00	C = 131.00												

REPLACE	: 1 - (RCPA) (26 5/8 x 43 3/4) which will carry 14.0 (cfs) under 0.1 (ft) of head													
	CULVERT DESIGN DATA		10.0	10.8	.00250	.000	6.4	9.4	0.7	2.2	14.0	(26 5/8 x 43 3/4) L= 40 ft. 1 - RCPA		
	SAFETY FACTOR = 1.00	C = 131.00												

REPLACE	: 1 - (RCPVE) (24 x 38) which will carry 11.0 (cfs) under 0.1 (ft) of head													
	CULVERT DESIGN DATA		10.0	10.8	.00250	.000	5.1	8.3	0.6	2.2	11.0	(24 x 38) L= 40 ft. 1 - RCPVE		
	SAFETY FACTOR = 1.00	C = 131.00												

REPLACE	: 1 - (RCPHE) (24 x 38) which will carry 11.0 (cfs) under 0.1 (ft) of head													
	CULVERT DESIGN DATA		10.0	10.8	.00250	.000	5.1	8.3	0.6	2.2	11.0	(24 x 38) L= 40 ft. 1 - RCPHE		
	SAFETY FACTOR = 1.00	C = 131.00												

CONCLUSIONS

Draincalc Release 4.0 software was written to serve as an engineering tool to accomplish the following objectives: 1) to expedite drainage and runoff calculations, 2) to expedite the design of open channel systems, and 3) to expedite the culvert and storm drainage design process whereby all commercially available culvert types are included in the design data base. The software package has been successfully field tested and has been released for licensing to Simplicity Systems, Inc. Commercial copies of the software are also available from the author, and Demo Disks are available for evaluation purposes. A metric version is being prepared at the time of this writing.

REFERENCES

1. Ami, S.R., **DRAINAGE PIPE TESTING MANUAL**, June 1987

2. Chow, V.T., Ph.D., **OPEN CHANNEL HYDRAULICS**, 1959, McGraw Hill Book Company

3. **CONCRETE PIPE DESIGN MANUAL**, 1980, American Concrete Pipe Association

4. **CORRUGATED PLASTIC PIPE MANUFACTURER'S ASSOCIATION**, Table of Standard Pipe Sizes, 1992

5. **ENGINEERING HANDBOOK FOR WORK UNIT STAFFS**, Louisiana, 1060; U.S. Soil Conservation Service

6. **HYDRAULICS OF CULVERTS**, 1964, American Pipe Association

7. King, H.W., Brater, E.F., **HANDBOOK OF HYDRAULICS**, McGraw Hill Book Company, 1976

8. Langlinais, S.J., **DRAINCALC USER'S MANUAL**, Simplicity Systems, Inc., 1990

9. **MODERN SEWER DESIGN**, First Edition, 1980, American Iron and Steel Institute

10. **NATIONAL ENGINEERING HANDBOOK, DRAINAGE**, U.S. Soil Conservation Service, 1961

11. Peckworth, H.F., **CONCRETE PIPE HANDBOOK**, 1966, American Concrete Pipe Association

12. Streeter & Wylie, **FLUID MECHANICS**, 6th Edition, McGraw Hill Book Company, 1971

IRRIGATION RETURN FLOW MECHANISM AND WATER QUALITY IN LOW LYING PADDY AREA

Masaharu KURODA*   Tetsuro FUKUDA**   Fatchan NURROCHMAD***

The operation and management of the irrigation system is characterized by reuse of return flow and drainage condition in low lying paddy area. A complex tank model was proposed to explain the water reuse mechanism and evaluated with actual water balance measurements. The conceptual definition of cyclic use of returning flow was presented for evaluating the water use efficiency in irrigation system. The water reuse mechanism is very effective for conserving irrigation water resources but it has very severe impact on water quality. The water quality was monitored at various monitoring points in the irrigation system from upper stream side to lower stream side in the low lying paddy area, such as in canal system, in creeks as temporally water storage and on paddy plots. The monitoring was conducted on not only in irrigation season (summer season) but also in non-irrigation season (winter season). Items for monitoring were as follows: electrical conductivity (EC), pH, COD, suspended solids (SS), total nitrogen (T-N), total phosphate (T-P), dissolved oxygen (DO) and so on. Especially hourly DO variations were measured to clarify the influences of photosyntesis and respiration activities of algae in ponded water in paddy plots and in creeks. According to results obtained, the water quality have considerable impact, and several suggestions are proposed for keeping sufficiently sustainable paddy cultivation in this area.

OUTLINE OF IRRIGATION SYSTEM AND PURPOSE OF INVESTIGATION

In a delta plain with creek network, the irrigation water is supplied to paddy plots using pipeline system with pumps in which outflow water from paddy plots to creek is reused as a returning water system. The water reuse mechanism is very effective for conserving irrigation water resources. Consequently, the reuse water as irrigation water, in this system, should be operated to keep good quality conditions, because the water quality decreases during n^{th} time reuse cycles and also water quality deterioration is accelerated by excess application of fertilizer in paddy fields.

This study was carried out in Kubota district which is located on Saga plain, Saga Prefecture, west Japan. The regional area for this study is, as illustrated in Fig.1, devided into three blocks, namely the upper, the middle and the lower blocks. The upper block serves as a regulating reservoir with buffer and storage functions for the middle and the lower blocks. The middle and the lower blocks have retarding basins with protection function from sea water influences and other hazards.

Each paddy plot in this area is placed along creek so the reuse of the irrigation water is easily performed (Kuroda et al, 1991). Most of the outflow (96%) from paddy plots return into creek network and is available to be used as irrigation water again (Ikushima and Kuroda, 1975).

*M. KURODA, Professor, **T. FUKUDA, Assist. Professor, and ***F. NURROCHMAD, Grad.Student, Agricultural Engineering Dept., Kyushu University, Fukuoka, Japan.

The purpose of this research is consisted of following three items:
Item 1 : Analyzing the reuse mechanism of return flow from paddy plots in the low lying creek area.
Item 2 : Investigating water quality in the area.
Item 3 : Conclusions on the relationship between the reuse of return flow and water quality.

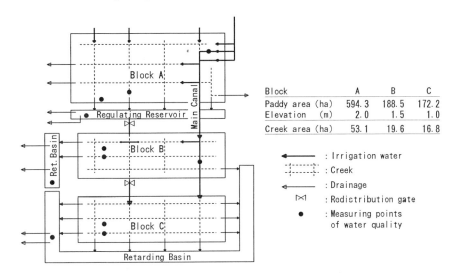

Block	A	B	C
Paddy area (ha)	594.3	188.5	172.2
Elevation (m)	2.0	1.5	1.0
Creek area (ha)	53.1	19.6	16.8

◀——— : Irrigation water
·⌐······⌐· : Creek
◀——— : Drainage
▷◁ : Redistribution gate
● : Measuring points of water quality

Figure 1. Layout of Irrigation System in Kubota District.

WATER BALANCE AND REUSE MECHANISM OF IRRIGATION WATER

Method of Analysis

Construction of tank model: The analysis on reuse water were carried out during rice planting seasons from 1985 to 1990 and will be continued in the following years.   A complex tank model was applied for analyzing the water balance and especially the quantity of reuse water. Figure 2 shows the construction of a complex tank model (Kuroda et al., 1991). The coefficients of paddy and creek tank model, as shown in Fig.2, were designed using some physical meaning of actual conditions and determined by Standardized-Davidon-Fletcher-Powell (SDFP) Method (Kadoya and Nagai, 1980).

The uppermost hole of coefficients of upper tank of paddy field model (a2 and h2) were designed taking into consideration heavy rainfall, the ponding depth of water in paddy field and the depth of levee (100mm). Coefficients of a0, h1 and a1 were designed taking into consideration the percolation value (96% of horizontal percolation and 4% of vertical percolation) and the mean ponding depth of water in paddy field.

The optimal combination of coefficients was obtained from minimizing the objective funtion J as shown in Eq.(1).

$$J = \sum_{i=1}^{N} \frac{(Q_{oi}-Q_{ci})^2}{Q_{oi}} \qquad (1)$$

where N : number of data, Q_{oi} = observed discharge, Q_{ci} = simulated discharge. The limiting conditions are: (1) all coefficients should be non negative; (2) sum of the hole coefficients should be less than 1; and (3) the

41

upper hole coefficients should not be less than the lower hole coefficients, are requested for making the optimization satisfied. Table 1 shows the coefficients of a complex tank model resulting from SDFP method.

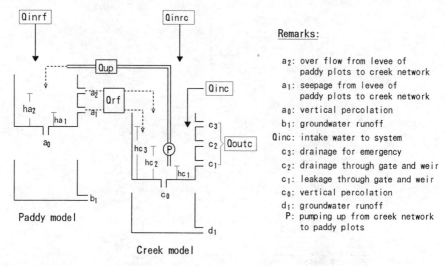

Figure 2. Construction of Complex Tank Model.

Table 1. Coefficients of Complex Tank Model

		Upper	Blocks Middle	Lower
Paddy Model				
	ha1 (mm)	100	100	100
	ha2 (mm)	10	10	10
	a0	0.008	0.008	0.008
	a1	0.250	0.250	0.250
	a2	0.600	0.600	0.600
	b1	0.001	0.001	0.001
Creek Model				
	hc1 (mm)	2692	1660	1728
	hc2 (mm)	1839	1181	1043
	hc3 (mm)	539	348	835
	c0	0.035	0.038	0.060
	c1	0.050	0.053	0.019
	c2	0.153	0.312	0.184
	c3	0.394	0.476	0.673
	d1	0.002	0.002	0.002

Irrigation season: In south west part of Japan, the irrigation season of paddy cultivation is from the middle of June to the begining of October (Table 2). The operation of daily intake water are carried out with taking into consideration the growing stages of paddy rice (Nurrochmad et al., 1992).

Table 2. Growing Stages of Paddy Rice.

```
----------------------------------------------------------------
         Growing stages                        Period
----------------------------------------------------------------

   Ia :  Puddling and transplanting    June 15  -  June 25
  IIa :  Tillering                     June 26  -  July 24
 IIIa :  Mid summer drainage           July 25  -  Aug. 10
  IVa :  Growing                       Aug. 11  -  Aug. 31
   Va :  Flowering                     Sep.  1  -  Sep. 10
  VIa :  Maturing                      Sep. 11  -  Oct.  6
 VIIb :  Ripening                      Oct.  7  -  Oct. 31
----------------------------------------------------------------
```

a Irrigation period
b No-irrigation period

Composition Ratio of Returning Water and Intake Water

The daily inflow of water into creek network is composed of the intake water from main canal and the returning water from paddy plots. Equation (2) presents the composition ratio of the returning water to the intake water into creeks, where R is the composition ratio.

$$R = \frac{\text{daily returning water from paddy plot to creek}}{\text{daily intake water into creek}} = \frac{Qrf}{Qinc} \tag{2}$$

The returning water from paddy plots flows into creek network, as creek elevation is lower than paddy plot elevation in usual in lowland paddy area, and the water from creek should be pumped up to paddy plots as irrigation water.

The daily flow of returning water from paddy plots into creek network (Qrf) can be evaluated using a complex tank model, in which returning water is the total amount of runoff from the upper tank of paddy tank model to the upper tank of creek tank model as shown in Fig.2..

For the upper block, the most of intake water (Qinc) is conveyed through main canal and an additional small amount of water is supplied from upper basin. For the middle and the lower blocks, the intake water (Qinc) is not only supplied through main canal but also from the regulating reservoir of the upper block as shown in Fig.1.

Figure 3 shows the frequency distribution of the composition ratio R on the growing stage II.

In the upper block, more than 50% frequencies in the distribution of composition ratio were included in a range from R=0.3 to R=0.5. The frequencies in the middle and in the lower blocks were in a range from 0.2 to 0.6 and from 0.4 to 0.8, respectively. The same tendency of the frequency distributions on R appeared from growing stage II to VI for the irrigation season during 1985 to 1990. Otherwise, in the growing stage I (puddling and transplanting period), the frequency distribution on R was unstable due to frequent rainfalls and the wide fluctuations of intake water operation. In this growing stage, the operator had to be very nervous to protect young paddy from excess flooding.

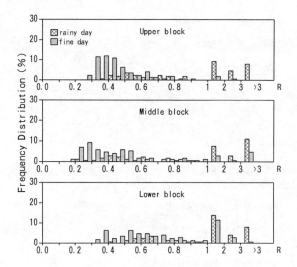

Figure 3. Frequency Distributions of Composition Ratio R on Growing Stage II.

Schematic of Water Balance in Paddy Plots and Creek Network System

The typical water circulation process in the paddy plots and creek network system is illustrated in Fig.5.(Kuroda and Cho, 1988).

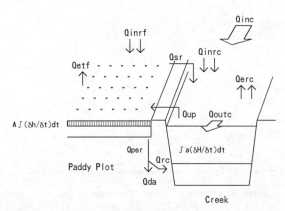

Figure 4. Illustration of Water Circulation in Paddy Plots and Creek Network System.

In creek irrigation system, the water supply to paddy plots from creek network is usually carried out by pumping (see Fig.4), since the water level in creek network is always lower than the surface of paddy plots.

The equations of water balance are given as follows. Water balance in paddy plots:

$$Q_{up} = Q_{etf} + Q_{per} - Q_{inrf} + A\int (\delta h/\delta t)dt + Q_{sr} \qquad (3)$$

Water balance in creek network:

$$Qinc = Qevc + Qup + Qoutc + \int a(\delta H/\delta t)dt - Qrc - Qrs - Qinrc \qquad (4)$$

Returning water:

$$Qrf = Qrc + Qsr \qquad (5)$$

in which Qup is water supply to paddy plots from creek network by pumping, Qetf is evapotranspiration of the paddy plots, Qinrf is effective rainfall to the paddy plots, A $\int(\delta h/\delta t)dt$ is variation of surface storage on the fields, Qsr is surface runoff from paddy plots, Qinc is water supply from main canals to creek network, Qevc is evaporation from creek network, Qoutc is runoff from creek network out of the system, $\int a(\delta H/\delta t)dt$ is variation in water storage of creek network, Qrc is seepage from the paddy plots to creek network, Qda is vertical downward percolation from the paddy plots , and Qinrc is rainfall to creek network.

Conceptual Definition of Cyclic Use of Returning Flow

The return water Qrf from paddy plots to creek network is around 60% of the irrigation water pumped up from creek network (Qup) (Ikushima and Kuroda, 1973), and is defined as

$$Qrf = 0.6*Qup \qquad (6)$$

in which Qrf = return water in a present day, and Qup = irrigated water in a preceding day.

In a steady state condition without rainfall, the following assumptions in equation 3, 4 and 5 might be allowable, i.e.
Qinrf = 0, Qinrc = 0, A $\int(\delta h/\delta t)dt$ = 0, $\int a(\delta H/\delta t)dt$ = 0, Qetf = constant, Qevc = constant and Qda = constant, X = Qinc - Qoutc and Qup = X + Qrf.

The cyclic use of returning water is therefore, conceptualy defined as:

The first cycle: $\qquad Qup1 = 0.6*Qup(0) + X(1)$ $\qquad\qquad (7)$

The second cycle: $\qquad Qup2 = 0.6* 0.6*Qup(0) + X(1) + X(2)$ $\qquad (8)$

The nth cycle: $\qquad Qupn = 0.6^n*Qup(0) + 0.6^{(n-1)}*X(1)+ ... + X(n)$ $\qquad (9)$

in which $X(i)=Qinc(i)-Qoutc(i)$ and $Qup(0)=X(0)$.

From the definition mentioned above, the cycle times of each block can be defined as Eq.(10).

$$R = \frac{0.6^n*X(0)+0.6^{(n-1)}*X(1)+ ... +0.6*X(n-1)}{X(0)+ .... + X(n-1)} \qquad (10)$$

Let $X(0)=X(1)= ... =X(n-1)$ be the constants variable of intake water. With the concepts we have already defined, the cycle times for n days are given by Eq.(11).

$$R = 3(1-0.6^n)/2n \qquad (11)$$

For the upper block, by substituting the composition ratio (R=0.3 to R=0.5) to Eq.(11), we obtain the cycle times (days) n which have a range, approximately, from 2 to 4 days. With the same concepts, for the middle block with R=0.2 to R=0.6 we obtain the cycle times n which have a range from 1 to 3 days and for the lower block with R=0.4 to R=0.8, 1 to 2 days are obtained as cycle times. In other word, for the 1, 2, 3 and 4 days cycle times, the irrigation

efficiency of water use is 100%, 160%, 196% and 216%, respectively.
The returning water used in the upper block will be able to be used as irrigation water again in the middle and in the lower block, so the irrigation efficiency of water use might be actually increased than the conceptual treatment mentioned above, but this fact will unfortunately influences the water quality used in this irrigation system, such as increasing nitrogen accumulation and so on.

On the other hand, as it is usual to have temporarily rainfalls during irrigation season, the storage water in creek network will be replaced by runoff of rainfalls. This phenomenon is effective to maintain good water quality in the paddy field irrigation system, but the irrigation efficiency of water use will decrease.

SURVEYING WATER QUALITY

Measuring Items

Field measurements were carried out from May 1991 to March 1992 and will be continued in the following years, not only during irrigation periods but also during no-irrigation periods. Measurement points for water quality are shown in Fig.1, i.e., main canal, creeks, paddy plots, regulating reservoir and retarding basins. Field measurements included air temperature, water temperature, dissolved oxygen (DO), electrica conductivity (EC), and pH. Factors analyzed in laboratory were suspended solids (SS), chemical oxygen demand (COD), total nitrogen (T-N) and total phosphate (T-P).

Restriction Index of Water Quality

Table 3 shows the water quality restriction index for paddy rice cultivation in Japan (Tabuchi, 1987).

Table 3. Water Quality Restriction Index.

Item	Restriction	Unit
Dissolved oxygen (DO)	more than 5	ppm
Electrical conductivity (EC)	less than 0.3	mS/cm
pH	6.0 - 7.5	
COD	less than 6.0	ppm
Suspended solids (SS)	less than 100	ppm
Total nitrogen (T-N)	less than 1.0	ppm

Hourly Variation of Water Quality

The 24 hours continous measuraments were carried out to analyze the variation of water quality in main canal, in creeks and in paddy plots of all blocks. Measured items were DO, EC and pH.

Dissolved Oxygen (DO): Figure 5 shows the hourly variation of global solar radiation and DO in a creek and a paddy plot of each block. Figure 5 indicate that there is a strong relationship between the hourly variation of DO and the hourly variation of global solar radiation for all blocks in the day time. The DO variation in paddy plots was larger than those in creek for propagating green algae as a result of photosynthesis in the day time and respiration at night.

A quality problem is evident at night, especially in the middle and in the lower blocks, because the value of DO in paddy plots is lower than the restriction index (5 ppm). This phenomenon suggests that the density of algae in paddy plots is rather too great. Similar phenomenon was pointed in previous report (Phuc et al., 1975).

The fluctuation of hourly variation of DO in main canal are not so wide than those in paddy plots and in creeks, because green algae is not able to grow in flowing water.

Electrical Conductivity (EC): Figure 6 shows the hourly variation of EC in creeks and paddy plots of all blocks. Hourly variation of EC was almost constant in main canal, in the upper block and in the middle block but in the lower block slight variation of EC value was observed.

Hydrogen Ion Concentration (pH): Figure 7 shows the hourly variation of pH in paddy plots of all blocks and in main canal. In the day time, alkaline ion in the water increased at night, acidity increased. pH and DO have a tendency increasing in the day time and decreasing at night.

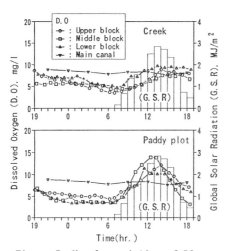

Figure 5. Hourly variation of DO
(Sept.2-3, 1991)

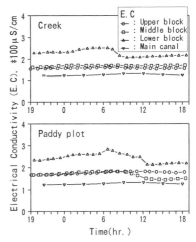

Figure 6. Hourly variation of EC
(Sept.2-3, 1991)

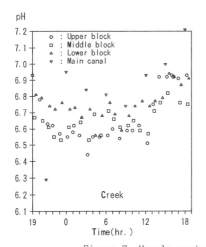

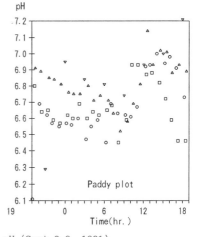

Figure 7. Hourly variation of pH (Sept.2-3, 1991)

Behavior of measured DO and pH may strongly suggest the photosyntesis and respiration processes of green algae in both paddy plots and creeks.

Periodically Changing of Water Qualities

Figures 8 and 9 show results for T-N, T-P, COD and EC.

Total Nitrogen: The values of T-N in the main canal, the upper block, the middle block and the lower block were higher than the restricted value (1ppm). It is suggested the T-N concentration of water in basin might be already influenced by excess application of nitrogen fertilizer.

Chemical Oxygen Demand: In the main canal and in the upper block, the value of COD do not show the wide fluctuation during irrigation season (see Fig.8). It is suggested that after 2 to 4 days reuse cycle, the water quality in the upper block is still suitable for irrigation use in the following blocks.

In August and September the value of COD in the middle and in the lower blocks increased more than restricted value (6 ppm, for example see Fig.9). It is understood, in August and September with small amount of rainfalls, the water quality will decrease because of increased irrigation efficiency of reused water as mentioned in the conceptual definition of the cyclic use of returning flow.

Electrical Conductivity: Just before the begining of the irrigation season, the EC value in the lower block, is rather high than other periods because of the condensation of contaminants in creek water. According to the location of each block, the EC values gradually increased from the upper block to the lower block (see Fig.8 and Fig.9). This tendency indicates the water quality decrease after n^{th} reuse cycles during irrigation season.

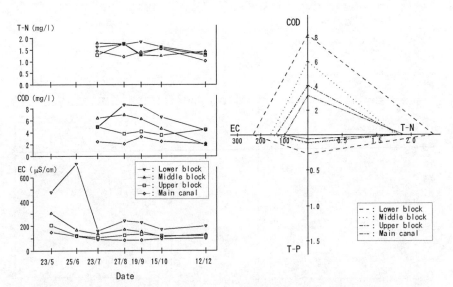

Figure 8. Variation Water Quality of Each Block.

Figure 9. Deportment of Water Quality Components (Sept.19, 1991)

CONCLUSION

The reuse mechanism of return flow in the irrigation system with creek network using the complex tank method was discussed. The conceptual definition of cyclic use of return flow was proposed to evaluate quantitively the irrigation efficiency with reuse mechanism.

Water quality indices such as EC, COD and T-N are gradually increased in the upper block, in the middle block and in the lower block in order (see Fig.9 and Fig.10). This fact suggests that the increased reuse cycles of irrigation water affects the increasing of the index values, since the returning water used in the upper block is being used in the middle block and in the lower block.

In continous clear days, irrigation efficiency of water use will be kept arround 200%. In the rainy day, storage water is being replaced by runoff from rainfalls, so the irrigation efficiency will tend to decrease. But the replacement of storage water by runoff is useful in maintaining suitable water quality conditions.

Acknowledgement

The writers are grateful to Tamotsu Funakoshi (Research Associate) and Misako Kojima (Grad. Student) for their sincere co-operations in field survey and laboratory works.

References

1. Ikushima, Y. and M. Kuroda. 1973. On the Water Budget after Land Readjustment for Heavy Clay Soil Paddy Field Close to Creek. Bulletin of Faculty of Agriculture Saga University. 35:31-49. (in Japanese).

2. Kuroda, M., T. Cho. 1988. Water Management and Operation of Irrigation System in Low Lying Paddy Area with Creek Network. Irrigation Engineering and Rural Planning, The Japanese Society of Irrigation, Drainage and Reclamation Engineering. 13:36-46.

3. Kuroda, M., T. Fukuda and F. Nurrochmad. 1991. Operation of Irrigation System and Water Management in Low Lying Paddy Area with Creek Network. Irrigation and Drainage, Proc. of the 1991 National Conference ASCE. 31-37.

4. Kadoya, M., A. Nagai. 1980. Techniques for Runoff Analysis, Journal of The Japanese Society of Irrigation, Drainage and Reclamation Engineering. 48 (12):51-59.

5. Nurrochmad, F., M. Kuroda and T. Fukuda.1992. Quantification Analysis On Factors Affecting Operation of Irrigation in Low Lying Paddy Area. Proc. of the ASAE. (under publishing).

6. Phuc, N., K. Tanabe and M. Kuroda. 1975. Variation of Dissolved Oxygen in the Flooding Water of the Paddy Fields. J. Fac. Agr., Kyushu Univ. 20: 47-60.

7. Tabuchi, T.(ed). 1987. Manual of Water Qualities for Agricultural Engineers The Japanese Society of Irrigation, Drainage and Reclamation Engineering. 17-19 (in Japanese).

ROTATIONAL GRAZING MODEL OF GOATS ON KUDZU-INFESTED FORESTLAND

A. Woldeghebriel*
R. N. Corley III
109 Milbank Hall
Tuskegee University
Tuskegee AL 36088

M. R. Murphy
University of Illinois
315 Animal Sciences Lab.
1207 West Gregory Drive
Urbana, ILL 62801

Funded by
USDA/ Forest Service, Southern Experiment Station Auburn Alabama

Simulation models of varying degrees of complexity have been used extensively to help understand the interaction between forages and animals grazing them. One of the major advantages of computer simulation models arises from the relative ease and lower expense of making computer runs and therefore, minimizing the requirement for costly and lengthy experiments. Modeling animal production to understand and predict the performance response of animals to dietary or environmental changes has become widely established in recent years. Normally, models develop as conceptual approaches to specific problems, but rapidly develop into computer simulation that require numbers (Robinson et al., 1990).

Simulation models, by nature, are also multivariate and thus make use pooled data from conventional studies. However, data from published research tend to be situation specific; and, therefore, when pooled by some commonality, they may introduce dissimilarities which can then affect the productive power of the model. Consequently, instead of making an absolute comparison between the output of the model and the experimental design it seemed more appropriate to observe if the conclusion drawn by the model agreed with the experimental data.

---

*A. WOLDEGHEBRIEL, Assistant Professor, R. N. CORLEY, Research Assistant, Tuskegee University, Tuskegee, Alabama and M. R. MURPHY, Associate Professor, University of Illinois, Urbana, Illinois

Angora goats are being introduced into the forest management system as a biological control for kudzu in some areas of Alabama. Kudzu (*pueraria lobata*) is a trailing or highly-climbing leguminous vine, native to eastern Asia. It was introduced into the eastern United States in 1876 as a soil erosion control measure. In this study a quantitative simulation model was developed which included angora goats in a forest management system to: (1) estimate forage yield and animal performance, and (2) predict how effectively the goats might keep kudzu under control.

Procedures:

The model (using the Stella II program on a Macintosh IIci) was designed to estimate: (1) net daily rate of forage production, (2) daily forage dry matter intake (DDMI), and (3) weight change of grazing goats (Fig. 1). The construction and validation of the model was difficult because, there are few relevant data available on kudzu. Therefore, some of the assumptions made in developing the model were: that grazing days per hectare could be used as a measure of grazing land productivity and the growth period of kudzu for one season was from March 1 to September 30 (adapted from the general forage growth model of Sibbald et al.,1979) with an estimated growth rate of 32 kg of dry matter (DM) /ha/d. Grazing was assumed to start May 1, after 61 d of undisturbed plant growth.

Intake was defined as the amount of herbage DM removed by animals each day. The period of occupation or length of stay of each paddock (8 d) was intentionally short to minimize the forced grazing of the animals on lower quality forages and to prevent excessive removal of photosynthetic material so that plant regeneration time would remain relatively short. The interval between successive grazing, or return time (RT), was calculated as the product of the number of paddocks minus 1 times the length of stay in each paddock. The 24 d RT of each paddock was considered adequate for growth between successive grazing cycles.

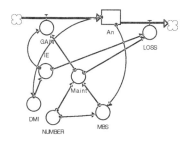

Figure. 1 Animal Growth Model

The equations used to establish the relationship between kudzu and the grazing animals were:

$$\frac{df}{dt} = \frac{dW}{dt} - (C+V) \text{ -------------------- (eq.1)}$$

Where:

$\dfrac{df}{dt}$ = net daily rate of forage produced = net accumulation rate,

$\dfrac{dW}{dt}$ = daily gross forage growth rate,

C = daily rate of consumption by the animal, and

V = daily rate of forage loss due to non-grazing causes

The growth rate of forage was defined as the rate of change in weight over time, and the net daily rate of forage produced, or the net accumulation rate (df/dt), was the difference between the daily gross forage growth rate (dw/dt) and the utilization rate (C + V) -eq 1 (Charles-Edwards et al., 1978). The amount of forage harvested at the end of the grazing season was calculated using eq. 2.

$$Hf = Ho + dt*(gz1+ gz2+ gz3 + gz4) \text{ ---------------- (eq. 2)}$$

where:
Hf = total harvestable forage, and
Ho = harvestable forage at time 0.

Growth rate of animals was defined as the rate of change in weight over time. The quantity of forage available to animals at any moment does not necessarily have a close relationship to the rate at which animals gain or lose weight. However, the rate of weight change (dm/dt) is a direct function of the amount of forage consumed (I) by the animals over the specified time period times the proportion of the useful or extractable energy (a_o), minus the rate at which energy is used to meet the maintenance requirement (Z) of the animal and energy used for moderate activity (A) provided that all other nutrients are adequate, (eq.3. adapted from Charles-Edwards et al.,1987).

$$\frac{dm}{dt} = a_o(I)-(Z+A) \text{ --------------------------- (eq.3)}$$

Where:

$\frac{dm}{dt}$ = rate of live weight change

I = amount of forage consumed over time (kg DM)
a_o = the proportion of the extractable energy (kcal/kg DM)
z = rate at which energy is used for maintenance (kg DMI equivalent/d), and
A = rate at which energy is used for moderate activity = .5 x Z (Mcal/d)

Energy and protein utilization was calculated using equations 4 and 5:

$$DMI = [.5^* \sin (2^*pi^*TIME/365) +3.0]^*Wt/100 \text{ ----- (eq. 4)}$$

IWt. = 40 kg
$DMI^\wedge$ = 40* .035 = 1.40 kg maximum
IE = $DMI^\wedge$*1.82 Mcal ME/kg DM = 2.548 Mcal
Mc = MBS *.10138 Mcal = 1.612 (NRC, 1981)

Where:

lwt = Average initial weight of goats,
IE = intake energy,
Mc = maintenance cost
MBS = metabolic body size $(W.^{75})$.

Equation 4 allows DMI to vary from 2.5 to 3.5% of body weight, but animals can not meet their requirements unless DMI is set to a minimum of 3.5% $(DMI^\wedge)$.

Therefore,
a. IF [IE > Mc + A], then weight gain occurs;
b. IF [IE < Mc + A], then weight loss occurs; and
c. IF [IE = Mc + A], then there is no change in weight.

The calculated net energy balance [IE - (Mc+A)] was 130 kcal ME/head/d in excess of what was needed for maintenance and moderate activity. According to the NRC (1981) the daily energy requirement is only 7.25 kcal ME/g weight gained. If the excess energy was used for growth, goats will gain at the rate of 17.93 g/d. If the excess energy is used for fiber production the amount of energy available for fiber production is only 43 Kcal ME/d (ME is used for fiber production with 33% efficiency). The ME and DP required/kg of fiber/y are 30 Kcal and 3 g/d, respectively, (NRC, 1981). Therefore, the average goat would have enough energy to produce 1.4 kg of fiber (30 kcal per kg). Even though energy is not a limiting factor, the bulk of the fiber produced is protein. Consequently, protein availability and utilization for each animal was calculated using eq. 5.

$$DPI = DMI* \%DP = (1.4 \text{ kg}*.107) = 149.8 \text{ g} ------------(eq. 5)$$

Where,
DPI = Digestible protein intake

Kudzu contains 10.7% digestible protein (DP) Morrison (1948).

The DP requirements of an average goat weighing 40 kg for the different activities are:
Mc+A = 64 g/d,
Growth (50 g/d) = 10 g/d, and
3 g/d/kg fiber/y (NRC, 1981);
therefore, assuming an average yield of 4 kg fiber/head/y, only 12 g of DP is needed for fiber production. This brings the total DP required per head to 86 g/d with 63.8 g/d of excess protein.

RESULTS

Grazing days was calculated as the product of the number of animals times the average number of days animals spent grazing each paddock.

Using DM availability as a measure of grazing land productivity, the grazing days of the area were estimated at 143 d/ha for the grazing season (250 d/ha/y equivalent). At the beginning of the grazing season, it was assumed that the initial herbage mass in each paddock was the same. This was later increased at the rate of 32 kg of DM/ha/d in paddocks 2, 3 and 4 for each additional day that they were not occupied by the goats. This pattern continued for paddocks 3 and 4 when paddock 2 was occupied, and for paddock 4 when 3 was occupied (Fig. 2). Dry matter yield was estimated at 5.5 t/ha/y (15.1 kg/ha/d) which was 1.5 t lower than was reported by Miles and Gross (1939). However, field data collected from ungrazed adjacent site during early and mid-growth periods of kudzu using the conventional hand plucking method from a portable grid system showed a much lower DM yield (3.6 t) with an accumulation rate of 9.9 kg/ha/d.

In a situation where the grazing period is more than one day, it is desirable to take into account the herbage production during the grazing period. The formula that is commonly used to estimate the magnitude of the herbage produced while animals are grazing is that of Linehan et al.

(1947). However, according to Lantinga (1985), the reliability of the Linehan equation is poor if the grazing period is more than 3 d. This is because of the assumed exponential growth pattern of ungrazed herbage, which can lead to underestimation of herbage produced and consumed.

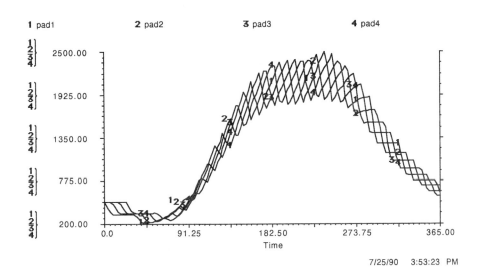

Figure 2.   Dry Matter Accumulation of Paddocks (First Year)

Lantinga (1985) also suggested that the larger the relative difference between the herbage mass at the start of the grazing period and the herbage mass in the undisturbed control at the end of the grazing period, the less accurately the Linehan equation predicts the quantity of herbage produced during grazing.

The model overestimated the regrowth potential of kudzu because the model assumed a fixed net growth rate (32 kg of DM/ha/d) for the entire grazing period. This means that the model did not consider the effect of grazing on subsequent growth. Additionally, the non-grazing loss was not included because it was assumed that the rate of non-grazing loss would be equal to the rate of daily growth during grazing. The amount of digestible kudzu per unit area was also expected to decrease with time but further losses of digestible material occurred with losses in pasture due to grazing and decay which the model did not take into account, hence again overestimating forage availability.

The total amount of herbage consumed was calculated as a daily average per goat over the entire grazing period times the number of goats grazing.

Total dry matter intake and animal weight gain for the entire simulation period were estimated at 1600 and 157.7 kg, respectively, with a feed conversion efficiency ratio of 10:1. Therefore, the estimated average weight gain of the goats was 34.5 g/d. However, the average daily gain of the animals started to decrease after 143 d of grazing. When grazing was extended 25 d beyond the estimated grazing period (Fig. 3), the goats started to lose weight. This type of body weight cycle normally occurs in year-round grazing situations (Charles-Edwards et al., 1978).

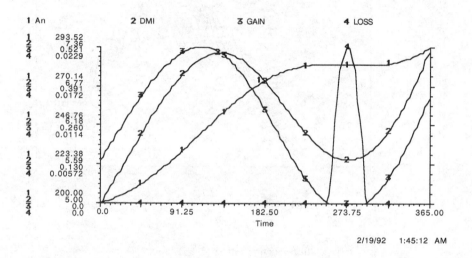

2/19/92   1:45:12 AM

Fig. 3   Intake and Weight Change of Goats (kg)

During the 1990 grazing season goats grazed continuously on a site stocked at the rate of 27 goats/ha and gained 160 g/h/d; did not gain weight the next year. This may mean that the goats had reached maturity and any excess energy obtained was used for fiber production. Other possible explanations for the lack of growth during the second growth season are lower dry matter accumulation in the pasture following the first year's intensive grazing, or reduced DMI.

As for the the effectiveness of the goats in controlling the kudzu, field observations of the paddocks occupied for three successive grazing cycles (32 goats/ha/y equivalent) showed that the goats kept the kudzu under complete control. The model also predicted a much lower peak (fig. 4) and a shorter growth period for kudzu during the second growth season possibly due to root storage depletion following repeated grazing cycles.

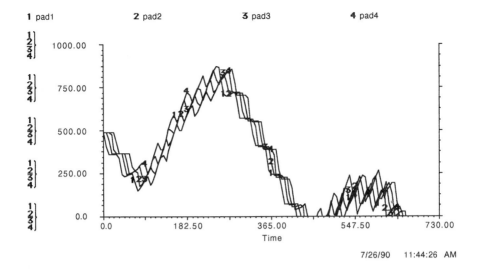

7/26/90   11:44:26 AM

Figure 4. First and Second Year Dry Matter Accumulation of Paddocks (kg)

While the model requires calibration, and further validation, it suggests rotational grazing may be an alternative to the traditional and expensive chemical control method used today in the southeastern United States. The model also estimated forage utilization and animal performance. In the absence of suitable experimental data on kudzu, many of the predictions made by the model cannot yet be adequately substantiated; however, errors in estimates of the number of grazing days and the dry matter yield are considered very low.

The major limitation of the present model is a lack of pertinent data. Little is known about the dry matter yield, growth behavior and even the nutritional value of kudzu to animals. Data collected for three growing seasons at the Experiment Station will be used to validate the model. The main focus of the preliminary research was to provide an analytical framework which would allow the multiple use of forestland while, at the same time maintain an adequate forage biomass as a soil cover to minimize erosion.

REFERENCES

1   Charles-Edwards, D. A., P. Tow and T. R. Evans. 1987. An analysis of
     the growth rate of pasture and animal production. Agricultural
     Systems, 25 : 245-259.

2.   Lantinga, E. A. 1985. Simulation of herbage production and herbage
     intake during a rotational grazing period; An evaluation   of Linhan's
     formula. Netherlands J. Agric. Sci. 33: 385-403.

3.   Linehan, P. A., J. Lowe and R. H. Stewart. 1947. The output of pasture
     and its measurement. Part II. J. Brt. Grassland Soci. 2: 145-168.

4.   Miles, I. E. and E. E. Gross. 1939. A compilation of information on
     kudzu. Mississippi Agric. Exper. Station Bull. No. 326.

5.   Morrison, F. B. 1948. Feeds and Feeding. 21st. Ed.

6.   NRC. 1981. Nutrient Requirements of Domestic Animals. Nutrient
     Requirements of Goats. National Academy of Science. National
     Research Council. Washington, DC.

7.   Robinson, P. H., G. Coto, M. D. Stern and D. M. Viera 1990.
     Interlaboratory variation in a diaminopimelic acid assay: Influence
     on estimated duodenal bacterial nitrogen flow. J. Dairy Sci.73: 2929.

8.   Sibbald, A. R., T. J. Maxwell and J. Eadie. 1979. A conceptual approach
     to the modeling of herbage intake by hill sheep. Agric. System. 4:
     121.

SOIL EROSION, RUNOFF AND WATER RELEASE CHARACTERISTICS

OF MEXICO SILT LOAM/MUNICIPAL SOLID WASTE MIXTURES

W.H. Neibling[1]   A.L. Thompson
Member ASAE   Member ASAE

Disposal of municipal solid waste (MSW) in an environmentally sound manner is one of our greatest challenges. Municipal solid waste production was estimated at 136 million metric tons in 1985 and is expected to continue to increase. Roughly 90 percent of this material is disposed of by landfilling (USEPA, 1989). A 1986 Wall Street Journal article estimated that by 1990 more than half the cities surveyed would exhaust landfill space (Morris and Seldman, 1986). One challenge then is to find environmentally safe ways to use this waste material in some positive manner, thus decreasing the volume of wastes that must be disposed by landfilling.

Investigations conducted in New York, New Jersey and Tennessee show that on an average, about 70% of municipal wastes by weight are degradable (paper, food and yard wastes, etc) (Besley and Reed, 1972). With curbside recycling to separate most non-degradable items such as metal cans, glass, oil and household chemicals, the degradable fraction would contain a low level of potentially harmful materials and could be land applied and incorporated. A 70% reduction in weight of material requiring landfill disposal would significantly lengthen the useful life of current landfills.

Claypan soils such as the Mexico series cover a large area of central and northeastern Missouri. These soils typically have a silt loam A horizon approximately 20 cm. deep overlying a much less permeable B horizon, or "claypan". Infiltration rates in the surface soil are moderate (1.5 - 5.1 cm/hr), but are quite slow (< 0.15 cm/hr) in the B horizon. Clay content of the surface layer is 15-27%, while at 20-28 cm. it is 35-50% and at 28-91 cm. it is 50-60%. Moist bulk density of the surface layer is 1.2-1.4 g/cc. wile it ranges from 1.25-1.45 at depths greater than 20 cm. (USDA, 1989). As the A horizon is removed by erosion, increasing amounts of the less permeable B horizon soil are mixed in the plow layer, progressively reducing infiltration rates, soil tilth, quality of seedbed and water available for crop use.

The addition of large quantities of organic matter to a soil such as the Mexico should in concept modify the pore size distribution and decrease soil bulk density. This is supported by field observations on Guelph silt loam (Webber, 1978) and Sango silt loam (Mays et al., 1973). Initial changes in soil properties from addition of uncomposted organic matter would be expected to decrease over time as the organic matter decomposed, similar in fashion to that from addition of manure (Meek et al., 1982). Since some materials such as lignins would decompose very slowly, benefits to the soil should be relatively long lasting.

---

[1]W.H. Neibling, Extension Water Management Engineer, Agricultural Engineering Dept., University of Idaho, Moscow, ID (formerly Assistant Professor, Agricultural Engineering Dept., University of Missouri, Columbia, MO) and A.L. Thompson, Associate Professor, Agricultural Engineering Dept., University of Missouri, Columbia, MO.

Contribution from the Missouri Agricultural Experiment Station.

In a related study on a Guelph silt loam soil near Guelph, Ontario, unsorted municipal garbage was ground, land applied at several rates and incorporated to a depth of 30 cm. by moldboard plowing (Webber, 1978). General findings were that soil carbon and nitrogen, and percent water stable aggregates increased with increments of solid waste added. Soil moisture retention at 0.04, 0.33 and 15 bars was not significantly affected by any treatment, nor was corn grain yield.

Incorporation of large quantities of organic matter in the surface layer of an uneroded Mexico soil should give a response similar to the Webber work since the soil characteristics were similar. Incorporation to a depth of one meter in the Mexico soil should improve bulk density, root penetration, infiltration and possible water holding capacity more than might be indicated by the Webber study due to the initial high clay content, high bulk density and resulting low infiltration rates of the B horizon of the Mexico soil relative to the Guelph silt loam.

PROCEDURE

The objective of this study was to determine possible changes in agronomic properties and therefore potential crop productivity of the Mexico silt loam soil (Fine, montmorillonitic, mesic Udollic Ochraqualfs) as affected by addition of the degradable portion of a typical municipal solid waste. The initial phase of the study involved examination of the literature to determine appropriate functional relationships between addition of organic material and changes in soil physical properties. Changes in properties for a Mexico silt loam could then be verified in the laboratory, and if improvement in crop productivity looked promising, the experiment could be scaled up for field study.

One established method to evaluate the relationship between soil physical properties and crop productivity is the Productivity Index (Neill, 1979; Kiniry et al., 1983) which was modified and validated for central Missouri conditions by Gantzer and McCarty (1987). This index considers crop productivity to be a function of bulk density, pH, available water holding capacity, and root water extraction pattern. Gantzer and McCarty (1987) and Thompson et al. (1992) found that for the Mexico silt loam, bulk density and available water holding capacity were the dominant factors. Therefore, to determine feasibility for increase of crop productivity by addition of ground MSW, relationships between MSW addition and bulk density and available soil water were required.

Review of Soil Physical Property/Amendment Addition Relationships

Bulk Density: Bulk density of the soil matrix depends on the particle size distribution of the soil solids, the degree of aggregation of these particles into larger aggregates of sand, silt, and clay, and level of compactive energy applied and the moisture content at which that compactive energy was applied. Bulk density of most agricultural soils is roughly 1.1 to 1.3 for freshly tilled soil and increases to 1.4 to 1.5 as consolidation occurs between tillage operations (Israelson and Hansen, 1979).

Addition of organic waste tends to decrease bulk density. For example, addition of 376 Mg/ha uncomposted, ground, MSW reduced bulk density of a Guelph silt loam from 1.38 to 1.17 (Webber, 1978) while addition of 327 Mg/ha of a composted MSW/sewage sludge mixture reduced bulk density of a Sango silt loam from 1.37 to 1.12 (Mays et al., 1973). Waste was applied twice in each study, in the first and third years of the Webber study and in two consecutive years in the Mays et al. study.

Long-term relationships between bulk density and organic matter may be inferred from studies on uncultivated soils. Linear change in bulk density per unit change in percent organic matter was 5.7% for Vermont forest soils (Curtis and Post, 1964), and 3.2% English forest soils (Adams, 1973).

Potential Available Water Content (PAWC): Potential available water content describes that portion of water held in the soil that can be extracted by a growing plant. It is defined as the difference in water contents at soil water tensions of 0.33 and 15 bars (field capacity and permanent wilting point, respectively). Field capacity is the moisture content of the soil after free water has been removed by internal drainage and is typically the water content of soil initially saturated by water 1-3 days after rainfall or irrigation. When water is removed by plants or by evaporation to permanent wilting point, plants will not recover when adequate moisture is then added to the soil. Available soil water is usually measured by equilibrating soil samples in pressure cells at 0.33 and 15 atmospheres of gauge pressure and then measuring water content.

Results are inconclusive regarding improvements in PAWC due to addition of organic materials. Webber (1978), using uncomposted MSW found a linear increase from 11.1 to 13 percent water by weight held at 15 bars when level of MSW application ranged from 0 to 376 Mg/ha. This MSW addition initially changed organic matter content from 4.1% to 6.5%. When multiplied by bulk density, no statistically significant difference in volumetric water content with MSW rate was found at any soil water tension level. Therefore no statistically significant change in available soil water was observed. However, Mays et al. (1973) found addition of composted MSW and sewage sludge increased PAWC from 11.1% to 15.3% as application rate was changed from 0 to 327 Mg/ha. This difference in response was perhaps due to the lower initial organic matter and greater increase in organic matter from 1.58% to 4.22% in the Mays et al. study.

Infiltration Rate: Increase in the quantity of water entering the soil surface by addition of organic wastes does not directly change the productivity of the soil as described by the PI. It does, however, make more water available to the plant per unit water applied by rainfall or irrigation and helps reduce soil erosion by decreasing surface runoff. Since no studies relating addition of MSW to infiltration rate were found, a similar study using manure is most directly applicable. Water intake rates showed a nearly linear increase with manure addition, with a 1 percentage point increase in organic matter decreasing infiltration time by 31%. Range of organic matter content studied was about 0.5 to 4%. Since this effect was shown to last only one year after the year of application, manure applications must be made at least in alternate years.

Soil Erodibility: Addition of organic matter improves soil infiltration and tilth characteristics (Meek et al., 1982), which tend to reduce soil erodibility (Wischmeier and Smith, 1978). Since most silt loam soils tend to be highly erodible, it was desirable to determine the potential for reducing erodibility through the addition of organic amendments.

The soil erosion process can be considered as composed of four processes: detachment of soil particles by raindrop impact, detachment by flowing water, transport downslope by raindrop impact and transport by flowing water (Meyer and Wischmeier, 1969). The detachment processes can be considered as a force/resistance model. That is, when detaching forces such as raindrop impact or flowing water exceed the resisting forces such as gravity and inter-particle cohesion (soil strength), detachment of particles from the soil mass will occur. An increase in inter-particle cohesion by addition of organic matter will decrease this component of the erosion process.

Once soil particles are detached from the soil mass they must be moved downslope for erosion to occur. Local movement can occur as transport by raindrop splash, with the majority of movement by transport due to flowing water. In many instances, erosion from a slope may be limited by the transport process, with more detached soil particles available for movement than can be moved by flowing water. Transport by flowing water is dependent on flowrate and velocity and is enhanced by raindrop impact (Neibling, 1984). Any factor that increases infiltration will decrease the runoff rate and therefore sediment transport and erosion. As a result, some soils with low soil strength such as sands can show low soil erodibilities due to their high infiltration rates.

Calculated change in soil physical properties due to amendment additions

Potential Available Water Content (PAWC): To assess the change in water holding capacity of a claypan soil due to organic matter addition, a relationship between soil physical properties and water held in the soil at specified tension levels developed by Gupta and Larson (1971), was used. They verified equation performance by comparison of predicted and measured water contents for 61 Missouri soils. Predicted volumetric water content of the soil for a given tension level is a function of percent sand, silt, clay, organic matter and bulk density of the soil. PAWC equals the sum of each of these factors multiplied by a coefficient. Based on previous discussion, addition of one application of 376 Mg/ha of MSW is assumed to reduce bulk density from an average value of 1.35 to 1.2 and increase organic matter from 1% to 19%. For a typical eroded Mexico silt loam soil, PAWC is then calculated to increase from 0.108 to 0.133 cm^3/cm^3.

Soil erodibility: The soil erodibility nomograph (Wischmeier and Smith, 1978) can be used to relate soil erodibility to soil physical properties. In this equation, soil erodibility (K) is related to percent 2-100um particles, % clay, % organic matter, soil structure and soil permeability. Since addition of organic material will not change the soil textural properties, the only way addition of MSW can change soil erodibility is through % organic matter, soil structure and soil permeability terms. A typical eroded Mexico silt loam has a soil erodibility of about 0.32. Based on previous discussion, one application of 376 Mg/ha of MSW is assumed to reduce bulk density from an average value of 1.35 to 1.2, increase organic matter from 1% to 19%, improve soil structure from "medium or coarse granular" to "fine granular", and increase soil permeability from "slow" to "moderate". Since the soil erodibility nomograph was only developed for organic matter content of 12 % or less, an organic matter content of 9.8% was used (that expected for 188 Mg/ha of MSW) to be conservative. Under these conditions, soil erodibility is reduced from 0.32 to 0.065. If periodic addition of MSW could maintain organic matter at 4%, soil erodibility would be reduced to 0.17, a considerable improvement.

Soil productivity index (PI): The aggregate effect on bulk density and PAWC of adding 376 Mg/ha of MSW to an eroded Mexico silt loam soil can be estimated with the PI approach discussed earlier. With an estimated decrease in bulk density from 1.35 to 1.20, and increase in PAWC from 0.108 to 0.133, change in PI was calculated to be from 0.46 to 0.64, a ratio of 1.38:1. These calculations are based on one application of MSW. Decomposition over time and repeated applications will give different results.

Laboratory testing of soil/MSW mixtures

Given the considerable predicted improvement in bulk density, PAWC, soil productivity and soil erodibility, the next step in evaluating potential soil property improvement was to conduct a series of laboratory experiments to determine results from one addition of MSW to an actual B horizon Mexico silt loam soil. Soil tests described below were performed on the following combinations of treatments:

Soil type:	Mexico B horizon
Refuse level:	0, 188, 376 Mg/ha oven dry weight
Refuse type:	uncomposted
Replications:	3

Soil tests performed include measurement of (1) pre- and post-rainfall bulk density (2) water release curves by standard pressure plate analysis of each soil mix, and (3) interrill erosion and infiltration as a function of time by the use of the USDA-ARS variable intensity rainfall simulator (Meyer and Harmon, 1979).

The soil was obtained from the University of Missouri South farm, sieved through an 8 mm. screen, air dried and stored until used. This is a standard procedure for erosion studies and aids in reproducibility of results from one sample to the next (Neibling, 1984). Soil/refuse mixtures were combined with a portable cement mixer. Uncomposted refuse was mixed from standard ingredients using a procedure developed for testing of degradable plastics at UMC. Refuse composition as percent by dry weight was 49.2% paper, 16.5% food waste, 17.5% lawn and garden waste, 4.5% wood chips, 8.4% rubber, leather and plastics, 2% textiles, and 1.9% rock and dirt (Hanks, 1967; Besley and Reed, 1972). Moisture content was approximately 60% on a wet basis.

The soil test boxes for rainfall simulation tests consisted of 0.3m wide by 1 m long metal boxes filled with a 1 cm. diameter perforated drainage system. Three cm. of fine sand was placed in each box and consolidated by impact shaking for 5 minutes. The sand layer was then covered with 15 cm. of soil or soil/refuse mix and again consolidated for a five minute period. This procedure produced a uniformly packed bed with an average bulk density of approximately 1.1. Bulk densities were determined for each test bed. Values were 1.0, 1.09, and 1.16 for the high, low, and no refuse treatments, respectively.

Each soil treatment was exposed to a three-storm sequence of rainfall at 64 mm/h. The first run was a 60-minute test under initially dry soil conditions. The second run followed 24 hours later under wet antecedent soil moisture conditions. After a 30-minute pause, the third run was made under very wet antecedent soil moisture conditions. Runoff samples were collected each minute for the first 5 minutes of runoff and at 5 minute intervals thereafter for each rainfall run.

Runoff rates were determined by measuring the weight of each timed runoff sample and sediment discharge rates by determining the oven-dried sediment weight of each times runoff sample. Four samples were taken following each run to determine post-rainfall bulk density by obtaining the oven dry weight of known volumes of soil containing aluminum rings buried in the soil before rainfall was applied.

Soil/refuse mixtures for water characteristic curve determination were mixed in the same manner as for the erosion tests. Because some of the refuse formed 2-3 cm. diameter clumps, it was necessary to reduce the maximum size of refuse for use in the 5 cm. diameter, 1 cm. tall cylinders used in the pressure cells. Representative samples of the refuse were passed through a 0.63 cm. screen and then mixed with the proper weight of soil. Large clumps retained on the screen were ground until they passed the screen. Three cylinders were used for each soil mixture treatment and pressure combination, for a total of 81 cylinders used. All cylinders and plates were then placed in pressure cells and exposed to pressures of 1/3, 1 and 15 bars (340,1020, and 15,300 cm. of water). Four days later, approximately 24 hours after no additional outflow from cells was detected, the samples were removed, and gravimetric moisture content determined.

RESULTS AND DISCUSSION

The results reported here are from the complete series of water characteristic curve tests but only from the first replication of the erosion and runoff tests. As a result, no firm conclusions can be drawn from the erosion and runoff data but certain trends can be noted.

Water Characteristic Curves

Water characteristic data were plotted in Figure 1 for both the A and B horizons with mixtures of no, low and high levels of refuse. From this plot it can be seen that gravimetric water content is approximately 3.5 percentage points greater for the soil from the B horizon compared to the A horizon at equivalent levels of capillary pressure head in the range of 340 to 15,200 cm. The addition of low and then high levels of refuse for these two soil profiles increased soil gravimetric water content in all cases. For the A horizon soil mixture, this increase was 1.5 and 4 percentage points, respectively at 340 cm. capillary pressure head, 0.75 and 2 percentage points, respectively at 1020 cm., and 0.1 and 1 percent, respectively at 15,300 cm.

For the B horizon, additions of low and high levels of refuse resulted in increases of 1 and 3 percentage points, 1 and 1.5 percentage points, and 0.5 and 1.5 percentage points, respectively for capillary pressure heads of 340, 1020 and 15,300 cm. The net result is that for each soil horizon-refuse mixture, there was at most a slight increase in water holding capacity. This finding is consistent with that of Webber, 1978, who found no significant change in water holding capacity when unsorted ground solid municipal waste was added to field plots of Guelph silt loam. However, results from multiple applications in a field condition could be different.

Runoff Rates

Runoff rate in mm/h is shown in Figure 2 for each of the three antecedent soil moisture conditions tested for the no refuse treatment. Runoff began 7 minutes after the start of rainfall and reached a near-equilibrium level 20 minutes after the start of rainfall, although the runoff rate did continue to slowly increase throughout the entire dry run. Runoff from the wet and very wet runs began within two minutes and reached an equilibrium level by 10 and 5 minutes, respectively on the wet and very wet runs. Since the rainfall rate was 64 mm/h, this steady state runoff rate represented a steady state infiltration rate of approximately 8 mm/h. Excavation of the soil following the run showed that the wetting front had advanced to a depth of 7 cm. in a soil of depth 15 cm. therefore surface and profile conditions, not boundary conditions, were limiting infiltration.

Runoff rate in mm/h is shown for the dry run for each of the soil/refuse treatments in Figure 3. Runoff response is similar for the no and low refuse levels. This might be expected since the low refuse level gave very little increase in surface cover. Runoff for the high refuse level began later than required significantly longer to reach an equilibrium level. The high level of surface cover appeared to provide some additional increase in roughness and surface storage, and provided protection against raindrop impact which delayed formation of a surface seal. Excavation following the run showed that the wetting front had reached approximately 9-10 cm. in the low refuse case and 12-15 cm. in the high refuse case, a 42% increase in infiltration due to the high refuse level.

Interrill Erosion Rates (sediment discharge rates)

Sediment discharge rate in g/min/m**2 is shown for each refuse level dry run in Figure 4 and for each of the wet runs in Figure 5. During the dry run, sediment discharge from the no and low refuse level runs was similar, as were the respective runoff rates. The sediment discharge rates for the no and low residue levels increased, peaked after 20 or 30 minutes, and then decreased during the rest of the run. This decrease could be due to the early removal of the easily eroded sediment, and to the formation of a surface seal which then limited the erosion rate.

Sediment discharge rates in the wet run are more than double those at the end of the dry run. This is due to an increase in the sediment concentration in the runoff since runoff rates were nearly the same during the two periods of comparison. This increase does not seem compatible

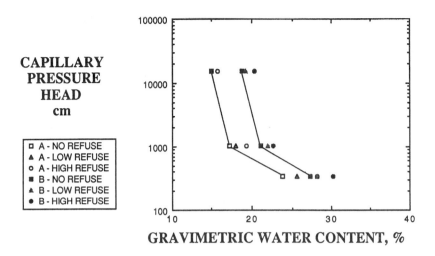

Figure 1. Capillary pressure head vs. gravimetric water content for three refuse levels of A and B horizon Mexico silt loam soil.

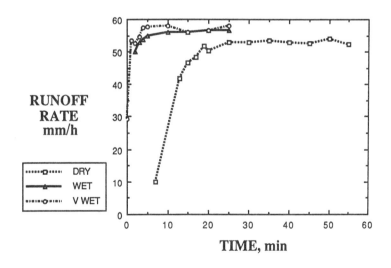

Figure 2. Runoff rate with time for the B horizon Mexico silt loam soil with refuse added.

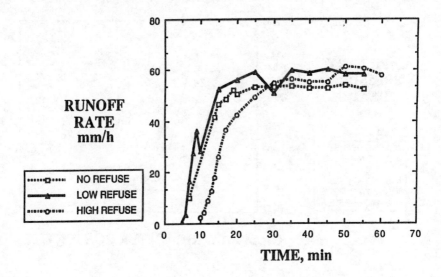

Figure 3.   Runoff rate with time for the dry run, B horizon Mexico silt loam soil.

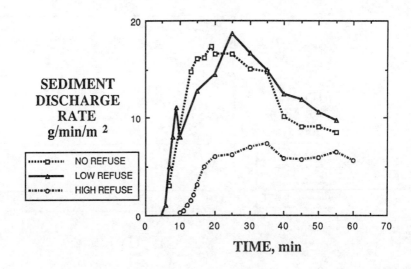

Figure 4.   Sediment discharge rate with time for the dry run, B horizon Mexico silt loam soil.

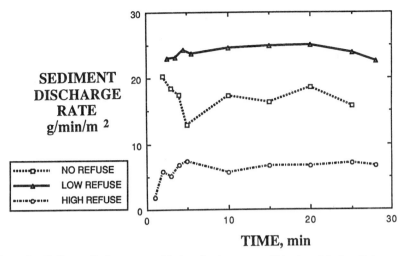

Figure 5.   Sediment discharge rate with time for the wet run, B horizon Mexico silt loam soil.

with the formation of a surface seal and is difficult to explain. It is hoped that the results of the two additional replications will help explain these results.

As before, the high refuse level was significantly different than the other two treatments, producing a consistently lower sediment discharge rate which reached an equilibrium level after about 40 minutes and continued at this rate during the wet run. The considerable surface cover present on the high refuse pan appears to limit erosion rates both by protection of the surface from raindrop impact and by limiting overland flow transport because of increased roughness.

SUMMARY AND CONCLUSIONS

Analysis of relationships between organic matter addition and soil physical properties from the literature were used to determine possible improvement in soil productivity and reduction in runoff and erosion. Based on favorable results, a laboratory study using the B horizon of a Mexico silt loam was initiated. Mixtures of the three refuse levels in both A and B horizon soil and a mix of A and B soils were tested to determine soil water characteristic curves by a standard pressure plate analysis. Differences between soils and between treatments within soils were consistent but small in magnitude. Increasing levels of refuse gave higher gravimetric water contents at the same level of capillary pressure head. Gravimetric water contents were always higher for the B horizon than for the A horizon at the same level of capillary pressure head.

Mixtures of the B horizon (claypan) of a Mexico silt loam soil and 0, 188 and 376 Mg/ha over dry weight of municipal solid waste were exposed to simulated rainfall at 64 mm/h for a two-hour sequence of runs. Infiltration and interrill erosion rates were determined for the first replication of this continuing study. Initial indications are that the runoff and interrill erosion response of the no and low refuse treatments are similar. The high refuse treatment gave a slightly delayed runoff response, and consistently lower interrill erosion rates relative to the no and low refuse treatments.

Because of the limited amount of data currently available for analysis, no specific conclusions regarding runoff, erosion or bulk density effects can be made at this time.

REFERENCES

1. Adams. W.A. 1973. The effect of organic matter on the bulk and true densities of some uncultivated podzolic soils. J. Soil Sci. 24:10-17.

2. Besley, H.E. and C.H. Reed. 1972. Urban waste management. J. of Environmental Quality. 1:78-81.

3. Curtis, R.O. and B.W. Post. 1964. Estimating bulk density from organic matter content in some Vermont forest soils. Soil Sci. Soc. Am. Proc. 28:285-286.

4. Gantzer, C.J. and T.R. McCarty. 1987. Predicting corn yields on a claypan soil using a soil productivity index. Trans. Am. Soc. Agric. Engrs. 30(5):1347-1352.

5. Gupta, S.C. and W.E. Larson. 1979. Estimating soil water retention characteristics from particle size distribution, organic matter percent, and bulk density. Water Resources Research. 15(6):1633-1635.

6. Hanks, T.G. 1967. Solid waste/disease relationships. U.S. DHEW Public Health Service, Cincinnati, OH. Publication No. 999-UIH-6, 179 pp.

7. Kiniry, L.C., C.L. Scrivner and M.E. Keener. 1983. A soil productivity index based upon predicted water depletion and root growth. University of Missouri-Columbia Research Bulletin 1051.

8. Mays, D.A., G.L. Terman and J.C. Dugan. 1973. Municipal compost: Effects on crop yields and soil properties. J. Environ. Quality. 2(1):89-92.

9. Meek, B., L. Graham and T. Donovan. 1982. Long-term effects of manure on soil nitrogen, phosphorus, potassium, sodium, organic matter, and water infiltration rate. Soil Sci. Soc. Am. J. 46(5):1014-1019.

10. Meyer, L.D. and W.C. Harmon. 1979. Multiple-intensity rainfall simulator for erosion research on row sideslopes. Trans. Am. Soc. Agric. Engrs. 22(1):100-103.

11. Morris D. and Seldman, N. 1986. New ways to keep a lid on America's garbage problem. Wall Street Journal. (April 15, 1986).

12. Neibling, W.H. 1984. Transport and deposition of soil particles by shallow flow on concave slopes. Unpublished Ph.D. Thesis. Purdue University, W. Lafayette, IN 171 pp.

13. Neill, L.L. 1979. An evaluation of soil productivity based on root growth and water depletion. M.S. Thesis. University of Missouri.

14. Thompson, A.L., C.J. Gantzer and R.D. Hammer. 1992. Productivity of a claypan soil under rainfed and irrigated culture. J. Soil and Water Cons. In Press .

15. USEPA. 1989. Standards for the disposal of sewage sludge: proposed rule 40cfr Parts 257 and 503. In: Federal Register 54, No. 23 (Feb. 6, 1989).

16. USDA. 1989. Soil survey of Randolph County, Missouri. U.S. Dept. of Agric., Soil Conservation Service. 98 pp.

17. Webber, L.R. 1978. Incorporation of nonsegregated, noncomposted solid wastes and physical soil properties. J. Environmental Quality. 7(3):397-400.

CHARACTERISTICS OF SUSPENDED SEDIMENT LOADS

AT THE AGRICULTURAL WATERSHEDS IN HOKKAIDO, NORTHERN JAPAN

T. NAGASAWA   Y. UMEDA   T. INOUE[1]

There are two viewpoints concerning conservation problems related to the agricultural land use of watershed. One is soil erosion at the hillslope including arable land, such as surface soil loss and destruction of the agricultural land base. Another problem is that the eroded soil on the slope is transported to the lower reaches of watershed by the river. The importance of the latter is greater because a wide area is being influenced by the river. It is necessary to explain the sedimentation mechanism through the river to lower reaches to understand various problems. And it is indispensable to understand the realities of sedimentation load by the river. So far, many studies have been performed on sedimentation of the river. Many of these studies have sampled water at fixed time intervals. The sampling require much labor and is not safe at high water. Therefore, it is difficult to take samples for a range of time. Especially, the data for flood conditions is not obtained easily. It is possible to understand the behavior of sediment transport in a large river even if the measurement interval is large because the change is gradual. However, the response is sensitive to the weather change in a small watershed river. Therefore, it is difficult to understand the actual conditions based on measurements of once in several hours or days. In this report, the actual conditions of suspended sediment transportation was examined by turbidity. As for turbidity, continuous self-recording is possible and handling is comparatively easy.

SUSPENDED SEDIMENT LOAD IN RIVER

Sediment load transportation by the river is classified as follows:

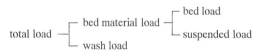

Suspended solid, SS is defined when the grain diameter is 1 μm-2mm. However, the material of 2mm or greater diameter is suspended and transported according to specific gravity and the velocity. Therefore, SS can be expressed as:

[SS] = [wash load] + [suspended load] + [a part of bed load]

SS will constitute a major part of total load. Turbidity is indicated according to the amount of the kaolin in water i.e., 1 ppm (or 1 degree), 1 liter of water contains 1 mg of kaolin. This index expresses "water impurity" quantitatively. The inorganic matter content can be neglected in the agro-forestry watershed. Therefore, SS is shown by the next expression:

[SS] = [suspended sediment] + [organic matter]

---

[1] The authors are: T. Nagasawa, Lecturer, Y. Umeda, Professor, and T. Inoue, Assistant Professor, Faculty of Agriculture, Hokkaido University, Sapporo, Japan.

And from TS = SS + DS

$$[\text{ suspended sediment }] = [\text{ TS }] - \{[\text{ DS }] + [\text{ organic matter }]\}$$
TS: Total Solids, DS: Dissolved Solids

The relative importance of the right hand second term is small when flood is compared with the amount of the entire suspended materials of river. After all, the suspended sediment can be considered about equal to TS during flood.

The value indicated with the turbidity meter does not show the suspended sediment concentration as it is. However, if the relation between the indication of the turbidity meter and TS value is confirmed separately, the suspended sediment concentration can be estimated. That is, the turbidity meter enables a continuous record of the suspended sediment concentration (Nagasawa, 1986).

INVESTIGATION WATERSHEDS

Mokoto River Watershed

This watershed is one of the coldest regions in Japan that face the Okhotskoe. The ground freezes in winter because there is less snowfall. Annual precipitation is about 850mm, and there are many fine days. Land is covered thick with volcanic ash soil derived from the volcanic gush. Figure 2 and Table 1 show the shape and parameters of the watershed. Land use of the watershed is 37% agricultural. Besides, there is natural vegetation such as *Sasa* and woods. Much of the agricultural land is grassland developed with the sloping land in the upper part of the watershed. The lower reaches parts along the river is arable land such as potato, beef, and corn.

Kutyoro River Watershed

The slope of this watershed is in south-north direction. The river flows into the Pacific Ocean. Ground surface is covered with volcanic ash soil. Two observation points were installed in the Kutyoro River. They are Oku-kutyoro point in the upper region and Hikari-basi point in the lower reaches region. Figure 3 shows the watershed shape and the position of the observation points. Watershed parameters are shown in Table 1. Land use of Oku-kutyoro watershed is mostly woodland. In Hikari-basi point watershed, the agricultural land use is 14%, woodland 80%, and the remaining is towns, roads, etc. There are grasslands in the watershed used for agricultural purposes. These grasslands have been reclaimed by the development project that had started in the 1970's. Moreover, the drainage canals and the river are improved in the middle and lower reach regions.

Kobetyanai River Watershed

Kobetyanai River flows into the Japan Sea. There are snowfall occurrence influenced by the seasonal wind from the Japan Sea. Surface layer of the watershed is clayey soil. Land use of the watershed in 1991 is arable land (reclaimed at improved slope) 11%, grassland (reclaimed at original slope) 4%, and remaining is woods or *Sasa* field. These agricultural lands had been developed during observation period of this study. Figure 4 shows the watershed shape and the position of the observation point. Parameters of watershed are shown in Table 1.

Table 1 Parameters of observed river watersheds

river	Mokoto	Kutyoro		Kobetyanai
observ. pt	Suehiro	Oku-kutyoro	Hikari-basi	Kobetyanai-basi
area(km^2)	49	29	100	14
main river length(km)	13	13	40	7
stream length(km)	53	29	74	13
mean width(km)	3.7	2.2	2.5	2.1
river density	1.08	1.00	0.74	0.91
form factor	0.23	0.17	0.06	0.32
arable land(%)	37	1	14	0-15*

* increased with development project

70

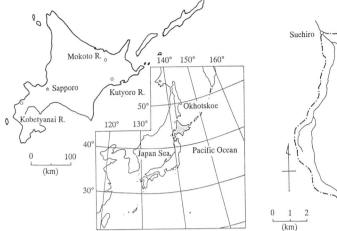

Fig. 1 Location of watersheds for the observation
in Hokkaido, northern Japan

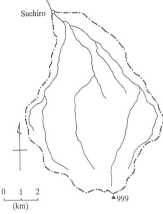

Fig. 2 Watershed of Mokoto River and location
of the observation point

Fig. 3 Watershed of Kutyoro River and location
of the observation points

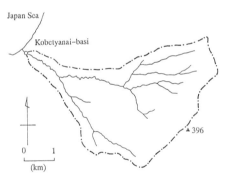

Fig. 4 Watershed of Kobetyanai River and
location of the observation point

OBSERVATION

Measurement of Rainfall, Discharge, and Suspended Sediment

The water level was continuously recorded by the water gauge set up in each observation point. And discharge was estimated from the H - Q curves. Rainfall amount was observed by the tipping-bucket rain recorder. The turbidity meter used to weigh the suspended sediment concentration was the optical scattering and continuous self-recording type (Hokuto Riken, MA-902). This meter assumes the luminescence diodes of the infrared rays wave length to be a source of light. It was a method which measures the turbidity by weighing the amount of the scattered light. A continuous recording at field can be obtained in accuracy using this apparatus.

Treatment of the Data

C (suspended sediment concentration, mg/l): C is obtained from converting the reading of turbidity meter, using calibration results such as Figure 6.

C_p (peak suspended sediment concentration, mg/l): Peak value of suspended sediment concentration.

Q_s (suspended sediment load, kg/s): Suspended sediment load that is passed at an observed cross section of the river at unit time. Product of C and Q.

L (total suspended sediment load, t): Total amount of suspended sediment load by a freshet.

l (specific suspended sediment load, t/100 km²): L per unit watershed area.

Q (discharge, m³/s), Q_p = (peak discharge, m³/s)

q_p (specific peak discharge, m³/s 100 km²): Q_p per unit watershed area.

D (hydrological parameter, d): Days until flood is greater than peak discharge.

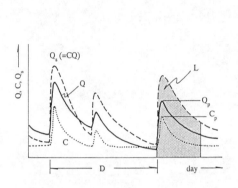

Fig. 5 Diagrammatic hydrograph of defining parameters for examination

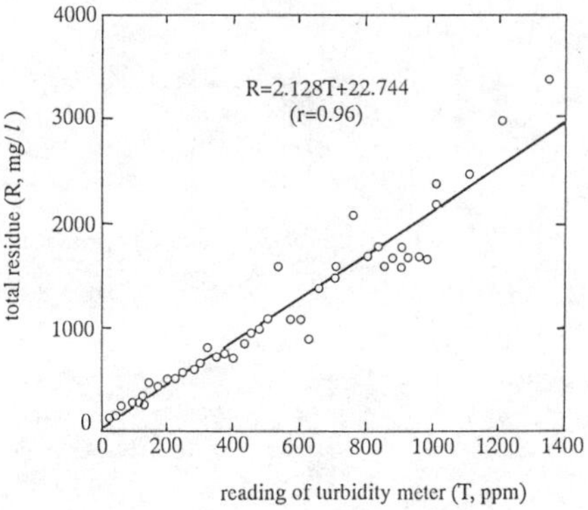

Fig. 6 Calibration of the reading of turbidity meter and total residue (example of Suehiro, Mokoto R.)

RESULTS AND DISCUSSION

Characteristics of Suspended Sediment Transportation with Rainfall

To explain the behavior of suspended sediment transportation with rainfall, various hydrological factors were examined. As a result, Q_p shows the highest correlation with suspended sediment. However, the correlation related to Q_p - C_p is low (Figure 7). On the other hand, the correlation related to Q_p - L is high (Figure 8). The reason is that L is shown by the product of C and Q. After all, if only Q_p is understood, L can be estimated in high accuracy.

Sediment in the riverbend is stored during the no rainfall period (Ebise, 1981). When ground surface in the watershed dries, the influence is shown in the sediment supply to the river (Aya, 1982). Like the above-mentioned reports, the hydrological conditions before flood exerts the influence on the suspended sediment transportation behavior. We had thought about D as a parameter concerning the hydrological condition before the flood. This parameter D is period until flood is greater than peak discharge of freshet. And L/ΣQ is an index of the sediment transportation. The potential for the sediment transportation in the watershed becomes large by increasing this index. In Figure 9, a significant correlation is not admitted, but L/ΣQ shows the increasing tendency as D increases.

Characteristics of Suspended Sediment Transportation in Snowmelt Period

As for the suspended sediment transportation behavior in snowmelt period, the suspended sediment concentration does not increase like the rainfall. However, the condition of comparatively high concentration and discharge continues for a long term. Therefore, the ration of the suspended sediment load in snowmelt periods to the annual total load is extremely large (Nagasawa, 1986).

The suspended sediment behavior in snowmelt period shows diurnal change corresponding to the air temperature (Figure 10). The behavior in snowmelt period differs from that of rainfall, but the relation between discharge and suspended sediment load is similar to the rainfall. That is, the peak discharge was confirmed as the most significant factor to decide the suspended sediment load (Figures 11, 12).

In snowmelt period, the ratio of the suspended sediment load to the discharge is small for the Mokoto River compared with rainfall flooding. One cause is the difference of the frequency of freshet. The frequency of freshet in snowmelt period is 3.8 days per event. On the other hand, the frequency in rainfall period is 9.8 days, and 2.6 times of the snowmelt period. Secondarily, the frequency of surface erosion can be pointed out. In snowmelt period, ground surface erosion caused by raindrops is insignificant. Soil loss is limited to the erosion of waterway in the snowmelt runoff. Therefore, the surface erosion over the whole watershed will not be great. For these reasons, even if the amount of surface runoff is similar to the rainfall, suspended sediment load in snowmelt period is relatively small. Anyway, in the river of snowy cold regions, a large amount of suspended sediment load is transported in the snowmelt period at early spring. It is very significant that this period is regarded as the critical erosion period in the snowy cold regions for agricultural land use and conservation planning of the watershed.

Land Use and Suspended Sediment Transportation of Watershed

Specific suspended sediment load, l and specific peak discharge, q_p were examined as a factor, comparing the suspended sediment transportation behavior between watersheds where the land use situation was different. It means that the sediment transportation is severe according to high l. The potential of the sediment transportation in watersheds was compared according to these factors (Figure 13). As a result, l is greater in order of Suehiro > Hikari-basi > Oku-kutyoro > Kobetyanai-basi. The results reflect the rate of agricultural land use in a watershed. As the degree of land use of the watershed increases, it is indicated that the potential of sediment transportation increases.

Annual Behavior of Suspended Sediment Transportation

The accumulation rate of the annual SS value is shown (Figure 14) for a one year period. In Oku-kutyoro, the rate of suspended sediment transportation is high in summer, July-August. There was a violent rainfall during summer, and a large amount of sediment transportation occurred by one flood. On the other hand, the rate of snowmelt period is extremely high in Suehiro, Mokoto River. That is, about a half of annual amount of suspended sediment transports at a short term during spring. If curves like this can be prepared according to many data, it can be an effective tool to examine the watershed conservation and management practices.

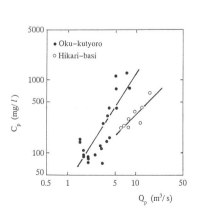

Fig. 7   Relationship between peak discharge, Q_p and peak suspended sediment concentration, C_p at the rainfall (Kutyoro R., 1990, '91)

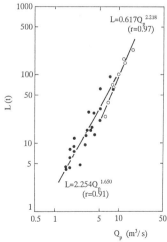

Fig. 8   Relationship between Q_p and suspended sediment load, L at the rainfall (Kutyoro R., 1990, '91)

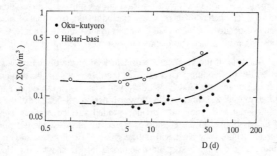

Fig. 9 Relationship between the retrospective duration over freshet, D
and the parameter of suspended sediment load, L / ΣQ
(Kutyoro R., 1990, '91)

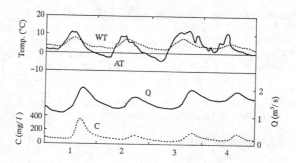

Fig.10 Change of air temperature, AT, water temperature, WT, discharge, Q
and suspended sediment concentration, C at the snowmelt period
(Suehiro, Mokoto R., 1990.4)

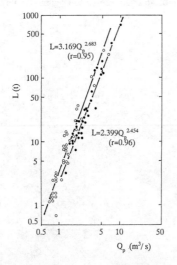

Fig.12 Relationship between Q_p and L of the freshets
at snowmelt and rainfall (Suehiro, Mokoto R., 1988, '89)

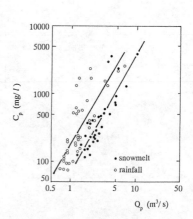

Fig.11 Relationship between Q_p and C_p of the freshets
at snowmelt and rainfall (Suehiro, Mokoto R., 1988, '89)

74

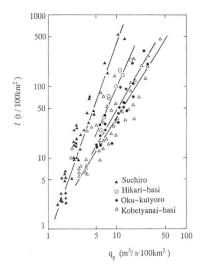

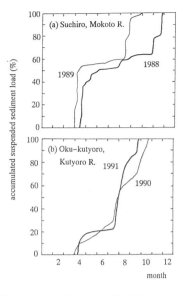

Fig.13 Relationship between specific peak discharge, q_p and specific suspended sediment load, l at rainfall

Fig.14 Accumulated suspended sediment load for a year

CONCLUSION

The agricultural land in the watershed exerts various influences on the entire regional ecosystem. For instance, it is working as a buffer to the undesirable factors in the watershed. However, it is possible that it become a pollutant load source depending on the conditions. At any rate, to maintain sustaining agricultural production in the region, the agricultural land watershed system should harmonize stably. In this research, conservation problems of the agricultural watershed were examined using suspended sediment as an indicator. Especially, conservation problem in the snowy cold condition was examined.

As for the suspended sediment that flows into the river, many factors are involved. Disaster prevention facilities, such as settling basins are set up around the sloping field. But, a complete obstruction of suspended solids is very difficult. The relation between various conditions and suspended sediment loads was examined to devise effective conservation methods. The suspended sediment transportation in snowmelt period was characterized by corresponding to the change of temperature-snowmelt-discharge. The amount of suspended sediment load in snowmelt is less than in rainfall, but the amount increases suddenly when there is rainfall in snowmelting. The process also depends on the soil properties, land use, and the weather conditions. Therefore, it is necessary to understand the actual conditions of each watershed for implementing conservation practices.

REFERENCES

1. Aya, S., Y. Iwasa. 1982. Yield and dispersion of turbidity in some rivers. Proc. Japanese Conf. Hydraulics 26:577-582.

2. Ebise, S., K. Muraoka, and K. Otsbo. 1981. Estimation of runoff suspended solid under heavy rain events in streams. Proc. Japanese Conf. Hydraulics 25:473-479.

3. Nagasawa, T., T. Kataoka, Y. Umeda, and J. Sakurada. 1986. Estimation of suspended sediment loads by a turbidity meter. Trans. JSIDRE 125:81-87.

4. Nagasawa, T. 1986. Behavior of suspended sediment loads from small watershed developed grassland. Trans. JSIDRE 125:89-94.

SEDIMENT ACCUMULATION IN SMALL WATER RESERVOIRS

UTILIZED FOR IRRIGATION

L. Janský[*]
Member ASAE

The sedimentation in small water reservoirs and proper management of forest cover in their watersheds are still unsolved problems in many regions, also in Czecho-Slovakia. The objective of this work is to examine and quantify the importance of forest stands and their integrated non-productive functions on sedimentation in small reservoir watersheds. Out of 193 reservoirs in use in Slovakia, 27 were analyzed quantitatively for sedimentary deposits (Fig. 1). The

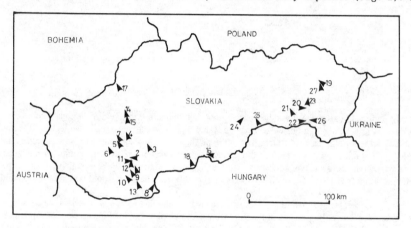

Figure 1. Locations of Surveyed Small Water Reservoirs

standard method of directly measuring the amount of accumulation of bed-load sediments was used. Data of sediment accumulation indicated that reservoir sedimentation deteriorates the ecological stability of the whole area. A methodological evaluation suggests a new simple regression method of assessing sedimentation intensity.

CHARACTERISTICS OF SMALL WATER RESERVOIRS

In 1981, the total volume of water in large reservoirs in Czecho-Slovakia was 4,380 million m^3 and that of small reservoirs 520 million m^3, totalling 4,900 million m^3 and covering an area of 92,730 ha (Zachar, 1987). In 1986 the Slovak Ministry of Agriculture and Food administered 193 reservoirs out of a total of 350 small water reservoirs in Slovakia. The 193 reservoirs had a total accumulation capacity volume of over 45 million m^3 with an area of 1,910 hectares (Janský,

[*]L. JANSKÝ, Soil Conservation Specialist, National Centre of Soil and Water Engineering in Bratislava, Czecho-Slovakia; recently visiting scientist, National Research Institute of Agricultural Engineering, Tsukuba, Japan.

1987). Those small reservoirs are distributed practically all over the eastern Czecho-Slovakia. According to the Czecho-Slovak standard small reservoirs are classified as water basins with a capacity of not more than 2 million m^3 of water with a maximum depth of 9 meters and with a hundred-year crest discharge not bigger than 60 $m^3 \cdot s^{-1}$.

Small water reservoirs have multiple functions: they help to increase the rain water flow rates, improve the total water balance within the catchment, enable more effective utilization of precipitations, protect the territory from floods, make possible fish breeding, create conditions for recreation, etc. They are also an important microclimatic and environment-forming factor at the local level in the biosphere. Until recently attention has focused mainly on reservoir use for irrigation of agricultural crops.

THE CONSEQUENCES OF SEDIMENTATION

Apart from the quantity of water, the main factor affecting the utilization and conservation of water is its quality. This is determined largely by the content of insoluble substances in the water. Pollution of surface waters and silting (sedimentation) of streams and small water reservoirs used for irrigation has increased because of erosion and has become a serious problem. The area of agricultural land affected by water erosion (1,520,000 hectares in 1987) and wind erosion (390,000 ha) in Slovakia is increasing. The area of compacted soils (750,000 ha), soils degraded and deteriorated by landslides and salt land is also increasing alarmingly (MAF, 1987).

Cutting the forest around small watersheds used for agricultural purposes affects flow rates, speeds runoff from spring areas and causes subsequent water budget deficits in these areas. Dams, irrigation canals, pipelines, culverts, headworks, weirs, pumping stations, drainage facilities, river training of small streams, etc. are often insufficient to compensate for the changed hydrological characteristics in watershed areas. Floods therefore occur more frequently in these modified mountainous and adjoining agricultural areas.

The operation of reservoirs is hampered by sedimentation of insoluble substances - sediments from the watershed - the product of erosion. Most importantly, sedimentation reduces the useful storage volume of the reservoir. This shortens the useful life-time of the reservoir and also causes the following problems;
- Deterioration of the quality of accumulated water
- Obstruction of reservoir flow control structures
- Reduction of flood control capability upstream of the reservoir due to damming-up of water caused by sediments
- Consequent decrease of the environmental quality (e.g. breeding grounds for mosquitos)
- Decrease in the sanitary standard of the environment
- Reduction in possibilities for recreation and tourism within the reservoir area.

The sedimentation problems of small water reservoirs are serious in Slovakia. At present, reservoirs are maintained mainly by sediment removal to keep the necessary storage volume. This is not very economical. Therefore an investigation on sedimentation of submountainous small water reservoirs was performed and the causes of sedimentation analyzed.

MATERIALS AND METHODS

Originally 33 out of 193 reservoirs were studied , but only 27 of them, with sufficient data were included into the regression analyses (Fig. 1, Table 1). The 27 basins were situated in altitudes from 135 to 380 m, their storage volumes ranged from 17,000 to 288,000 m^3, and the maximum flooded area ranged from 1 to

Table 1. SUMMARY OF THE RESERVOIR AND WATERSHED DATA

Reservoir	Watershed area (km^2)	Reservoir flooded area (ha)	Reservoir capacity (10^{3}m^3)	Non-forested watershed area (km^2)	Average annual sediment accumulation (m^3)
1.Pl. Vozokany	20.1	17	164	18.09	7 554
2.Veľký Ďúr	10.2	10	130	10.20	3 762
3.Drženice	17.5	7	98	12.25	3 676
4.Mankovce	18.0	3	50	9.00	188
5.Kolíňany	17.0	13	106	15.30	1 474
6.Čápor	13.1	8	128	13.10	556
7.Jelenec	11.1	7	174	5.55	1 861
8.Bajtava	5.5	7	48	4.95	721
9.Dedinka	16.4	15	246	14.76	4 326
10.Dubník	12.5	14	240	12.50	2 360
11.Maňa	6.2	8	169	6.20	960
12.Trávnica II.	25.3	20	288	20.24	7 478
13.Svodín	9.8	14	221	9.80	4 171
14.Brezolupy	24.0	7	90	9.60	3 143
15.Nedašovce	28.0	6	60	14.00	1 174
16.Rátka	0.8	1	17	0.48	250
17.Bolešov	11.1	2	26	4.44	544
18.Glabušovce	8.7	14	180	6.96	580
19.Karná	2.0	2	17	1.20	578
20.Košic.Olšany	3.5	2	25	2.80	505
21.Poľov	5.1	5	75	5.10	971
22.Trstená pri H	8.4	2	34	5.88	864
23.Vyš. Kamenica	11.4	2	32	7.98	2 972
24.Gemer.Teplica	3.7	14	257	2.22	1 067
25.Hrušov I.	2.6	4	36	1.82	1 150
26.Nižný Žipov	3.5	9	146	3.50	1 270
27.Bor-Továrne	7.5	8	203	3.75	1 464

20 hectares. The medium depth of the reservoirs was 0.69 to 2.54 m. The watershed areas varied between 0.8 and 28.0 km^2 with an average of 11.2 km^2, all classified as small watersheds according to Czecho-Slovak standards. The percentage of forests was 0 - 60%, mostly of the altitudinal 1. and 2. vegetation zones with forest-types of *Ulmeto-Fraxinetum* (UFr), *Carpineto-Quercetum* (CQ) and *Fageto-Quercetum* (FQ).

Because of the relatively small size of the water reservoirs direct measurement of sedimentation in emptied reservoirs was possible, though very work-intensive and time-consuming. According to Walling (1988), such a survey has several advantages, e.g. it provides a meaningful estimate of sediment yield averaged over a period of several years and there should be less uncertainty associated with the resulting sediment yield values. Sediments yields also include both the bedload and the suspended load. The methods of measurement are described in Fig. 2. In the regular grid sampling, the volumes between cross-sections of the reservoir were calculated as an average of sediment cross-section area times the distance between cross-sections and summed over the total area. In the irregular sampling, the average depth of all samples was multiplied by the total area. The second type of measurement was used only in a few cases when the access to the whole emptied reservoir area was difficult due to insufficient drainage.

Verification of the measured sedimentation was tried by the method of calculating rainwash erosion using modifications of the Universal Soil Loss Equation and considering sediment delivery ratio. However, it was found that such equations are more suitable for soil erosion calculations on smaller, homogenous areas. Therefore, when this type of equation was used for average annual soil loss

a) Regular Grid Sampling - Water Reservoir "Kolíňany"

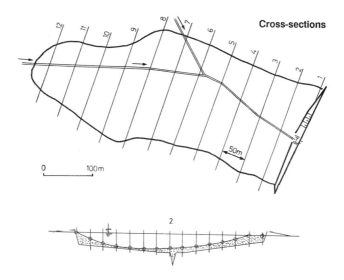

b) Random Sampling - Water Reservoir "Nedašovce"

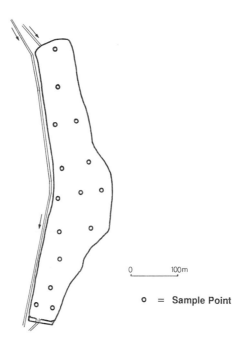

Figure 2. Two Examples of Sampling the Reservoir Sedimentation

estimation and annual sediments accumulation in reservoirs for the larger watersheds with an area of 0.8 - 28.0 km^2, the results did not correlate well with the directly measured values. Thus a regression method of Janský (1988) was applied to estimate the amount of stored sediments in the 27 reservoirs from data of forested and non-forested area of the watershed.

RESULTS

Results of sedimentation measurements are in Table 1. Calculations showed that the amount of sedimentation was 4.8 - 83.6 % of total storage capacity. Annual deposits ranged from 188 to 7,554 m^3, meaning an annual decrease of their storage volume of 0.32 - 9.30 %. For the majority of reservoirs it was estimated, that the sedimentation will fill them much sooner than is their anticipated, designed period of use (100 years). Maintenance is needed every 9 to 25 years, on average once in 15 years. Annual sediment yield deposit accumulating in individual reservoir was between 10.4 - 442.2 $m^3 \cdot km^{-2}$. Total amount of money to remove the sediment and to repair damages of the 193 reservoirs averaged for one year, was about Kčs 15 - 20 millions (Czechoslovak crowns; 1984 cost estimate).

The results of regression analysis showed that total non-forested watershed area correlates well with the amount of sediments accumulated in the reservoir over a period of several years. Linear regression for this relationship is (Fig. 3):

$$y = - 182.115 + 273.091 \ x \tag{1}$$

where   y   is annual accumulation of sediments in the reservoir $(m^3 \cdot year^{-1})$;
      x   is non-forested watershed area (km^2);

with a correlation coefficient R = 0.725. This equation fits the data better than the slightly different relationship of Janský (1988).

A even better regression is obtained by using the quadratic function (Fig. 3):

$$y = 667.860 + 14.478 \ x^2 \tag{2}$$

with a correlation coefficient   R = 0.779.

In fact, these two equations provide simple and time-saving method for approximation of small water reservoir silting by using available data about watershed forest cover. This equation is valid for small reservoirs (with capacity up to 300 thousand m^3) and for small watersheds with an area up to approximately 30.0 km^2. Identification of further factors affecting resulting sedimentation could improve the usefulness and accuracy of this method appreciably.

CONCLUSIONS

From the synthesis of our knowledge about natural conditions around small water reservoirs and the regression analysis results it is concluded, that generally the greatest soil conservation effect in small water reservoir watersheds is formed by forest. Silting is mostly affected by the proportion and distribution of forested and forestless areas in the watershed. However, the effect of the total area of watershed must also be considered. The results emphasize the importance of forests in small water reservoir watersheds for soil conservation and erosion control. This means that close cooperation between small watershed control and agricultural and forest soil use is needed.

A forest with a dense canopy, good undergrowth and an undisturbed litter layer have the most significant effect on surface runoff and thereby on the intensity and course of erosion. Forest reduces surface runoff from the watershed

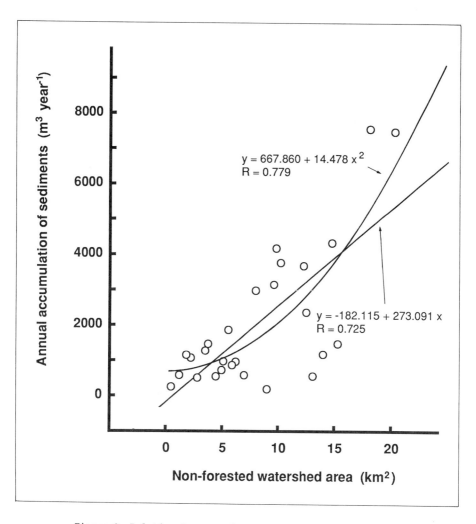

Figure 3. Relation Between the Non-forested Watershed Area
and Average Annual Accumulation of Sediments in the Reservoir.

by increasing interception and infiltration of rainfall. This results in a decreased intensity of erosion processes in the watershed area and especially in the river beds. This favorable effect of forest cover has been proved in experimental watersheds by many authors who have compared the erosion effects of runoff from areas with different amounts and quality of forest cover.

As Fig. 3 shows, forest area of only about 10 km² will significantly decrease the annual accumulation of sediments in water reservoir to one half, in this case this means nearly 1 500 - 4 000 m³·year⁻¹ for central European conditions. Therefore erosion control by forest area management is quite feasible, especially in small watersheds.

Many studies have dealt with the problems of runoff from watersheds, suspended sediment transport by rivers, sediment delivery ratio, etc. However, all these factors and management activities in watersheds must be considered as a part of a comprehensive picture of large-scale, cumulative effects (Sidle and Hornbeck,

1991). Such studies require a long-term commitment and a multidisciplinary approach.

ACKNOWLEDGEMENTS

The author thanks Dr. Ilkka Havukkala for critical reviewing of the manuscript. National Institute of Agricultural Engineering in Tsukuba, Japan is thanked for facilities. Financial assistance from The Nomura Foundation in Tokyo, Japan, enabling me to present this work is gratefully acknowledged. The opportunity given by Slovak Ministry of Agriculture and Food in Bratislava to survey for several years the reservoir sedimentation in the territory of Slovakia is greatly appreciated.

REFERENCES

1. Janský, L. 1987. The economic efficiency of government-operated small water reservoirs in Slovakia. Ekonomika poľnohospodárstva 26:136-139. (In Slovak).

2. Janský, L. 1988. Impact of forest on the sedimentation in small water reservoirs. (PhD. Thesis). Faculty of Forestry, Zvolen, 140. (In Slovak with summary in English and Russian).

3. Sidle, R.C. and J.W. Hornbeck. 1991. Cumulative effects: A broader approach to water quality research. J. Soil & Water Conservation 46:268-271.

4. Slovak Ministry of Agriculture and Food (MAF). 1987. Environmental programme for Slovak agriculture towards 2000. Bratislava, 150. (In Slovak).

5. Walling, D.E. 1988. Measuring sediment yield from river basins. In: R. Lal (Ed.) Soil erosion research methods. Soil and Water Conservation Society, Ankeny, Iowa. 39-73.

6. Zachar, D. et al. 1987. Water utilization and conservation in Czecho-Slovakia from the standpoint of agriculture and forestry. Veda/Academia, Praha, 568. (In Slovak with summaries in English, German and Russian).

***

DETECTION OF GROUNDWATER VEIN STREAM BY GROUND TEMPERATURE PROSPECTING

T. Okuyama[*]

To collect information concerning geological structure and the depth of water table, seismic and electrical prospecting or test boring are commonly practiced. But it is difficult to know the actual movement of groundwater by these methods. Measurement of ground temperature through the boring holes has been widely practiced to investigate geothermal resources, and also used for deducing groundwater flow from the recharge zone to the discharge zone (Cartwright, 1974). Takeuchi(1980,1981) studied the relationship between the groundwater vein stream and landslide disasters. He confirmed the usefulness of 1 m depth temperature anomaly in determination of the vein stream.

Recently, large scale land reclamation is a common practice in Japan, and disturbance of groundwater streams occurs over the reclaimed areas. Consequently, unexpected landslide and water logging on upland fields are frequently brought about.

In this study, the feasibility of the ground temperature anomaly in the distribution of the groundwater vein stream was assessed first. Secondly, this technique was greatly improved and modified for the determination of the vein stream in the large scale reclaimed land, especially for upland crop and orchard. In this paper, principle and measurement technique of this method, and its usefulness for land reclamation and land conservation are discussed.

FORMATION OF GROUNDWATER VEIN STREAM

Water filtration rate through soil layers is chiefly dependent upon the magnitude of permeability of the soil layer and hydraulic gradient in it.

The magnitude of permeability is governed by the size and continuity of micropores formed in-between soil particles. Gravel and sand layers, generally possess greater permeability than silt- or clay-dominant layers. If there are gravel- and/or sand rich strata in the profiles, water is preferably flowing into the layer and accumulate there.

Macropores and cracks in the profile accelerate water movement. Such soil water pipes are formed of material rock fissure or joint, alternative swelling and shrinking of soil layers, and moles' activities.

PRINCIPLE AND METHOD OF THE TEMPERATURE PROSPECTING

Ground Temperature

Heat is mainly transferred between soil layers in terms of heat conduction. Diurnal change of vertical distribution of ground temperature in a profile was simulated based on the assumptions that ground temperature was a constant at the bottom of the profile, and that varied within the range of plus/minus 6°C of the surface temperature (Fig. 1). Great temperature

*Soil Physicist, Tohoku National Agricultural Experiment Station, Morioka, Japan

fluctuation is observed only in shallow surface layers and the ground temperature approaches to the constant temperature at 0.5 m depth from the surface. Previous studies confirmed that seasonal variations in the temperature could be neglected at and below the 10 m depth, hence annual temperature variations in groundwater in deep strata is far smaller than that of shallow layers.

Figure 2 shows an example of the monthly variations in air temperature, ground temperature at 1 m depth (Hereafter, referred to as T(1m)), and groundwater temperature in central Japan. The air temperature does not sharply reflect that of the groundwater. In some seasons, difference between T(1m) and the temperature of groundwater which is kept in deep strata and forms vein streams is maximized up to +/- 10°C. Thus, the groundwater vein stream can be located in terms of measurement of T(1m), which is lower in summer and higher in winter in the area with groundwater vein stream than in the area without it. In this context, spring and autumn are not suitable for the application of this technique.

Figure 3 shows the ground temperature measured at 3 cm and 1 m depth from the surface. Variations in T(3cm) is far greater than that in T(1m).

Correlation between them is very low (r=-0.066), hence T(3cm) is affected rather by air temperature than by the ground thermal status. This indicates that one meter-deep drilling for the measurement is required to obtain reliable data by this method.

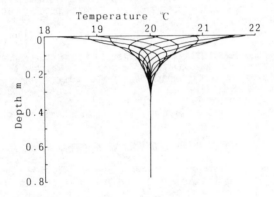

Figure 1. Simulated Diurnal Change in Ground Temperature.
Simulation was conducted under the following condition:
Boundary temperature in the ground: 20°C
Surface temperature: 20±6°C

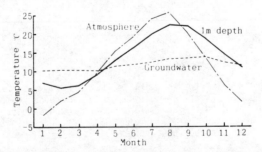

Figure 2. Seasonal Variation of Atmospheric, 1 m Depth and
Groundwater Temperature in Central Japan.

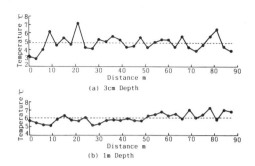

(a) 3cm Depth

(b) 1m Depth

Figure 3. Change of the Ground Temperature at Different Depth in March, with Increased Distance from the Edge of the Survey Line.

T(1m) varies according to such land properties as geologic structure, soil type, land use and season. The temperature difference due to these factors reaches up to plus/minus 2°C (Takeuchi, 1980). Great attention, therefore, should be paid in the application of this technique to a huge area and long-term prospecting.

Method of the Temperature Prospecting

Determination of Location Measured: First of all, we should decide where to draw prospecting lines based on topographical and geological information, and preparatory investigation. It is recommended to dig out holes used for temperature measurement on the prospecting lines within 5 meter interval. A motor-driven auger is a considerable labor-saving tool to drill the holes with 2 cm in diameter and 1 m in depth.

Measurement of 1 m Depth Temperature: Temperature at the bottom of the holes is measured with platinum RTD (Resistance Temperature Device) sensors attached to the edge of 1.2 m plastic pipes. Platinum RTD is a temperature sensor with great accuracy and stability. A temperature indicator with the accuracy of 0.01 °C was newly designed for this measurement. Immediately after drilling the holes, the platinum RTD sensor was set in each hole. At least 5 minutes are required for the temperature equilibrium between the sensor and the ground. This procedure was repeated on all the holes. Two persons can measure about 100 holes a day.

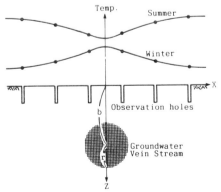

Figure 4. Supposed Temperature Anomaly Due to Groundwater Vein Stream.

Analysis: To predict the depth and the scale of a veinstream, ground temperature distribution at steady state is calculated using co-ordinates, in terms of supposing that there is a cylindrical vein stream as a heat source in the ground in parallel with land surface (Fig. 4). The following assumptions were made to simplify calculation of the 1 m depth temperature anomaly.

1) Heat is transferred only by conduction in the profile.
2) The land surface is an infinite plane and vein stream possesses infinite length.
3) Soil layers are homogeneous with respect to thermal transfer.

The steady state equation of thermal conductance for two dimensions is defined as,

$$\partial^2 T/\partial x^2 + \partial^2 T/\partial z^2 = 0 \tag{1}$$

The boundary conditions are

$T = Tw \qquad ; \quad x^2 + (z-b)^2 = r^2$

$\partial T/\partial z - hT = 0 \; ; \; z = 0$

Tw: groundwater temperature
b : depth to the vein center
r : radius of the vein
h : cooling coefficient, based on Newton's law of cooling

Approximate solution of the 1 m depth temperature at distance x is obtained by the following equation (Yuhara, 1955).

$$\tag{2}$$

$$T(1m) = \frac{T_w - T_u}{\log\frac{b+a}{b-a}} \left[\log\frac{(1+a)^2 + x^2}{(1-a)^2 + x^2} + \frac{4(1+a)}{h((1+a)^2 + x^2)}\right] + T_u$$

where
Tu : natural 1 m depth temperature
a : $(b^2 - r^2)^{0.5}$

Tu is obtained as the maximum temperature in summer or the minimum one in winter measured on the survey line. Tw is measurable by using a well or a spring. The depth and the radius of the vein are determined by trial and error method to minimize the difference between simulated values and measured ones. PPA portable computer is very useful for this calculation on the field.

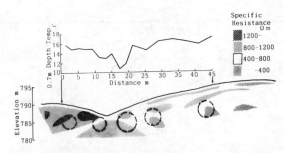

Figure 5. Comparison of Ground Temperature Distribution with Apparent Resistivity.

FIELD STUDIES

Comparison with Electrical Prospecting

The ground temperature prospecting was compared with the well-established electrical prospecting using the same survey line on a hill slope in Nagano Japan in September 1986. In this experiment, the survey line was set with crossing a small stream and 0.7 m deep holes were drilled at every 4 m on the line. Due to hard rocks, the holes could not be drilled down to 1 m depth. Electrical prospecting was practiced with dipole-dipole electrodes array (Takeuchi, 1989).

The upper half of Fig. 5 shows the temperature distribution along the survey line. In September, T(1m) is lower than that in the area without the stream, therefore the location and the scale of groundwater vein streams were presumed by low temperature anomaly and shown by five circles in the lower half of Fig. 5. The profile is divided into four parts in terms of apparent resistivity and shown also in the lower half of Fig. 5. In the electrical prospecting, it is confirmed that gravel or sand layer have much higher resistivity than clayey layer does. The circled areas give a good agreement with those with resistivity more than 800 Ωm. It is suggested, therefore, that groundwater vein has a great tendency to be located in the gravel layer, because it has high permeability as previously discussed.

Groundwater Survey at a Reclaimed Field

Water logging due to high groundwater table are often observed in reclaimed upland fields especially in mountainous areas. An orchard with a slope of 12 % was reclaimed on a hill slope in Ishikawa Japan in 1982, however since then apple trees planted at the bottom of slope were frequently damaged by water logging. Mother rock is mainly composed of sandstone and mudstone.

Ground temperature prospection was practiced to investigate the

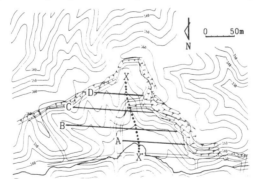

Figure 6. Survey Line Installation in the field (Ishikawa, Japan).

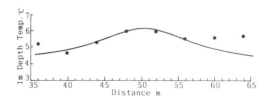

Figure 7. Comparison of Measured and Simulated T(1m) near the Point Intersected between Lines D and X-X'.

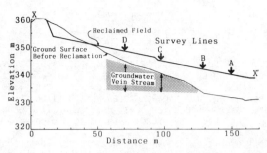

Figure 8. The Cross Section of the Slope Surveyed along the Line X-X'.

groundwater movement in this area using four survey lines (A, B, C, D in Fig. 6) in March 1989. T(1m) was measured every 4 m on each line. Average temperature of lines A, B, C, and D were 6.85°C, 6.07°C, 5.60°C and 5.32°C, respectively. Thus, the temperature increased as the slope went down. Groundwater temperature in tile drainage was 11-12°C, therefore, it was apparent that T(1m) was increased by groundwater heat. Line X-X' in Fig. 6 shows the track of a natural stream before the area was reclaimed.

Figure 7 shows the T(1m) actually measured and the simulated temperature anomaly using Eq. (2) based on the assumption that there is a groundwater vein stream at the intersection of line X-X' and the survey line D. The depth and the radius of the vein stream were estimated to be 10 m and 6 m, respectively in terms of best fitting the simulated values to the measured. A similar temperature anomaly was observed in line C, but no anomalies could be seen in both lines of A and B. This fact indicates that the groundwater vein stream exists under the area between the line C and D as shown in Fig. 8. It was supposed that the groundwater vein streamed along the line X-X' and separated from the line B before reclamation. However, the banked soils plugged water seepage, and consequently the water table went up.

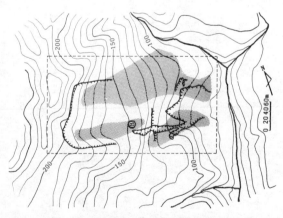

Figure 9. Outline of the Field Surveyed in the Landslide Area (Chiba, Japan).
(⊤⊤:Landslide scarp. Dotted areas denote the presumed groundwater vein stream.)

Groundwater Survey at a Landslide Area

Groundwater flow is closely related to landslide disasters. Therefore, underground drainage is usually installed to avoid expected hazardous landslide. Survey was conducted to clarify relationship between the landslide and the location of groundwater vein stream. The field was located in Chiba, Japan, and mainly used for rice and flower cultivation. The ground temperature prospecting was practiced at 20 m intervals for 400 × 200 m area (Fig. 9) in September 1991.

T(1m) is affected not only by the groundwater vein stream but also by such many other factors as elevation and land use. The elevation difference of slope surveyed was 160 m, and land use in the area varied from forest, flower cultivation to bare land. To eliminate the influence of environmental factors and only to detect the temperature decrease due to the groundwater vein stream, the point where the temperature was 0.5 degree lower than the average temperature of the four points surrounding it was selected as its location. The location of groundwater vein streams are shown by dotted area in Fig. 9. They are agreed well with the area of landslide scarps.

Five holes (66 mm in diameter and 20 m long) were almost horizontally drilled into the slope about 5 m apart from one another and installed with plastic pipes as an underground drainage at point B in Fig. 9. The runoff obtained from two pipes were combined to measure, however, almost all the water was drained out of only one pipe. Figure 10 shows the amount of groundwater discharge from March to April in 1992. Flow rate was so small that it couldn't be measured by a flow meter between rainy days (period marked X in Fig. 10), but it jumped up suddenly when it began raining. This fact indicates that groundwater forms narrow and limited vein stream in the ground and its flow rate reflects rainfall. Ground temperature prospecting is, therefore a suitable method to detect the groundwater vein stream, hence can be used to decide the installation places of underground drainage.

Water temperature in the brook located at the bottom of the landslide area was measured to evaluate the effect of the groundwater vein on the brook in February 1992. The water temperature ranged from 6 to 7 °C, and decreased as the brook downstream. At the place where extension of the bottom of presumed groundwater vein streams and the brook meet, the water temperature was increased to 8 °C. Temperature of groundwater in a test boring in the area was about 13 °C. This fact also supports that the presumed location of groundwater vein which supplies a substantial amount of warmed water to the brook, is correct.

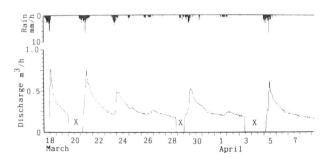

Figure 10. Time Course of Discharge through Underground Drainage Installed at Point B in Fig. 9.

CONCLUSIONS

The ground temperature prospecting was proved to be a very useful tool to detect the location of the groundwater vein stream. It was confirmed that the groundwater vein was localized in gravel and/or sand layers determined by a high electric resistivity in the electrical prospecting. Such layers have great permeability and a substantial amount of water is flowing in and accumulate. Banking on these layers should be associated with an adequate drainage system to drain excess water. Since the groundwater vein stream is closely related to localized slope failure in the areas with a great landslide frequency, therefore, drainage borings should be installed in the right places to drain excess groundwater efficiently, hence in the groundwater vein stream.

Ground temperature prospecting is an inexpensive and labor-saving technique for the survey of shallow groundwater vein stream, therefore, can provide valuable information necessary for design and installation of adequate underground drainage systems.

REFERENCES

1. Cartwright, K. 1974. Tracing shallow groundwater system by soil temperatures. Water Resour. Res. 10(4):847-855

2. Takeuchi, A. 1980. Method of investigating groundwater-vein streams by measuring one-meter-depth temperature in landslide areas Part 1. J. Jap. Assoc. Groundwater Hydrology 22(2):11-39

3. Takeuchi, A. 1981. Method of investigating groundwater-vein streams by measuring one-meter-depth temperature in landslide areas Part 2. J. Jap. Assoc. Groundwater Hydrology 23(1):1-27

4. Takeuchi, M., et al. 1989. Reservoir geology in water resources development project. Proc. 7th Afro-Asian Regional Conference, International Commission on Irrigation and Drainage 1-B:124-134

5. Yuhara, K. 1955. Geothermal prospection of underground heat source. Society of Exploration Geophysicists of Japan 8(1):27-33

MACROPORE FLOW EFFECT ON INFILTRATION, THROUGHFLOW, AND SURFACE RUNOFF ON A RECLAIMED SURFACE-MINED WATERSHED

Michael D. Guebert   Thomas W. Gardner

Newly reclaimed surface-mined watersheds in central Pennsylvania exhibit low steady-state infiltration rates (1-2 cm/hr) and produce runoff dominated by infiltration-excess overland flow. However, within four years after reclamation, infiltration rates on some mine surfaces approach pre-mined rates (8 cm/hr). Importantly, as infiltration rate increases, the volume of infiltrated water increases, but the total porosity of minesoil matrix remains constant. Furthermore, there is little change in the surface discharge volume, indicating that infiltrated water continues to contribute to the basin surface discharge by the processes of throughflow and return flow.

The hydrologic response of the minesoil is dominated by rapid macropore flow within the unsaturated topsoil. Application of fluorescent dyes on the reclaimed surface reveals preferred flowpaths through macropores surrounding the numerous large rock fragments in the topsoil. These macropores are hypothesized to have formed by differential expansion and contraction between the topsoil matrix and the coarse fragments during freeze/thaw and/or wet/dry cycles.

The development and integration of a macropore network on reclaimed surface-mined watershed has a significant, direct effect on infiltration, throughflow, and return flow contribution to surface runoff. As infiltration rates increase through time and slightly delayed macropore return flow increases, the peak runoff rate is reduced, therefore reducing the potential for severe gully erosion on the reclaimed site. In addition, throughflow water remains predominantly in the topsoil horizon, and therefore has limited contact with potentially acid-producing backfill. Better understanding of macropore flow process in reclaimed minesoils will help investigators evaluate past strategies and develop new reclamation techniques that will optimize the long-term effluent and groundwater quality while minimizing the short-term surface erosional effects of mining and reclamation.

INTRODUCTION

Surface runoff from a watershed can be generated along two distinctly different flow paths: infiltration excess overland flow and subsurface throughflow (Dunne, 1978) (Fig. 1.a). Infiltration excess overland flow occurs when rainfall rate exceeds the infiltration rate of the soil (Horton, 1933). Throughflow occurs when rainfall infiltrates and travels through the hillslope soil mantle, reaching the stream channel before reaching the general groundwater zone (Whipkey, 1965). Overland and throughflow runoff processes are associated with distinctly different runoff hydrograph shapes (Dunne, 1978). On hillslopes with low infiltration rate, infiltration excess overland flow dominates the surface runoff hydrograph, producing a hydrograph with a short time to peak, a high peak runoff, and a rapid recession (Fig. 1.b). Hillslopes with high infiltration rate may have a significant throughflow contribution to the surface runoff hydrograph. Infiltrated water flows more slowly through the soil than at the surface, therefore producing a hydrograph with a relatively longer time to peak, lower peak runoff, and slower rate of recession (Fig. 1.b).

In response to altered soil physical conditions, infiltration rates of several newly reclaimed surface-mined watersheds in central Pennsylvania are an order of magnitude lower than surrounding undisturbed forest soils (Jorgensen and Gardner, 1987; Lemieux, 1987; Guebert, 1988). Because of reduced infiltration, surface runoff on mined land is dominated by infiltration excess overland

Michael D. Guebert, Assistant Professor, Department of Geography and Geology, Middle Tennessee State University, Murfreesboro, TN 37132

Thomas W. Gardner, Professor, Department of Geosciences, The Pennsylvania State University, University Park, PA 16802

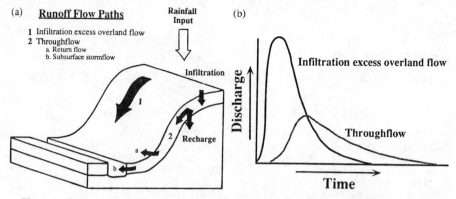

Figure 1. Surface Runoff Flow Paths and Associated Hydrograph Shapes (after Ritter, 1990).

flow (Gryta and Gardner, 1983; Jorgensen and Gardner, 1987; Lemieux, 1987), producing up to 50 % of rainfall per event as surface runoff (Ritter, 1990; Guebert, 1991), compared to up to 10 % on nonmined pasture land in central Pennsylvania (Rawitz et al., 1970).

While changes in infiltration rate in response to natural soil genesis and vegetation change occur over 10^3 to 10^4 years (Ritter, 1990; based on rates of pedogenesis from Birkeland, 1984), steady-state infiltration rates on some newly reclaimed surface mines in central Pennsylvania increase from 0.5 cm/hr to 5 cm/hr, an order of magnitude, in just 3 to 4 years (Jorgensen and Gardner, 1987; Lemieux, 1987). As infiltration rate increases, the volume of infiltrated rainfall increases. However, total porosity calculated from bulk density samples in the upper few centimeters of mined land remains low (40 %) during the first 3 (Ritter, 1990) to 4 (Jorgensen, 1985) and up to 9 years (Lemieux, 1987) following reclamation.

It is hypothesized that increase in infiltration rate on surface-mined land is predominantly controlled by development of macropores in the near-surface minesoil horizon. Macropores represent a small percentage of the total volume of the minesoil (<5 %) and are undetected by bulk density and porosity measurements. However, entrance of rainwater into macropores greatly increases infiltration rate (Beven and Clarke, 1986; Edwards et al., 1988) by increasing the volume of storage that must be filled before surface runoff is initiated and by providing additional surface area for matric infiltration at depth (Beven and Germann, 1981).

Intuitively, as infiltration on mined surfaces increases through time, a smaller percentage of rainfall contributes to surface runoff as infiltration excess overland flow. Steady-state infiltration rates on one surface-mined watershed near Snow Shoe, Pennsylvania increased from 2.4 cm/hr in Year 1 (1987), the first year after reclamation, to 3.9 cm/hr in Year 2, and to 4.8 cm/hr in Year 3 (Ritter, 1990). However, there was no significant difference in the volume of surface runoff per rainfall volume between Years 1, 2, and 3, on the basis of discriminant analysis (Ritter, 1990). It was inferred that infiltrated rainfall on the Snow Shoe watershed leads to increased throughflow resulting in continued contribution to surface runoff by return flow.

Given the observed increase in mine surface infiltration, the lack of increase in near surface porosity, and the inferred increases in throughflow and in return flow, the purpose of this study is to investigate the existence of macropores on a surface-mined watershed and determine the effect of development of macropres on infiltration, throughflow, and surface runoff. To accomplish this, a study watershed was established on the #26 mine operated by R. S. Carlin, Snow Shoe, Pa., located near the town of Snow Shoe in northwestern Centre County, and situated along the eastern edge of the Allegheny Plateau, in the main bituminous coal field. The Snow Shoe watershed has a total drainage area of 32.3 hectares, and reclamation was completed in 1987. The third-order drainage network present on the Snow Shoe watershed was manually installed during reclamation and has remained unchanged since its implementation (Ritter, 1990). Precipitation and runoff were measured on an event basis by continuous strip-chart recorders monitored from August, 1987 (Year 1) to November, 1990 (Year 4) (Guebert, 1991). In Year 2 (1988), two throughflow collection pits modified from designs by Atkinson (1978) and Whipkey (1965) were installed on an approximately planar, topsoiled hillslope within the Snow Shoe watershed, and collected throughflow from the topsoil (0-15 cm) and upper backfill (15-100 cm) from a one-meter wide face (Guebert, 1991).

CHARACTERISTICS OF MINESOIL MACROPORES

Surface mining for coal in central Pennsylvania dramatically alters the surface physical properties from their pre-mine condition (see Guebert and Gardner, 1992, this volume for brief review). The disturbed and highly compacted nature of surfaces immediately following reclamation produces very few macropores. However, macropores in the form of soil cracks ranging from a few tenths of a millimeter to two millimeters in width, have formed in the topsoiled surface in the Snow Shoe watershed within two years. The cracks are found in the soil matrix adjacent to coarse fragments greater than approximately one centimeter, and connecting coarse fragments separated by less than approximately 7 cm. Cracks directly beneath coarse fragments exposed at the surface connect to other coarse fragments in the underlying matrix and are notably larger; up to 5 mm in width. Macropores are hypothesized to have formed by differential expansion and contraction between the topsoil matrix and the coarse fragments during feeze/thaw and/or wet/dry cycles as the matrix repeatedly shrinks open and swells closed against the fragment. The physical properties of particle size distribution and coarse fragment size and content regulate the effectiveness of the climatic induced differential expansion and contraction through the shrink-swell capacity and water holding capacity of the minesoil matrix. Vegetation type and percent cover may also be important for minesoil crack development. Roots concentrate along the coarse fragment surfaces (Pedersen et al., 1978) and may help keep the cracks open during wet periods, allowing the continued flow of water.

To determine the connectivity of the cracks, and consequently their potential to increase infiltration and rapidly transport water downslope, small volumes (0.5 to 2 liters) of dyed water were poured directly into cracks exposed beneath, and adjacent to, 5 separate surface coarse fragments approximately 10 cm in diameter. Subsequent excavation revealed dye stained cracks located within the topsoil matrix and surrounding coarse fragments in the topsoil. Several separate and discrete dyed flow paths through cracks were observed for each dye application. The general vertical depth of dye penetration was 10 to 12 cm, with the exception of one path that penetrated 16 cm to the base of the topsoil along the surfaces of 5 closely spaced coarse fragments. The maximum net, lateral, downslope distances for each of the five dye applications were 15, 16, 20, 25, and 33 cm. In general, dyed water tended to flow along narrow, discrete paths, the length of which depended upon the abundance and proximity of coarse fragments. Dyed paths generally stopped when the distance between coarse fragments exceeded about 5 cm, or possibly when the small volume of dyed water was insufficient to cause further penetration.

EFFECT OF MACROPORES ON INFILTRATION, THROUGHFLOW AND SURFACE RUNOFF ON A RECLAIMED WATERSHED

Effect of Macropores on Infiltration

Macropores present in a soil and open to the atmosphere have an important effect on infiltration. The interaction between the macropore and matric flow domains in the minesoil environment depends upon the supply of water to the macropores in relation to the hydraulic conductivity of the matrix. The initiation of macropore flow requires a supply of water exceeding all losses to the matrix, whether at the soil surface or within the macropore (Beven and Germann, 1982). Because of the highly disturbed and compacted nature of newly reclaimed minesoils, matric hydraulic conductivity is extremely low (1 to 2 cm/hr; Jorgensen and Gardner, 1987). At rainfall intensities in excess of the low matric infiltration rate, water is available at the surface for entrance into the macropores.

Average steady-state infiltration rates, weighted by percent cover of each surface of the Snow Shoe watershed, increase during the first three years following final reclamation from 2.4 cm/hr in Year 1, to 3.9 cm/hr in Year 2, and to 4.8 cm/hr in Year 3 (Ritter, 1990). However, average near-surface total porosity for the Snow Shoe watershed remained constant at 38.6 ± 4.4 % (n=5) in Year 1, 38.0 ± 11.5 % (n=24) in Year 2, and 39.9 ± 6.7 (n=10) in Year 3 (data from Ritter, 1990). Infiltration rate is a function of matric suction and hydraulic conductivity, which are strongly affected by the physical properties of the soil (Schwab and Frevert, 1981). Because total porosity remains low on mined land, matric infiltration rate remains low in the years following reclamation, and the observed two-fold increase in infiltration at the minesoil surface is predominantly controlled by macropores.

The volume of water infiltrated during all 30-minute infiltration tests on surface mines in central Pennsylvania (Jorgensen, 1985; Lemieux, 1987; Guebert, 1988; Ritter, 1990) increases with years since reclamation (Fig. 2). By year 4, infiltration rate has reached its maximum and the population has become bimodal. It is hypothesized that tests having high infiltrated volume occur on surfaces containing a population of macropores, such as the topsoiled surface on the Snow Shoe watershed.

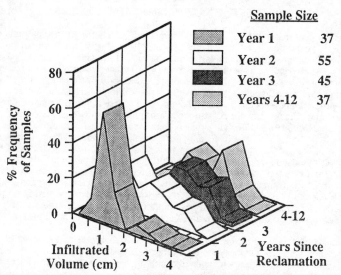

Figure 2. Frequency Distribution of Infiltrated Volume During 30-Minute Rainfall-Simulation Infiltration Tests Conducted on Mined Surfaces in Central Pennsylvania (from Ritter, 1990).

Effect of Macropores on Throughflow

The integration of minesoil cracks into a minesoil macropore network provides an important mechanism for rapid flow of water through the topsoil horizon. The effectiveness of macropores for transmitting throughflow downslope depends upon their size, spatial distribution, and connectivity (Beven and Germann, 1982; McDonnell, 1990). For macropores to be important in producing rapid throughflow, the supply of water to the macropores must be in excess of lateral losses to the surrounding minesoil matrix, as for infiltration. On minesoils, matric conductivity is low (1-2 cm/hr; Jorgensen and Gardner, 1987) and little loss of water occurs from macropores to the matrix.

To verify the expected increase of throughflow on the Snow Shoe watershed, two throughflow collection pits were installed at the mid-point and near the base of an 86-meter long, approximately planar hillslope within the watershed. Both pits collected throughflow from the topsoil horizon (0-15 cm) and the upper backfill horizon (15-100 cm) at one meter wide vertical faces. The topsoil layer is normally composed of stockpiled material quite different than that of backfill material. In general, topsoils have finer texture, higher structural porosity, more abundant organic matter, and higher water retention values than underlying backfill (Pedersen et al., 1980), while backfill material is composed of broken and pulverized overburden and may occupy up to 25 % more volume than undisturbed bedrock (Van Voast, 1974).

Throughflow occurs predominantly in the topsoil horizon. Volumes of topsoil throughflow are 2 to 4 times greater than volumes of backfill throughflow. As much as 70 % of the total throughflow collected from the upper one meter of minesoil occurs in the 15 cm thick topsoil horizon. Flow in the backfill horizon is dominated by vertical drainage toward the water table (ground water recharge is 10-20 % of monthly rainfall; Guebert, 1991), and is a direct function of rainfall volume. This indicates that the physical conditions of the minesoil material sufficient for development of macropore-controlled, lateral throughflow are better developed in the topsoil horizon.

Topsoil throughflow volume per rainfall volume increases from Year 2 to Year 4 (Fig. 3). Although data were not collected in Year 1, relative to infiltration rates on surrounding forest soils (8 cm/hr; Jorgensen, 1985; Guebert, 1988), the low infiltration rate on that surface (2.5 cm/hr) indicates that very little rainfall infiltrated the minesoil surface and flowed laterally. By Year 4, both the upper and lower pit topsoil horizons produce large throughflow volumes per rainfall volume (approximately 30 to 40 %, but up to 65 % of runoff). The difference in the upper and lower pit volumes in Year 3 suggests that the physical properties that control the efficiency of macropore throughflow develops sooner in the lower portion of the slope than in the upper portion of the slope.

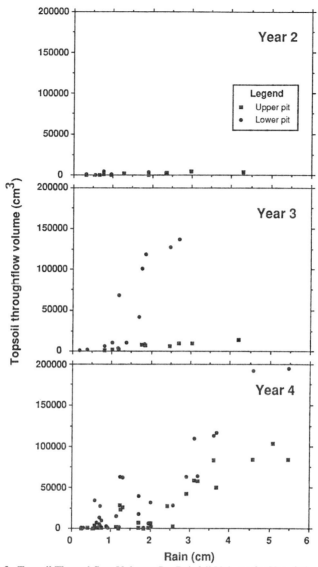

Figure 3. Topsoil Throughflow Volumes Per Rainfall Volume for Year 2 through Year 4.

In Years 3 and 4, the throughflow collection pits were equipped to measure cumulative throughflow volume during a single event. For a double peak storm in Year 3, initiation of topsoil throughflow lags behind initiation of rainfall by 2.3 hours and peak throughflow discharge lags behind peak rainfall by 3.4 hours (Fig. 4). However, in the second event, throughflow responds very quickly to rainfall. Initiation of increased throughflow lags the initiation of the second rainfall by only 5 minutes, and throughflow peak discharge lags the rainfall peak by less than 30 minutes (Fig. 4). The short time lag of topsoil throughflow discharge, in combination with the low effective porosity and shallow depth of wetting, indicates that the dominant mechanism for throughflow is not matric throughflow. The calculated lag time for water to infiltrate the minesoil matrix at 1-2 cm/hr, percolate 15 cm through the topsoil, build a saturated layer, and flow laterally downslope to the collection pit would be on the order of 10 to 30 hours rather than the less than two hour lag times commonly measured at the throughflow pits. Depending on the antecedent moisture and the rainfall conditions, initiation of throughflow may begin as quickly as 5 minutes after the start of rain.

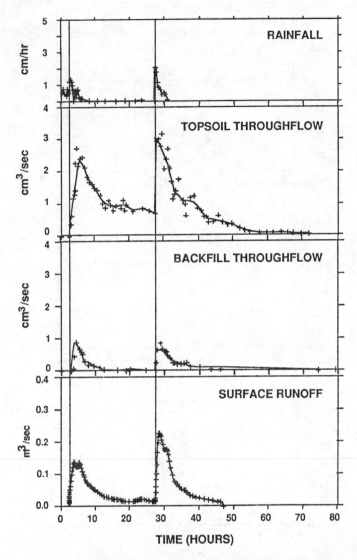

Figure 4. Rates of Rainfall, Topsoil and Backfill Throughflow and Basin Surface Runoff for a Double-peak Event (October, 19-20, 1989).

Effect of Macropores on Surface Runoff

Intuitively, as infiltration on mined surfaces increases through time, a smaller percentage of precipitation contributes to surface runoff as infiltration excess overland flow. However, while basin average infiltration rates have doubled from Year 1 (2.4 cm/hr) to Year 3 (4.8 cm/hr) (Ritter, 1990), the rainfall-runoff relationships are not significantly different between years 1, 2, and 3 on the basis of discriminant analysis (Ritter, 1990). Because there is no significant change in surface runoff volume for Year 1 through Year 4, yet there is at least a two-fold increase in the infiltrated volume, infiltrated rainfall must contribute to the surface storm runoff hydrograph by the process of return flow.

Return flow on the Snow Shoe watershed occurs primarily by macropore flow, not by matric flow. Soil probe observations in the Snow Shoe minesoil reveal a saturated wetting front no deeper than 4 cm and the lack of a saturated layer at the base of the topsoil. Although matric return flow probably does not occur at the base of the hillslope on the Snow Shoe watershed, return flow is released from the water-filled macropores in the topsoil. Macropores present in the topsoil horizon, open to the atmosphere, appear to be laterally connected, but become vertically discontinuous at the topsoil/backfill contact. This minesoil macropore network of vertically discontinuous cracks acts as a natural hillslope drain system that receives rainfall input along its length and discharges it near the base of the hillslope. Water infiltrates the surface, flows downslope in the macropores, accumulates in the macropore network from upslope and begins to flows out near the base of the slope, producing return flow.

The increase in the return flow contribution to the surface runoff hydrograph, should, theoretically, be reflected in the shape of the hydrograph (Fig. 1.b). The primary effect of any throughflow contribution to surface runoff is to lengthen the hydrograph along the time axis, by lagging the return flow contribution relative to the infiltration excess overland flow contribution (Dunne, 1978; Gray, 1970). By the process of return flow, throughflow on the Snow Shoe watershed contributes to the surface runoff hydrograph, effectively reducing the average peak discharge (Fig. 5) and extending the recession limb with no loss in total runoff volume. Peak runoff per rainfall volume for all events on the Snow Shoe watershed decreases for each year from Year 1 to Year 4 (Fig. 5). Surface runoff for Year 1, having the lowest infiltration, is dominated by infiltration excess overland flow and is characterized by flashy runoff hydrographs, with a high peak runoff per rainfall volume. The runoff hydrograph for Year 4, having the highest infiltration rate, and presumably the greatest return flow contribution, has the lowest peak runoff per rainfall volume.

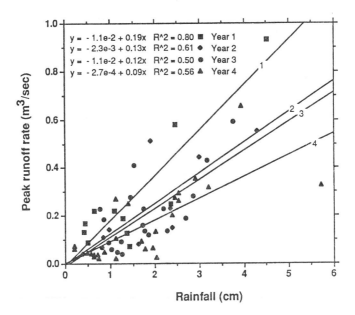

Figure 5. Peak Runoff Rate Per Rainfall Volume, Year 1 through Year 4.

To illustrate the typical shape of the runoff hydrograph, particularly the peak runoff rate and recession limb, one storm from each year, Year 1 through Year 4, was selected as an example for that year (Fig. 6). In an attempt to remove the effect of rainfall characteristics and antecedent soil moisture conditions on the shape of the runoff hydrograph, storms were selected for similarity in total volume, average intensity and duration of rainfall, and in antecedent precipitation (Guebert, 1991). The most significant changes in the shape of the runoff hydrograph from Year 1 to Year 4 occur in the systematically reduced peak runoff and lengthened recession curve (Fig. 6). Given the nearly constant rainfall characteristics, both changes in the runoff hydrograph shape are inferred to be the result of increased macropore return flow.

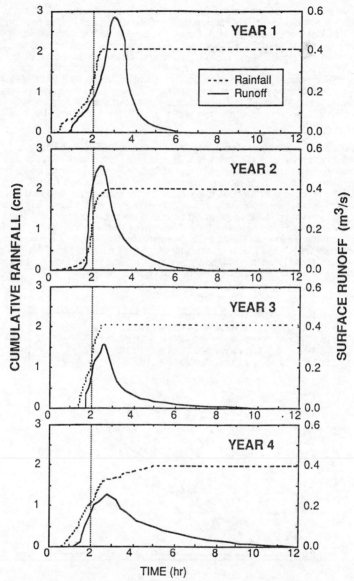

Figure 6. Example Storm Hydrographs for Year 1 through Year 4.

SUMMARY AND CONCLUSIONS

Development and integration of macropores on surface-mined land following reclamation are the fundamental controls on increases in infiltration and throughflow. Macropores provide a pathway for the inflow of surface water, increased surface area for matrix infiltration below the surface, and a mechanism for rapid flow through the topsoil. On the Snow Shoe watershed, steady-state infiltration rates recover rapidly during the first three years following reclamation, and volumes of throughflow discharge increased systematically from year 2 to year 4 in the topsoil. Comparison of rainfall and throughflow timing indicates a very quick response to rainfall input via macropore flow.

The development of a minesoil macropore network also provides an efficient mechanism for rapid return flow contribution to surface runoff. The presence of macropores affects the shape of the surface runoff hydrograph in two ways. First, by providing a pathway for increased infiltration, less rainfall is available for infiltration excess overland flow contribution to the hydrograph, effectively reducing the instantaneous discharge rate. Second, by providing a mechanism for increased topsoil throughflow, a hillslope with sufficiently steep topography may have a large portion of the infiltrated rain returned to the surface, with a certain time lag, effectively increasing the recessional flow of the surface runoff hydrograph.

In conclusion, the infiltration, throughflow, and surface runoff response to rainfall on watersheds disturbed by surface mining in central Pennsylvania is fundamentally controlled by the development and integration of macropores within the topsoil horizon. In the first year following reclamation, minesoils lack macropores, have low average infiltration rates, and produce high-peak, short-duration runoff hydrographs dominated by infiltration excess overland flow. Surfaces with high peak runoff rates have the greatest potential for unstable channelized flow and high erosional rates. The result is large erosion gullies on the disturbed land (Gryta and Gardner, 1983) that expose the buried (and potentially acid-producing) mine spoil. In addition, changes in channel geometry and clogging of the channel with sediment occur in the watershed downstream (Touysinhthiphonexay, and Gardner, 1984). As macropores develop in subsequent years, infiltration increases, and throughflow may significantly contribute to the surface runoff hydrograph by return flow. Infiltration excess overland flow may continue to dominate the runoff volume, but the percentage of return flow contribution becomes large enough to effectively reduce the peak runoff rate and extend the recession limb of the surface runoff hydrograph, thereby reducing the potential for severe gully erosion on mined land. At the same time, infiltrated water remains largely within the topsoil as throughflow, thus limiting the contact with spoil material and subsequent production of acid mine drainage. Better understanding of macropore flow processes in minesoils will help investigators evaluate past strategies and develop new reclamation technologies that will minimize the adverse effects of both short-term surface gully erosion and long-term subsurface generation of acid mine drainage.

ACKNOWLEDGMENTS

This project was sponsored in part by a grant from the United States Department of Energy, by a Fellowship from the Pennsylvania Mining and Mineral Resources Research Institute, by the Krynine Memorial Fund at The Pennsylvania State University, and by a Faculty Research Grant from Middle Tennessee State University.

REFERENCES

1. Atkinson, T.C., 1978. Techniques for measuring subsurface flow on hillslopes, in: Kirkby, M.J. (ed.), Hillslope Hydrology, John Wiley and Sons, New York, 389pp.

2. Beven, K.J. and R.T. Clarke, 1986. On the variation of infiltration into a homogeneous soil matrix containing a population of macropores. Water Resources Research, 22(3):383-388.

3. Beven, K. and P. Germann, 1981. Water flow in soil macropores, 2, A combined flow model. Journal of Soil Science, 32:15-29, 1981.

4. Beven, K. and P. Germann, 1982. Macropores and water flow in soils. Water Resources Research, 18(5):1311-1325.

5. Birkeland, P.W., 1984. Soils and Geomorphology. Oxford University Press, New York, 372pp.

6. Dunne,T., 1978. Field studies of hillslope flow processes, in M.J. Kirkby (ed.), Hillslope Hydrology, John Wiley and Sons, New York. p. 478-490.

7. Edwards, W.M., L.D. Norton and C.E. Redmond, 1988. Characterizing macropores that affect infiltration into nontilled soil. Soil Science Society of America Journal, 52:483-487.

8. Gray, D.M. (ed.), 1970. Handbook on the principles of hydrology. Canadian National Committee for the International Hydrological Decade, Ottowa, Canada.

9. Gryta, J.J., and T.W. Gardner, 1983. Epidosic cutting and filling within gully-fan systems in disequilibrium. Geological Society of Americal, Abstracts with Programs, 15:587.

10. Guebert, M.D., 1988. Relationship of remotely sensed SPOT data to infiltration capacity of surface mined land in central Pennsylvania, M.S. thesis, Department of Geosciences, The Pennsylvania State University, University Park, PA. 37pp.

11. Guebert, M.D., 1991. Macropore flow on a reclamed surface-mined watershed in central Pennsylvania: Control on hillslope and surface hydrogogy, Ph.D. dissertation, Department of Geosciences, The Pennsylvania State University, University Park, PA. 85pp.

12. Guebert, M.D., and T.W. Gardner, 1992. Remote sensing of infiltration rates on a reclaimed surface-mined watershed. in: Land Reclamation: Advances in Research and Technology, Proceedings of the 1992 International Synposium, American Society of Agricultural Engineers, this volume.

13. Horton, R.E., 1933. The role of infiltration in the hydrological cycle. Transactions of American Geophysical Union. 14:446-460.

14. Jorgensen, D.W., 1985. Hydrology of surface mined land: a determination of minesoil control on infiltration capacity, and runoff modelling of distrubed watersheds. M.S. thesis, Deptartment of Geosciences, The Pennsylvania State University, University Park, PA. 127pp.

15. Jorgensen, D.W., and T.W. Gardner, 1987. Infiltration capacity of disturbed soils: temporal change and lithologic control. Water Resources Bulletin 23:6:1161-1172.

16. Lemieux, C.R., 1987. Infiltration characteristics and hydrologic modeling of disturbed land, Moshannon, PA. M.S. thesis, Department of Geosciences, The Pennsylvania State University, University Park, PA. 150p.

17. McDonnell, J.J., 1990. A rationale for old water discharge through macropores in a steep, humid catchment. Water Resources Research, 26(11):2821-2831.

18. Pedersen, T.A., A.S. Rogowski, and R. Pennock, Jr., 1978. Comparison of morphological and chemical characteristics of some soils and minesoils. Reclamation Review. 1:143-155.

20. Pedersen, T.A., A.S. Rogowski, and R. Pennock, Jr., 1980. Physical characteristics of some minesoils. Soil Science Society of America Journal 44:2:321-328.

21. Rawitz, E., E.T. Engman and G.D. Cline, 1970. Use of the mass balance method for examining the role of soils in controlling watershed performance. Water Resources Research 6(4):1115-1123.

22. Ritter, J.R., 1990. Surface hydrology of drainage basins disturbed by surface mining and reclamation, Central Pennsylvania, Ph.D. dissertation, Department of Geosciences, The Pennsylvania State University, University Park, PA. 162p.

23. Schwab, G.O. and R.K. Frevert, 1981. Soil and Water Conservation Engineering. Wiley and Sons, New York. 525p.

24. Touysinhthiphonexay, K.C., and T.W. Gardner, 1984. Threshold response of small streams to surface coal mining, bituminous coal fileds, Central Pennsylvania. Earth Surface Processes and Landforms, 9:43-58.

25. Van Voast, W.A., 1974. Hydrologic effects of strip coal mining in southeastern Montana--emphasis: One year mining near Decker. Montana College of Mineral Science and Technology, Butte, Montana.

26. Whipkey, R.Z., 1965. Measuring subsurface stormflow from simulated rainstorms--a plot technique. USDA, Forest Service, Central States Forest Experiment Station, Research Note CS-29, 6pp.

SALT MOVEMENT IN A SHALLOW DRAINED SOIL

WITH AN ARTESIAN PRESSURE

A.A. GHAEMI[1]   L.S. WILLARDSON[2]

The purpose of this research was the determination of salinity variation in a vertical soil profile and the effect of shallow plastic-lined mole drains on salinity levels in an irrigated soil affected by artesian pressure. The results indicated that salt concentration increased with depth from 45 cm below the soil surface to a maximum value at 2 to 3 meters below the ground surface even though the piezometric surface in the area is two meters above the soil surface. The salinity variations with depth were compared for three different drain spacings: 6 meters, 12 meters, and 24 meters. It was observed that the highest salt concentration was in the 6 meter drain spacing and the lowest concentration was found in the 24 meter spacing.

INTRODUCTION

Millions of acres of once-productive land in the world have been abandoned because of salt accumulation in the soil. For example, most of the irrigated land in Iran, more than 50% of the irrigated land in Syria, and about 20% of irrigated land in the United State suffer from depressed yields due to excess soil salinity (Yaron, 1981). Any soluble salt contained in irrigation water is always concentrated in the soil solution as a result of direct evaporation from the soil surface and plant transpiration that extracts water from the root zone.

The preservation and conservation of irrigated land from a salinity standpoint becomes more critical when a soil of low hydraulic conductivity (high in clay or fine textured) overlies an artesian aquifer. The upward movement of water from artesian pressure may be great enough to cause water logging and to, keep salt in the root zone of the crops. The upward gradient also prevents downward seepage of water that normally provides the necessary leaching for salinity control. Subsurface drainage systems must be provided under such conditions to avoid an adverse salt buildup in the root zone, to provide sufficient aeration for plant growth, and to control water table height (Bazaraa et al., 1986).

For the maintenance of salt balance, the quantity of salt in the water applied to the surface of the land should be equal to or less than the quantity of salt carried away by percolation below the root zone. This statement may at times be modified, because some ions may be precipitated in the soil as insoluble compounds (Raymond, 1961, James et al., 1982, and van Schilfgaarde et al., 1974). The salt balance includes all processes that contribute to inflow, outflow and the change of dissolved salt in the soil profile.

---

[1] A.A. Ghaemi, Former Graduate Student at Utah State University. Department of Irrigation, College of Agriculture, Shiraz University, Shiraz, Iran. Islamic Republic of Iran.

[2] Professor Biological and Irrigation Engineering, Utah State University, Logan, Utah 84322-4105 U.S.A.

In a large area of the Cache Valley in Utah, in part of the Nile Delta, and in other irrigated areas developed in the arid and semi-arid regions in the world, the presence of fine textured soils of low permeability overlying artesian aquifers cause an upward water flow from the confined aquifers toward the soil surface. This can lead to waterlogging and salt build-up in the soil and in the root zone of crops (Bazaraa et al., 1986)

Experimental plastic-lined mole drains were installed in 1983 at a depth of 75 cm on the Utah State University Drainage Farm to control salt accumulation and prevent waterlogging. The average annual precipitation in Cache Valley is approximately 400 mm (16 inches) most of which normally occurs as snow. Data indicate that the water table rises in spring, mainly from snowmelt. During the summer, due to evapotranspiration, the water table moves downward, and it continues falling during the winter (SCS, 1974). Leakage from the artesian aquifer is low and therefore does not contribute a significant amount of water to the root zone, but the groundwater flow gradient in the soil is vertically upward.

The research was initiated to determine, by soil analyses, the salinity variation in a vertical soil profile affected by artesian pressure for a full year and to determine the affect of shallow plastic-lined mole drains on salinity level (Ghaemi, 1987). Salt balance was determined during one irrigation by measuring the volume and EC of the drainage effluent and the irrigation water applied.

PROCEDURE

The research, which started in August 1986, was carried out on the Drainage Farm of Utah State University. The general soil description for the farm identifies a heavy soil (Salt Lake Silty Clay), gently sloping (0-3% slope), and poorly drained (SCS, 1974). The farm has a full pasture grass cover. Eighteen plastic-lined mole drains (Figure 1) were installed in the north-central part of the farm in 1963 at a depth of 75 cm. The drains were spaced 6, 12, and 24 meters apart (Willardson and Peterson 1965)

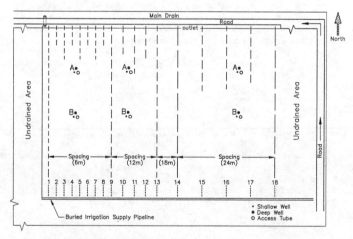

Figure 1. Sketch showing plastic lined mole drain locations, neutron probe access wells, and observation wells in the area of study at USU Drainage Farm (not to scale).

A total of 144 soil samples were taken midway between drains from six different locations in the field, in 30 cm depth intervals from the ground to 360 cm deep at two different times during the year. Samples were collected in September 1986, one week after harvest, and a second set of samples was taken at the same locations at the beginning of the growing season in April 1987. All samples were collected by hand auger. Soils were air dried in the laboratory. The dry samples were grounded and passed through a 2 mm sieve. About 200 gram sub-samples were taken from each soil sample and a saturation soil paste was prepared by adding distilled water to the samples while stirring with a spatula. The saturated soil was left standing overnight and the saturation condition was rechecked. A portion of saturated soil paste from each samples was oven dried at 105 C° to determine saturation percentage (SP%). Saturation extracts were also obtained from the saturation soil paste for each sample by using a vacuum filter funnel system. A portion of the soil water extracts were then used to determine electrical conductivity (EC_e) in deciSiemans per meter, dS/m, chloride concentration (Cl) in meq/l, and the pH. Tables 1 and 2 show the values of SP%, EC_e, Cl, and pH from the saturation soil extracts obtained in the 6 meter drain spacing area by the two samplings.

Table 1. Electrical Conductivity (dS/m), Chloride (meq/l), Saturation Percentage (SP%), and pH for samples from the 6 meter spacing (drains 4-5 (A)). September 12, 1986

Depth (cm)	ECe (dS/m)	Cl (meq/l)	SP%	pH
0-30	2.98	1.30	68.00	8.64
30-61	1.10	1.25	67.00	8.66
61-91	3.20	20.30	69.60	8.61
91-122	8.05	43.30	98.00	8.17
122-152	11.06	70.90	100.10	7.96
152-183	12.59	108.40	87.20	7.84
183-213	12.30	106.40	91.10	7.55
213-244	10.90	105.60	93.20	7.75
244-274	17.92	146.50	90.50	7.57
274-305	17.10	143.10	83.40	7.61
305-335	15.82	142.40	67.80	8.04
335-366	17.73	186.50	69.85	7.49

Twelve permanent water table observation wells made of PVC pipe with 1.8 cm inside diameter were installed at the midpoint between drains. Six wells were 90 cm deep and six were 300 cm deep. The pipes were perforated except in the upper 30 cm. The perforated sections of the PVC pipes were wrapped with synthetic nylon drain envelope material and were capped at the bottom. The replicated water table observation wells were spaced 90 meters apart in a north-south direction. Wells which were close to the outlet were marked as (A) and the wells to the south, furthest from the outlet, were denoted as (B). Water table fluctuations were monitored by measuring the water table depth from the ground surface in the observation wells using a bell sounder device once a week. Due to snowmelt starting in February, the water table normally rises to the ground surface.

Table 2. Electrical Conductivity (dS/m), Chloride (meq/l), Saturation Percentage (SP%), pH for 6 meter spacing (Drains 4-5 (A)).   April 11, 1987 (*)

Depth (cm)	ECe (dS/m)	Cl (meq/l)	SP%	pH
0-30	3.32	2.60	66.00	7.15
30-61	2.09	3.21	66.50	7.62
61-91	4.57	16.97	69.70	8.01
91-122	7.83	32.10	98.20	8.21
122-152	10.65	47.92	99.10	7.96
152-183	12.39	62.02	85.90	7.72
183-213	12.17	59.85	93.40	7.54
213-244	11.30	52.69	93.00	7.83
244-274	18.15	90.17	92.10	8.31
274-305	15.54	80.57	87.70	8.15
305-335	16.52	89.33	65.60	8.12
335-366	17.39	90.59	67.10	8.19

* Soil samples were collected before irrigation.

Adjacent to each set of observation wells, neutron probe access tubes (PVC pipe 5 cm ID and 300 cm long) were installed. These tubes were also capped at the bottom to prevent the entry of water into the pipe when the water table is high. A neutron meter was used to measure change in volumetric water content of the soil profile once a week through the year. Readings with the neutron meter were recorded at depths of 23, 46, 75, 105, 135, 165, 195, 225, 255, and 285 cm with a count time of 15 seconds at each depth. The following calibration equation was used:

$$P_v = -0.033 + 0.286 \ (R_s/R_{std})$$

where:

P_v = Volumetric water content
R_s = The count in the soil
R_{std} = The average of counts in the shield

On May 1, 1987 the first irrigation was applied using a side-roll sprinkler system. Depths of irrigation water application were determined using catch cans. During each irrigation, drain discharge was measured when the water table rose to a level that caused the shallow drains to begin functioning. Drain discharge rate was measured two times a day. Samples of the drainage and irrigation water were collected to determine electrical conductivity, chloride concentration, and pH.

RESULTS

The main objective of the research was to study the salinity variations in the vertical soil profile and to determine the effect of shallow plastic-lined mole drains on salinity level. Since the general behavior of salinity and water table fluctuation were similar in the three different drain spacings, only the results of sampling locations between the 6 meter drains have been discussed. There were no dramatically different effects of drain spacing on either water table level or salt removal.

Figure 2 shows the volumetric soil profile water contents at location A in the 6 meter drain spacing area for September 1986 and April 1987. Changes in water content were greatest in the top 152 cm, and were almost constant at depths below 152 cm. The water table fluctuated between 152 and 180 cm. The changes in soil moisture content were due to evapotranspiration, precipitation, irrigation, and some upward flow from the artesian aquifer. The smaller variation in P_v below 152 cm was due to the presence of a water table and little or no moisture extraction by the few roots in this zone. Variation in P_v was highest in the upper 120 cm, the most active depth for the grass roots.

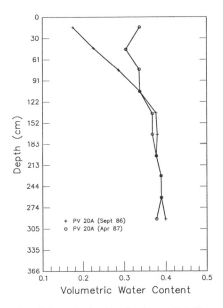

Figure 2. Change in volumetric soil moisture content with depth at 20A drain spacing from September 1986 to April 1987.

Water table fluctuation was significantly responsive to snowmelt, irrigation, and evapotranspiration. Figure 3 shows the total soil profile water content and water table fluctuations for locations 20 A and B during a one year period. Snowmelt, starting at the beginning of February, and a total amount of 113 mm of precipitation from November 22, 1986 to April 10, 1986 raised the water table from 186 cm to 130 cm during this period. Evapotranspiration during March and April lowered the water table about 20 cm. The first irrigation at 20 A started on May 5 and continued for 24 hours. The application rate was 11 mm/hr. The watertable rose to within 10 cm of the soil surface at the midpoint of the 6 meter drain spacing locations. The 264 mm of water applied also increased the soil moisture content in the top of 152 cm from 456 mm on May 5 before irrigation to 561 cm on May 6 after the irrigation.

Figure 3 also shows that during the winter, when the soil surface layers are colder than the subsoil, the water in the soil has a tendency to migrate in the soil profile due to heat potential differences, and cause the water table depth to increase even though there is no root extraction of water. The water table gradually moved downward at an average rate of 2.8 mm per day from August 21 to January 8, 1987. The total amount of 96 mm of rainfall during the period from January 8 to April 3, 1987 and the snowmelt in the second week of February caused the water table to rise from a depth of 186 cm on January 8 to 130 cm below the soil surface in mid-March.

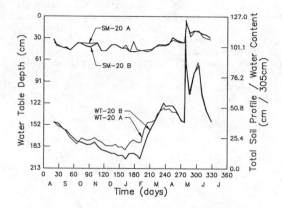

Figure 3. Relationship of soil moisture content to water table fluctuation at locations 20 A and B, from August 21,1986 to June 22, 1987.

Figures 4 and 5 show the variation with depth of average electrical conductivity (EC_e) and percent salt in the soil (PSS) at sampling locations in 6, 12, and 24 meter drain spacings for the two sampling dates. Percent salt in a soil profile can be estimated by the following equations:

$$P_{sw} = (mg/l)/10000 = 0.064 \ EC$$

$$PSS = (P_{sw} \cdot \theta_m)/100$$

P_{sw} is percent salt in water and θ_m is mass water content of the soil. Figures 4 and 5 show that the EC_e values increase with depth below 45 cm. The maximum salt concentration is approximately 300 cm deep due to the leaching of salt from the upper layers and the upward movement of water from the artesian aquifer. The irrigation water used came from the artesian aquifer and had an EC_e of 22 dS/m.

During irrigation, the drain discharge was measured twice daily, at 8:00 A.M and 4:00 P.M. when the drains were flowing. The average discharge rate for the 24 meter drain spacing was 4.34 l/m and the EC of the drain effluent was 1.5 dS/m on May 4, 1987. On May 5, the average discharge at the same locations was 1.84 l/m and EC was 1.79 dS/m. For the 6 meter drain spacing, the drain discharge was 0.5 l/m and 3.27 l/m and the EC of the drain effluent was 1.3 and 1.2 dS/m on May 6 and May 7, respectively. The total volume of water removed by these drains was computed. The kilograms of salt removed by the drains was estimated as follows:

$$Salt \ Removed(kilograms) = (V) \ (EC) \ (0.845)$$

where:
V = Volume of water drained in cubic meters, EC = Electrical conductivity of drainage water in dS/m and 0.845 is a conversion factor developed from U.S. Salinity Laboratory (1954) equations.

The amount of salt removed by one drain at the 24 meter spacing was 38.82 kg, while the total amount of salt removed by drains 5 and 6 (6 meter spacing, Figure 1) was 8.45 kg and 5.17 kg respectively. Using the depth of water applied (264 mm), the drain spacing, and the drain length (180 m), the total volume of irrigation water applied was computed and the total amount of salt added to the soil by irrigation water was also computed. Table 3 shows the quantities of salt added by irrigation water and the amount of salt removed by drainage water

106

through individual drains. Less than eight percent of the salt added was removed by the drains.

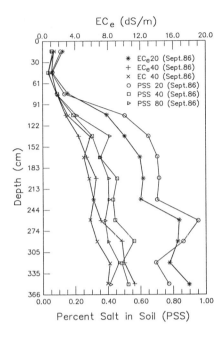

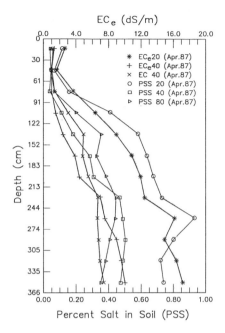

Figure 4. Relationship of average electrical conductivity and percent salt in soil with depth at locations 20,40, and 80 for soil samples of September, 1986.

Figure 5. Relationship of average electrical conductivity and percent salt in soil with depth at locations 20,40 and 80 for soil samples of April, 1986.

Figures 4 and 5 also show that the salt concentration in the soil in the 6 meter spacing area is highest, is lowest in the 24 meter spacing and is higher in the 12 meter spacing than in the 24 meter spacing. Similar results were observed for chloride concentration in the vertical soil profile. The maximum chloride
concentration was also near the 300 cm depth. The higher salt content in the narrow drain spacing may be related the artesian
condition or a difference in soil types within the drained area.

Table 3. Salt-In and Salt-Out at selected locations in the 6, 12, and 24 meter drain spacing areas.

Number of Drain	Drain water (m³)	Quantity of Salt-Out	Irrig. water (m³)	Quantity of Salt-In	Salt remain (kg)	Salt removed (%)
16	34.04	38.82	1140.48	530.04	491.22	7.9
11 12	6.47	5.19	570.24	265.02	259.83	2.0
6	8.16	8.45	285.12	132.51	124.06	6.8
5	5.43	5.17	285.12	132.51	127.34	4.1

Figure 6 shows the salt concentration profiles for September 1986 and April 1987. The vertical interval between the curves at the 1.5 meter depth is the distance (48 cm) that the salt profile moves in response to water extraction during the growing season (the difference between the April and September position). The difference between September and April salt profile position is due to leaching caused by rainfall and snowmelt. The maximum salt content at the 3 meter depth and the low salt content near the surface indicates that it is possible to maintain a favorable salinity condition in the upper profile even in a poorly drained soil by trying to keep a deep water table. The EC of the artesian water deeper in the profile is 0.55 dS/m.

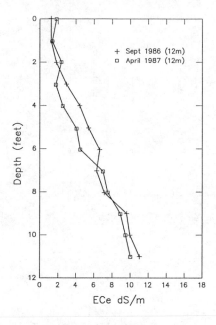

Figure 6. Salt concentration profiles in the 12m drain spacing in September 1986 and April 1987.

The shallow plastic-lined mole drains were effective in reducing excess water in the upper level of the soil profile following the rise in the water table from snowmelt and irrigation. However, the long term lowering of the water table for all the area was due to evapotranspiration by the pasture grass. Figure 3 shows that the water table dropped rapidly in the months from April to October even though the water table was below the level of the drains. The slowly permeable subsoil and the flat topography essentially eliminates lateral seepage out of the area. The artesian pressure gradient prevents deep percolation losses, so, the only way to remove water from the profile is with the plants. The indications of the results are that by keeping the water table low by evapotranspiration and by avoiding raising the water table to levels near the surface, the salt can be kept deep in the profile in spite of the artesian pressure. The winter precipitation, which is salt-free, helps leach the salts downward if the water table is low at the time spring snowmelt occurs.

CONCLUSIONS

Artesian pressure does not create root zone and soil surface salinity problems if the vertical seepage rate is much lower than the evapotranspiration rate. Having a deep water table, due to plant extraction of water, at the time natural precipitation occurs will result in vertically downward translation of the salinity profile and removal of salinity from the surface soil layers. A deep water table is important to salinity control where deep artificial drains cannot be installed. Shallow drains can prevent water logging in the deeper rootzone but are not effective for salinity control.

REFERENCES

1.   Bazarra, A. S.; Dayem, A.; Amer, A.; Willardson, L. S. 1986. Artesian and anisotropic effects on drain spacing. Journal of Irrigation and Drainage Engineering. 112 (1): 55-65.

2.   Ghaemi, Ali A. 1987. Salt Movement in a Shallow Drained Soil With an Artesian Pressure. M.S. Thesis. Dept. Bio. and Irrig. Engr. Utah State Univ. Logan, Utah.

3.   James, D. W.; Hanks, R. J.; Jurinak, J. J. 1982. Modern irrigated soils. New York: John Wiley and Sons, Inc.

4.   Raymond, A. H. 1987. Leaching requirements in irrigation. Journal of the irrigation and Drainage Division, ASCE. 87 (IR1):1-51961.

5.   SCS. 1974. Soil Survey of Cache Valley Area, Utah. U.S. Department of Agriculture. Washington, D.C.

6.   U.S. Salinity Laboratory. 1954. Diagnosis and Improvement of Saline and Alkali Soils. USDA handbook No.60.

7.   van Schilfgaarde, J., Bernstein, L., Rhoades, J. D.; Rawlins, S. L. 1974. Irrigation management for salt control. Journal of the irrigation and Drainage Division, ASCE. 100 (IR3) : 321-338.

8.   Willardson, L.S. and H.B. Peterson. 1965. Crop and Soil Management Over Shallow Plastic-Lined Mole Drains. Unpublished Research Report. USDA-ARS (SWC 6-g2 Utah-Ld-2) Logan, Utah.

9.   Yaron, D. 1981. Salinity in irrigation and water resources. New York: Marcel Dekker, Inc.

A SHALLOW MICRODRAIN SYSTEM TO CONTROL EROSION AND LEACH SALTS ON SLOPING LANDS.

V.I. SARDO*   D. PARLASCINO*
Member ASAE

Soil erosion and salt accumulation are the main causes of deser-fication in the Mediterranean environment, depending on the typi-cally autumn- concentrated, high-intensity precipitation pattern and/or the often poor quality of irrigation water.
The total amount of precipitations could in fact often be suffi-cient to leach out salts accumulated by irrigation water if a si-gnificant percentage of rainfall were not lost as runoff due to precipitation intensity exceeding water intake capacity of soil.

This in turn brings about a more serious impact on sloping soil losses through erosion, deriving from the typically erosive pre-cipitations and from the water intake rate lowered by surface sealing and impaired soil permeability as a result of increased colloids peptization depending on salt load.

Microdrains in sloping soils appear to be a promising solution for alleviating at the same time the problems of soil erosion and salt accumulation;from time to time a system of shallow micro-drains has been advocated to reduce runoff through the increase of infiltration ,namely through an intervention on the Hortonian mechanism,e.g.Breckenbridge et al.(1985),Fausey (1982),Jarrett et al.(1980),Kastanek(1988)

MATERIALS AND METHOD

A research has been conducted at plot scale and observations ha-ve been made at field scale to assess the effectiveness of micro-drains. The results of the observations are reported as a case study below. Researches at plot scale have been carried out on a loamy sand soil in order to assess the effectiveness of shallow microdrains in increasing intake rate of water and in leaching out salts. The main properties of the soil are reported in table 1.

V.I. Sardo, Associate Professor, Istituto di Idraulica Agraria, University of Catania, Italy and D. Parlascino, Dr. Chem., ENI-CHEM Agricoltura, Gela, Italy.

Table 1 - Some selected physical properties of the soil in the experimental plots.

Texture% (ASTM classification)				Median particle diameter (mm)	Consistency limits %				Infiltrability[*] mm/h
Gravel	Sand	Silt	Clay		liquid limit	plastic limit	plasticity index	shrinkage limit	
11	51	33	5	.18	34	22	12	19	26

[*] As measured by means of a double cylinder infiltrometer

Two standard Wischmeier plots were used, with dimensions of m. 22,0 x 2,5 and a slope of 9%; microdrains were installed at a depth of about 350 mm. Microdrains were pvc corrugated slotted pipes with a diameter of 50 mm, embedded in gravel with mean particle diameter of about 10 mm; they were laid down on a herringbone pattern with four short laterals at the distance of 5 meters and two manifolds, one on each plot, collecting water into two tanks downstream (fig. 1).
Overland flow was captured in a gutter and collected into two separate tanks. Plots were separated by means of iron sheets protruding about 200 mm above soil level.

Rain was simulated by means of self-compensating, slow-rotating sprinklers manufactured in Israel by DAN Sprinklers, with a nominal flow rate of 240 l/h (actually 233 l/h), installed at a distance of m 2,5 x 2,0: this brought about a maximum precipitation of 46,6 mm/h, when all the sprinklers were operating simultaneously.
However they could be excluded as desired, so that 75%, 50% or 25% could operate simultaneously.
One control group upstream included a gate valve, a filter and a totalizing water meter; water was distributed under a head of about 400 kPa.

Each set of experiments included a "pre-wetting" run, with the simulator operating 30 minutes at the maximum precipitation rate (46,6 mm/h) in order to thoroughly wet the surface layer; this was followed by ordinary runs, lasting 30 or 60 minutes, with various precipitation rates.
The "pre-wetting" run appeared necessary because during the preliminary calibration trials the influence of antecedent soil moisture conditions was evidenced, and this suggested a standardised procedure as above described.

One further factor affecting results was vegetation cover, which made runoff range between 5% to 75% plus, all other conditions being identical, under 100% operating sprinklers.

Since the high infiltration rate of the soil made the microdrains not very effective even under the highest precipitation rate (100% sprinklers operating) an additional immission of water was necessary, by means of a hose applying about 1 l/s during 30 minutes at the upper side of the plots: under such conditions the equivalent precipitation rate was raised to about 112 mm/h, which triggered the operation of the microdrains (fig. 2).

Water in the collecting tanks was measured and sampled every ten minutes; samples were analysed for solid transport and solutes.

RESULTS AND DISCUSSION

The Plot-Scale Trials

The hydrograph with cumulated curves (fig. 2) shows the uneffectiveness of microdrains under 46,6 mm/h precipitation rate, due to the elevated natural drainage in the soils, and their utility under the higher precipitation rates, their action making up for about 25% of overland flow.

This may prove particularly useful with highly erosive precipitations, above 50 mm/h; research is in progress to assess the effectiveness of microdrains in the protection of less permeable soils. The results of measurements showed a susprisingly high degree of scattering, with a coefficient of variation of the order of 23% over 30 runs under identical conditions.

Water analysis showed a remarkable difference between surface and drained water, as evidenced in table 2, thus demonstrating the potential of drains in maintaining salt balance. Of course the generally low salinity level depends both on the good quality of irrigation water and on the high natural drainability of soils that avoided salt accumulation.

Table 2 - Main properties of water

	Suspended solids	NO_3^-	Ca^{++}	Na^+	K^+	Mg^{++}	pH	EC
	%	ppm	ppm	ppm	ppm	ppm		μS/cm
Irrigation water	.021	7.0	17	83	9	23.3	7.98	446
Overland water	.738	27.9	34	84	4	7.3	8.30	504
Drainage water	.030	33.2	64	78	6	8.4	8.27	596

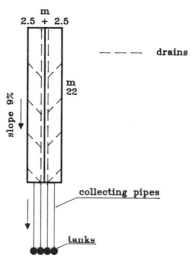

Fig. 1 – Lay-out of the experimental setup

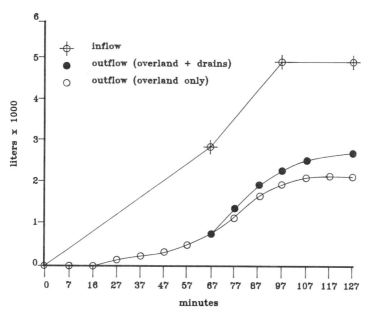

Fig. 2 – Hydrograph with cumulated curves

The Field Observations: A Case Study

The protection with microdrains has been tried in an industrial citrus grove with the surface of about 15 ha (37 acres) under varying soil conditions, with slopes of 12-25% and a clay content up to 52%. The grove is located in Eastern Sicily, at a latitude of approximately 37°50' and an elevation of about 130 masl. The maximum recorded 24-hours precipitation is 339 mm; though such an extreme event is exceptional, intensities above 50 mm/hour are rather frequent. The draining system includes pvc corrugated, slotted drains with a diameter of 50 mm, at the depth of 350 mm embedded in gravel and installed at the distance of 5 to 6 meters, as described elsewhere (Sardo, 1992). The open ditches are spaced more widely than usual (about 100 m) as a consequence of the presence of subsurface drains.

Although no accurate measurement has been possible in this case, four years' experience show that the solution is fairly effective in protecting the soil from erosion, since runoff and solid transport have been considerably reduced.

The effectiveness of this draining system is demonstrated by its long seepage time after the end of precipitations and the impressive amount of water discharged. It seems very likely in the light of such observations and of the results thus far achieved with the rain simulator that the action of microdrains in accelerating soil drying and therefore in influencing soil moisture conditions may substantially reduce runoff rate (Bagley, 1976; Sardo et al., 1992). It would also appear that a beneficial action of drains results, consisting in venting air entrapped in the soil, thus enhancing infiltration and reducing runoff, as suggested by Breckenbridge et al. (1985) and Jarrett et al. (1980).

CONCLUSIONS

The principle of using a shallow, narrow-spaced microdrain system to increase infiltration through the reduction in runoff is by no means new but seems to deserve further exploration. It is particularly attractive in the light of its action which helps to combat soil erosion and at the same time concurs to alleviate the problem of salt accumulation. Both the plot-scale research and the field-scale observations encourage a deepening of the knowledge of this technique to gain a better insight into its possibilities, limits and implications.

REFERENCES

1 - Bagley, G:R: 1976 - Drainage for increased crop production and a quality environment - Proc. 3rd Nat.l Drainage Symposium. p. 3-5

2 - Breckenbridge, R.P.; Jarrett, A.R. and Hoover, J.R. 1985. Runoff reduction by venting with shallow subsurface drainage TRANS. of the ASAE:476-479

3 - China, S.S. and Jarrett, A.R. 1983. The effect of simulated rainfall and soil air entrampment on soil erosion. ASAE paper 83-2070

4 - Fausey, N.R. 1982 - Small diameter tubing for shallow drainage applications. Proc. 2nd Int.l Drainage Workshop. p. 64-68

5 - Jarrett, A.R.; Hoover, J.R. and C.D. Paulson. 1980 Subsurface drainage air entrapment and infiltration in sand. TRANS of the ASAE:1424-1427

6 - Kastanek, F. 1988. Drainage problems in mountainous areas. Agric. W. Management, 14(1988):169-174

7 - Sardo, V. 1992. An Integrated Approach to Soil Conservation, Irrigation and Drainage in a Sloping land. Proc. of the VII Int.l Citrus Congress - Acireale (Italy), March 1992.

8 - Sardo, V.; Vella, P.; Zimbone S.M. 1992: Preliminary Field Investigations with a Rainfall Simulator. Proc. 1st Int.l ESSC Congress - Silsoe (UK) 6-10 April 1992

9 - Skaggs, R.W. and Khaleel, R. 1982 - Infiltration. - Hydrologic modeling of small watersheds (p 135) ASAE monograph n.5

APPLICATION OF EXCESS DAIRY MANURE TO ALFALFA TO REDUCE

GROUNDWATER POLLUTION

Jayaram Daliparthy[*], Stephen J. Herbert[*] and Peter L. M. Veneman[*]

Many dairy farms in the northeastern United States have a high ratio of livestock per acre of cropland. High density confinement of animals offer economies of scale but often results in problems with manure disposal. The amount of nitrogen availability in the farm often exceeds the amount required for the production of corn. In Lancaster County, Pennsylvania, manure applications average over 90 Mg ha^{-1} (Young et al., 1985). Similar rates have been determined for dairy farms in Massachusetts. Fields closest to the barn or manure storage area often receive manure applications at rates far above crop requirement. In addition to the manure, many farmers apply commercial fertilizer. Only a small amount (less than 20%) of the nitrogen input into forage production leaves farms in the form of milk, meat or wool (Ryden, 1984). Since dairy farms also import nitrogen in purchased feed grains along with commercial fertilizer, there is a continuous increase in nitrogen to the total system. This often results in overapplication of nitrogen from manure and commercial fertilizer especially on corn fields. Some of this nitrogen may be lost as nitrate to groundwater (Brinton, 1985; Westerman et al., 1985; Young et al., 1985).

Manure application to perennial forages in addition to the application to corn on dairy farms would greatly increase the land area for spreading, decreasing the amount spread on any field and thus lessening the potential of nitrate leaching. Field observations have shown that alfalfa reduces the nitrate concentration in soil profiles (Mathers et al., 1975; Schertz and Miller, 1972). On a drained peat soil (Levin and Leshem, 1974) where alfalfa was grown, no nitrate was found in the soil profile whereas under cotton, nitrate accumulated to toxic concentrations. Alfalfa is thought to remove large amounts of nitrate from the soil despite its ability to symbiotically fix atmospheric nitrogen. Alfalfa is often grown in rotation with corn, and is the preferred perennial forage legume by farmers. This research was designed to evaluate the impact of dairy manure applications on alfalfa and the associated environmental concerns of such applications on two coarse textured soils in southern New England.

---

* Department of Plant and Soil Sciences, University of Massachusetts, Amherst, MA 01003.

MATERIALS AND METHODS

Experiments were established in 1990 on one and two-year old stands of alfalfa. The Deerfield farm soil is a Hadley fine sandy loam (coarse-silty, mixed, nonacid, mesic Typic Udifluvent) low in organic matter with a very fine sandy loam textured soil solum. The Sunderland site had Agawam soils (coarse-loamy, mixed, mesic Typic Dystrochrept) consisting of a fine sandy loam mantle of coarse sands.

Experimental Design: Five treatments were laid out in four randomized blocks in bordered plots 3m x 6m. Treatments were:

1. Check (no manure or no N fertilizer)
2. Low manure (112 kg N ha^{-1} yr^{-1} equivalent)
3. High manure (336 kg N ha^{-1} yr^{-1} equivalent)
4. Low N fertilizer (112 kg N ha^{-1} yr^{-1} from NH_4NO_3)
5. High N fertilizer (336 kg N ha^{-1} yr^{-1} from NH_4NO_3)

Liquid dairy manure (0.33% total nitrogen, 0.145% ammonia nitrogen and 0.185% organic nitrogen) was applied to alfalfa in 1990 immediately after the 1st cutting. Phosphorus and potash fertilizers were applied in amounts equivalent to amount of P and K in the high manure treatment. Harvest management was a 3-cut system with the first cut at full bud and the next two at 10% bloom.

Soil solution monitoring: Porous ceramic cup suction water samplers were installed in June 1990 in 75% of the plots covering 3 replications at depths of 30, 60, 90 and 120 cm. Samplers were sealed at the top with Bentonite. Water samples were collected twice a week during the growing season and biweekly during the late fall. Water samples were collected June to the end of November, 1990 and spring samples were collected again in April, 1991. Water samples were analyzed for nitrates by the cadmium reduction method using a Technicon auto analyzer. Statistical analysis of data was performed using the SAS statistical software program.

RESULTS AND DISCUSSION

Frequency of water samples exceeding 10 mg L^{-1} nitrate-N : Temporal variability in leachate nitrate-N concentrations during the period (June 1990 to May 1991) was appreciable, and the covariance was also high. At the Sunderland site, where soils were coarser textured, plots at the high manure rate had a greater frequency exceeding the 10 mg L^{-1} drinking water standard as compared to check plots and the low manured plots (Fig. 1). This did not occur at the other site where frequency of samples exceeding 10 mg L^{-1} was similar for both manure treatments and the check. Low manure plots exhibited a similar frequency of water samples exceeding 10 mg L⁻¹ of nitrate N as found in the check plots. The differences in nitrate-N concentration between check plots and low manure plots were not significant at both experimental sites. The nitrogen fertilizer treatments exhibited a high frequency of water samples exceeding 10 mg L⁻¹.

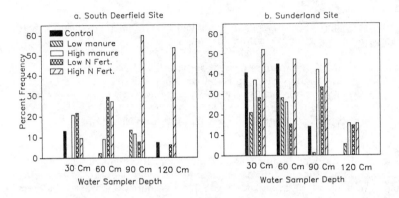

Fig. 1: Frequency of water samples exceeding 10 mg nitrate-N L⁻¹
(June 1990 to May 1991)

The interaction between treatments and depths was significant. Nitrate-N concentrations in water samples collected from 60 cm and 90 cm depths were comparatively higher, and the difference among treatments was distinct. High concentrations of nitrate-N were observed even at a depth of 120 cm, especially in the high nitrogen fertilizer plots but not in control or low manure plots. Generally, the nitrate-N in water samples was high immediately after a rainfall event with a delayed response with soil depth.

Nitrates in Summer and Fall Water Samples: Nitrate-N concentrations in water samples varied over time. Nitrate concentrations peaked 30 to 100 days after spring fertilizer or manure application (Figs. 2 and 3). At the Sunderland site, the water samples collected in the first two months, after application of manure and fertilizer (July and August) showed higher concentrations of nitrates. Thereafter, the concentrations were comparatively low, whereas at the South Deerfield site higher concentrations were observed from September onwards. This may be due to the coarser soil at Sunderland site, which may have resulted in faster percolation of rain water transporting nitrates. Also differences in soil texture at the two sites may have resulted in more rapid mineralization and nitrification in the sandier Sunderland site. At the South Deerfield site nitrate-N concentrations in the summer months were low except for one sample which

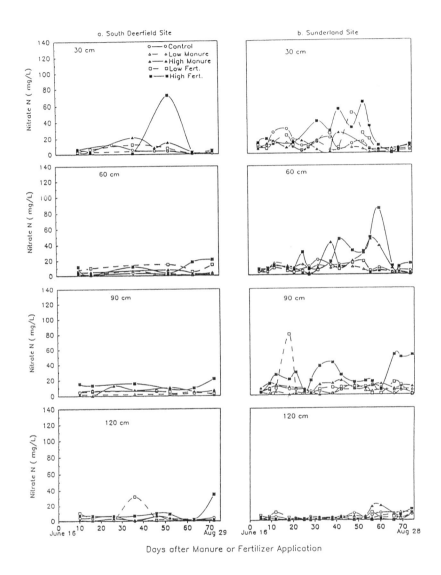

Fig. 2: Nitrate nitrogen concentration in porous cup water samples from various depths during the Summer of 1990.

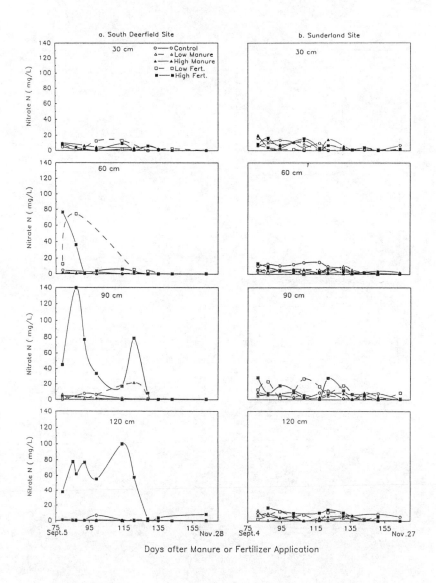

Fig. 3: Nitrate nitrogen concentration in porous cup water samples from various depths during the Fall of 1990.

showed approximately 70 mg nitrate-N L⁻¹ 50 days after the high fertilizer application.

Nitrate concentrations in water samples collected September to November were lower at the Sunderland site compared to the South Deerfield site (Fig. 3). High fertilizer plots at South Deerfield showed significantly high concentrations of nitrates even at deeper depths, whereas low manure and high manure plots did not show any significant amounts of nitrates.

Nitrates in Spring Water Samples: Nitrate-N concentrations in the soil water samples in the following spring were low and did not show any differences among treatments at both sites (Fig. 4). Water samples from all the treatments showed less than 6 mg L⁻¹ nitrate-N.

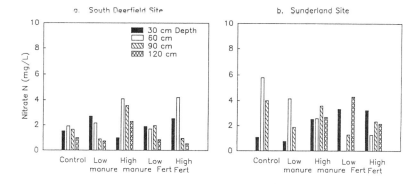

Fig. 4: Nitrate nitrogen concentration in porous cup water samples during the Spring of 1991.

CONCLUSIONS

Application of manure at the lower rate resulted in significantly lower concentrations of nitrate-N at both sites as compared to high and low fertilizer treatments. Low manure plots exhibited a similar frequency of soil water samples exceeding 10 mg L⁻¹ of nitrate-N as in the check plots. At the Sunderland site, where soils were coarser textured, high manured plots showed a greater frequency of nitrate-N exceeding the 10 mg L⁻¹ drinking water standard as compared to the check plots and the low manured plots. This did not occur at the South Deerfield site where frequency of samples exceeding 10 mg L⁻¹ was similar for both manure treatments and the check. Nitrogen fertilizer treatments had a greater frequency of samples exceeding 10 mg L^{-1} at both the sites. These preliminary results suggest that if the trends observed continue in succeeding years of this study farmers could reduce excess nitrogen in crop live stock farms by applying the manure on alfalfa, at rates of 45 to 67 Mg ha^{-1} depending upon soil type, without an adverse effect on groundwater quality. Such a practice may enable farmers to reduce overapplications of manure to corn fields.

REFERENCES

1. Brinton, W.F.,Jr. 1985. Nitrogen response of maize to fresh and composted manure. Biological Agricultural and Horticulture. 3:55-64.

2. Levin, I. and Y. Leshem. 1974. Using forage crops to reduce nitrate accumulation in Hula peat soils. Proc. 5th Scientific Conf. of the Israel Ecolog. Soc., Technion-Israel Inst. of Technol., Haifa, Israel.

3. Mathers, A.C., B.A. Stewart, and B. Blair. 1975. Nitrate nitrogen removal from soil profiles by alfalfa. J. Environ. Qual. 4:403-405.

4. Schertz, D.L. and D.A. Miller. 1972. Nitrate N accumulation in the soil profile under alfalfa. Agron. J. 64:660-664.

5. Westerman, P.W., L.M. Safley, J.C. Barker, and G.M. Chescheir, III. 1985. Available nutrients in livestock waste. Proc. 5th International Symposium on Agricultural Wastes, Chicago. pp295-307.

6. Young, C.E., B.M. Crowder, J.S. Shortle, and J.R. Alwang. 1985. Nutrient management on dairy farms in southeastern Pennsylvania. J. Soil Water Conservation 40:443-445.

INTERPRETATION OF THE STORET DATABASE FOR ATRAZINE IN

GROUND WATER USING A GEOGRAPHIC INFORMATION SYSTEM

Robert T. Paulsen   Allen E. Moose   Vicki Whitledge

The U.S. Environmental Protection Agency's (USEPA) STORET database for atrazine was analyzed using a Geographic Information System (GIS) to determine: 1) How the publicly available database (STORET) for atrazine in ground water related to the results from other studies including the USEPA's National Pesticide Survey (NPS); 2) If there existed any geographical trends in the data; and, 3) The general quality of data in STORET. As a matter of practicality and so that the results would be directly usable by the USEPA, the GIS used was the same package utilized by the USEPA in the recent review of atrazine residues in ground water.

The STORET database confirms that in general atrazine was detected in less than 10 percent (6.6%) of the 4,224 wells sampled in 34 states and when detected ususally found in trace quantities (less than 0.5 parts per billion (ppb)). The occurrence of atrazine in ground water above the Health Advisory was limited to less than 1 percent (0.7%) of detections. Over 50 percent of the data was generated by the U.S. Geological Survey (USGS) and can be considered of good quality complying in general with Good Laboratory Practices for sample collection, preservation, and analysis. This conclusion was supported by the detailed field and analytical protocols maintained by the USGS. These protocols were similar to those required of pesticide manufacturers, by USEPA, in completing water quality studies.

There appears to be two geographic regions where the bulk of detections, including those exceeding the 3.0 ppb Health Advisory, are common. Thematic maps for atrazine in ground water showed that the Northern Corn Belt, defined by Minnesota, Iowa, and Nebraska contains the most detections, the Mid-Atlantic states of Maryland, Delaware, New Jersey, and Pennsylvania also show considerable detections of atrazine.

Overall, the STORET database for atrazine in ground water is of good quality. Few wells were poorly located and those with inaccurate locations generally had no detections of atrazine. Researchers should have confidence in using STORET in their projects.

R.T. Paulsen, Director of THE PAULSEN GROUP - Independent Research Company, Bowie MD; A.E. Moose, Professor of Pysics, Southampton College, NY; and, V. Whitledge, Earth Scientist -THE PAULSEN GROUP, Bowie MD.

INTRODUCTION

The occurrence and distribution of pesticides in ground water has been widely researched over the past decade. The results of this research are at times conflicting. The results of the U.S. Environmental Protection Agency's (USEPA) latest national pesticide survey (NPS) have recently been released (USEPA, 1990). The results of the 1,290 well survey suggest that pesticide residues may be detected in 4.2 and 10.4 percent of the private and community water supply wells, respectively. However, in general, less than 1 percent of the wells contained pesticide residues exceeding health advisories.

Atrazine was one of the 127 chemicals searched for in the NPS. Atrazine, (2-chloro-4-ethylamino-6-isopropylamino-s-triazine), is a water soluble triazine herbicide widely used across the United States as primary weed control in corn, sorghum, sugarcane, and in many non-crop areas. Atrazine has been applied for weed control since 1958 (USDA, 1988; Gilliom et al, 1985) at an average rate of 61 million pounds of active ingredient during the period 1966-82 (USDA, 1983). The annual applications ranged from 24 million pounds in 1966 to a maximum of 90 million pounds in 1976.

The USEPA requested that the CIBA-GEIGY Corporation, the primary registrant of atrazine, perform a Data Call-In for atrazine. The Data Call-In included, in part, the results of atrazine in ground water sampling programs from 103 separate published references (8,474 samples) and CIBA-GEIGY sponsored studies which included 1,918 samples from 489 wells distributed across the United States. The CIBA-GEIGY Corporation analyzed these data using a (microcomputer based) Geographic Information System (Balu and Paulsen, 1991). The results of that analyses suggested that atrazine was detected above the Health Advisory 3.4 percent of the time and that the majority of occurrences (62 percent) were associated with point source contamination.

STORET is a computerized database which was developed to contain all available water quality data. Individual agencies and States were asked to input the results from monitoring programs into the database. STORET contains data that resides in the USGS WATSTORE database and individual states databases. An updated and detailed analysis of the atrazine in ground water data stored in the USEPA STORET water quality database has been completed. This analysis utilized the GIS, mentioned above, to determine if the existing data for 6,052 samples from 4,224 wells distributed across 34 States supported or contradicted CIBA-GEIGY's findings or those of the USEPA NPS.

OBJECTIVES

The objectives of this study were to determine: 1) How the publicly available database (STORET) for atrazine in ground water related to the USEPA NPS and the CIBA-GEIGY databases; 2) If there existed any geographical trends in the data; and, 3) The general quality of data in STORET.

METHODS

Data Collection

CIBA-GEIGY's prior review (Balu and Paulsen, 1991) included a STORET summary up to the year 1988, the current review includes data collected as late as May 1990 an addition of 1,850 samples. The type of data retrieved from STORET parallels that requested by USEPA in a Data Call-In. A detailed list of input fields is available from the authors upon request.

In May of 1990, a request was made to the USGS National Water Data Exchange (NAWDEX) program to retrieve all data pertaining to the sampling of atrazine in ground water and surface water available in the USEPA STORET database. In the past there have been concerns regarding the quality of the data stored in STORET, this issue will be addressed in a later section entitled Quality Of Data .

Data Compilation

Data for each well was tabulated on a separate sheet of computer print out. These sheets were separated, sorted by State and County and collated. The structure of the database (the data fields required) follwed guidlines prepared by the USEPA for a Data Call-In. The pertinent data were obtained from the hard copy and entered into database management software. In addition to the obvious data (for example, State and County, sample date, atrazine concentration,) it was usually possible to determine the type of well sampled, analytical detection limit, and if the sampling and analytic programs met or nearly met Good Laboratory Procedures (GLP). However, even with interpretation and personal communications with the original collecting agencies, generally 70 percent or less of the data fields were completed. The data fields for well location and atrazine concentrations were complete in all cases.

Quality of Data

USGS field and laboratory procedures are well documented and these protocols often are more detailed than those used by researchers cited in the published literature. The Techniques of Water Resources Investigations of the USGS Series Reports (TWRI) document, in detail, various sampling and analysis techniques and are similar to GLP protocols required by the USEPA. Wells sampled and analyzed by the USGS were generally in compliance with GLP. Attempts were made to contact individual agencies to obtain information regarding field and laboratory GLP compliance.

Each record of the electronic database was manually checked against the raw data in order to assure that no transcription errors existed. The GIS was used to check the validity of well locations. For example, a well stated as being sampled in Utah should plot within the boundaries of the State of Utah. If a well appeared to be incorrectly plotted, the electronic data was checked against the original data. The location check exercise illustrated the value of GIS in data accuracy and QA/QC (Quality Assurance / Quality Control) functions.

<u>Data Analysis</u>

The data were imported into the GIS for analysis. The MAPINFO GIS is a desktop computer based mapping system that allows a user to display and analyze data geographically. The following statements outline MAPINFO's general features (Mapping Information System Corporation, 1989):

> 1. MAPINFO can analyze and graphically display data distributions and trends within geographic areas and can also incorporate map information into presentation quality graphics.

> 2. MAPINFO can create, manipulate, and analyze color maps of states, counties, or any other data that can be shown on a map. A map of any area from 52 square feet to 12,000 miles wide can be created and the user can pan, zoom, and interactively find ground water data anywhere on the map.

> 3. Using the thematic and filtering features, the system will use database information to assign different symbols to different points or different types of shading to specific map areas based on user search criteria.

RESULTS AND DISCUSSION

Figure 1 illustrates the distribution of the 4,224 wells sampled. The 63 wells located on the islands of Hawaii are not shown but are included in the database.

<u>Quality Of Data</u>

Of the 4,224 wells, 51.4 percent (2,170 wells) were located, sampled, and analyzed by the USGS. This means that over half of the database generally meets GLP and can be considered valid. In this paper, data for the 2,170 wells is expressed as the GLP Subset.

The latitude and longitude data were inaccurate for 22 wells in 9 states (CA - 5, HI- 3, IA- 1, IL-1, MD- 2, MO- 1, NJ- 2, VA- 3, and WV- 4). These 22 wells plotted outside of the State boundary from which they were collected. Of the misplotted wells, atrazine was reported in four (CA- 1, HI- 1, IA- 1, and MD- 1). Figure 2 shows the three misplotted wells in Virginia. The latitude and longitude errors reside in the original data and were not a function of the GIS plotting progams.

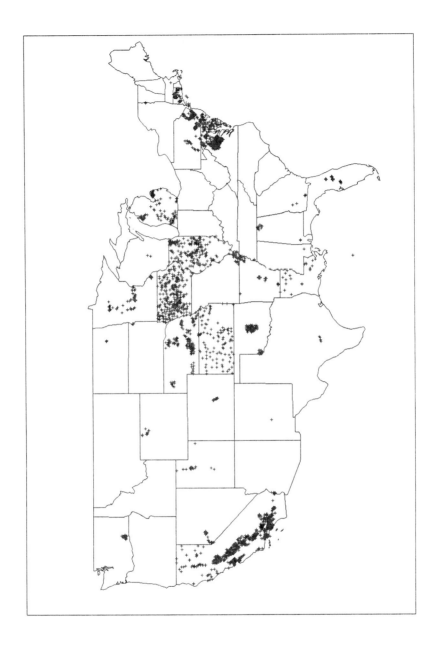

Figure 1. Distribution Of Wells In The STORET Database Sampled For Atrazine In Ground Water.

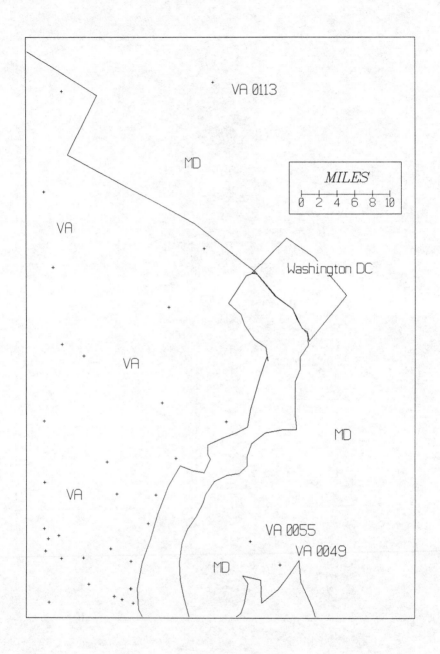

Figure 2. Map Of Northern Virginia Showing Misplotted Wells Sampled For Atrazine.

The average of the detection limits was 0.34 ppb with a range of 0.01 ppb to 10 ppb. The median and the mode of the distribution was 0.10 ppb. The average detection limit of the GLP wells was 0.16 ppb.

Atrazine In Ground Water Above A Detection Limit Of 0.30 Ppb.

For the entire database, 279 wells (6.6 percent) had reported average atrazine concentrations equal to or exceeding 0.3 ppb. The majority of these wells (71 percent) are distributed in three regions: 1) The Mid-Atlantic Region, PA, NJ, DE, MD, (also included is Connecticut); 2) The Michigan Basin; and, 3) The Northern Corn Belt (MN, IA, and NE). Figure 3 shows a thematic map of these regions.

GLP subset: For GLP wells, 187 wells (8.6 percent) had reported average atrazine concentrations equal to or exceeding 0.3 ppb. The majority of these wells (90 percent) are distributed in two regions: 1) The Mid-Atlantic Region, PA, NJ, DE, MD, (also included is Connecticut); and, 2) The Northern Corn Belt (MN, IA, and NE). Figure 4 shows a thematic map of these regions.

Atrazine In Ground Water Above The Lifetime Health Advisory Of 3 Ppb

The percentage of wells with the average atrazine concentration equal to or exceeding the Health Advisory (HA) was minor at 0.7 percent (31 0f 4,224) of the entire database. The percentage of wells with a one time detection (low concentration) of atrazine equal to or exceeding the HA was 0.6 percent. Most of the wells with average detections above the HA were found in the Northern Corn Belt (61 percent) particularly along the Platte River in Nebraska and in northwest Iowa, areas of high atrazine use.

GLP Subset: The percentage of GLP wells with the average atrazine concentration equal to or exceeding the HA was again minor at 0.7 percent (15 of 2,170) of the database. The percentage of wells with a one time detection (low concentration) of atrazine equal to or exceeding the HA was 0.5 percent. As with the database as a whole, the wells with average detections above the HA were found in the Northern Corn Belt (87 percent) particularly along the Platte River in Nebraska and in northwest Iowa.

Relationship Between Aquifer Regions In Iowa And Atrazine Detections

There were a significant number of detections of atrazine in the northwest region of Iowa. It has been thought that the eastern karst areas and the central Iowa alluvial aquifers should have the most detections given the existence of sinkholes and permeable soils, respectively. However it was shown here that many detections occur in the sandstone aquifers of northwestern Iowa (Fig. 5). The aquifer boundaries displayed (Fig. 5) were digitized from a map prepared by the USGS (USGS, 1985, p 213). Possibly, these detections are associated with permeable soils overlying the Dakota Aquifer. It is possible that these detections are from wells in the alluvial aquifers above the sandstone aquifer. Further insight into this problem may be gained by the use of additional GIS boundaries for: atrazine use, age of well, depth to bedrock, fracture traces, and soil texture.

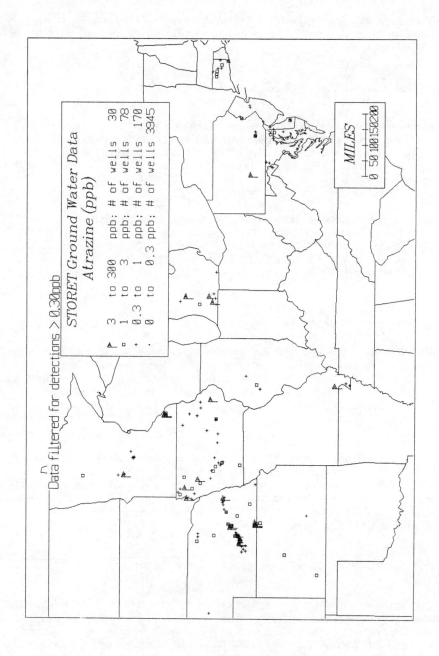

Figure 3. Thematic Map Of Central And Eastern United States Showing The Location
Of Wells And Atrazine Concentration For All Wells With Detections Equal
To Or Exceeding 0.3 ppb.

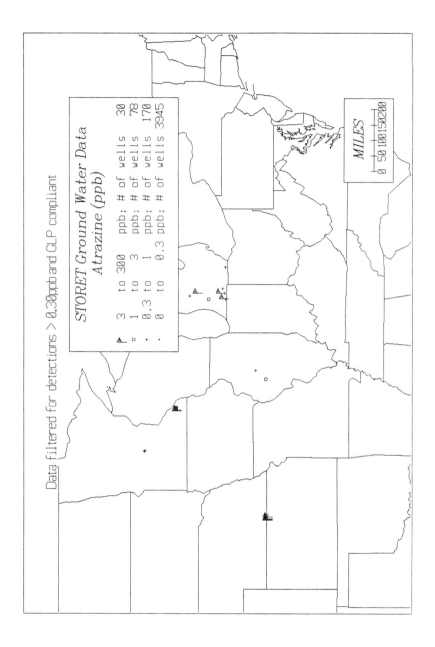

Figure 4. Thematic Map Of Central And Eastern United States Showing The Location Of Wells With Atrazine Concentration Equal To Or Exceeding 0.30 ppb For Wells Considered To Have Been Sampled And Analyzed Using Good Laboratory Practices.

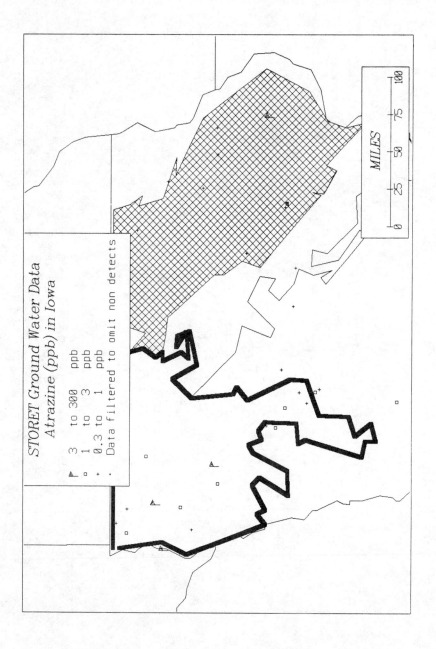

Figure 5. Thematic Map Of Iowa Showing Location Of Wells Sampled For Atrazine, Concentration In Samples, And Aquifer Boundaries. Stipple Pattern Denotes Major Alluvial Aquifers; Hatch Pattern Denotes Karst Aquifers; And, Open Pattern Denotes Sandstone Aquifers. (Aquifer Delineations USGS, 1985).

Relationship Between Storet Database And Results From NPS

According to the results of the NPS (USEPA, 1990 - a copy of the raw data was obtained from Ms.Briskin, USEPA-Office of Drinking Water) atrazine was detected in 1.3 percent (7 of 539 wells) of the public water supplies and 1.3 percent (10 of 751 wells) of the domestic supplies. The highest detection was 7.01 ppb for a domestic well. The median concentrations for public supplies and domestic supplies were 0.26 and 0.28 ppb, respectively.

Atrazine was detected above 0.3 ppb 6.6 percent of the time in the STORET database. The median of the average atrazine concentrations was 0.31 with a mode of 0.10 ppb. Atrazine was detected above the HA only 0.7 percent of the time with a maximum concentration of 700 ppb for a well in Alabama.

CONCLUSIONS

Based on this analysis, the STORET database for atrazine in ground water compared favorably with results from other studies. The STORET database confirms that in general atrazine was detected in less than 10 percent of the wells sampled and usually detected in trace quantities (less than 0.5 ppb). The occurrence of atrazine in ground water above the HA was limited to less than 1 percent of detections.

There appears to be two geographic regions where the bulk of detections, including those exceeding the 3.0 ppb HA, were common. The primary region of detections was the northern corn belt, defined by Minnesota, Iowa, and Nebraska. This was not surprising considering that these are areas of considerable atrazine use. The lack of STORET data for Wisconsin was anomalous since it is known that Wisconsin has an active program for sampling for atrazine and Wisconsin should be added to the northern corn belt delineation. The secondary region of detections was the Mid-Atlantic States of Maryland, Delaware, New Jersey, and Pennsylvania which showed considerable detections of atrazine. The state of Connecticut was also included in this region.

Within these two geographic regions distinct zones of detections could be mapped. Although intuitively we expected to see more detections associated with alluvial aquifers and karst aquifers, areas of fractured sandstone aquifers (northwestern Iowa) appear to show many detections. The source of these detections was not clearly evident from this analysis.

Overall, the STORET database for atrazine in ground water is of good quality. Few wells were mislocated and those with inaccurate locations generally had no detections of atrazine. Over 50 percent of the data was generated by the USGS and were considered of good quality complying in general with Good Laboratory Practices for sample collection, preservation, and analysis.

Finally, based on this study, the STORET database can be considered of reasonably good quality and investigators interested in using STORET should feel comfortable with the general validity of the data.

ACKNOWLEDGMENTS

The authors would like to acknowledge and thank the U.S. Geological Survey Water Resources Division for the arduous task of retrieving, packaging, and shipping the data for this study.

REFERENCES

Balu, K and Paulsen R.T.. 1991. Interpretation of Atrazine in Groundwater Data Using A Geographic Information System. in: Weigmann, D.L. (Ed). Pesticides in The Next Decade: The Challanges Ahead. Virginia Water resources Center, Blacksburg, VA. pp. 431 - 446.

Gilliom, R.J., Alexander, R.B., and R.A. Smith. 1985. Pesticides in the Nation's Rivers, 1975-1980, and Implications for Future Monitoring: U.S. Geological Survey Water Supply Paper 2271.

Mapping Information Systems Corporation. 1989. MAPINFO-Desktop Mapping Software: Users Guide. MAPINFO Corp., Troy, New York.

U.S. Department of Agriculture. 1983. Agricultural Resources-Inputs, Situation and Outlook Report. U.S. Department of Agricultural, Economic research Service, IOS-2.

U.S. Department of Agriculture. 1988. Agricultural Resources-Inputs, Situation and Outlook Report. U.S. Department of Agricultural, Economic Research Service, AR-9.

U.S. Environmental Protection Agency. 1990. National Survey of Pesticides in Drinking Water Wells - Phase I Report. U.S. Environmental Protection Agency, Washington, DC. NTIS# PB91-125765, 476 p.

U.S. Geological Survey. 1985. National Water Summary 1984. U.S. Geological Survey Water Supply Paper 2275, 467 p.

Surface Runoff Samplers for Nutrient Assimilation Measurement in a Restored Riparian Wetland

George Vellidis,   Matt C. Smith,   Robert K. Hubbard,   Richard Lowrance
MEMBER   MEMBER   MEMBER
ASAE   ASAE   ASAE

Abstract: A recently restored riparian wetland is being evaluated as a bioremediation site for nutrients moving downslope from an animal waste application site. In question is the short-term effectiveness of the restored wetland in enhancing the quality of the water leaving the site. Networks of shallow ground water wells and surface runoff collectors are being used to monitor nutrient concentrations and nutrient assimilation as surface and ground water moves through the wetland. A 600 mm H-flume at the wetland outlet measures the quantity and quality of surface water discharged from the wetland. Runoff is sampled at two locations entering the wetland and at two locations near the stream flow. At each location, the runoff is collected in a gutter, passed through a flume, and redistributed through a slotted gutter. Composite samples from each runoff event are collected with a low-cost automated sampler and analyzed for NO_3-N, NH_4-N, TKN, PO_4-P, Total P, and Cl. The restoration effort is described and the design, installation, and performance of the runoff samplers are discussed in detail.

Excessive pollutant loadings from nonpoint sources have been proven to have significant ecological effects on the receiving waters of lakes (Powers et al., 1972; Schelske and Stoermer, 1972) streams (Hynes, 1969), and estuaries (Fraser and Wilcox, 1981; Myers and Iverson, 1981). Traditionally, intensive agricultural land use has been considered a source of nonpoint source pollution and in many areas, rainfall runoff and subsurface flow from land application of farm animal waste has been shown to provide significant loadings of nutrients to receiving waters unless appropriate management techniques are employed.

Recent research has shown that riparian ecosystems can be used to control nonpoint pollution. Lowrance et al. (1984, 1985a, 1985b) and Peterjohn and Correll (1984) demonstrated during studies of coastal plain agricultural watersheds that riparian forest ecosystems are excellent nutrient sinks and buffer the nutrient discharge from surrounding agroecosystems. They showed that nutrient uptake and removal by soil and vegetation in the riparian forest ecosystem prevented agricultural upland outputs from reaching stream channels. They concluded that the riparian ecosystem can serve as both a short and long-term nutrient filter and sink if above-

The authors are: G. VELLIDIS and M.C. SMITH, Assistant Professors, Biological and Agricultural Engineering Department, Coastal Plain Experiment Station, University of Georgia, Tifton, GA 31793-0748, R.K. HUBBARD Soil Scientist, and R. LOWRANCE, Ecologist, USDA-ARS, Southeast Watershed Research Laboratory, Tifton, GA 31793-0946.
Supported by funds from the U.S. Geological Survey through the Georgia Water Resources Research Institute and by State and Hatch funds allocated to the Georgia Agricultural Experiment Stations.
Mention of commercially available products is for information only and does not imply endorsement.

135

ground vegetative biomass is periodically harvested to ensure a net uptake of nutrients. Riparian wetlands have also been shown to function as nutrient sinks and filters for land treated waste application of municipal sewage in the past (Turner et al., 1976; Sloey, 1978). Although mature riparian forests have been shown to be excellent nutrient sinks and buffers, little research has been conducted on the short-term effectiveness of newly established riparian forests. The work reported here is evaluating the bioremediation potential of a recently restored riparian wetland.

The wetland is located at the University of Georgia's Coastal Plain Experiment Station in Tifton, Georgia. It is directly downslope from an animal waste land application research site where a 5.6 ha center pivot irrigation system is being used to apply liquid manure derived from flush cleaning of a dairy cow confinement area. The waste application site is primarily used to evaluate the development of an environmentally safe and economically sustainable year-round minimum tillage forage production system using farm animal manure as the only fertilizer. A major thrust of the project is to evaluate the impact of land application of the farm animal waste on groundwater beneath the proposed forage production system (Vellidis et al., 1991a). A detailed monitoring program is used to determine the concentrations and cumulative amounts of NO_3-N, NH_4-N, Total N, PO_4-P, Total P, Ca, K, Mg, and Na applied through the waste, assimilated by the crops, stored in the soil, or leached to shallow ground water.

The northern section (2 ha) of the land application site drains downslope directly into the wetland. Surface runoff and ground water from this section flow through the wetland before being discharged to the first order stream which drains the wetland. The stream discharges into a constructed farm pond. The wetland (.92 ha), which was forested until 1985, is easily distinguished from the surrounding agricultural area by its vegetation, which consists mostly of wetland grasses and rushes (*Juncus sp.*), and its soil, which is Alapaha loamy sand, a deep, poorly drained soil commonly found along drainageways. Plinthite is found below a depth of 1 m and typically acts as an aquitard.

The forage production site is comprised primarily of Tifton loamy sand soil with a plinthic layer at a depth of 1-1.5 m. As in the wetland, the plinthite typically acts as an aquitard and during periods of high rainfall, is responsible for the formation of transient perched water tables. Water movement to the wetland from the upslope areas is primarily through subsurface flow. In the summer and autumn, surface runoff generally occurs only during intense rainfall events. During the winter months, when the soil profile is often saturated, runoff events are frequent and stream flow through the wetland is evident.

The site provides a unique opportunity to study the potential remediating effects of a wetland on the nutrient loading of the stream. To capitalize on this opportunity, this study was initiated to evaluate the feasibility and effectiveness of reestablishing a forest in a riparian wetland and using it as a bioremediation site for nutrients moving downslope from the animal waste application site. In question is the short-term effectiveness of the restored wetland in enhancing the quality of the water leaving the site.

METHODS

Wetland Restoration

The wetland was partially restored in February 1991 by reintroducing a combination of native trees over 0.47 ha (Fig. 1). The trees will be grown for eventual harvest as pulpwood, timber wood, or both. Pines and hardwoods were selected as a combination that would provide fast growth and year round nutrient uptake. Slash pines (*Pinus elliottii* Engelm.) were planted on the upslope portions of the wetland while Yellow poplar (*Liriodendron tulipifera* L.), tupelo gum (*Nyssa sylvatica* Marsh.) and green ash (*Fraxinus pennsylvanica* (Borkh.) Sarg.) saplings were planted in the wettest areas. The trees were planted with 1.5 m spacing within rows and 3 m spacing between rows to permit seasonal mowing for biomass removal (Vellidis et al., 1991b; 1992).

Native grasses and forbs have been allowed to reestablish themselves amongst the trees. In April 1992, marsh cordgrass (*Spartina patens* (Aiton) Mulh.), a perennial grass, was established along the perimeter of the wetland (0.45 ha) to act as a transitional zone between the forage production system and the riparian forest (Fig. 1).

Water Quality Measurement

A combination of surface runoff collectors, flumes, and monitoring wells were installed to monitor surface runoff and shallow ground water in the restored riparian wetland and the

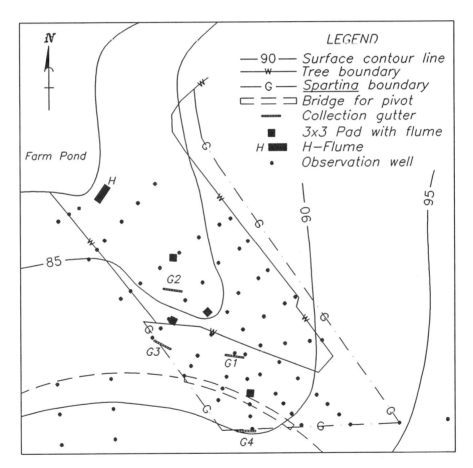

Figure 1. Map of the Dairy Wetland Restoration site showing the network of monitoring wells and the location of the 4 collection gutters and flumes.

agricultural uplands (Fig. 1). The resulting data are expected to provide specific information on nutrient uptake and removal processes in the riparian wetland and on changes in nutrient content of surface runoff and shallow ground water moving through the riparian zone.

Nutrient movement and concentrations in shallow ground water are being tracked and sampled in the north quadrant of the agricultural upland with 18 monitoring wells installed at depths of 3 and 6 m. In the wetland, ground water is monitored with 63 wells located within the wetland and on its perimeter on a 10 m grid (Fig. 1). The wells were installed to the plinthic layer - from 1 to 1.5 m in depth and are sampled biweekly.

Surface runoff is sampled at two locations entering the wetland, and at two locations near the stream flow. At each location, the runoff is collected in a gutter, passed through a 200 mm Modified Tucson Flume, and redistributed through a slotted gutter. Collection gutters G4 and G3 (Fig. 1) were installed at the boundary of the wetland and the agricultural area and sample runoff leaving the forage production system. Collection gutter G1 was located downslope from G4 at the boundary of the perennial grass zone and the hardwoods to sample surface water that has traveled approximately 20 m through the wetland. Gutter G2 was located downslope from G3 at the boundary of the pines and hardwoods to sample water that has passed through approximately 25 m of wetland. A 600 mm H-flume installed at the wetland outlet to measure surface water quantity discharged into the farm pond. The flume's location is denoted by the letter *H* in Figure 1. The location of the surface water collectors is expected to provide specific information on nutrient uptake and removal by wetland soil and vegetation types as the nutrient front discharged from the land application site migrates through the wetland. The outlet flume is expected to provide data on the overall effectiveness of the wetland.

The collection gutters were fabricated from galvanized sheet metal. Their bottoms slope towards the center to facilitate water flow towards a 75 mm outlet pipe. An overhang prevents rainfall from entering the gutters directly. The gutters are 3.6 m long, 50 mm wide, and range from 10 mm deep at each end to 120 mm deep at the center. They were installed so that the gutter collection lip was slightly below the soil surface. To prevent erosion at the lip, a fiberglass resin epoxy was used to coat approximately 50 mm of the soil immediately adjacent to the lip. The epoxy was also used to bond the lip to the coated soil.

The flumes were equipped with Belfort 5-FW1 strip chart stage recorders and installed on prepoured 1×1 m concrete pads to ensure a solid base that would remain level throughout the study (Fig. 2). To overcome the elevation difference between the flume inlets and the concrete pad (0.3 m), the flumes were, by necessity, located 10 to 20 m downslope from the collection gutters. As a result, water released through the redistribution gutters bypasses a portion of its potential flow path through the wetland. The G1 and G2 collection gutters were therefore strategically located to avoid collecting water released from the G4 and G3 redistribution gutters.

Runoff Sampler Design

Composite water samples of runoff events are collected from the five flumes with battery-powered peristaltic pumps (Fig. 2). During runoff events, the pumps are switched on by electro-optic liquid level switches installed in the flume stilling wells. To prevent overflow of the 13 L glass sample jars during extended runoff events, programmable cycle timers are used that permit the pumps to cycle on and off. A list of components is given in Table 1.

Figure 2. A flume and the associated sampling instrumentation on a concrete pad.

Figure 3 presents the circuit diagram for the automated water sampler. The key components are the Gems electro-optic liquid level switch and the Macromatic cycle timer. The switches require a 5 VDC excitation dropped down from the 12 VDC supplied by the deep cycle marine battery. The switches are 55 mm long and 16 mm wide and can be mounted vertically or horizontally.

Table 1. Automated runoff sampler components and their cost in 1992.

Item	1992 Cost
Tat Engineering electric peristaltic pump #410-66Q	$250
Gems electro-optic solid state level switch #138167	$55
Milwaukee Electronics Macromatic cycle timer #SS65126	$60
Potter Brumfield current sensitive DPDT relay #T85N11D114-05	$6
LM340-T5 IC voltage regulator	$2
Momentary contact SPST switch	$1
PCB terminal strip and box enclosure	$5
12 V 34 Amp-hr deep cycle marine battery	$60
LED for monitoring switch state (optional)	$1
13.25 L (3.5 gal) solution bottles	$60
Total Cost	**$500**

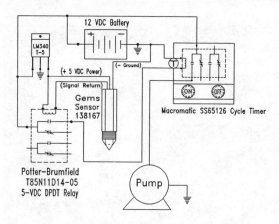

Figure 3. Circuit diagram of the automated surface runoff water sampler.

In this case, they were attached to threaded rods and mounted vertically in the stilling wells so that the conical prism surface (Fig. 4) was slightly above the stilling well water level when flow out of the stilling well ceased. The switches contain an infrared LED and a light receiver. Light from the LED is directed into the prism which forms the tip of the sensor (Fig. 4). With no liquid present, light from the LED is reflected within the prism to the receiver. When rising liquid immerses the prism, the light is refracted out into the liquid, leaving little or no light to reach the receiver. Sensing this change, the receiver actuates electronic switching within the unit to operate an external control circuit. Therefore, when the water level rises in the stilling well during a runoff event, the switch activates the timer. The liquid level switch has a repeatability of $\pm$ 1 mm (IMO, 1990) and is actuated by liquid level rise of less than 2 mm.

The cycle timers are programmable for 'on' and 'off' times of between 0.6 s and 24 hr. The on and off times are selected based on seasonal variation of runoff event duration. During winter in southern Georgia, low intensity runoff events commonly last 2 or 3 days. To obtain daily 12 L composites, an on time of 15 seconds with an off time of 80 minutes was used. In the summer, when runoff events result from thunder storms and are typically short lived, the timer is reprogrammed to be on for 15 seconds out of every 5 minutes.

To avoid passing the sample through the peristaltic pump, the glass sample jars (carboys) were installed, in line, between the intake and the pump. Sample was transported to the carboys through a 6 mm (OD) Teflon intake tube attached to the level floor section of the flume. At the carboy, the tube passed through a 2-hole stopper. The vacuum line was attached to the stopper with a hose barb. The carboy acted as a vacuum reservoir in addition to being a receptacle for the samples and flow of sample into the carboys occurred over a considerably longer period than the 15 s that the pump was in operation. Sample volume and flow duration were, consequently, inversely proportional to the volume of water already in a carboy.

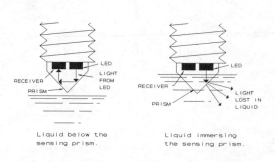

Figure 4. Liquid level switch operating principle. Adapted from (IMO, 1990).

Elevation of the intake tube outlet within the carboy affected volume and flow duration of the first sample due to initial elevation head differences. Figure 5 presents the two scenarios evaluated for this study; a) the outlet end of the intake tube was pushed through the stopper so that the tube protruded 200 mm into the carboy, thus, the inlet and outlet of the tube were at the same elevation, and b) the outlet of the intake tube was at the stopper and therefore 200 mm above the inlet.

For both scenarios, 18 samplings were required to accumulate approximately 12 L of sample. Average volumes were 676 mL and 661 mL, respectively. Corresponding average flow durations were 2.01 and 1.62 minutes. The difference between the two scenarios was essential caused by the decreased flow duration and sample volume that resulted from the energy spent to overcome the elevation difference between the inlet and outlet of the intake tube during the first sampling. The intake tube retained its prime during the subsequent samplings so that volumes and flow durations were the same for both scenarios (Fig. 5).

Hinged sheet metal covers fabricated in the dimensions of the concrete pads completely enclose all instrumentation on the pads. Water exiting the flumes enters the redistribution gutters (Fig. 2). These rectangular gutters are 3.6 m long, 100 mm wide, and 100 mm deep with flat bottoms that rest on the soil surface. Slots 50 mm tall × 2 mm wide were cut into the downslope face of the gutters at 100 mm intervals for uniform redistribution of collected water. Because the slots are somewhat restrictive during even moderately low flow rates, water tends to accumulate in the gutters and the resulting head forces relatively uniform flow through the slots. With large flow rates, water fills the gutter and exits from the slots and over the top of the gutter (Vellidis et al., 1992).

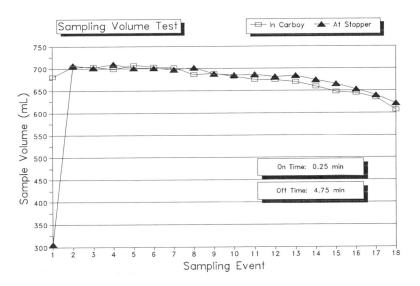

Figure 5. Volume collected per sampling event with an on time of 0.25 min and an off time of 4.75 min.

141

RESULTS

Instrument Performance

The automated sampler system was evaluated extensively in the laboratory to determine its reliability and repeatability. The system performed flawlessly except when the liquid level switch was exposed to intense external light. To avoid similar problems, it is recommended that the switch be shaded from direct sunlight and that it be installed more that 50 mm from a reflective surface. Energy consumption varied with duration of on time and frequency of simulated runoff events. During winter, the combination of low temperatures and frequent sampling requires that the batteries be recharged at monthly intervals. During the rest of the year, the interval can be increased to 6 or 8 weeks. Because the liquid level switches have no moving parts and use solid state switching, maintenance requirements consist of an occasional wipe-down cleaning of the prismatic tip of the sensor to ensure adequate light refraction when the tip is immersed. Automated samplers were installed in the field at each of the flumes on 01 May 1992. Since then, composite water samples have been successfully collected during each runoff event registered by the stage recorders.

Sampling Strategy

Samples from each runoff event and from the biweekly sampling of the monitoring wells are analyzed for nutrient concentrations (NO_3-N, NH_4-N, Total N, PO_4-P, and Total P). Water samples from the stream at the wetland outlet are collected periodically and compared to background level samples (collected before waste application began) to evaluate nutrient loading of the stream.

Soil samples for denitrification and inorganic N measurements are taken monthly at 5 depth increments to 0.3 m. Gaseous loss of N from the soil through denitrification is measured in intact core samples (Lowrance and Smittle, 1988). Nitrogen inputs by symbiotic nitrogen-fixation are estimated from the literature.

Nutrient accrual and storage in above ground vegetation is estimated from nutrient concentrations in woody plant tissue, community species composition, biomass estimates, and plant age at the end of each year. Evaluation of the wetland as a bioremediation site will be accomplished by maintaining a nutrient budget for the riparian system over the life of the project.

SUMMARY

A recently restored riparian wetland is being evaluated as a bioremediation site for nutrients moving downslope from an animal waste application site. In question is the short-term effectiveness of the restored wetland in enhancing the quality of the water leaving the site. Networks of shallow ground water wells and surface runoff collectors are being used to monitor nutrient concentrations and nutrient assimilation as surface and ground water moves through the wetland. A 600 mm H-flume at the wetland outlet measures the quantity and quality of surface water discharged from the wetland. Runoff is sampled at two location entering the wetland and at two locations near the stream flow. At each location, the runoff is collected in a gutter, passed through a flume, and redistributed through a slotted gutter. An automated low-cost water sampler was designed and installed at each flume to collect a composite water sample for each runoff event. The composite samples are analyzed for NO_3-N, NH_4-N, TKN, PO_4-P, Total P, and Cl.

REFERENCES

1. Fraser, T.H., and W.H. Wilcox. 1981. Enrichment of a subtropical estuary with nitrogen, phosphorus and silica. Pages 481-498 in B.J. Neilson and L.E. Cronin, editors, Estuaries and nutrients. Humana, Clifton, NJ.

2. Hynes, H.B.N. 1969. The enrichment of streams. Pages 188-196 in Eutrophication: causes, consequences, correctives. National Academy of Sciences, Washington, D.C.

3. IMO. 1990. GEMS Liquid level switches. IMO Industries Inc., Plainville, CT.

4. Lowrance, R., R. Leonard, and J. Sheridan. 1985a. Managing riparian ecosystems to control nonpoint pollution. *J. Soil Water Cons.* 40(1):87-91.

5. Lowrance, R., and D. Smittle. 1988. Nitrogen cycling in a multiple-crop vegetable production system. *J. Environ. Qual.* 17:158-162.

6. Lowrance, R.R., R.L. Todd, and L.E. Asmussen. 1985b. Waterborne nutrient budgets for the riparian zone of an agricultural watershed. *Agric. Ecosyst. Environ.* 10:371-384.

7. Lowrance, R.R., R. Todd, J. Fail, Jr., O. Hendrickson, R. Leonard, and L. Asmussen. 1984. Riparian forests as nutrient filters in agricultural watersheds. *BioScience* 34:374-377.

8. Myers, V.B., and R. I. Iverson. 1981. Phosphorus and nitrogen limited phytoplankton productivity in northeastern Gulf of Mexico estuaries. Pages 569-582 in B.J. Neilson and L.E. Cronin, editors, Estuaries and nutrients. Humana, Clifton, NJ.

9. Peterjohn, W.T., and D.L. Correll. 1984. Nutrient dynamics in an agricultural watershed: Observations on the role of a riparian forest. *Ecology* 65(5):1466-1475.

10. Powers, C.F., D.W. Schults, K.W. Malueg, R.M. Brice, and M.D. Schuldt. 1972. Algal responses to nutrient additions in natural waters. American Society of Limnology and Oceanography Special Symposium 1:141-154.

11. Schelske, C.L., and E. F. Stoermer. 1972. Phosphorus, silica, and eutrophication in Lake Michigan. American Society of Limnology and Oceanography Special Symposium 1:157-170.

12. Sloey, W.E., F.L. Spangler, and C.W. Fetter, Jr. 1978. Management of freshwater wetlands for nutrient assimilation. In R.E. Good, D.F. Whigham, and R.L. Simpson (eds.), Freshwater wetlands: Ecological Processes and Management Potential. Academic Press, New York, NY.

13. Turner, R.E., J.W. Day, Jr., M. Meo, P.M. Payork, T.B. Ford, and W.G. Smith. 1976. Aspects of land treated waste application in Louisiana wetlands. In D.L. Tilton et al., (eds.), Freshwater wetlands and sewage effluent disposal. Univ. Mich., Ann Arbor, MI.

14. Vellidis, G., S.T. Henry, C.D. Perry, and R.K. Hubbard. 1991a. Methodology and instrumentation for assessing the water quality impacts of a dairy waste land application system. ASAE Paper No. 91-2598, ASAE Int'l. Winter Mtg., Chicago IL, Dec. 1991.

15. Vellidis, G., R.R. Lowrance, M.C. Smith, and R.K. Hubbard. 1991b. Restoration of a riparian wetland for agricultural water quality improvement. ASAE Paper No. 91-2507, ASAE Int'l. Winter Mtg., Chicago IL, Dec. 1991.

16. Vellidis, G., R.R. Lowrance, R.K. Hubbard, and M.C. Smith. 1992. Evaluating the effect of a restored wetland on nutrient movement from a farm animal waste application site. Technical Completion Report for USGS Project No. 14-08-0001-G2013(06), Environmental Resources Center, Georgia Institute of Technology, Atlanta.

ACKNOWLEDGEMENTS

The authors acknowledge with gratitude the contributions made by Mr. Mike Gibbs who was responsible for the design and assembly of the electronic circuits and Mr. Greg Tucker who was responsible for instrument installation, sample collection, and equipment maintenance.

WETLAND RESTORATION FOR FILTERING NUTRIENTS FROM AN

ANIMAL WASTE APPLICATION SITE

R. K. Hubbard*   G. Vellidis*   R. Lowrance*
Member ASAE   Member ASAE

Recent research has shown that riparian forest ecosystems are excellent nutrient sinks and buffer the nutrient discharge from surrounding agroecosystems. A new research facility at the University of Georgia's Coastal Plain Experiment Station in Tifton, GA, is evaluating the impact of land application of farm animal waste by center pivot irrigation on groundwater quality. Surface runoff and shallow groundwater from one treatment area receiving 800 kg ha^{-1} yr^{-1} of nitrogen in animal waste drain directly downslope into an adjacent wetland. The wetland, which was forested until 1985, is on Alapaha loamy sand, a deep poorly drained soil, and is underlain by plinthite which acts as an aquitard below 1 m depth. The wetland was restored in winter 1991 by reintroducing trees to the existing perennial grasses and forbs. Networks of shallow groundwater wells were established both in the animal waste application area and in the wetland for measurement of nutrient concentrations. The animal waste area also has solution samplers for determining water quality in the root zone. Surface runoff measuring and sampling devices were installed in the wetland. Nutrient concentrations in surface runoff and groundwater, nutrient accrual and storage in above ground vegetation, and losses of nitrogen due to denitrification are being tracked in the wetland as the woody vegetation matures. Preliminary results indicate that the effectiveness of the riparian ecosystem as a living filter relates to growth stage and maturity of the vegetation.

Reclamation of land to its original function in the landscape ecosystem is becoming increasingly important. Under natural conditions (pre-agricultural) each segment of the landscape had plant and animal species unique to position, soils, and micro-climate. As land was developed for agriculture, the typical practice was to first clear and drain the uplands, and later clear and drain the lower wetter areas. In certain physiographic areas, such as the Midwest, many wetlands were completely drained so that row crop agriculture could encompass the entire landscape except for occasional drainage ditches. In other physiographic regions, such as the coastal plain of the southeastern part of the U.S., soils of the wetland areas were not very suitable for agricultural production, so more of these areas were left intact. However, considerable segments of the riparian wetlands in the southeastern U.S. coastal plain have been deforested, and this land use practice has continued until recently.

Early settlers to the eastern part of the United States often viewed wetlands as wasted lands that needed to be drained and brought into crop or animal production. This philosophy persisted until very recently, and in some cases still persists. Recognition of the importance of wetlands first gained national attention during the environmental awareness movement of the 1970's. However, the emphasis at that time was primarily on retaining existing wetlands so that flora and fauna could be preserved. Provisions of the 1985 and 1990 Farm Bills have provided financial penalties for farmers who drain and convert wetlands to crop production.

---

*R.K. HUBBARD, Soil Scientist, USDA-Agricultural Research Service, Southeast Watershed Research Laboratory, Tifton, GA; G. VELLIDIS, Assistant Professor, University of Georgia, Coastal Plain Experiment Station, Tifton, GA; and R. LOWRANCE, Ecologist, USDA-ARS, SE Watershed Research Laboratory, Tifton, GA.

Research started in the late 1970's showed another role for riparian and wetland zones. Extensive studies (Asmussen et al., 1979; Yates and Sheridan, 1983) of nutrient budgets in riparian areas of the Tifton Upland in the coastal plain of Georgia examined nitrate losses from cropped areas and riparian wetland zones, and nitrate loads in streamflow. It was estimated that 96 percent of the nitrate was retained, utilized, or transformed in the heavily vegetated riparian forests of the Coastal Plain (Yates and Sheridan, 1983). Stream outflow loads of nitrate on a mixed-use agricultural watershed were found to be lower than nitrate loads input by rainfall (Asmussen et al., 1979).

A series of studies (Lowrance et al., 1983; Lowrance et al., 1984a; Lowrance et al., 1984b; Lowrance et al., 1984c; Lowrance et al., 1985) in the 1980's measured streamflow and shallow groundwater quality in the same physiographic region and found reduction in nitrate levels in waters leaving the riparian zone as compared to the agricultural upland. Phreatic nitrate nitrogen, ammonium nitrogen, and organic nitrogen inputs to the riparian zone were 74 percent, 8 percent, and 18 percent of total nitrogen load, respectively. Streamflow nitrate nitrogen, ammonium nitrogen, and organic nitrogen outputs were 18 percent, 2 percent, and 80 percent of the total nitrogen load, respectively. Total annual nitrogen inputs to the riparian zone averaged 12.2 kg ha^{-1} yr^{-1} in precipitation, 29 kg ha^{-1} yr^{-1} in subsurface flow, 10 kg ha^{-1} yr^{-1} in surface runoff, and 10.6 kg ha^{-1} yr^{-1} as N fixation for a total of 61 kg ha^{-1} yr^{-1}. Losses of nitrogen in streamflow averaged 13 kg ha^{-1} yr^{-1}. The change in both form and amount of nitrogen between edge of field and stream were due to processes occurring within the riparian forest. It was projected that in this physiographic region, total replacement of riparian forest with a mixture of crops similar to those grown on the upland would increase present mean annual nitrate concentrations in streamflow from 0.20 mg L^{-1} to an estimated 4 mg L^{-1}. Conversion of this land to one-third cropland, one-third pasture, and one-third riparian forest potentially would increase nitrate nitrogen and ammonium nitrogen loads in streamflow by as much as 800 percent.

A North Carolina Coastal Plain study on soils having significant shallow subsurface flow showed that from 10 to 56 kg ha^{-1} yr^{-1} of nitrate moved from cropped fields in subsurface drainage water (Jacobs and Gilliam, 1985). Natural riparian vegetation downslope from the cropped fields resulted in a substantial portion of the nitrate in the drainage water being removed. The investigators attributed this primarily to denitrification. Buffer strips less than 15 m wide caused significant losses of nitrate before runoff water or subsurface flow reached the stream. It was also noted in this study that while soybean production had increased 760 percent since 1945, with commensurately more nitrogen fixation, and while fertilizer use had increased 400 percent since 1945, the research results showed no proportional increase in the nitrogen content of most coastal plain streams. It was concluded that from an environmental view, the most effective system for removing nitrogen is a natural drainageway bordered by poorly drained soil and dense riparian vegetation. Another North Carolina study found no increase in nitrate in streams over the last 50 years in that state despite increases in fertilizer application (Gilliam and Terry, 1973).

Riparian forests consisting of mature trees (30-75 yrs old) are known to be effective in reducing nonpoint pollution from agricultural fields (Lowrance et al., 1985). At least three separate studies at different sites in the Gulf-Atlantic Coastal Plain region have shown that concentrations and loads of nitrogen and phosphorus in subsurface flow and surface runoff are markedly reduced after passage through a riparian forest (Jacobs and Gilliam, 1985; Lowrance et al. 1983, 1984; Peterjohn and Correll, 1984). What is not known is the effect on water quality of riparian forest ecosystems with immature trees.

In 1991 a research project funded through the LISA (Low Input Sustainable Agriculture) program entitled "Development of an environmentally safe and economically sustainable year-round minimum tillage forage production system using farm animal manure as the only fertilizer" was started. This study is being conducted by a multidisciplinary scientific team at a site where screened dairy wastes are applied to 5.6 ha by center pivot. During the experimental design stages of the project it was recognized that a formerly forested riparian zone existed downslope from the center pivot area, and that nutrients from the upland site would impact this area via surface runoff, shallow subsurface flow, or drift from the center pivot.

A decision was made to restore the wetland to forested condition and to determine the effects of the wetland on water quality during the restoration process. The specific objectives for the restoration were to:

a. Measure nutrient (nitrogen, phosphorus) concentration changes in surface runoff and shallow groundwater as they move through the wetland.
b. Determine nutrient uptake and removal by soil microbial processes and vegetation in the wetland.
c. Evaluate the wetland as a potential bioremediation site.

WASTE HANDLING AND APPLICATION TO UPLAND AREA

The University of Georgia Coastal Plain Experiment Station dairy herd averages 90 lactating cows. These animals are confined to an outside lot with shelters over the freestall and feeding areas. Water released from the milking barn or an alternate exterior holding tank is used to flush the manure to a 35 m^3 waste holding tank. The manure-laden water from the waste holding tank is then pumped over a stainless steel separating screen using an automatically controlled pump with chopper blades. Large solids, consisting mainly of sand, undigested portions of feed, and bedding material, slide from the screen while the finer solids and liquid pass through the screen. The liquids then flow to a lagoon with a storage capacity equal to 3 to 4 weeks of wastewater production. The material from this lagoon is used for application to the upland site.

A 5.6 ha center pivot irrigation system (Fig. 1) is being used to apply the liquid manure from the lagoon. The waste is applied to four pivot quadrants at nitrogen application rates of 400, 600, 800, and 1200 kg ha^{-1} yr^{-1}, respectively. These rates were selected so that the lowest rate is restrictive to plant growth and the highest rate is excessive for maximum plant growth based on nitrogen uptake rates calculated from previous experiments (Johnson et al., 1984). The cropping system consists of overseeding of abruzzi rye (*Secale cereale* L.) into Tifton 44 bermudagrass (*Cynodon dactylon* L.) sod in the fall, followed by minimum tillage planting of silage corn (*Zea mays* L.) into the bermudagrass and rye stubble in the spring, followed by summer crops of hay or silage from the residual bermudagrass.

The north quadrant of the pivot, which receives a nitrogen application rate of 800 kg ha^{-1} yr^{-1} drains downslope into a wetland area (Fig. 1). This area (.92 ha), which was forested until 1985, was distinctly different from the upslope areas in vegetation at the start of the upland study. The vegetation before restoration was primarily wetland grasses and rushes (*Juncus sp.*).

WETLAND RESTORATION

The soil at the wetland site is Alapaha loamy sand, a deep, poorly drained soil commonly found along drainageways. Plinthite is commonly found beginning about 1 m, and this is then underlain by the Miocene age Hawthorn Formation. Both the plinthite and the Hawthorn Formation are only very slowly permeable and hence act as aquitards.

The wetland was partially restored in February 1991 by reintroducing a combination of native trees over 0.47 ha (Fig 2). The trees will be grown for eventual harvest as pulpwood, timber wood, or both. Slash pine (*Pinus elliottii* Engelm.) and yellow poplar (*Liriodendron tulipifera* L.) were selected as a combination that would provide fast growth and year-round nutrient uptake. The pines were planted on the upslope portions of the wetland while the poplars were planted in the wettest areas. The trees were planted with 1.5 m spacing within rows and 3 m spacing between rows to permit seasonal mowing of herbaceous vegetation.

Evaluation of the planted trees in April 1991 indicated potential very low survivorships of the poplars. A decision was made to replant with different tree species to ensure a satisfactory stand of hardwoods. Accordingly blackgum (*Nyssa sylvatica* Marsh.) and green ash (*Fraxinus pennsylvanica* (Borkh.) Sarg.) saplings were introduced to the hardwood area in April 1991. In April 1992, marsh cordgrass (*Spartina patens* (Aiton) Mulh.), a perennial grass, was established along the perimeter of the wetland (0.45 ha) to act as a transitional zone between the forage production system and the riparian forest.

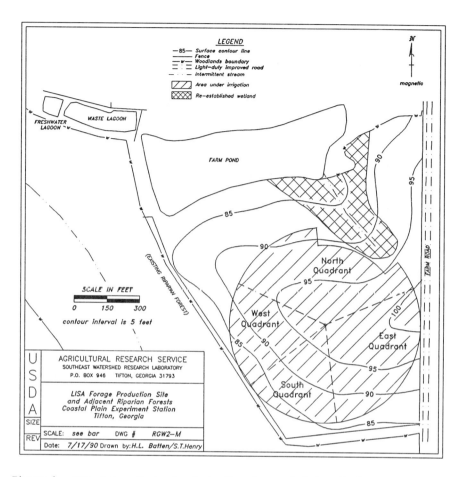

Figure 1. The Dairy Waste Land Application and Dairy Wetland Restoration Research Facilities. The Circle Indicates the Area Irrigated by the Center Pivot Waste Application System. The Wetland Is Indicated by the Cross-Hatched Area.

WATER QUALITY MEASUREMENT

Measurement of quality of waters entering the wetland, moving through the wetland, and exiting the wetland are being made using a combination of monitoring wells, surface runoff collectors, and flumes (Figs. 1 and 2). Nutrient movement and concentrations in the upland root zone and in shallow groundwater are being tracked in the north quadrant using both solution samplers and a network of 18 monitoring wells. The solution samplers are installed at 0.5 m, 1.0 m, 1.5 m, and 2.0 m depths. There are six samplers per depth for a total of 24 in the north quadrant, and they are located on miniplots within the quadrant. The solution samplers are constructed from 1 bar, high flow ceramic cups, 48 mm diameter X 60 mm long, attached to a 300 mm long, 48 m OD schedule 40 PVC pipe with epoxy.

Nine of the 18 shallow groundwater wells in the north quadrant are at 3 m depth, while the other nine are at 6 m depth. These wells are placed in a rectangular pattern so that flow net calculations of water movement can be made. The wells are constructed of 50 mm I.D. schedule 40 PVC pipe with 0.8 m of slotted well screen glued at the bottom end.

In the wetland and around it's perimeter groundwater is monitored with 63 wells (Fig 2). The wells are installed to a depth of 1 m and are fully

147

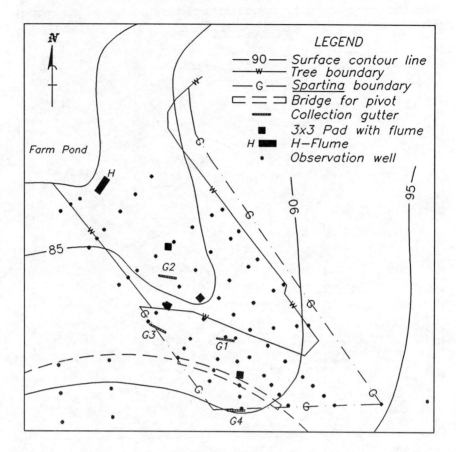

Figure 2. Map of the Dairy Wetland Restoration Site Showing the Network of Monitoring Wells and the Location of the Four Collection Gutters and Flumes.

slotted up to the soil surface. They were constructed from 50 mm diameter schedule 40 PVC by attaching a section of well screen to a nonperforated section of pipe. A biweekly sampling schedule is used for measuring the depth to the water table in both the upland and wetland wells, and also for collecting samples for nutrient analyses. Tapedown from the top of the well to the water surface is accomplished using a plastic tape with a metal "blooper" attached. Water samples from the upland wells are collected using a bladder type pump while those from the wetland are collected using a peristaltic pump. Water samples from the solution samplers in the upland are collected on the same biweekly schedule.

Surface runoff is sampled at two locations entering the wetland and at two locations near the stream flow. At each location, the runoff is collected in a gutter, passed through a 200 mm Modified Tucson Flume, and redistributed through a slotted gutter. The gutters were fabricated from galvanized sheet metal and are 3.6 m long, 50 mm wide, and range from 10 mm deep at each end to 120 mm deep at the center. The flumes are equipped with Belfort 5-FW1 strip chart stage recorders. Composite water samples are collected from the flumes with battery-powered peristaltic pumps.

Collection gutters G4 and G3 (Fig 2) were installed at the boundary of the wetland and the agricultural area and sample runoff leaving the forage production system. Collection gutter G1 is located downslope from G4 at the boundary of the perennial grass zone and the hardwoods, and samples surface water that has traveled approximately 20 m through the wetland. Gutter G2 is located downslope from G3 at the boundary of the pines and hardwoods and samples water that has passed through approximately 25 m of wetland. A 600 mm H-flume installed at the wetland outlet measures surface water quantity and quality discharged into the farm pond. The flume's location is denoted by the letter H in Figure 2.

Water samples from the upland are analyzed for nitrate nitrogen, ammonium nitrogen, total nitrogen, phosphate, total phosphorus, calcium, potassium, magnesium, and sodium concentations. Water samples from the surface runoff collectors and shallow wells in the wetland are analyzed for nitrate nitrogen, ammonium nitrogen, total nitrogen, phosphate, and total phosphorus concentrations.

EVALUATION OF WETLAND RECLAMATION AND WATER QUALITY

This study is in the beginning stages; and, consequently, results at this time are limited. Results from the study fall into two categories: (1) evaluation of success in reestablishing wetland species in the area, and (2) determination of the effect of the restoring vegetation on water quality.

Evaluation of the riparian zone reclamation will be made through observations of the success of the planted species. The initial difficulties with the poplar trees were believed to be due primarily to the fact that they were supplied from a mountain nursery rather than a coastal plain nursery. At the time of preparation of this paper, the planted Spartina grass is showing some difficulties in getting established, primarily because of lack of rainfall. Evaluations of community species composition will be made periodically throughout each year of the study. Evaluations of nutrient concentrations in woody plant tissue, biomass estimates, and plant growth will be made annually. This information will be useful in serving as a guide for reestablishing other riparian areas in the Coastal Plain and other areas of the Southeast.

Evaluation of the wetland as a bioremediation site will be accomplished by maintaining a nutrient budget for the riparian system over the life of the project. This budget will include the observations of surface and shallow groundwater quality plus results from soil samples. Soil samples for denitrification and inorganic nitrogen measurements are being taken monthly at 5 depth increments to 0.3 m. Gaseous loss of nitrogen from the soil through denitrification are measured in intact core samples (Lowrance and Smittle, 1988). Nitrogen inputs by symbiotic nitrogen-fixation will be estimated from the literature. Measurement of water quality at this time shows both nitrate nitrogen and ammonium nitrogen entering and leaving the wetland without the major changes in concentrations generally associated with mature trees. It is anticipated that the effectiveness of the wetland ecosystem as a bioremediation system will increase as the trees mature.

REFERENCES

1. Asmussen L.E., J.M. Sheridan, and C.V. Booram, Jr. 1979. Nutrient movement in streamflow from agricultural watersheds in the Georgia Coastal Plain. Trans., ASAE 22:809-815, 821.

2. Gilliam, J.W., and D.L. Terry. 1973. Potential for water pollution from fertilizer use in North Carolina. Ext. Circ. No. 550. N.C. State Univ., Raleigh.

3. Jacobs, R.C., and J.W. Gilliam. 1985. Riparian losses of nitrate from agricultural drainage waters. J. Environ. Qual. 14:472-478.

4. Johnson, J.C., R.E. Hellwig, G.L. Newton, J.L. Butler, and E.D. Threadgill. 1984. Use of liquid dairy cattle waste to produce Tifton 44 bermuda grass forage. 4th Annual Solar and Biomass Energy Workshop, Atlanta, GA, April 17-19, 1984.

5. Lowrance, R.R., R.L. Todd, and L.E. Asmussen. 1983. Waterborne nutrient budgets for the riparian zone of a agricultural watershed. Agr. Ecosystems Environ. 10:371-384.

6. Lowrance, R.R., R.L. Todd, and L.E. Asmussen. 1984a. Nutrient cycling in an agricultural watershed: I. Phreatic movement. J. Environ. Qual. 13:22-27.

7.   Lowrance, R.R., R.L. Todd, and L.E. Asmussen. 1984b. Nutrient cycling in an agricultural watershed: II. Streamflow and artificial drainage. J. Environ. Qual. 13:27-32.

8.   Lowrance, R.R., R. Todd, J. Fail, Jr., O. Hendrickson, Jr., R. Leonard, and L. Asmussen. 1984c. Riparian forests as nutrient filters in agricultural watersheds. BioScience 34(6):374-377.

9.   Lowrance, R., R. Leonard, and J. Sheridan. 1985. Managing riparian ecosystems to control nonpoint pollution. J. Soil and Water Cons. 40: 87-91.

10. Lowrance, R. and D. Smittle. 1988. Nitrogen cycling in a multiple-crop vegetable production system. J. Environ. Qual. 17:158-162.

11. Peterjohn, W.T. and D.L. Correll. 1984. Nutrient dynamics in an agricultural watershed: observations on the role of a riparian forest. Ecology 65(5):1466-1475.

12. Yates, P., and J.M. Sheridan. 1983. Estimating the effectiveness of vegetated flood plains/wetlands as nitrate nitrogen and orthophosphorus filters. Agr. Ecosystems and Environ. 9:303-314.

THREE CASE STUDIES OF SUCCESSFUL WETLAND REHABILITATION IN ALASKA

USING NEWLY DEVELOPED WETLAND CULTIVARS

S. J. Wright[*]

WETLANDS IN ALASKA

The issues associated with wetlands and emotions generated by these land forms are extremely strong in Alaska. Whereas some states may have lost over 90% of the estimated wetlands in existence in the 1780s, Alaska's estimated loss is 0.1% (Dahl, 1990). The estimated 200,000-acre (81,000 hectare) loss in Alaska since the 1780s, places the state in the same numeric loss category of New Hampshire, a state less than 1/60th the size of Alaska (Dahl, 1990).

Alaska's immense size is reflected in the overall size of wetland within it's borders. Of Alaska's land surface, 45.3% or 170,000,000 acres (44,050,000 hectares) is wetland (Dahl, 1990).

Needless to say, issues such as "no net loss" are important in Alaska. Development in Alaska can easily be brought to an abrupt halt with a restrictive or unrealistic wetland policy. Alaskans, however, do not for the most part, promote rampant destruction of valuable wetland resources.

Rehabilitating damage to wetlands in Alaska is a relatively new art. The Alaska Plant Materials Center has been on the leading edge in this activity since 1980. This report will deal with three case studies involving the rehabilitation of damaged wetlands. Full function was not measured on these sites, however, the attempt was to reestablish known wetland vegetation species.

PLANT MATERIAL

The studies described in this report relied, for the most part, on native species. In this report, native species means that the species can be found growing naturally in the geographic region. Table 1 lists the species, cultivar and the species' indicator status as listed in Wetland Plants of the State of Alaska 1986 (Reed, 1986).

'Arctared' red fescue, Festuca rubra, was released in 1965 as a revegetation species showing extreme hardiness throughout Alaska (Hodgson, 1978). The overly aggressive, sod-forming nature of this species often makes this cultivar unacceptable in reclamation. However, in erosion control the cultivar is outstanding. The cultivar was cooperatively developed by the University of Alaska Agricultural Experiment Station and the USDA.

'Egan' American sloughgrass, Beckmannia syzigachne, was released by the Alaska Plant Materials Center in 1990 as a wetland rehabilitation cultivar (Wright, 1991a). This has been the state's first cultivar developed solely for wetland restoration. Additionally, the species has wildlife benefits by providing forage and seed for waterfowl.

---

[*]STONEY J. WRIGHT, Manager and Agronomist, Alaska Plant Materials Center, Palmer, Alaska.

'Kenai' polargrass, <u>Arctagrostis</u> <u>latifolia</u>, is a variety recommended for forage and revegetation from the central interior to southern portions of Alaska (Mitchell, 1987). This species has potential in wet areas in portions of Alaska. This cultivar was developed by the Alaska Agriculture and Forestry Experiment Station at Palmer, Alaska.

'Alyeska' polargrass, <u>Arctagrostis</u> <u>latifolia</u>, is a cultivar developed by the University of Alaska Agricultural Experiment Station. The prime purpose for this cultivar is revegetation in interior and western Alaska (Mitchell, 1979). The species is adapted to moderately wet areas.

'Sourdough' bluejoint, <u>Calamagrostis</u> <u>canadensis</u>, is a cultivar with a wide range of adaptability. The species occurs throughout Alaska on both dry and wet sites. The cultivar was developed by the University of Alaska Agricultural Experiment Station for revegetation in northern latitudes (Mitchell, 1979).

'Norcoast' Bering hairgrass, <u>Deschampsia</u> <u>beringensis</u>, was released in 1981 by the University of Alaska Agricultural Experiment Station as a forage and revegetation grass in northern areas. Norcoast is recommended for revegetation use in coastal regions of western Alaska to southwestern Alaska and possibly in the northern maritime regions (Mitchell, 1985).

'Tundra' glaucous bluegrass, <u>Poa</u> <u>glauca</u>, was originally collected in Arctic Alaska. The cultivar was released by the University of Alaska Agricultural Experiment Station for revegetation in extreme northern areas with severe environmental conditions (Mitchell, 1979).

'Caiggluk' tilesy sagebrush, <u>Artemisia</u> <u>tilesii</u>, was developed and released by the Alaska Plant Materials Center in 1989 as a reclamation species. This forb has a wide range of adaptations throughout Alaska (Wright, 1991b).

Table 1. Species Used in the Wetland Studies

Common Name	Scientific Name	Cultivar	Status
Polargrass	Arctagrostis latifolia	Alyeska	Facultative Wetland
Polargrass	Arctagrostis latifolia	Kenai	Facultative Wetland
American sloughgrass	Beckmannia syzigachne	Egan	Obligate
Bluejoint	Calamagrostis canadensis	Sourdough	Facultative
Hairgrass	Deschampsia beringensis	Norcoast	Facultative
Red Fescue	Festuca rubra	Arctared	Facultative Upland
Glaucous bluegrass	Poa glauca	Tundra	Upland
Tilesy sagebrush	Artemisia tilesii	Caiggluk	Upland

STUDY SITES

The Alaska Plant Materials Center is involved with other wetland and emergent species, however, this paper only deals with three selected projects (Figure 1). These projects are located at the Red Dog Mine port site north of Kotzebue, Eielson slough east of Fairbanks and the Kenai River wetland east of the city of Kenai.

Figure 1. Study Site Locations.

Red Dog Port Site

The Red Dog site is roughly 60 meters from the coastline of the Chukchi Sea. The
disturbance requiring restoration was a small (1.5 ha) disposal pit located on
NANA Regional Corporation property. The site was opened but never used for solid
waste disposal (Figure 2). The U. S. Army Corps of Engineers and U. S. National
Park Service stipulations required the site to be rehabilitated. Due to the site
location in a wetland area and proximity to the sea coast, excess water was a
significant problem.   In addition to surface fresh water, the site was also
subject to occasional storm surges causing brackish conditions in the area.
Prior to seeding, the area was graded and contoured to the best possible
condition using a D-6 class dozer. Based on seasonal water depth and elevation,
a revegetation plan consisting of four mixes was developed around native species.
Only the two mixes used in high moisture areas are discussed in this report
(Table 2).

Figure 2. Red Dog Port Site, June 1988.

153

Figure 3. Red Dog Site, September 1990.

Table 2. Red Dog Port Site Seed Mixes.

Mix #	Species	Soil Conditions	% of Mix By Weight
1	Norcoast Bering Hairgrass	Saturated or Flooded	50
1	Arctared Red Fescue	Saturated or Flooded	30
1	Egan American Sloughgrass	Saturated or Flooded	15
1	Caiggluk Tilesy Sagebrush	Saturated or Flooded	5
2	Tundra Glaucous Bluegrass	Wet Upland	40
2	Arctared Red Fescue	Wet Upland	30
2	Alyeska Polargrass	Wet Upland	30

Both mixes were seeded at a rate of 44.8 kg ha^{-1}. Fertilizer (20-20-10) was applied at a rate of 504 hg ha^{-1}. All seeding and fertilization was conducted with hand operated equipment (Wright, 1990).

In 1989, the Alaska Plant Materials Center was asked to assist in restoring a
wetland disturbance covering approximately .04 ha. This disturbance was the
result of an illegal fill. A plan was prepared and accepted by the U. S. Army
Corps of Engineers. The plan relied entirely on species native to the area and
adapted to saturated soil on sites where prolonged seasonal flooding may occur.

Figure 4. Photograph of the Kenai Site, June 1989.

Figure 5. Kenai Site, September 1991.

155

The area was seeded with the mix in Table 2 at a rate of 22.4 kg ha^{-1} and fertilized at a rate of 560 kg ha^{-1} 20-20-10 (Wright, 1992).

Table 3. Kenai River Seed Mix.

Species	Percent by Weight
Egan American Sloughgrass	50
Sourdough Bluejoint	25
Norcoast Bering Hairgrass	25

Past seeding evaluations of the site occurred on September, 1989 and August, 1991. During the September, 1989 site visit the entire site was under one meter of water due to flooding of the Kenai River. This condition lasted for roughly 30 days.

Figure 6. Pile Driver Slough, 1985.

PILE DRIVER SLOUGH (EIELSON)

During a road construction project near Eielson, Alaska, a wetland adjacent to an overflow channel was damaged by fill and equipment movement. The Corps of Engineers required site restoration and the Alaska Plant Materials Center responded with a plan using native American sloughgrass, a wetland species. The disturbance was relatively small but typical of wetland disturbances in Alaska. The fill and equipment tracks were leveled and contoured to recreate a natural topography. During June, 1985, the site was hand seeded with sloughgrass at a rate of 11.2 kg ha^{-1}. The area was then fertilized with 20-20-10 at a rate of 504 kg ha^{-1} (Wright, 1989).

156

Figure 7. Pile Driver Slough, August 1987.

RESULTS AND CONCLUSIONS

The species presently being used in Alaska for wetland rehabilitation seem to be performing well. At the Red Dog site, the original sedge communities have been temporarily replaced with grasses. Reinvasion of the original community is expected. The sites at Kenai and Eielson were originally grass communities and the seeded species appear quite natural.

Table 4. Success of Wetland Seedings.

Site	Cover	Composition	Vigor	Native Reinvasion
Red Dog	90	60% Sloughgrass 30% Hairgrass 10% Tilesy Sage	Excellent	Sedges Cotton Grass Some Willow
Eielson	85	50% Sloughgrass	Good	Bluejoint
Kenai	98	75% Sloughgrass 20% Hairgrass 5% Bluejoint	Excellent	Forbs Sedge

Based on the performance of Egan American sloughgrass in these studies, this cultivar will become very important in wetland rehabilitation. This species' non-aggressive growth habit will not prevent reinvasion of other native plant material.

Until sedge and cotton grass seed becomes commercially available, Egan sloughgrass is the only truly obligative wetland species available in quantity. This cultivar should be used in all situations for the present time. Additional studies with this cultivar are being conducted in Canada, South Dakota and Utah in an attempt to determine the cultivar's value in temperate areas.

157

Norcoast hairgrass performance is also quite acceptable. While the species is not significant in waterfowl habitat, it is nonetheless important for wetland rehabilitation.

Sourdough bluejoint, while in limited supply and costly, small amounts of seed should be used in wetland rehabilitation mixes.

The following mix seems to be ideal for Alaska's wetland disturbances.

Table 5.   Preferred Wetland Seed Mix.

Species	Percent By Weight
Egan American Sloughgrass	60
Norcoast Bering Hairgrass	35
Sourdough Bluejoint	5

The mix listed in Table 5 will perform well if broadcast seeded at a rate of 22 kg ha^{-1}. Drill seeding could halve the seeding rate. Fertilizer rates can be developed for local conditions, but 500 to 560 kg ha^{-1} of 20-20-10 seems to work well in Alaska.

This report weighs the term "rehabilitation" with respect to total wetland reclamation. This author is not convinced that all the factors in a disturbed wetland can be recreated by artificial means. However, some components such as vegetative cover can be matched or temporarily replaced with appropriate commercially available species. Until additional wetland species become available, this represents the best available technology to superficially reclaim a wetland.

The other major conclusion is the cost effectiveness of wetland restoration. Much of the criticism associated with wetland rehabilitation and restoration is based on the fact that many techniques being proposed are punitive, and not cost effective. Developing plant material and techniques that are inexpensive and practical is the key to acceptance of wetland reclamation. When this occurs, wetland values will be accepted and reclamation will be accepted as a standard cost of doing business. Until then, the wetland issue will remain nothing more than an issue.

REFERENCES

Dahl, T. E. 1990. Wetlands Losses in the United States 1780's to 1980's. U. S. Department of Interior, Fish and Wildlife Service, Washington, D. C. 21.

Hodgson, H. J., R. L. Taylor, L. J. Klebesadel, A. C. Wilton. 1978. Registration of Arctared Red Fescue. Crop Science, Vol 18:524.

Mitchell, W. W. 1979. Three Varieties of Native Alaskan Grasses for Revegetation. Circular 32. Agricultural Experiment Station, School of Agriculture and Land Resources Management, University of Alaska. Fairbanks, Alaska. 9.

Mitchell, W. W. 1985. Registration of Norcoast Bering Hairgrass. Crop Science. Vol 25:708-709.

Mitchell, W. W. 1987. Notice of Release of Kenai Polargrass. Agroborealis. Vol 19 No:5.

Reed, P. B. 1986. Wetland Plant List, Alaska. U. S. Department of Interior, Fish and Wildlife Service, Washington, D. C. 22.

Wright, S. J. 1989. Final Report of Data and Observations Obtained from the Chena Flood Control Project Evaluation Plots Located Near North Pole, Alaska. Alaska Department of Natural Resources, Division of Agriculture, Plant Materials Center, Palmer, Alaska. 14.

Wright, S. J. 1990. Final Report of Data and Observations Obtained from the Red Dog Mine Evaluation and Demonstration Plots. Alaska Department of Natural Resources, Division of Agriculture, Plant Materials Center, Palmer, Alaska. 16.

Wright, S. J. 1991a. Registration of 'Egan' American Sloughgrass. Crop Science. Vol. 31, No. 5. 31:1380-1381.

Wright, S. J. 1991b. Registration of 'Caiggluk' Tilesy Sagebrush. Crop Science. Vol. 31, No. 5. 31:1380.

Wright, S. J. 1992. Unpublished Data, Kenai River Wetland Rehabilitation Project. Alaska Department of Natural Resources, Division of Agriculture, Plant Materials Center, Palmer, Alaska.

QUANTIFICATION ANALYSIS ON FACTORS AFFECTING OPERATION

OF IRRIGATION IN LOW LYING PADDY AREA

Fatchan NURROCHMAD*   Masaharu KURODA**   Tetsuro FUKUDA***

The quantification analyses were carried out for evaluation the factors affecting the actual operation of irrigation system by water associations in low lying paddy area. The Quantification Method "I" developed by Hayashi was applied for the analyses. The daily series of operated irrigation water were specified as objective variables (outside criterion variables). The explanatory variables were chosen as: (1) daily progress of rainfall, (2) growing periods of paddy, (3) moon calendar affecting drainage conditions in low lands, (4) influences of preceding irrigation process, (5) labor's conditions (Sunday or weekday), and so on. Each explanatory variable (item and category) was given as dummy variable such as 1 or zero. Analyses were tried for three areas of various conditions in which one was free drainage available and others were strongly restricted drainage. Obtained results were reasonable and suitable to explain the characteristics of individual operation of irrigation system for areas in conditions above mentioned.

OUTLINE OF WATER OPERATION SYSTEM

It is very important to predict the amount of intake water for supplying paddy fields throughout an irrigation season. In south west part of Japan, the irrigation season is from middle of June to beginning of October and it can be devided into 6 stages as : (1) puddling and rice transplanting stage, (2) tillering stage, (3) mid summer drainage stage, (4) growing stage, (5) flowering stage and (6) maturing stage.

This study was carried out in the low lying paddy area with creek network reclaimed from the swamp with dikes. Irrigation operation in this area is characterized by utilizing the storage and buffer function of those creeks (Kuroda et al., 1991). Figure 1 shows the layout of the area of this study. This area devided into 3 blocks namely A, B and C blocks.

In the block A, irrigation water is mainly supplied from main canal to creeks. In the blocks B and C, irrigation water is supplied not only from main canal but also from buffer reservoir or creeks from upper blocks through water redistribution gates to creek as shown in Fig.1. Buffer reservoir has two main purposes i.e. collector drain for block A and irrigation water resources for blocks B and C.

It seems to be natural that the water demand for supplemental irrigation to paddy plots would be decreasing due to rainfall events. But in actually, the intake water for irrigation is not directly decreasing due to rainfall. The amount of daily intake water does not show the reasonable correspondence to daily rainfall as shown in Fig.2.

---

*F. NURROCHMAD, Grad.Student, **M. KURODA, Professor, and ***T. FUKUDA, Assistant Professor, Agricultural Engineering Dept., Kyushu University, Fukuoka, Japan.

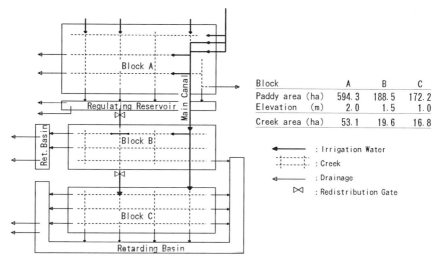

Figure 1. Layout of the Area of Study.

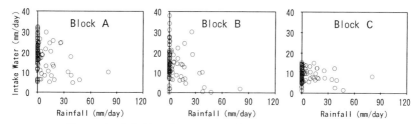

Figure 2. Relation Between Intake Water and Rainfall

In this study, a specified quantification method was applied for clarifying the prediction of daily intake water operation.

METHOD OF ANALYSIS

It is suggested the operation of daily intake water is not only affected by one factor as (1) daily rainfall of the preceding day, but also influenced by other factors as : (2) daily rainfall tendencies in several previous days, (3) daily intake water of the preceding day, (4) daily intake water tendencies in several previous days, (5) growing stage of paddy rice in the irrigation season, (6) moon calendar affecting drainage conditions in low lands and (7) labor's conditions (weekday or holiday). Those factors were used as items and categories of the quantification method. The quantification method I developed by Hayashi (1991) was applied in this analysis.

The daily intake water has a numerical value (mm/day) as an objective variable or outside criterion variable. It is tried to predict such quantitative objective variable by the combinations of several quantitative indexes.

Term C(jk) is quantitative index in the kth category of jth item explained in the following chapter.

The item-category response $\delta i(jk)$ was given as dummy variable written as following Eq.(1).

$$\delta i(jk) = \begin{cases} 1 : \text{means yes, if } i^{th} \text{ day responds to } C(jk) \\ 0 : \text{means no, if } i^{th} \text{ day do not respond to } C(jk) \end{cases} \qquad (1)$$

The category weight $x(jk)$ was given as the explanatory variables in the kth category of the jth item. Then the effect of each category is expressed as the multiplying of $x(jk) * \delta i(jk)$.

Equation (2) presents the simulated daily intake water $Y(i)$ (mm/day) in the ith day of the irrigation season.

$$Y(i) = \sum_{j=1}^{R} \sum_{k=1}^{cj} \{x(jk) * \delta i(jk)\} \qquad (i=1,2,\ldots.n) \qquad (2)$$

in which : n is number of days during irrigation season, R is number of items and cj is number of categories.

For normalyzing the numerical treatments, the Eq.(2) is converted into Eq.(3) using the mean of the outside variables $\overline{Y}$.

$$Y(i) = \overline{Y} + \sum_{j=1}^{R} \sum_{k=1}^{cj} \{X(jk) * \delta i(jk)\} \qquad (3)$$

in which $X(jk) = x(jk) - 1/n * \sum_{l=1}^{cj} \{n(jl) * x(jl)\}$

The purpose of this analysis is to obtain the suitable set of category weigts $x(jk)$ for explaining suitable set of objective variable $Y(i)$. The method of least square shown in Eq. (4) was applied for making a good prediction of the category weights.

$$Q = \min \sum_{i=1}^{n} \{y(i)-Y(i)\}^2 \qquad (4)$$

in which $y(i)$ is the measured daily intake water (mm/day) and $Y(i)$ is the simulated daily intake water (mm/day) as objective variable.

Item (1), Daily Rainfall of the Preceding Day (RPD)

The operation of intake water was influenced strongly by the daily rainfall of the preceding day (Kuroda et al, 1990). Item (1) consists of 3 categories i.e. no rain C(11), little rain C(12) and heavy rain C(13). No rain C(11) was the case of no rain in preceding day. Little rain C(12) was the case of rainfall less than 15 mm/day in preceding day (this amount is almost equivalent to the water requirement in this area 15.3 mm/day as pointed by Ikushima and Kuroda, 1973). Heavy rain C(13) was the case of rainfall larger than the water requirement in preceding day.

Item (2), Rainfall Tendencies in Several Previous Days (RSD)

Item (2) was characteryzed by the rainfall tendencies in several previous days (for example in 5 days). Item (2) is grouping into 3 categories i.e. small C(21), medium C(22) and large C(23) as shown in Fig.3.

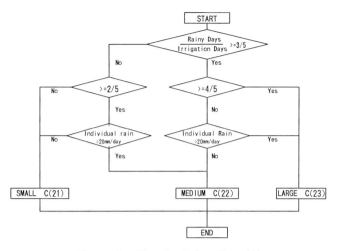

Figure 3. Flowchart for Item (2).

Item (3), Daily Intake Water in The Preceding Day (IPD)

Item (3) was considered the intake water of the preceding day and consisted of 3 categories i.e. small C(31), medium C(32) and large C(33). Small C(31) was the case of the amount of intake water less than 10 mm/day in the preceding day. Medium C(32) was the case of the amount of intake water arranging from 10mm/day to 20mm/day in the preceding day and large C(33) was the amount of intake water in the preceding day larger than 20 mm/day.

Item (4), the Tendencies of Intake Water in Several Previous Days (ISD)

The suggestion of item (4) was influenced by characteristic of the intake water (I-W) tendencies in several previous days (for example in 5 days). Item (4) consisted of 3 categories i.e. little C(41), medium C(42) and heavy C(43) as shown in Fig. 4.

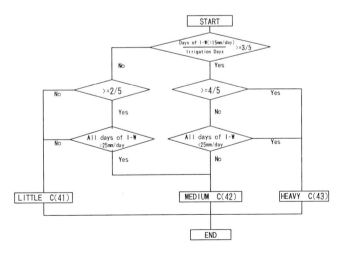

Figure 4. Flowchart for Item (4).

163

Item (5), Growing Stage of Paddy Rice in the Irrigation Season (IRS)

As defined above mentioned, the irrigation season in Japan was began in the middle of June and ended in the beginning of October. Item (5) was considered into 6 categories during irrigation season (see Table 1).

Table 1. Growing Stage of Irrigation Season.

Category	The stage	Date
I C(51)	Puddling and transplanting	June 15 — June 25
II C(52)	Tillering	June 26 — July 24
III C(53)	Mid summer drainage	July 25 — Aug. 10
IV C(54)	Growing	Aug. 11 — Aug. 31
V C(55)	Flowering	Sep. 1 — Sep. 10
VI C(56)	Maturing	Sep. 11 — Oct. 6

Item (6), Moon Calendar (MOC)

Moon calendar affecting drainage conditions in low lands was considered as item (6). Item (6) consisted of 2 categories i.e. low level C(61) and high level C(62). Neap tide in the moon calendar was categoryzed as low level and the other tides were classified as high level.

Item (7), Labor's Condition (LAC)

Labor's condition was characteryzed by workdays (presented by Monday through Friday), Saturday as a half day and Sunday as a holiday. Item (7) consisted of 3 categories i.e. workday C(71), a half day C(72) and a holiday C(73).

Figure 5. shows a flowchart for simulating the daily intake water into each block.

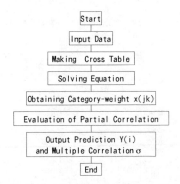

Figure 5. Flowchart for Simulating

RESULT AND DISCUSSION

Category Weight

This study was carried out for 6 years irrigation seasons for analyzing the daily operation of intake water by the water association throughout irrigation season for each year. All of the items used in the simulation were classified as independent factors.

Figures 6, 7 and 8 show the category weights resulting from the simulating daily intake water into block A, block B and block C, respectively, during irrigation seasons from 1985 to 1990 for 6 years irrigation seasons.

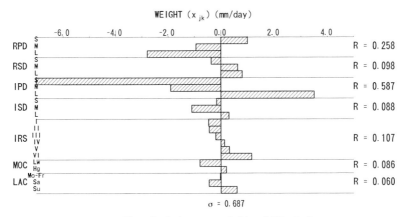

Fig. 6. Category-weight of Block A.

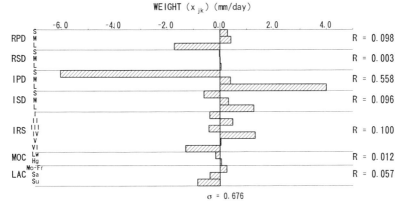

Fig. 7. Category-weight of Block B.

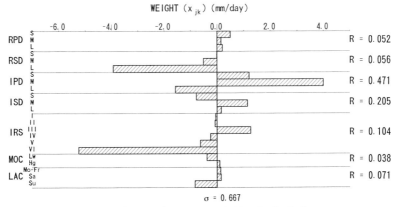

Fig. 8. Category-weight of Block C.

The distinctive character of each item will be discussed as following on each block.

Block A : The mean value of simulated ($\bar{Y}$) and measured intake water ($\bar{y}$) were shown in Table 2 for irrigation seasons of six years. The mean value of intake water in block A (19.1mm/day) was a little bigger than the water requirement (15.3mm/day) (Ikushima and Kuroda, 1973).

The present day intake water was strongly affected by the intake water in preceding day (partial correlation coefficient R=0.587) but was slightly influenced by the long term tendencies of the intake water during several previous days (R=0.088). From the view point of the coefficient correlation between those two factors and the present day intake water above mentioned, it is to say that both of those items were the independent each other.

The rainfall event in preceding day influenced the operation of intake water in present day (R=0.258), and the long term tendencies of the rainfall events in several previous days did not clearly affect (R=0.098) the present day operation. It is clarified the water operation in present day is usually carried out depending on both the operation of intake water and the rainfall event in preceding day.

The operation of intake water in present day also related to the growing stages throughout the irrigation season (R=0.107).

Tidal phenomenon did a little affect the operation of intake water in present day (R=0.086).

Weekdays as the last factor for simulating gave a little responses to the operation of intake water in present day (R=0.060). It was concluded the operators in this irrigation system managed the operation of intake water throughout weekdays. The multiple correlation coefficient (σ) between the measured daily intake waters and the simulated those using dummy variables is shown in Table 2. The value of coefficient σ is reasonable.

Table 2. Simulated and Measured Results on Each Block

Year	Block A Mean Value(mm/day)		Block B Mean Value(mm/day)		Block C Mean Value(mm/day)	
	Simul. ($\bar{Y}$)	Meas. ($\bar{y}$)	Simul. ($\bar{Y}$)	Meas. ($\bar{y}$)	Simul. ($\bar{Y}$)	Meas. ($\bar{y}$)
1985	18.8	19.4	16.7	19.0	13.5	13.6
1986	18.6	18.0	12.5	12.2	11.9	12.2
1987	20.0	21.0	11.5	11.0	16.0	17.3
1988	21.5	22.6	15.9	15.8	15.2	16.1
1989	16.4	14.3	11.6	10.1	10.8	9.1
1990	18.9	18.8	14.0	14.0	9.8	9.0
6 years mean	19.1	19.1	13.7	13.7	12.8	12.8
σ	0.687		0.676		0.667	

Block B : As shown in Table 2, the mean value of intake water (13.7mm/day) was a little smaller than the water requirement (15.3mm/day). It is suggested the operators are nervous for operating intake gates because the surface elevation of block B is almost equal to mean sea water level.

The present day intake water was strongly affected by the intake water in preceding day (partial correlation coefficient R=0.558) and was a little influenced by the long term tendencies of the intake water during several previous days (R=0.096). From the view point of the coefficient correlation between those two items and the present day intake water above mentioned, it is clear that both of those items were the independent each other.

The rainfall event in preceding day slightly influenced the operation of intake water in present day (R=0.098) and the long term tendencies of the rainfall events in several previous days (R=0.003) did not affect the present day operation. It is clarified the water operation in present day is usually carried out depending only on the operation of intake water in preceding day and was not influenced by the rainfall event.

The operation of intake water in present day also related to the growing stages throughout the irrigation season (R=0.100).

Tidal phenomenon did not affect the operation of intake water in present day (R=0.012).

The excess water in block B will be able to be drained directly into the retarding basin. It can be concluded the existing of both regulating reservoir in the upper block and the retarding basin in the lower part of block B were very useful for protecting block B from flooding.

Weekdays as the last factor for simulating gave a little responses to the operation of intake water in present day (R=0.057). The multiple correlation coefficient (σ) between the simulated and the measured is shown in Table 2. The value of coefficient σ is reasonable.

Block C : As shown in Table 2, the mean value of intake water (12.8 mm/day) was a little smaller than the water requirement (15.3 mm/day). It is suggested the operator is very severe for operating intake gates because the surface elevation of block C is a little lower than mean sea water level.

The present day intake water was affected by the intake water in preceding day (partial coefficient correlation R=0.471) and also influenced by the long term tendencies of the intake water during several previous days (R=0.205). From the view point of the coefficient correlation between those two factors and the present day intake water above mentioned, it is clarified the operation of intake water in present day is usually carried out carefully in small amount and almost constant during irrigation season (R=0.104) because of the restricted drainage condition.

Both of the rainfall event in preceding day (R=0.052) and the long term tendencies of the rainfall events in several previous days (R=0.056) gave little influences on the operation of intake water in present day.

Tidal phenomenon did not give influence on the operation of intake water in present day (R=0.038).

Weekdays as the last factor for simulating gave a little responses to the operation of intake water in present day (R=0.071). The multiple correlation coefficient between the simulated and measured is shown in Table 2. The value of coefficient σ is reasonable.

Simulated Results of Daily Intake Water

As pointed above mentioned, the simulated daily intake waters was obtained during irrigation seasons from 1985 to 1990 using Eq.4. Figure 9 shows the relation between the simulated and the measured daily intake water in block A in 1990. The measured data had a range from 5mm/day to 35 mm/day and the simulated data had a range from 7mm/day to 29mm/day. The amplitude of simulated intake water is smaller than the measured intake water but from Fig.6 and Fig.9, we would be able to say the phase of simulated intake waters were well fitted with the measured intake waters. The wide amplitude in

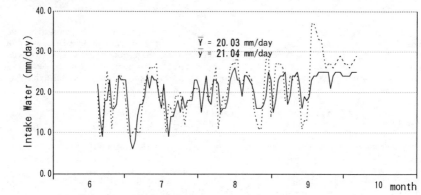

Figure 9. Simulated and Measured Daily Intake Water in Block A
(solid line : simulated;   dotted line : measured)

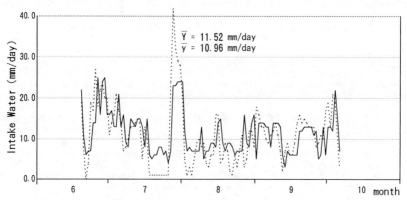

Figure 10. Simulated and Measured Daily Intake Water in Block B
(solid line : simulated;   dotted line : measured)

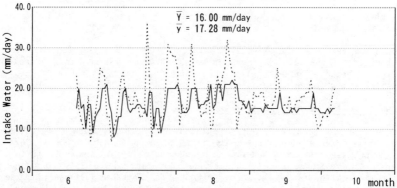

Figure 11. Simulated and Measured Daily Intake Water in Block C
(solid line : simulated;   dotted line : measured)

operation of intake water was mainly affected by the intake water and rainfall event in preceding day.

Figure 10 shows the relation between the simulated and the measured daily intake water in block B in 1990. The amplitude of simulated intake water (4mm/day to 24mm/day) was little smaller than the amplitude of measured intake water (0mm/dat to 38 mm/day). The phase of simulated intake waters were fitted with the measured intake waters. The amplitudes of both the simulated and the measured in block B were very similar to those of in block A. It means the creek networks in block B which is laid on the middle area of this irrigation system role as regulator and buffer function for block C.

As shown in Fig. 11, the absolute mean value of intake waters was relatively small and the amplitude of the simulated and measured intake water in block C was smaller than those in block A and in block B. This fact tells the daily operation of intake water was controlled well in relative small amount from block B by the water association because of the restricted drainage conditions.

CONCLUSION

The operation of daily intake water in block A is strongly affected by the intake water operation and rainfall event of the preceding day, but the operation of daily intake water both in blocks B and C were not remarkably affected by the rainfall event in preceding day. The operation of daily intake water in blocks A and B has a wide amplitude, but the phase of simulated intake waters were fitted with the measured intake waters each others. The amplitude of daily intake water operation in block C is relatively small.

From the result mentioned above, the analysis of predicting daily intake water operation by applying quantification method especially using category weights was effectively useful. It can be suggested that the actual operation in the irrigation system by the water association has to be concerned by giving attention to the characteristics of each block.

The procedures and results presented by this study would be applicable in other irrigation systems with similar conditions.

REFERENCES

1. Hayashi, C. (ed). 1991. Quantification, Theory and Data Treatment. Asakurashoten:10-48 (in Japanese).

2. Ikushima, Y. and M. Kuroda. 1973. On the Water Budget after Land Readjustment for Heavy Clay Soil Paddy Field Close to Creek. Bulletin of Faculty of Agriculture, Saga University. 35:31-49 (in Japanese).

3. Kuroda, M. and T. Fukuda. 1989. Operation and Water Management of Paddy Field Irrigation System in Low Lying Creek Area. 17th Afro-Asian Regional Conf. ICID. 1-C:168-177.

4. Kuroda, M., T. Fukuda, F. Nurrochmad and M. Kojima. 1990. Management Loss of Irrigation Water in Low Lying Creek Area. Annual Congress, The Japanese Society of Irrigation, Drainage and Reclamation Engineering. 128-129 (in Japanese).

5. Kuroda, M., T. Fukuda and F. Nurrochmad. 1991. Operation of Irrigation System and Water Management in Low Lying Paddy Area with Creek Network. Irrigation and Drainage. Proc. of the 1991 National Conference ASCE, 31-37.

WETLAND RESTORATION, ENHANCEMENT, OR CREATION --

A New Chapter in the USDA-SCS Engineering Field Handbook

William H. Boyd   Randall L. Gray
Member ASAE

In response to a growing national emphasis on wetland restoration the Soil Conservation Service (SCS) developed a new Chapter for the SCS Field Handbook, entitled "Restoration, Enhancement, or Creation of Wetlands." The SCS developed this chapter through an inter-agency and inter-disciplinary committee to assure adequate consideration of both biological and engineering sciences and to provide a general technical reference for wetland restoration, enhancement and creation activities.

HISTORICAL BACKGROUND

During the last fifty years there has been a growing understanding and appreciation of the ecological and economic values of wetlands. As society became aware of these values, legislation was passed to provide for wetland protection. The more significant of the wetland protection laws are Section 404 of the Clean Water Act (P.L. 92-500), 1985 Food Security Act (P.L. 99-198), and the 1990 Food, Agriculture, Conservation and Trade Act (P.L. 101-624).

There is a growing emphasis being placed on wetland restoration to increase the Nation's wetland base. For example, the National Research Council (1992) published a report calling for the restoration of 10 million acres of wetlands by 2010. In addition, the President's Domestic Policy Council has established a committee to address opportunities for restoring wetlands on both federal and non-federal lands.

To address the goal of wetland restoration, the 1990 Food, Agriculture, Conservation and Trade Act established the Wetlands Reserve Program (WRP). This program allows for the

William H. Boyd, P. E., Environmental Engineer, Engineering Staff, Midwest National Technical Center, USDA Soil Conservation Service, Lincoln, Nebraska.

Randall L. Gray, PhD., Staff Biologist, Ecological Sciences Staff, South National Technical Center, USDA Soil Conservation Service, Fort Worth, Texas.

United States Department of Agriculture to enter into long
term agreements with landowners to restore and protect up to
1 million acres of wetlands by 1995. In addition to the
WRP, there are numerous other federal, state and private
programs focusing on restoration of wetlands.

The USDA Soil Conservation Service has developed and
maintained close working relationships with private
landowners and with Soil and Water Conservation Districts.
Through these relationships they have provided technical
assistance to restore and manage wetlands for over fifty
years. The 1990 WRP has increased the opportunity for SCS
to be involved in this type of activity by delegating
technical authority for wetlands restoration to the SCS in
consultation with the U. S. Fish and Wildlife Service. This
emphasis on wetland restoration has challenged SCS to take a
fresh look at existing technology and to develop new tools
to assist conservation planers in restoring wetlands.

DEVELOPMENT PROCEDURE

As part of the SCS response to this challenge, Chapter 13 of
the SCS Engineering Field Handbook entitled "Dikes, Levees
and Wetland Development", was proposed for revision in 1990.
Because success in applying this technology depends on
several disciplines, the scope of this chapter was expanded
beyond the predominate engineering focus of previous
chapters of the SCS Engineering Field Manual. SCS assembled
a team of engineers, biologists, and landscape architects to
work on this revision. In addition, biologists, ecologists,
and engineers were solicited from the Army Corp of
Engineers, Environmental Protection Agency, and Fish and
Wildlife Service. The Tennessee Valley Authority, Duck's
Unlimited, faculty from the University of Minnesota and the
California State Polytechnic Institute, and a private
consultant also participated in the initial technical review
of the first draft. This inter-agency and inter-
disciplinary team was necessary to adequately address the
complex nature of the challenges presented in restoring
wetland systems.

The team first met to define the scope and determine the
contents of the chapter. After a tentative agreement was
reached assignments were made to small groups to produce
first draft copies of the various sections. These draft
copies were completed and the chapter was sent out for the
initial inter-agency review. The team met again to discuss
the technical comments from the review. Once all the
comments were discussed, the engineers on the team reviewed
the predominantly "biological" sections of the chapter, and
the others reviewed the predominantly "engineering"
portions. Following this internal review the team met for a

general discussion of the recommended changes and the
sections were returned to the small groups to rewrite their
sections. The second draft was thus completed and sent out
for another general inter-agency review. Subsequently, four
selected members of the team met to consider the technical
comments from this second general review and to make
necessary changes in the document.

TECHNICAL CONTRIBUTIONS

The revised Chapter 13 was renamed "Wetland Restoration,
Enhancement, or Creation." The chapter is not a policy
document nor does it a set standards or minimum criteria.
It is a technical document written to provide field personal
with a guide to planning, design, implementation,
maintenance, and monitoring of wetland restoration,
creation, and enhancement projects.

This chapter presents a procedure to plan wetland systems
according to functional objectives. This approach to
planning recognizes that the functions wetlands preform in a
landscape are identifiable and that wetland systems can be
designed to target those functions. The fifteen wetland
functions addressed in the chapter are:

1. Education and research,
2. Erosion control,
3. Fish and shell-fish production or habitat,
4. Flood storage,
5. Flood conveyance,
6. Food production,
7. Habitat for threatened and endangered species,
8. Historic, cultural, and archaeological,
9. Open space and aesthetic quality,
10. Recreation,
11. Sediment control,
12. Timber production,
13. Water supply,
14. Water quality improvement, and
15. Wildlife habitat.

Each of these functions are described with an explanation of
how they interact with other functions and with recommended
considerations for planning and design.

In the planning section of this chapter, individual wetlands
systems are considered as components which are inter-
connected with the other components in even larger landscape
systems. Because of this, landscape features such as the
location of other wetlands systems are considered in site
selection and evaluation. Special emphasis is given in this
section to soils, hydrology, and vegetation, as well as to
impacts on fish and wildlife, problem plants and animals,

use and spatial organization, recreation potentials, aesthetic quality and open space, cultural features, and to social, economic, and environmental impacts and evaluations.

The design section begins with recommendations for design data collection. At a minimum, the chapter calls for the information in surface feature surveys to include:

1. A location sketch showing property boundaries, benchmarks, permanent features, orientation, and wetland location,
2. Profiles and cross sections describing typical or critical parameters of existing conditions, and
3. Location and elevation of necessary soil borings.

The geotechnical investigation should include soil borings when structures are involved which reveal:

1. The elevation of the water table,
2. The position, thickness, and classification of each soil layer, and
3. The existence of any buried foreign materials.

An examination of the hydrologic system calls for the development of a water budget which quantifies the volumes and rates of water entering, leaving, and stored within a wetland. The section on the water budget identifies, describes, and suggest ways to develop numerical values for the major factors in the water budget equation including:

1. Precipitation,
2. Storm water runoff,
3. Evaporation and transpiration,
4. Base surface flow,
5. Ground water flow,
6. Pumped water,
7. Tidal flows,
8. Surface water storage, and
9. Pore water storage.

This is followed by a brief discussion of the hydroperiod which includes a list of ways in which the factors of the water budget can be manipulated to provide the hydroperiod necessary for the intended function.

The major equations describing flow characteristics of wetland systems are classified and discussed under the headings of depressional, riverine, and tidal flow systems. Included in this section are recommended "n" values for Manning's equation for conditions in wetland systems with flows greater than one foot in depth. A procedure to estimate appropriate "n" valued for flows less than one foot in depth is also provided which uses the same SCS retardance class curves currently used in the design of vegetated waterways.

The section on structural components discusses earthen dikes and levies and includes guidance for determining the height, settlement allowance, fill materials, cutoff trench, stability, and berms of these dikes. A table in included to provide design recommendations for the minimum top width, side slope, freeboard, and berm width for dikes based on the height of the dike and whether the dike is constructed of mineral or organic soils. This information is purposefully general in nature so that it may be applied outside of the scope of wetland development.

The discussion of water control structures includes a discussion of the major equations describing weir, orifice, and pipe flow. Recommendations are also included for the design of vegetated emergency spillways. In the section discussing drainage are recommendations for the blocking of existing surface and subsurface drains and a brief discussion of substrate sealing to prevent excessive seepage loss.

The vegetative design section identifies factors affecting plant selection including:

1. Goals and objectives,
2. Water supply,
3. The nature and condition of the substrate,
4. Water depth,
5. Slope,
6. The length of the growing season,
7. Surrounding habitats and land uses,
8. Wind and wave energies,
9. Currents and velocities, and
10. Cost.

Included in this discussion are sections on natural colonization, planting, propagule types, time of planting, site preparation, equipment, and nuisance species control.

Following the design section is a section on implementation. The major topics in this section are quality control during construction, dewatering, pollution control, construction of dikes and levees, installation of conduits and pilings, construction equipment, and some special considerations for handling wetland soils. This section also includes information pertaining to the management and planting of vegetative materials.

The chapter concludes with guidance pertaining to monitoring and a discussion of the management of major types of wetland systems. In the appendix is a "Wetland Planning Checklist" that can be filled out for an individual site and a "Site

Visit Checklist" that may be used as a part of the monitoring program.

While SCS does have a proven history of success in wetland restoration, enhancement, and creation, this chapter does not purport to be the "last word" on any of the subjects which it addresses, rather it is intended to be a dynamic document that can be supplemented and revised as knowledge and experience continues to grow in the field.

REFERENCES

National Research Council, 1992, Restoration of Aquatic Ecosystems: Science, Technology, and Public Policy. National Academy Press, Washington, D. C. 552 pp.

OVERVIEW OF RECENT COASTAL PROJECTS IN ALASKA USING

BEACH WILDRYE (ELYMUS MOLLIS)

S. J. Wright[*]

THE SPECIES BEACH WILDRYE

Beach wildrye Elymus mollis is an easily identifiable grass species common throughout coastal and insular Alaska. The nomenclature, as well as overly agressive taxonomic fractioning, has caused some confusion about this species. This species (or subspecies) has been called by a number of common and scientific names. Klebesadel (1985) listed no less than 13 common names including: "dune grass", "American Dune grass", "Lyme grass", "beach ryegrass", "sea lymegrass", "Siegle de mer", "Strand wheat", "Strand Oats", "wild wheat", "Sand-meal grass", "dune wildrye", and "beach wild-rye".

Genus and species names applied to this species are nearly as confusing as the common names. Lymus mollis is presently being proposed as the scientific name of the species. However, this report will use Elymus mollis, reluctantly recognizing the taxonomic segregation from the Eurasian form Elymus arenarius. To further muddle the issue of nomenclature, species of Amomophilia are at times confused with beach wildrye because of that genus' common name "beach grass".

This report uses Beach wildrye synonymously with Elymus mollis, except where material of European origin is specifically sited as Elymus arenarius, or in describing the circumpolar range of the E. arenarius complex which includes E. mollis.

Range and Habitat

By definition, Elymus mollis is the North American phase/variety of Elymus arenarius complex. The range of E. mollis is described as being along the coast of Alaska to Greenland, south to Long Island, New York and central California, along lakes Superior and Michigan, also eastern Siberia to Japan (Hitchcock 1950). Within this range, the species occupies a specific niche. It is most often on sandy beaches forming belts along the shore (Hulten 1968).
The species habitat is further defined as being spits, sea beaches, tidal flats, sea cliffs and lakeshores (Welsh 1974). While usually associated with coastal dunes, the species can be found along large inland lakes occupying the same relative shoreline areas as in the marine coastal areas (Klebesadel, 1985).

Description of Species

Elymus mollis is a perennial grass with stout culms, pubescent below the spike. It ranges in height from 60 to 120 centimeters, with numerous overlapping basal leaves. The strong stout rhizomes spread widely. Leaves are 7 to 25 cm wide (Hitchcock 1950).

---

[*]STONEY J. WRIGHT, Manager and Agronomist, Alaska Plant Materials Center, Palmer, Alaska.

Both seed and seed heads are relatively large. This grass is not a heavy seed producer in Alaska because many of the potential florets do not produce seed (Klebesadel, 1985). The rhizomes of beach wildrye are large and vigorous, promoting rapid spread of individual plants to cover small areas (Klebesadel, 1985). This can occur in a short period of time as noted in this report.

Historic Use of Beach Wildrye

The most obvious historic use of beach wildrye has been as a forage, especially in Alaska. The species was rated inferior in yield and value. Nonetheless, beach wildrye has a long history for use as a forage crop in Alaska (Klebesadel, 1985).

Other significant uses throughout the species' range include: thatching for shelters, basketry and cordage, and the seed and rhizome have been used as a food source. Klebesadel concluded in 1985 that "A logical use for beach wildrye may be soil stabilizing species in coastal or inland, sandy situations. The species could be planted with seed harvested from native stands or from fields planted for seed production.

Artificial selections might identify lines more productive of seed than the general population. Beach wildrye could also be propagated vegetatively with transplants or rhizome segments in a procedure called sprigging (Klebesadel, 1985).

The need for additional research into Beach wildrye was also noted by W. W. Woodhouse, "Research needs...propagation and planting requirements and procedures for less frequently planted species such as American Dunegrass [Beach wildrye]..." (Lewis 1982).

DEVELOPMENT OF COASTAL RESTORATION TECHNIQUES
AND PLANT MATERIALS IN ALASKA

Initial investigation regarding the potential of beach wildrye as a revegetation species occurred during the 1970s following Department of Energy activities on Amchitka Island. These ecological studies are well documented and, for the most part, can be attributed to Clifford Amundsen, University of Tennessee.

Large-scale plantings of beach wildrye were not attempted until 1987 when the Alaska Plant Materials Center, in cooperation with the U. S. Army Corps of Engineers, Alaska District, and the U. S. Air Force Alaskan Air Command, implemented an 11 hectare planting on Shemya AFB (Wright, et al, 1987). This project relied, in part, on the initial small-scale planting activities conducted on Amchitka and Adak by the University of Tennessee (Amundsen, 1986), as well as a one-year study on Shemya Island (Wright, 1986). Activities on Shemya not only addressed the potential of transplanting locally acquired beach wildrye sprigs, but also transplanted sprigs and seed produced at Palmer, Alaska.

Following the successful project on Shemya, other large-scale or significant plantings occurred on Adak Island (Wright, 1990a), Port Clarence, Alaska, and Red Dog Mine north of Kotzebue (Wright, 1990b). Limited plantings have also occurred in the Kuparuk oil field and a coastal wetland in Anchorage. Figure 1 shows the location of planting sites.

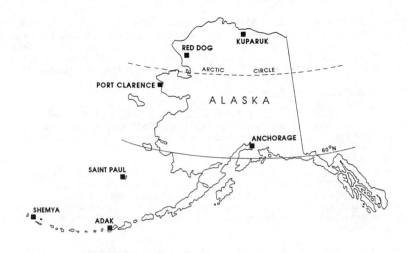

Figure 1. Location of Study Sites.

In addition to the species' adaptability for cost-effective revegetation and erosion control, soil requirements and planting seasons were evaluated. An incidental observation occurred on St. Paul Island regarding the species tolerance to traffic.

While much data has been obtained regarding the actual use of the species in revegetation, the studies have also resulted in the release of two cultivars for commercial production (Wright, 1991a, 1991b).

TRANSPLANTING TECHNIQUES

In order for large-scale transplanting of beach wildrye to become an accepted revegetation method, the techniques must be simple, cost-effective and provide satisfactory results. Mechanization of as much of the harvesting and planting procedure as possible is the critical aspect of simplicity and cost-effectiveness.

Harvesting

Harvesting can, in some cases, be accomplished economically by hand. For instance, the limited plantings at the Red Dog Mine port site were efficiently collected by hand as the source material was readily available on an exposed coastal beach. In most cases, standard backhoes are quite acceptable. This technique relies on moving sod blocks to a site where workers can easily remove the sprigs.

Front-end loaders will also function in this role. They tend to be slower and not as efficient because the sod blocks are often upset, forcing the harvest crew to hunt for the sprigs. The vibration and force exerted on the excavated blocks loosens the soil, usually sand, to the point where the sprigs can be easily removed by hand in large, relatively clean and undamaged culms. These are then further divided into individual sprigs for planting.

Figure 2. Mechanized Harvesting of Beach Wildrye.

A technique for harvesting employed at the Plant Materials Center uses a standard potato digger. This method is not expected to gain acceptance with general contractors due to the specialized and fragile nature of a potato digger. Potato diggers are expected to gain acceptance in commercial production of Beach wildrye.

Planting

Planting can also be accomplished by standard hand and shovel method, provided disturbances are less than one acre. On larger sites, mechanization is the only cost-effective method. Modifying standard construction equipment, which is usually on site, to prepare planting beds is quite simple. For example, the small dozer used on Shemya was modifed by means of welding "tiger teeth" to the bottom of the blade (Figure 3). Back-blading the area to be sprigged provided a well prepared site that eliminated the need for shovels or any other hand held tool. A very simple and successful planting method referred to as "drop and stomp" emerged from this project (Figure 4). Beach wildrye sprigs can be placed in any position and will resume growth, thereby eliminating the need for careful upright planting (Wright, 1990a). Negative gravitropic growth resumes quickly from inverted seed blocks (Amundsen, 1986) indicating haphazard and rough treatment of the sprigs is acceptable.

The use of mechanical tree planters has been attempted on production ground with good results. It is unlikely that general contractors will use this type of equipment. Instead, they will rely on standard construction equipment.

Figure 3. Modified Dozer Blade Used to Prepare Planting Site.

Figure 4. Drop and Stomp Planting Method.

Time Requirements

Time required to transplant beach wildrye sprigs is a major concern. Based on time studies on Shemya, one laborer could dig and prepare 400 sprigs per hour, while one laborer could plant 350 sprigs per hour. The planting rate per hectare on Shemya was 49,400 sprigs. Based on records obtained over the 11 hectare project, a total of 148 man hours were needed to tranpslant one hectare (Wright, 1987). This rate of preparing and planting was also verified at Adak and Port Clarence. Small-scale plantings at the other sites slightly exceeded the Shemya rate. In areas where density is not as critical as Shemya, the per hectare manpower requirements can be greatly reduced.

The number of sprigs used per hectare on Shemya exceeded the actual need, however, success was crucial. It has been determined that a planting rate of 24,700 sprigs per hectare is sufficient under normal circumstances (Wright, 1987). The higher rate is only justified for the most highly disturbed and erosive sites. These numbers are in contrast to the 58,000 sprigs per acre (143,260 per hectare) called for by Carlson, (1991).

Success Rates

The first major planting at Shemya produced results far in excess of expectations. The plantings at Adak, Red Dog and Port Clarence also produced excellent results. The plantings at both Kuparuk and Fish Creek (Anchorage) are in the initial stage of evaluation, however initial success rates are acceptable.

Figure 5. Shemya Planting Site, May, 1987.

Figure 6.   Shemya Site, August, 1988.

Table 1.   Percent Survival of Locally Collected Beach Wildrye Sprigs Related
            to Soil Characteristics.

Location	Soil Characteristics					Size of Planting Site	Success Rate
	Sand	Silt	Clay	Organic (LOI)	Gravel >2mm		
Shemya	91	6	3	4	–	11 ha	98%
Adak	85	10	5	2	–	2 ha	93%
Shemya	83	12	5	3	–	<.2 ha	98%
Red Dog	42	2	4	–	52	.4 ha	99%
Port Clarence	8	1	–	–	91	.8 ha	70%
Kuparuk	45	6	5	1	44	<.04 ha	98%
Fish Creek	22	61	12	–	5	<.04 ha	90%

The studies shown in Table 1 should suggest to the reader that transplanting
Beach wildrye is very successful and relatively cost effective.   These results
dispute the 25% transplant survival rate suggested by Carlson, et al (1991).

One major drawback usually pointed out for this species, is that the window or time period for successful planting is very limited. Carlson (1991), states "American dunegrass (Beach wildrye) must be planted when dormant". This point has been dismissed in Alaska. Table 2 will list various planting times attempted by the author throughout Alaska. High success rates have been reported at all sites regardless of planting time. This may be in part due to the relatively cool temperatures and cloudy conditions typical of all of the planting sites in Alaska.

TABLE 2. Seasonal Planting Study.

Date	Location	Success
May 15	Shemya	98%
June 23	Adak	93%
July 12	Shemya	98%
July 18	Adak	99%
August 17	Adak	98%
August 23	Anchorage	90%
September 15	Adak	99%

Rate of Spread

By taking advantage of the species ability to spread vegetatively, the number of sprigs used per acre can be greatly reduced. On Shemya, the length of first year rhizomes have been measured and have exceeded 1.5 meters in length. This incredible ability for vegetative spread is well documented in a July 1985 planting on Shemya. This planting relied on transplants spaced 3 meters within rows and .9 meters between rows. During a site evaluation conducted in August 1991, this planting had created a dense, solid stand 10.6 to 12.1 meters wide. This plot extended lengthwise an additional 9.1 meters from the original plot. Sand accumulation on the plot had also created a dune 24 meters high. Spacing of transplants is only dictated by the erosive nature of the planting site and the degree of protection sought. Uniformity of spacing is critical, otherwise unwanted dune formation may result (Wright, 1991c).

PROBLEMS ASSOCIATED WITH BEACH WILDRYE

Competition With Other Species

The aggressive vegetative growth habit of Beach wildrye is limited when mixed with other species of grass. This was evident at the production fields established at the Plant Materials Center when timothy, Phleum pratensis, and Kentucky bluegrass, Poa pratensis, invaded the field. This intolerance was also noted on Adak (Amundsen, 1986). On Shemya, Beach wildrye transplants appear to withstand a higher degree of competition from hairgrass, Deschampsia beringensis, than from fescues, Festuca rubra (Wright, 1991c). This trait of Beach wildrye must be considered if one intends to use the species in conjunction with other revegetation grasses.

Tolerance to Traffic

This robust and vegetatively aggressive species appears to be quite intolerant to any significant degree of traffic. Following the 1987 grounding of the M/V All Alaskan on St. Paul Island in Alaska, a rescue trail through naturally occurring stands of Beach wildrye was monitored. Attempts to preclude further traffic on the rescue trail were ineffective. Even occasional use by light footprint traffic, such as four and three-wheelers, has created a significant scar beyond the recovery rate of Beach wildrye (Wright, 1990c).

Concluding that soil compaction was in itself responsible for the lack of regrowth, has little merit as the sandy nature of the dunes at St. Paul are not susceptible to intense compaction. On foot trails crossing Beach wildrye stands leading to popular fishing spots on the Kenai River, compaction seems to be the cause of Beach wildrye elimination. However, the soils in these areas tend to contain significant amounts of fine, silty material.

COMMERCIAL CULTIVARS OF BEACH WILDRYE

As a result of a Beach wildrye evaluation program started in 1976 and the off-site investigation on the Aleutians and coastal Alaska, two cultivars were released by the Plant Materials Center in 1991. Both cultivars should be commercially available by 1994.

The cultivar 'Reeve' Beach wildrye (of Norwegian origin, therefore the nomenclature Elymus arenarius applies) was released as a seed producing variety (Wright, 1991a). Natural stands of Beach wildrye are notorious for not producing seed. This collection not only produces commercially viable quantities of seed, but also exhibited the hardiness and adaptation needed in Alaska.

The second cultivar, 'Benson' Beach wildrye, is of Alaskan origin and is intended for sprigging or transplanting on highly erosive sites where establishment by seed would be impractical or impossible (Wright, 1991b).

CONCLUSIONS

Beach wildrye is extremely effective in stabilizing coastal areas. It is particularly effective for controlling erosion on sandy sites and active dunes.

If a disturbance is a significant problem and extraordinary measures are needed to control sand or erosion, Beach wildrye transplants are both economically and biologically feasible methods of control. Success rates, if properly conducted, are very high and the results justify the additional expense of transplanting versus seeding. This species is very tolerant of rough handling associated with mechanized planting and harvesting. Non-skilled labor can be used without jeopardizing success.

Design and layout of the project is the most critical if preventing dune formation is desired. If a wild, natural appearance is desired, layout and spacing is less important.

In Alaska, Beach wildrye can be planted from early May through September with no significant change in success rates. The species will become increasingly important in environmental restoration and coastal rehabilitation, as well as a bioengineering measure to control coastal erosion through it's range.

REFERENCES

1. Amundsen, C. C. 1986. Central Aleutian Tundra, Ecological Manifestations of Maritime Tundra Landscapes in the Central Aleutian Islands (Amchitka, Adak), Alaska. DOE-AS05-76EV04180. University of Tennessee, Knoxville, Tennessee.

2. Carlson, J., F. Reckendorf and W. Ternyik. 1991. Stabilizing Coastal Sand Dunes in the Pacific Northwest. Agriculture Handbook 687. United States Department of Agriculture, Washington, D. C.

3. Hitchcock, A. S. 1950. Manual of Grasses of the United States. United States Government Printing Office, Washington, D. C.

4. Hulten, E. 1968. Flora of Alaska and Neighboring Territories. Stanford University Press, Stanford.

5. Klebesadel, L. J. 1985. Beach Wildrye Characteristics and uses of a Native Alaskan Grass of Uniquely Coastal Distribution. Agroborealis. 17:31-38.

6. Lewis III, R. R. 1982. Creation and Restoration of Coastal Plant Communities. CRC Press, Inc. Boca Raton, Florida.

7. Welch, S. L. 1974. Anderson's Flora of Alaska and Adjacent Parts of Canada. Brigham Young University Press, Provo, Utah.

8. Wright, S. J. 1986. Beach Wildrye (Elymus arenarius) Sprigging on Shemya Air Force Base, Lateral Clear Zone - A Qualitative Study in Response to Questions Arising From Contract DACA 85-86-C-0042. State of Alaska, Division of Agriculture, Plant Materials Center.

9. Wright, S. J., L. H. Fanter, and J. M. Ikeda. 1987. Sand Stabilization Within the Lateral Clear Zone at Shemya Air Force Base, Alaska Using Beach Wildrye, Elymus arenarius. State of Alaska, Division of Agriculture, Plant Materials Center and U. S. Army Corps of Engineers, Alaska District.

10. Wright, S. J. 1990a. Final Report of Data and Observations Obtained From the Adak Naval Air Station Evaluation Plot Network, 1988-1990. State of Alaska, Division of Agriculture, Plant Materials Center.

11. Wright, S. J. 1990b. Final Report of Data and Observations Obtained From the Red Dog Mine Evaluation and Demonstration Plots. State of Alaska, Division of Agriculture, Plant Materials Center.

12. Wright, S. J. 1990c. An Overview of the Alaska Plant Materials Center's Work with Beach Wildrye, Elymus arenarius (E. mollis). Proceedings of the Public Symposium. Restoration Following the Exxon Valdez Oil Spill. March 26-27, 1990. Restoration Planning Work Goup. Anchorage, Alaska.

13. Wright, S. J. 1991a. Release Notice - 'Reeve' Beach Wildrye. State of Alaska, Division of Agriculture, Plant Materials Center.

14. Wright, S. J. 1991b. Release Notice - 'Benson' Beach Wildrye. State of Alaska, Division of Agriculture, Plant Materials Center.

15. Wright, S. J. 1991c. Assessment of Revegetation on the Aleutian Islands - Adak, Amchitka, Shemya and Attu. State of Alaska, Division of Agriculture, Plant Materials Center.

DRAINAGE AND SOIL COMPACTION IMPROVEMENTS

TO THE U. S. MILITARY ACADEMY PARADE FIELD

L. D. Geohring   A. J. Palazzo   R. W. Duell   R. C. Jones[1]
Member ASAE

Turfgrass is the predominant, most suitable and traditionally preferred land surface cover for the parade field of the United States Military Academy (USMA) at West Point, New York. The turfgrass cover is preferred because it is aesthetically pleasing, tolerates foot and light vehicle traffic, is relatively low in cost to establish and maintain, and provides an open space park-like setting and recreational area for the cadets and officers who reside in adjacent housing. It also provides important sound and thermal buffering close to the high walled, triangular-shaped Washington Hall Barracks Complex. Since the parade field is the center of numerous marching activities, the turfgrass is subjected to severe foot traffic. Parade reviews occur several times per week, regardless of weather conditions, and usually consist of 12 squadrons each eight cadets wide. This 96-man front proceeds in unison across the parade field as other cadets follow in file. A full Brigade review involves 4000 cadets. This intensive and continued foot traffic loading, especially during adverse wet weather conditions, flattens and damages the turfgrass directly while simultaneously inducing soil compaction. As a result, maintaining turfgrass vigor, density and quality on the parade field is a continuous management problem.

Because of the high visibility and continual use of the parade field, it is important to maintain a healthy, green, uniform sward. For 15 years prior to this project, turf vigor continued to decline. Randomized drainage and soil improvements and the addition of soil amendments carried out in the past were not sufficient to sustain a healthy turfgrass cover throughout. The turf was exhibiting discoloration and gradual death leading to bare soil areas. The discoloration occurred as a result of the darker green Kentucky bluegrass (Poa pratensis L.) being overtaken by the weedy type, lighter green annual bluegrass (Poa annua L.) which was more tolerant and adaptable to the wet, compact soil conditions. The barren spongy areas were not only unsightly but were becoming slippery and hazardous. The boundaries of the barren areas were gradually expanding and lawn maintenance was becoming increasingly difficult. Routine maintenance procedures were no longer effective in sustaining turfgrass vigor.

[1]L. D. Geohring, Sr. Extension Assoc., Dept. of Agricultural and Biological Engineering, Cornell University, Ithaca, NY; A. J. Palazzo, Research Agronomist, U. S. Army Cold Regions Research and Engineering Lab, Hanover, NH; R. W. Duell, Assoc. Professor, Dept. of Soils and Crops, Rutgers/Cook College, New Brunswick, NJ; and R. C. Jones, Agronomist, U. S. Military Academy, West Point, NY.

Although major restoration of the area was considered necessary, the factors causing the gradual decline of turfgrass vigor were not well understood. Consequently, a restoration project was initiated to evaluate the problem, develop recommendations, and to implement procedures for reclaiming the area. This paper will discuss the findings of the site investigation and focus on the soil reclamation efforts which were performed.

SITE DIAGNOSIS

Climate

The USMA location is at Latitude 41°23'N and Longitude 73°58'W within a cool, humid climatic zone. The site is characterized by cold winters and mild to hot summers. Mean monthly and annual precipitation is 9.73 cm and 116.6 cm, respectively. The lowest average monthly precipitation generally occurs in February with 7.7 cm. The wettest month is in July with 11.0 cm. The least amount of precipitation recorded in any one year occurred in 1931 with 76.2 cm, and the highest annual amount occurred in 1952 with 165 cm. A 100-year return period storm event would result in approximately 7.6 cm of precipitation in 1 hour or up to 18 to 20 cm within 24 hours.

Precipitation exceeds evapotranspiration by approximately 10 cm on an annual basis. On a monthly basis precipitation usually exceeds evapotranspiration except during the summer months of June, July, and August. During the summer evapotranspiration from turfgrass can be as high as 7.6 mm/day often necessitating supplemental irrigation. The most intensive use of the parade fields is during the spring and fall, however, when excess water is typically the norm.

Temperatures average -2.7° C during the coldest winter month of January and 23.8° C during the hottest summer month of July. The freeze-free growing season averages 180 days with the last spring freeze generally occurring between March 31 and May 14, and the first fall freeze occurring between September 26 and November 24.

Topography

A detailed topographic survey to document the surface topography and existing structures in a 0.83 ha triangular portion of the approximately 6.1 ha parade field was carried out using a 7.6 m grid spacing (See Fig. 1). Existing USMA facility maps of utilities and storm drains for the adjacent Washington Hall Barracks Complex were consulted to tie-in elevations and establish reference points. The triangular area was the focus of the restoration because all the cadets traverse this area when they enter the parade field.

A maximum elevation difference of 85 cm was observed from the highest to the lowest point in the surveyed area. An average downward slope of 1.9% occurs as one moves from the high area around the Washington Monument in an eastwardly transect towards an existing surface inlet. A 0.5% slope occurs in the swale area (lowest portion) between the surface inlets. Since a minimal positive grade exists in the swale area, a small section between the dry well and most northerly surface inlet occurs as a depressional area.

187

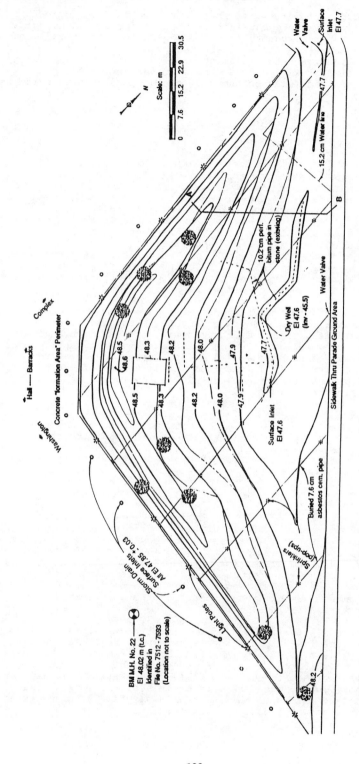

Figure 1. Plan view of topography and drainage at USMA parade field restoration site.

The entire parade field sits on an escarpment approximately 48 m above (overlooking) the Hudson River which is only 0.5 km away. The Hudson River is about 1 m above sea level at this location and subject to tidal influences. Nevertheless, this areal and topographic landscape position of the parade field indicates that an adequate drainage outlet exists, and any high water table which occurs is the result of a localized effect.

Soils

The general soils survey for the USMA parade field location indicates the native soil was a coarse-loamy, mixed, mesic Typic Fragiochrepts. This soil is a deep, well to moderately well drained soil which formed in glacial till deposits and has a dense fragipan occurring at approximately 1 m depth. The fragipan can restrict downward water movement and limit root penetration. This soil also tends to be low in organic matter and acidic. Because the site was disturbed during barracks construction, the existing soil has been modified and differs from its original characteristics.

Subsurface soil borings to 12.2 m depth obtained in 1964-65 prior to the construction of the Washington Hall Barracks Complex provide some additional soils information. According to this data, the soil is relatively deep sand and gravel deposits (of varying proportions) with occasional cobbles and small boulders occurring more frequently with depth. Bedrock was observed at 9.5 m depth at one location, but was deeper than 12 m for most of the area. No significant silt, clay or other stratifying layers exist according to these soil borings. Groundwater was observed in many of the drill holes and occurred at approximately 6.1 m below the surface. The groundwater was determined to be of a perched nature, perhaps being restricted by the bedrock formation which lies above the level of the adjacent Hudson River.

Additional soil sampling of the surface soil was carried out to better characterize this disturbed site. Within the top 7.5 cm of soil, the average particle size analysis consisted of 48% sand, 41% silt, and 11% clay resulting in a loamy soil texture. The particle sizes were distributed quite uniformly with no single particle size dominating to any extent. At 10 to 15 cm of soil depth, the particle size changed slightly to 54% sand, 34% silt and 12% clay resulting in a more fine sandy loam or sandy loam soil texture. The soil at the 10 to 15 cm depth contains a greater percentage of very coarse and fine sand material. At 30 cm depth, the soil is 57% sand, 31% silt and 12% clay resulting in a coarse sandy loam texture. No deep soil exploration pits were made to avoid premature disturbance of the parade field.

The available water holding capacity of the soil was measured to be 0.135 and 0.11 cm/cm for the 7.5 and 15 cm layers, respectively. The coarse grain texture and cemented nature of the soil did not allow the use of hand tools to appropriately sample bulk density or implement hydraulic conductivity measurements. However, observations of water movement and soil moisture above and below the 15 cm soil depth after a 2.5 cm application of water indicated the top soil became saturated while the underlying layer remained dry. The presence of a relatively shallow, impermeable layer resulted in a perched water table condition. The soil permeability apparently decreased significantly in this underlying layer.

Soil strength is a primary determining factor which controls the penetration of roots through sandy hardpans. Most grasses cannot develop root growth pressures which are great enough to overcome penetration forces exceeding 4 MPa (especially when the pore size is also small) so cell growth and root elongation ceases in soils having this strength (Fryrear and McCully, 1972). A soil of this strength also has a very different pore size distribution and permeability than a similar textured soil which is not compacted. A soil layer with more than 3 to 4 MPa penetration resistance not only becomes a restrictive layer to root growth but also acts as a restrictive layer to air and water movement (Bower, 1981).

A soil cone penetrometer, which measures soil strength, was used to locate and map the impermeable, dense layer. Penetrometer measurements were made using the Cornell Soil Penetrometer equipped with a standard 12.8 mm diameter cone base (ASAE S312.2). The hand operated penetrometer traces the necessary force (penetration resistance) with depth to provide a graphical output. The penetrometer is capable of displaying an upper penetration resistance of 4.1 MPa over a depth of 30 cm (Terry and Wilson, 1952). To determine the locations and demonstrate the importance of the dense layer, forty-five penetrometer probings were conducted in a grid pattern and in locations of poor turfgrass vigor, better turfgrass vigor, and the healthiest turfgrass. The penetrometer results which correspond to turfgrass condition are shown in Fig. 2. The areas of poor turfgrass correlate well to the depth of the dense, compacted layer especially when it is found within less than 10 cm of the soil surface. The average depth to the restricting layer (defined as a penetration resistance greater then 3.4 MPa) was approximately 12 cm. Approximately 0.32 ha (39% of the area) consists of soil with less than 10 cm of permeable soil depth. In locations where the turfgrass was almost nonexistent, the restrictive layer occurred within 5 cm of the soil surface. Approximately 0.02 ha (2% of the area) had less than 5 cm of permeable soil depth.

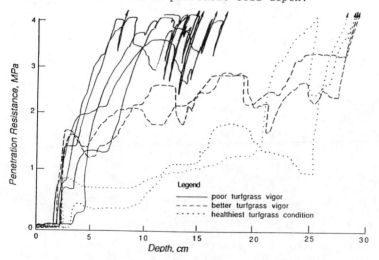

Figure 2. Soil penetration resistance under different existing turfgrass conditions.

Existing Drainage

The existing surface drainage of the area is quite good with numerous storm drains and surface inlets strategically located to collect surface runoff (See Fig. 1). Surface slopes are adequate in most of the area so water will not pond for any extended duration. One exception is the depressional area between the dry well and a surface inlet to the north. Although an existing tile line is below most of this depressional area, a rapid runoff event causes ponding to a 5 cm depth.

The subsurface drainage of this site is influenced primarily by the soil's compacted layers. As water moves downward through the more permeable upper topsoil layer it's impeded by the less permeable underlying layer causing a perched water table. With the shallow restrictive layer that exists in much of the area, the saturated (perched water table) zone occurs within the turfgrass rooting zone. Since turfgrasses require oxygen, the plant roots die back or will not grow into this saturated layer. The topsoil depth and root zone which is more permeable is quite shallow so there is little capacity for rooting or to store excess water. Figure 3 illustrates how the restricting layer is influencing the subsurface drainage across transect AB (transect AB is shown in Fig 1). As downward water movement is impeded, a saturated zone develops just above the restricting layer. Since the restricting layer is also sloped, the perched water moves downward and laterally along it. Where the existing soil surface contour and the restricting layer converge, the entire root zone becomes saturated and a seepage zone develops. The combination of shallow soil and a seepage zone are causing the decline of turfgrass vigor and the initiation of a barren, spongy area midway down the slope. Adjacent to the existing drain at the top of the slope, the turfgrass vigor was also poor. At this location the slope of the restricting layer flattens causing the perched water table to again rise to the surface. As a result, the turfgrass root zone depth is being limited by saturated conditions caused by a combination of poor surface drainage and an accumulation of seepage.

Inspection of the existing dry well (outlet) and some of the older bituminous drain lines was carried out to determine their condition (See Fig. 1 for locations). The dry well is constructed of stones and mortar and has an open storage area for approximately 1.9 kL. The bottom of the dry well was usually observed to be dry indicating it should provide a sufficient outlet and that high water tables throughout the site and soil profile are not a problem. A slug infiltration test for the dry well was performed and it did not fill above 30 cm from the bottom when approximately 190 L/min were discharged into it. For all practical purposes, the dry well appears to be a suitable drainage outlet for the small contributing area. Four existing random tile lines discharged into the dry well and three of these existing lines, for a total of 57 m, were inspected and determined to be free from sediment and debris. Despite the appearance that these lines should be functional, the turfgrass above them revealed no differences. Determination of the depths and grades of the existing lines and inspection of the fourth line was not carried out until the restoration project.

Turfgrass Irrigation Management

The ordinarily satisfactory irrigation was actually exacerbating turfgrass decline in the compacted and poorly drained

191

areas. Since the available water holding capacity of the
uncompacted 5 cm root zone depth would be only 6.8 mm, a peak
turfgrass evapotranspiration rate of 7.6 mm per day would consume
all the available water in less than a day giving the appearance
of droughtiness. When a typical 2.5 cm application was made every
three or four days (the usual schedule), any area with less than
20 to 25 cm of soil depth would become partially saturated by the
perched water table. Consequently, irrigations to overcome the
reduced available water and droughty appearance of some shallow
soil locations actually led to saturated conditions and further
decline in vigor of the Kentucky bluegrass while promoting the
growth and spread of the less desirable annual bluegrass.

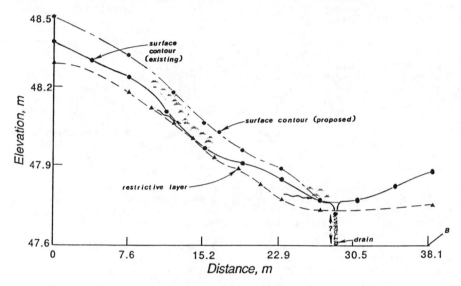

Figure 3. Surface contour and restricting
layer prior to reclamation work.

SOIL AND SITE DETERIORATION PROCESS

The decline of turfgrass vigor, density and quality at the
USMA parade field is attributed to several inter-related
conditions. Wet soils often occur because of the cool, humid
climate or irrigations. Marching traffic, when the soil is wet,
contributes soil compaction. These compressive forces consolidate
the soil pore space of the topsoil and the underlying soil. A
decreased pore space restricts water and air movement and alters
the water retention characteristics of the soil leading to a
greater incidence of the soil being in a wet condition and more
susceptible to further compaction. As the process is repeated,
root zone conditions gradually deteriorate until the turfgrass can
no longer be sustained. The turfgrass roots will not penetrate
the dense, consolidated underlying layer, nor will they tolerate
the saturated conditions in the topsoil layer. Root growth is
reduced and there is greater incidence for disease and weed
(especially annual bluegrass) development. Even turfgrass species

192

which are more tolerant of intense traffic cannot maintain good sod forming and recuperative qualities under these conditions.

The existing loam and sandy loam soil texture in an uncompacted state should be a desirable texture for supporting turfgrass growth. This soil texture would generally exhibit good overall characteristics of nutrient retention, water availability, and permeability. However, this soil was detrimentally affected by compaction because of the well distributed grain sizing. Furthermore, since the clay content is not high, natural wetting and drying cycles do not cause this soil to shrink and swell to ameliorate any compaction which occurs. Consequently, any compaction of this soil is accumulative and irreversible.

The surface and subsurface drainage of this soil type, when in a natural uncompacted state, is not likely to cause major problems for turfgrass growth. However, compaction has altered the topographical and internal drainage characteristics. Saturated conditions occur because of the reduced pore space of the topsoil, the underlying restricting layers, and the seepage and surface water which ponds in depressional areas. The existing surface inlets and random subsurface drains have probably reduced the incidence of soil compaction but the traffic pathways and compaction were more widespread than the existing drain network. The continued compaction gradually altered the soil water movement and storage characteristics to a condition where turfgrass growth was not sustainable.

RECLAMATION PROCEDURES

DRAINAGE IMPROVEMENTS

To enhance the aeration exchange of the topsoil layer and reduce the incidence for compaction, an intensive combination surface and subsurface drainage system was designed and installed for part of the USMA parade field. The subsurface drain spacing calculations for this site condition using a steady state analysis resulted in a decision to use a 3 m spacing. A parallel pattern type system was thus layed out perpendicular to the predominant surface grade and installed with a chain trencher (See Fig. 1). The drainage trenches were excavated to grade so all collected water would flow to the dry well. A cross-section of a typical combination drainage lateral trench is shown in Fig. 4. Part of the main collector is different from the lateral trench in that a 10 cm diameter pipe was placed on the bottom of a 30 to 40 cm wide trench. The combination trench design, which uses graded coarse sand and stone backfill material, will allow excess surface water to percolate through the backfill and will also intercept any subsurface water which may become perched and move laterally in the profile. Approximately 2 km of perforated corrugated plastic drainage tubing and trench was installed. The spoil material (i. e., sod, compact soil, stones, previously buried construction debris, etc.) was excavated and removed because it was unsuitable as a backfill. Approximately 52 m^3 of stone, 365 m^3 of coarse sand, and 620 m^2 of filter fabric was used in the backfill process. Some of the existing drains which were disturbed during the excavation were repaired. However, some existing drains were found within 15 cm of the surface which explains why these were not very functional.

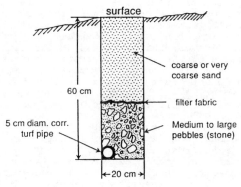

Figure 4. A typical lateral trench cross-section for
a combination surface and subsurface drain.

To facilitate surface drainage, 440 m^3 of coarse sandy loam
topsoil fill material was spread over the area after subsoiling
was performed. The particle size analysis of this material
consisted of 74% sand, 20% silt and 6% clay. The topsoil fill was
smoothed and graded to fill depressions and to provide a new
uniform surface slope across the area (See Fig. 1). The topsoil
modification will enhance the surface drainage, provide some
additional rooting depth, and provide a better soil medium which
should be more resistant to compaction.

Alleviation of Compaction

After the subsurface drainage was installed, a single leg,
winged subsoiler was used to shatter the soil compaction. The
subsoiler penetration depth was approximately 20 to 25 cm and it
was pulled through on a 0.8 m spacing perpendicular to the
drainage trenches. A second, shallower subsoiling operation was
also made perpendicular to the first pass to more uniformly
disturb and loosen the entire area. The resulting cloddy surface
was then roto-tilled, to a 10 cm depth, prior to the placement of
the additional top soil fill and regrading operation. Although a
deeper subsoiling depth may have provided better long term soil
conditions, inadequate tractor horsepower and traction prevented
deeper penetration on this compacted site. Since future
compactive traffic was not going to be eliminated, deeper
subsoiling may also have caused excessive and undesirable
resettlement. Furthermore, deeper subsoiling would have resulted
in excessive debris being brought to the surface. Soil
penetrometer measurements performed after site restoration were
more variable than those taken beforehand, however, the results
indicate the average depth to the underlying restricting layer is
now approximately 20 to 25 cm.

After the coarse sand topsoil fill material was added and the
site regraded to the new topography, 22.7 t of arcillite (a
calcined clay) soil amendment material was spread within the
marching traffic lanes. Since these lanes will be subject to
continuing compaction, the addition of this amendment was to
further modify and enhance the soil to resist this compaction.

SUMMARY

The predominantly Kentucky bluegrass turf on the parade field of the USMA at West Point, N.Y. was gradually disappearing as a result of continued compaction abuse from marching activities. Routine maintenance efforts were not successful in sustaining the turfgrass. A site analysis using a soil penetrometer revealed that about 40% of the parade fields entrance area consisted of less than 5 to 10 cm of topsoil underlain by an impermeable layer. The compacted topsoil and shallow impermeable layer were restricting air and water movement and root development causing the turf to die. Existing random drainage was not effective in removing excess water and preventing further compaction.

The site reclamation process to minimize future compaction and to restore soil physical conditions so turfgrass could be sustained, consisted of installation of an intensive surface and subsurface combination drainage system, subsoiling, and the addition of soil amendments which are more resistant to compaction. Drainage trenches were excavated to a 60 cm depth on 3 m spacing. The trenches were fitted with a 5 cm diameter perforated plastic pipe and then backfilled with a layer of stone and coarse sand to the surface. Subsoiling was used to alleviate the existing compaction and to reclaim a more permeable rooting zone to 20 to 25 cm depth. A coarse sandy loam topsoil fill was added to regrade the surface topography and also to provide additional soil depth. Arcillite was also added to amend the soil in the march traffic lanes to be more resistant to compaction. Although continued site maintenance has been essential, the turfgrass developing from the Kentucky bluegrass sod placed immediately after reconstruction is sustaining itself well after 3 years of marching activity.

ACKNOWLEDGEMENT

Funds for this reclamation work at the USMA were provided by the Facilities Engineering Assistance Program (FEAP) of the U. S. Army under the direction of Dr. Vic Diersing, Engineering Housing and Support Center, Ft. Belvoir, VA.

REFERENCES

1. American Society of Agricultural Engineers. 1991. Soil Cone Penetrometer Standard 313.2. *In:* Standards, Engineering Practices, and Data, (38th Edition) American Society of Agricultural Engineering, St. Joseph, MI. p. 591.

2. Bower, H.D. 1981. Alleviating Mechanical Impedance. *In:* Modifying the Root Environment to Reduce Crop Stress, American Society of Agricultural Engineering Monograph 4, ASAE, St. Joseph, MI. pp. 21-57.

3. Fryrear, D.W. and W.G. McCully. 1972. Development of grass root systems as influenced by soil compaction. J. Range Management. 25:254-257.

4. Terry, C. W. and H. M. Wilson. 1952. The Cornell Soil Penetrometer. Agricultural Engineering Journal. 33:425.

SOME EXPERIMENTS RESTORING HYDROLOGICAL CONDITION OF

PEATLAND IN HOKKAIDO, JAPAN

T. INOUE[*]   Y. UMEDA[*]   T. NAGASAWA[*]

Hokkaido has some two hundred thousand ha of peatland, mainly on the lower reaches of the rivers such as Ishikari, Teshio and Kushiro. During this century, the greater part of these peatlands have been reclaimed into paddy field for rice cultivation and grassland for daily farming. Meanwhile, requirements for the conservation of natural conditioned peatland became large concern. In such cases, restoration of hydrological condition of peatland is necessary.

Some experiments are implemented for the restoration of hydrological condition of peatland in Hokkaido. One case is to dissolve influence of water logging by the road banking which cross the peatland of Kiritappu, eastern Hokkaido. From the hydrological research performed before and after the reconstruction of the road, the effectiveness of devices improving groundwater condition is cleared. Another attempt is to avoid excess drain from conserved bog of Sarobetsu, northern Hokkaido. For this object, vinyl sheets have been put vertically in the peat to insulate water movement. As a result, the pattern of fluctuations of groundwater table changed on some part under influence of vinyl sheet.

The agricultural engineering technology has many experiences on land management. Some of these technology are very useful and valuable for the field of conservation of natural environment. In this report, we will mention some of the attempts performed in Hokkaido, Japan, for the wetland restoration and conservation.

ROAD RECONSTRUCTION WITH CONSIDERATION TO MIRE HYDROLOGY

Kiritappu Mire

The mire is located in the eastern Hokkaido. The mire, facing Pacific Ocean on its eastern side, extends for about 10km from north to south, and has a width of about 3km. The mire is rather flat in topography, and its elevation does not exceed 5m above sea level. According to the soil survey made by Hokkaido National Agricultural Experimental Station(1966), peatland in Kiritappu is composed in large portion of fens distributed in its southern part and of bogs in the center. This central part of the mire was designated for conservation as a natural monument in 1922. The depth of peat layer is about 1 to 1.5m in average. One of the characteristic features of the peat layer in Kiritappu is that several layers of volcanic ash are contained between peat layers.

In the center of peatland where bogs are distributed, a road is crossing through from the Chanai Town to the urban district of Kiritappu. This road cross the central part of the protected area mentioned above. The road has already appeared on the map of Land Survey Department published in 1897, but it probably was only a footpass or rutted road without any improvement. During the period from 1966 to 1967, this road has been improved by banking, but it is still not paved. Recently, according to the growth of the traffic, the road reconstruction was again planned.

Hydrological Survey

Together with reconstruction planning, the environmental survey was carried (Umeda et al., 1985). As the result of the survey, unbalance in hydrological condition on both side of the road was identi-

---

[*]T. Inoue, Assistant Professor, Y. Umeda, Professor, and T. Nagasawa, Lecturer, Dept. of Agricultural Engineering, Faculty of Agriculture, Hokkaido University, Sapporo, Japan

fied. Some differences in vegetation was also known from the survey, which seems to be caused by the change of hydrological condition after road banking.   The south side of the road, which is the lower side of water flow, has the vegetation of *Moliniopsis japonica* and *Myrica gale* community, with *Eriophorum vaginatum*.   The north side of the road, which is upper on the water flow, has similar vegetation with south, but it includes *Phragmites communis* too.

According to the survey of groundwater level, the difference of groundwater condition on both side of the road was apparent. In upper side, the record indicated very high water level after rainfall, which cause the water-logging condition. Figure 1 shows a cross section along the observation line and several measurements of the groundwater surface. As it is shown in Fig.1, the water level on the northern (upper) side of observation line is apparently increased by the damming effect of the road. The highest peak of groundwater recorded on the water level recorder appeared on August 23, 1984. Even in August 27, the water level was still high in the northern (upper) side of the road. The groundwater level at the same day on the southern (lower) side of the road, however, did not show much difference from the groundwater level recorded on August 3.

The influence of banking was clearly visible also in the results of the continuous measurements of groundwater fluctuations on 4 points in observation line (Fig.2). In this figure also the behavior of the water table, calculated by the tank model for peatland groundwater level(Umeda et al., 1985) are shown by dotted lines. The graph of point N'-30 shows a specific pattern of water level fluctuations. Here, the peak of water level shows time lag of about one day from the peak of rainfall. The height of rise due to the rainfall is considerable, and the rate of water level decline is also large, compared to those of other 3 observation sites. Apparent decline of the water level in all sites start after the lowering of water table in N'-30. High water table is kept in these sites at the time when the water level in N'-30 is also high. It seems that the continuation of such high water table in N'-250 was caused by backing of the water from the road banking, while in S'-30 and S'-250 it is due to the continuous supply of seepage water from the upper side of the road.

Devices for Suitable Groundwater Condition

After these assessment, the road reconstruction plan was decided with consideration to the mire hydrology. Two major points of this plan are as follows.

1) To avoid excess drainage through the ditch alongside the road.
2) To ensure the water movement through the road banking for well-balanced groundwater condition on both side of the road.

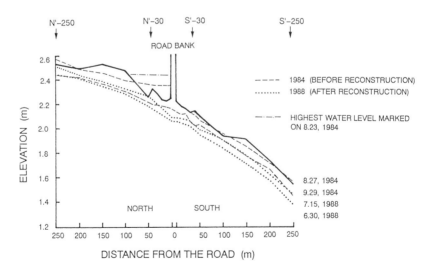

Fig. 1   Cross Section of Observation Line on Kiritappu with Some Measurements of Groundwater Table Before/After the Road Reconstruction. The Arrows on the Top Show the Location of Water Level Recorders.

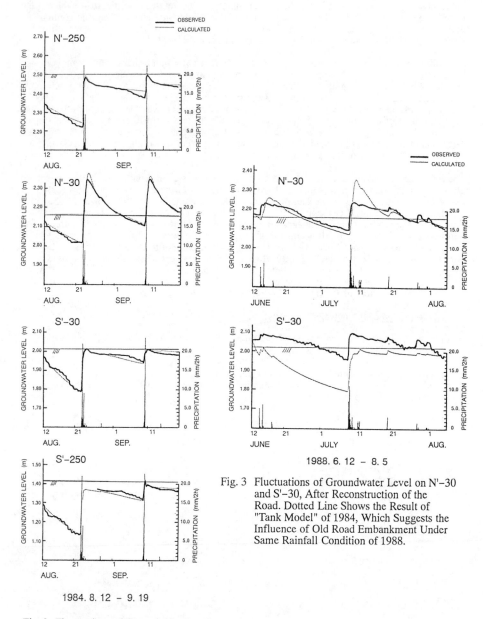

1984. 8. 12 – 9. 19

Fig. 2 Fluctuations of Groundwater Level on
Observation Line N'–S', Before Recon-
struction of the Road. Dotted Line
Shows the Result of "Tank Model"

1988. 6. 12 – 8. 5

Fig. 3 Fluctuations of Groundwater Level on N'–30
and S'–30, After Reconstruction of the
Road. Dotted Line Shows the Result of
"Tank Model" of 1984, Which Suggests the
Influence of Old Road Embankment Under
Same Rainfall Condition of 1988.

198

The old ditch   existed on the northern (upper) side of the road, but it already lost its function after long period of abandon. When the reconstruction was set out, the ditch was not renewed, but it was changed into several series of pools by means of kind of weir built by the peat. In case of heavy rain, the excess water can run over the weir, but in ordinary conditions, the water will keep relatively high position, and excess drainage from the ditch is avoided.

Also to ensure the water movement through the road banking, large diameter pipe was laid under the embankment. This pipe connects the pools on both side of the road, so that the water from the upper side of the road can smoothly move to the lower side.

Result of Road Reconstruction

In Kiritappu Mire, these pools and pipes were built   each 100m in distance. The reconstruction work were done during 1985 to 1986. After the reconstruction works, a follow-up study was carried. From the continuous measurement of groundwater level, very similar patterns of groundwater level fluctuations are obtained from both side of the road (Fig. 3). The water-logging condition on the upper side of the road was disappeared, and also the groundwater level in lower side of the road get slightly high in average. It is more clear when the actual groundwater level is compared with the result of former tank model. The calculation suggests the supposed groundwater level under former condition on same rainfall occurred during the follow-up study. The result of tank model calculation on N'-30 suggests possibility of high water level after the rainfall, but actual water level does not arise as high as the calculation. These evidences indicate the dissolution of water-logging condition on upper side of the road, and well-balanced groundwater flow across the road.

The vegetation also shows sign to change. The result of vegetation survey on 1991 indicates the reduction of *Phragmites communis* on the upper side of the road. Also, the *Shpagnum* hummock appeared clearly on the both side of the road. These results suggest that the vegetation of this area has a similar pattern, which is caused by the control of groundwater level.

INSTALLATION OF VINYL SHEET BARRIER IN PEATLAND

Sasa and Hydrological Condition of Sarobetsu Mire

Sarobetsu Mire is one of the largest peatland in Japan, including fen and bog vegetation. Large portion of this peatland has been designated as a national park. The problem of this peatland is that the part of original bog vegetation seems to be occupied by *Sasa palmata* community, a kind of bamboo grass which prefer the dry condition. The aerial photographs show that the *Sasa* vegetation mainly covers the western part of the mire, that is nearer to the River Sarobetsu (Fig.4). A large number of naturally formed ditches are also identified from the aerial photographs on the same area. Umeda and Shimizu(1985) have described this naturally formed ditches. Also Umeda et al.(1988) suggest that these ditches perform main portion of drainage from bog area to the River Sarobetsu. This seems to be the main reason for the distribution of *Sasa* at the same area with the distribution of ditches.

As a matter of fact, however, the change of vegetation, from bog plant to *Sasa*, is not a matter of very rapid time sequence. Recent five year study on Sarobetsu Mire did not capture *Sasa* invasion into the bog vegetation. But it is still problem for the national park to prevent bog vegetation under adequate condition. This is the reason for the experiment to be conducted on conserving hydrological condition of Sarobetsu Mire.

The condition of groundwater was investigated on both bog and *Sasa* vegetation. The range of fluctuations of groundwater level is narrow in bog, and it is rather high constantly. In contrast, the groundwater level in *Sasa* vegetation is quite different from that of bog. The range of fluctuations are rather wide, and water level deeply declines especially in the summer season under less rainfall. The leaf area index of *Sasa* shows good correlation with depth of groundwater level, especially with the deepest record during dry season (Fig. 5). It is also discovered from small-scale field examination that the growth of *Sasa* can be restrained by keeping the groundwater level in high condition with narrow range of fluctuations. This examination was executed by making a barrier in the natural ditch by blocks of peat, or a sheet of thin plywood, to dam up the water behind the barrier. As a result, those *Sasa* raised near the ditch easily dead in short period, and *Moliniopsis japonica* replaced its position.

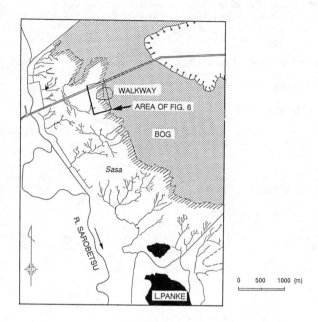

Fig. 4 Distribution of *Sasa* and Naturally Formed Ditches in Sarobetsu Mire.

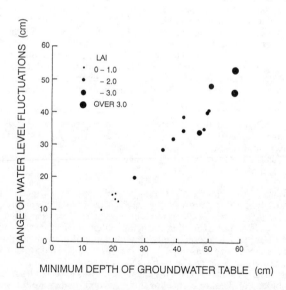

Fig. 5 The Relation Between Leaf Area Index of *Sasa* and Groundwater Level.
(after Fujita et al., unpublished)

Installation of Vinyl Sheet Barrier

After confirming the result of small–scale examination of damming–up, a series of vinyl sheets was installed in the margin of bog vegetation, to conserve groundwater condition in wide region. The sheet has been located at the transitional point of gradient which is the topographical shoulder so that the influence may effect more farther. The length of barrier is 550m, and its route installed roughly parallel to the contour line. With this, the straight line was avoided to not to make ill-matched landscape (Fig.6, Fig.7).

The thickness of vinyl sheet is 0.3mm, its width is 1200mm, and the length is 30m for each roll. A trencher combined with special equipment for installing the vinyl sheet was used. This installing machine is originally used for controlling water loss from the rice paddy. The contact pressure was reduced and rubber crawler was attached, for the trafficability of the equipment and to prevent vegetation damage. By using this machine, the trench of 15cm wide and 1.2m deep was excavated, and the vinyl sheet was automatically installed vertically just after the excavation.

The installation was carried on the afternoon of August 27 and 28 morning, 1991. The actual in-stallation took only a half day. The damage of vegetation caused by moving equipment is very slight, but the dumped peat formed a ridge of about 50cm wide. This ridge, however, was hidden by the vegetation, and its curved route also made itself invisible.

Hydrological Effect

8 years of continuous measurement on groundwater level has been conducted on 3 points in this area (E, bog vegetation; W, bog vegetation with *Sasa* frontier; and WW, *Sasa* vegetation). Based on the tank model analysis, the fluctuating patterns of groundwater level in these 3 points show no sign of change for 8 years. For identifying the effect of the barrier, another measuring point (Wb) was added at 60m upper side of the barrier in 1991. The measurement of this year started one month before the installation of the barrier, terminated on the end of November.

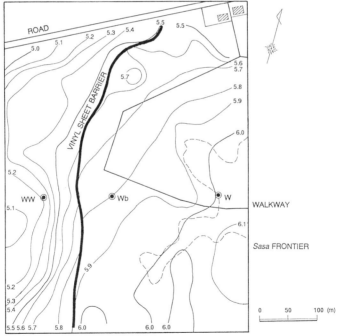

Fig. 6 Location of Vinyl Sheet Barrier and Water Level Recorder (WW, Wb, W) in Sarobetsu Mire. Point E situates 200m East of Point W.

201

The continuous records of groundwater level on 4 points are shown in Fig.8. The gradual change of fluctuating pattern on Wb is apparent. This tendency is especially clear after rather heavy rainfall on the end of September. The reason for the time lag between installation of the barrier and the start of pattern change of groundwater level fluctuation,   seems to be caused by less rainfall during September, and by the time needed for water storage behind the barrier.

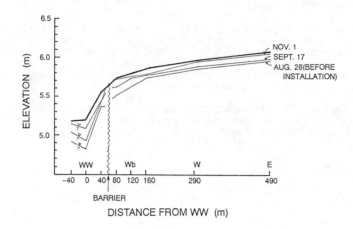

Fig. 7 Cross Section of the Observation Line in Sarobetsu Mire.

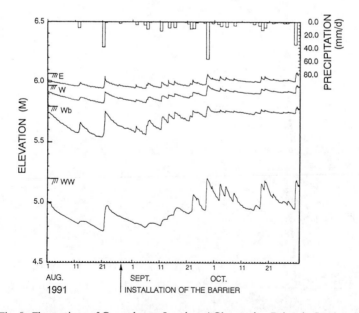

Fig. 8 Fluctuations of Groundwater Level on 4 Observation Points in Sarobetsu Mire.

CONCLUSIONS

Although the change in hydrological condition happens in short span of time, the change in vegetation ordinary takes rather long period. So it is important to continue the follow–up investigation on this kind of matter. Both two examples of hydrological restoration/conservation experiments show capability of managing groundwater condition on peatland. In case of Kiritappu, the vegetation also shows tendency to change. We need some more time to conclude the effectiveness of vinyl barrier against *Sasa* vegetation of Sarobetsu, but at least it seems to be effective for maintaining the groundwater condition of existing bog vegetation.

On the application of these devices, it is important to carry topographic and hydrological survey beforehand. The condition of groundwater level, its direction of flow, and the area of expected effect, etc., will become clear by these assessments. In Kiritappu, the topographic survey was conducted for the width of 500m along the road. In Sarobetsu, the area of about 600m x 500m is surveyed with a net of 40m meshes, to draw the counter line of 10cm interval. Continuous measurement of groundwater level is another important observation for evaluating the groundwater condition of wetland. The fluctuations of groundwater level is one of the expression of on–situ water balance, so that it is possible to interpret the present condition of wetland. The tank model for peatland groundwater level may help the interpretation, and also can be used for the evaluation of the restorational/conservational devices.

REFERENCES

1. Hokkaido National Agricultural Experimental Station. 1966. Soil Survey Report No.17 : 26–35 (in Japanese)

2. Umeda, Y. and T. Inoue. 1985. The Influence of Evapotranspiration on the Groundwater Table in Peatland. J. Fac. Agr. Hokkaido Univ., Vol. 62, Pt. 2 : 167–181

3. Umeda, Y., T. Tsujii and T. Inoue. 1985. Influence of Banking on Groundwater Hydrology in Peatland. J. Fac. Agr. Hokkaido Univ., Vol. 62, Pt. 3 : 222–235

4. Umeda, Y. and M. Shimizu. 1985. On Natural Channels in Sarobetsu Peatland. Memoirs Fac. Agr. Hokkaido Univ., Vol. 14, No.3 : 281–293 (in Japanese with English summary)

5. Umeda, Y., T. Tsujii, T. Inoue, M. Shimizu, and Y. Konno. 1988. The relation of Groundwater Depth to Invasion of *Sasa* in Sarobetsu Peatland. Memoirs Fac. Agr. Hokkaido Univ., Vol.16, No.1: 70–81 (in Japanese with English summary)

DEVELOPMENT OF EROSION STANDARDS FOR USE IN THE REHABILITATION

OF URANIUM MINES IN NORTHERN AUSTRALIA

P W Waggitt[1]   S J Riley[1]
Member ASAE

As society has become more aware of the need to preserve the environment whilst still developing resources so the issue of mine rehabilitation has taken on ever greater importance. Regulatory Authorities and mining companies need a set of criteria that will allow them to confirm objectively the success of rehabilitation of mine sites prior to discharging responsibilities for maintenance (Roederer, 1985; Ellis, 1989). An example is the broad goal and objectives for rehabilitation of the Ranger Uranium Mine (in the Alligator Rivers Region of the Northern Territory of Australia) agreed to by the Commonwealth of Australia and Northern Territory Governments (OSS, 1990, p.59). The three main objectives relate to erosion, revegetation and radiological safety. In order to assist in achieving this goal work on developing standards is being undertaken by the appropriate agencies of the two Governments and the mining companies.

This paper describes the process of development of "erosion standards" and their potential for use in the rehabilitation of present day uranium mines in the Northern Territory of Australia. The signficance of erosion is discussed, the role of standards in design and assessment is outlined and issues related to risk, reliability and time are presented. Finally, the key issues, the constraints and the process of standards development are discussed.

THE ALLIGATOR RIVERS REGION - THE EROSION ISSUE

The Alligator Rivers Region (ARR) of Australia lies in a seasonally wet tropical environment. The World Heritage listed Kakadu National Park (KNP) lies wholly within the ARR. (Fig 1). At present there are two operational uranium mines in the region. One, Nabarlek, has recently been 'mothballed' but rehabilitation is due to be completed by the end of 1995. The other, Ranger (which is surrounded by the KNP), is likely to remain operational for 20 years or more. Environmental Requirements currently require that after mining all tailings be contained "below-grade" within the mined-out pits (OSS, 1990, Appendix 13, ER29). At Nabarlek this was done in the course of operations but at Ranger there is an above ground tailings dam covering approximately 100 ha. The inclusion of this tailings dam within an artificial hill is being studied by the mining company as their preferred rehabilitation option (Unger et al., 1989) In both cases there will be elevated landforms constructed as part of the rehabilitation works. These structures must have a high erosional stability to reduce the risk of impact to the environment to the lowest level that can reasonably be achieved.

Fluvial erosion is the principal erosion process in the ARR. The average annual rainfall is approximately 1500 mm and falls mostly between September and May with approximately 80% falling in the period December to March (Armstrong and Reid, 1989). High intensity rain storms of the early wet season can result in highly erosive events (Riley and East, 1990). The open

---

[1]P.W.Waggitt and S.J.Riley, Office of the Supervising Scientist, PO Box 461, Darwin NT 0801, Australia

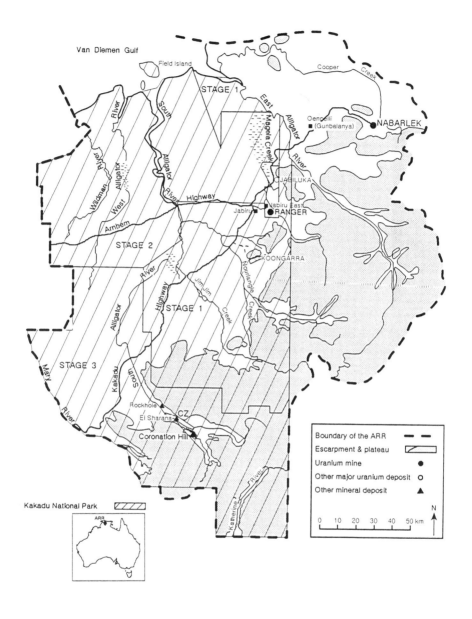

Figure 1. Alligator Rivers Region, Northern Territory, Australia.

woodland vegetation and the sparse surface cover associated with the end of the dry season expose the mineral soil surface to erosion (Story et al., 1969). The dominant erosion processes in disturbed areas in the ARR are rilling and gullying. The erosion potential will be greatest during the early stages of the rehabilitation, before vegetation cover has been established (Duggan, 1991).

Waste rock at Ranger Uranium Mine, dominated by chloritic schist (Milnes, 1986), is highly weatherable and the seasonally wet, tropical environment is conducive to rapid weathering. Large boulders, competent when dumped, break-down into fine gravels, micaceous sands and clays in a matter of years. This waste rock will comprise the majority of engineered landforms and the cover for tailings, low grade ore, and other potential contaminants.

The highly erodible waste rock, the contaminants contained within the structures, mainly tailings and/or low grade ore, and the downstream ecosystem in the Kakadu National Park environment, taken in combination, will require the use of demanding erosion control measures. Such measures should be based on design standards that have been drawn-up to ensure protection of the environment to an acceptable level.

STANDARDS IN A DESIGN AND ASSESSMENT ENVIRONMENT

Before mining is completed regulatory authorities will set standards for use in designing rehabilitation. Such standards do not yet exist for the ARR but examples are found elsewhere (eg. as suggested by US Dept Energy, 1982,p.25 for mines in USA). When the rehabilitation work is completed these standards will also be the criteria for making an objective assessment of its success or failure , as is the case with the US Code of Federal Regulations (1989). Such an assessment would determine if further work, and expenditure, by the mining company is necessary.

The standards must be achievable and likely to succeed. For example, the period of assessment and/or management after final rehabilitation should be compatible with assessing the probability that the work is lasting and self-sustaining. The presence of contaminated material and radionuclides within a rehabilitated site presents further concerns. For example, CFR 40 suggests active management and monitoring of such a site for thirty years after rehabilitation (US Code of Federal Regulations, 1989, 264.117).

RISK AND RELIABILITY

There are unlikely to be precise answers to all the questions concerning the erosional stability of rehabilitated landforms. Firstly, it is difficult to predict the nature of soil development on the rehabilitated waste rock dumps 100, 500 or 1000 years into the future; yet this information will be required for erosion modelling (Ahnert, 1987; Kirkby, 1985). Secondly, the temporal sequence of processes that will trigger erosion and affect rehabilitation can only be poorly predicted. It is not possible to forecast reliably the sequence and magnitude of: i) events in a wet season (Riley, 1991b), ii) the total rainfall in successive wet seasons (McQuade et al., 1991) and iii) major climatic change (Wasson, 1992).

An issue in defining the standards will be setting the degree of risk or the probability of a decision being wrong. An example would be the criteria used to judge whether gullying is unacceptable within the period set aside for monitoring rehabilitation. Assume that there is a criterion for the maximum gully depth that develops in a given period. Over that period no major storm events may have occurred, falsely suggesting that gully development is of minor concern and rehabilitation is successful. It would be more appropriate to use a "gully development model" to compare measured gully development with that predicted. If the model predicted less gully development than had occurred then rehabilitation would be a failure requiring remedial action. However, a deterministic model may not suffice, because within an area of 4

206

km^2 (the area to be rehabilitated at Ranger) only 2 or 3 gullies out of 100 may fail to meet the model's predictions. Does this mean that rehabilitation has failed to meet specifications? Clearly, the predicted depth of gully incision must be assessed within a pre-set confidence range. The number of times the model will accurately predict gully incision needs to be firmly based on probabilistic analysis, with levels of acceptance clearly defined.

STANDARDS IN A TEMPORAL CONTEXT

Erosion rates will vary with time. It is likely that initial erosion rates will be high while the rehabilitated surface settles, excess loose material is removed and the ecosystem develops. If the rehabilitation is successful then the rate of erosion will decline to a "steady state" value, which will indicate negative feedback in the erosion system (Chorley and Kennedy, 1971). Unsuccessful rehabilitation will be indicated by erosion rates greater than predicted limits (Flack and Thames, 1986). Greater erosional stability may arise through negative feedbacks within the system. For example, the removal of fines may leave an erosionally stable lag gravel. Successful rehabilitation will be indicated by a decrease in the erodibility of the surface. Alternatively the system may become unstable, with positive feedbacks dominating. Gully initiation, with consequent increase in slope gradients, exposure of bare areas and development of concentrated flow zones, is an example of this (Wells, 1982; Abt, 1986; Bocco, 1991). Gully erosion will probably be the most important erosion process on rehabilitated lands (Shelton et al., 1984).

KEY ISSUES

Erosion can have impacts both on- and off-site. There are specific concerns about on-site effects of erosion. Where the rehabilitated area includes a cover designed to contain uranium mill tailings, a major concern will be that erosion may breach the cover and allow release of the tailings and other radionuclides. In such cases attention will be focussed not on average erosion rates but on the extremes of localised erosion that might lead to such a breach. Gully and mass movement erosion will be the focus of concern in this case, although tunnel erosion (piping) may become an issue. The on-site and off-site effects of erosion are clearly linked, primarily by surface water movement. Goundwater processes may also be important in mass movement through erosion arising from seepage lines. Geochemical changes may also influence erosion.

Amongst the key parameters to be considered in developing erosion control standards are:
(i) the average rate of erosion; (ii) the spatial distribution of different types of erosion; and (iii) the maximum depth of erosion.

These parameters need to be considered in the context of:
(i) changes in erosion rates over time; (ii) changes in erodibility over time; and (iii) probable erosion rates under more severe climatic regimes.

The list of issues relevant to provisional standards presented below is not intended to be exhaustive, but rather indicates the major areas of concern where research efforts have been concentrated and discussions are on-going.

- Selective use of topsoil
- Standard of regrading for final land surfaces
- Design event for flood protection
- Maximum catchment area for drainage works
- Silt trap capacity
- Use of energy absorbing structures in drains
- Batter slopes on the final landform
- Runoff to pass through silt traps & wetland filters

207

Sedimentation

The impact of discharges into the environment, particularly the aquatic ecosystem, has been the subject of considerable research by the Office of the Supervising Scientist (OSS, 1989). The geomorphic impacts could be substantial for the lower Magela floodplain, which is downstream of Ranger. Wasson (1991) suggests that erosion on the rehabilitated area 3.5 times greater than the natural rate would lead to significant contamination of the floodplain sediments. As erosion on the waste rock dumps could be up to 100 times greater than natural, there is potential for extensive contamination of the flood plain.

The possible impact on the channel of Magela Creek is less certain. Roberts (1991) reports natural transport rates of 5000 tonnes per year for fine grained sediments. Erosion products from the waste rock dump could substantially increase this with consequent effects on the morphology of Magela Creek.

CONSTRAINTS IN SETTING THE STANDARDS

In the process of deriving standards, several physical factors that will constrain the standards have been identified. Amongst these are the natural denudation rate, wash loads and sediment transport in receptor streams, decay processes in gully development and existing water quality standards.

Denudation rate

The rehabilitation goals and objectives required that the target denudation rate must be comparable to that on the surrounding lowlands (<0.1 mm/yr). Average slopes on these lowlands are less than 2%, ie. approximately five times less steep than those initially proposed by the mining company for the rehabilitated landscape (Unger et al., 1988).

As erosion is dependent on climatic factors these must be incorporated into an assessment. Low rates of erosion may only indicate low intensity erosion events during the assessment period, and it will be necessary to check if critical thresholds of erosivity were exceeded.

Wash loads

The impact of the discharge of fine-grained material and solutes into receiving waters will depend on the dilution of the material and the bio- and geo-chemical concentration processes. In the seasonally wet tropics the timing of the discharge of such materials is very important. Receiving streams commonly have lower discharges in the early stages of the wet season. Thus dilution will be lower than during later, higher flow regimes. The wash load concentration of the surrounding streams is ~13mgL^{-1} (Duggan, 1991; Roberts, 1991) yet rainfall simulation experiments on Ranger's waste rock dump have shown suspended sediment concentrations in excess of 500mgL^{-1}. Thus dilution of runoff may need to be greater than 40.

Sediment load

Wasson's suggestion (1991) is that the downstream environment could tolerate no more than an annual addition of 500 tonnes of sediment. This is equivalent to a denudation rate over the Ranger site of 0.1mmy^{-1}.

Gully development

Observations suggest that gullies develop rapidly on new landforms and then stabilise. A relevant standard would have to recognise that gully development

- Factor of Safety for construction
- Retention of ponds for post-mining use
- Maintenance period post rehabilitation works
- Use of passive management systems
- Water quality standards.

In the course of developing standards to address the key issues a number of specific concerns have been identified. Examples of some of these concerns are listed below.

Mass movement

Changes as a result of mass movement, particularly subsidence, can be treated in terms of the maximum permissible area and depth of subsidence. Acceptable disruption of the drainage lines caused by subsidence and mass movement can be specified in terms of the impact on drainage network and channel incision.

Soil erosion and depth

A limit which will influence the erosion standards is the minimum soil depth required for successful and continuing plant growth (Alexander, 1988). Rates of soil erosion should not be permitted to exceed the rate of soil formation.

Settling basins

Not all material eroded from a site is potentially damaging to the off-site receiving areas nor will all eroded materials be transported great distances. Most rehabilitation designs incorporate settling basins and sediment traps, which should mean that only the finer grained sediments escape into streams and receiving areas (Riley and Waggitt, 1992). However, it is often these finer grained sediments that are the carriers of the most damaging pollutants such as heavy metals and nutrients (Hart et al., 1986).

The efficiency of settling basins needs to be assessed, not only by the size of the particles that they retain, but also by their long term viability. A settling basin that fills in a century only delays the release of materials.

A further concern about settling basins is that they may induce adverse geochemical conditions. Seasonally anoxic conditions have been recorded in local billabongs (Hart and McGregor, 1982).

First flushes

First flush and depletion effects of erosion need to be taken into account in assessing the off-site impacts. Erosion simulation and monitoring experiments currently being carried out on the waste rock dump at Ranger have shown that suspended sediment concentrations can decrease by an order of magnitude during runoff events and over the Wet season. As a consequence of this there are concerns about the emphasis that should be given to the first flush in setting erosion standards.

Cumulative impacts

The impact of discharge on receiving areas may be cumulative and take a long time to reach a level where environmental change will be noticed (Ramamoorthy and Baddaloo, 1991; Westman, 1985). Critical thresholds may not be reached for several centuries. Thus, long term impacts must be assessed, however crudely, before the discharge of materials can be determined as benign. Standards adopted for off-site effects of erosion will need to be based on assessment of the timing and quantities of solutes and particulates discharged and long term accumulation effects of such discharges.

may be rapid initially but decrease with time.

Water quality

It is suggested that the predicted maximum concentration of discharged contaminants, when considered as being diluted by receiving waters at their minimum predicted flow rates should not exceed established water quality standards.

ITERATIVE PROCESS OF DEVELOPMENT OF STANDARDS

The rehabilitation design process is iterative, as illustrated by Beedlow et al (1982), with the standards defining the optimum design (Fig 2). Several research projects are currently underway and planned, which should lead to the specification of standards or, at the least, definition of the boundary conditions for the standards. Thus, the development of standards is an ongoing process involving constant review in the light of scientific findings.

Certain "standards" are likely to dominate, for example average denudation rate will control acceptable rill and gully erosion rates.

Finally, when "standards" have been set, they will need to be applied in conjunction with other assessment processes not included here, such as cultural attitudes, aesthetics and the economics of implementation of rehabilitation. The whole rehabilitation operation needs to be carried out in accordance with the "best practicable technology" as defined in the Environmental Requirements that govern all aspects of the protection of the environment in relation to uranium mining operations in the Northern Territory of Australia.

CONCLUSION

This paper outlines some of the issues and the processes in the development of a set of "standards" for use in the design of the final rehabilitation of uranium mines in the ARR. Research suggests that rilling and gullying will be the primary processes of erosion. Furthermore, gullying, because of its potential to incise deeply into the rehabilitated landforms and release radionuclides, will be of primary concern to the regulatory authorities. The standards to be set for erosion will, therefore, have to take into account the technical requirement to reduce gully formation to the lowest level reasonably achievable whilst still conforming to the requirements of the other objectives of the rehabilitation program.

REFERENCES

1. Abt,S.R., Falk,J.A., Nelson,J.D., Johnson,T.L. 1986. Gully incision prediction on reclaimed slopes. ASCE Water Forum 86.,412-419.

2. Ahnert,F. 1987. Approaches to dynamic equilibrium in theoretical simulation of slope development. Earth Surface Processes and Landforms, 12,3-15.

3. Alexander,E.B. 1988. Strategies for determining soil-loss tolerance. Environmental Management, 12(6),791-796.

4. Armstrong,A., and Reid,A. 1989. Environmental auditing at Ranger. Proceedings North Australian Mine Rehabilitation Workshop No.11, 95-100.

5. Beedlow,P.A., McShane,M.C., Cadwell,L.L. 1982. Revegetation/rock cover for stabilisation of inactive uranium-mill tailings disposal sites. US Dept of Energy UMT-0210.

6. Bocco,G. 1991. Gully erosion: processes and models. Progress in Physical Geography, 15(4),392-406.

7. Chorley,R.J. and Kennedy,B.A. 1971. Physical geography: a systems approach. Prentice Hall, London. 370pp.

8. Duggan,K. 1991. Mining and erosion in the Alligator Rivers Region of Northern Australia. Commonwealth of Australia. Office of the Supervising Scientist Open File Record OFR-81.

9. Ellis,D. 1989. Environments at risk: case histories of impact assessment. Springer-Verlag, Berlin. 330pp.

10. Flack,P. and Thames,J.L. 1986. A method for establishing base line soil loss rates on surface mine sites. Symposium on Mining, Hydrology, Sedimentology and Reclamation, University of Kentucky, Lexington, p.283.

11. Hart,B.T., Ottaway,E.M., Noller,B.N. 1986. Nutrient and trace metal fluxes in the Magela Creek system, Northern Australia. Ecological Modelling,31, 249-265.

12. Hart,B.T. and McGregor,R.J. 1982. Water quality characteristics of eight billabongs in the Magela Creek catchment. Commonwealth of Australia. Office of the Supervising Scientist Research Report RR-2.

13. Kirkby,M.J. 1985. A model for the evolution of regolith-mantled slopes in M.J.Woldenburg (ed) Models in geomorphology. Binghampton Symposium in Geomorphology. International Series No.14. Allen and Unwin, NY, 213-237.

14. McQuade,C., Lee,A., Gillies,S. 1991. Rainfall analysis for mine water management system design and operation. Proceeding 4th International Mine Water Congress, Ljubljana, Slovenia, Yugoslavia. Sept 1991, Vol2., 295-303.

15. Milnes,A.R., Riley,G.G., Raven,M.D., 1986. Rock weathering, landscape development and the fate of uranium in waste-rock dumps and the low grade ore stockpile. CSIRO Division of Soils, Adelaide. Rehabilitation of Waste Rock Dumps, Ranger No.1 Mine, Northern Territory. Chapter 1.

16. Office of the Supervising Scientist. 1989. Annual research summary 1987-88. Australian Govt Publishing Service, Canberra.

17. Office of the Superivising Scientist. 1990. Annual report 1989-90. Australian Govt Publishing Service, Canberra.

18. Ramamoorthy,S. and Baddaloo,E. 1991. Evaluation of environmental data for regulatory and impact assessment. Elsevier, Amsterdam.

19. Riley,S.J. and East,T.J. 1990. Investigation of the erosional stability of waste rock dumps under simulated rainfall. Commonwealth of Australia. Office of the Supervising Scientist Technical Memorandum TM-31.

20. Riley,S.J. and Waggitt,P.W. 1992. The potential fate of particulate contaminants from the rehabilitated Ranger Uranium Mine. American Society of Civil Engineers Water Forum 92, Baltimore, (in press).

21. Roberts,R.G. 1991. Sediment budgets and Quaternary history of the Magela Creek catchment, tropical Northern Australia. PhD. Thesis, University of Wollongong. 565pp.

22. Roederer,T. 1985. Reclamation standards and objectives. Proceedings of Workshop on engineering and Hydrology research needs for phosphate mined lands of Idaho. US Dept Agric Forest Service. Intermountain Research Station. Report No. GTR-INT-192, p.12

23. Shelton,C.W., von Bernuth,R.D., Tyler,D.D. 1984. Prevention of gully formation and associated water degradation in West Tennessee. Tennessee

Water Resources Research Centre, Knoxville. Research Project Technical Completion Report #102 UT Publication No. R0102550-29-004-85.

24. Story,R., Williams,M.A.J., Hooper,A.D.L., O'Ferrall,R.E., McAlpine,J.R. 1969. Lands of the Adelaide-Alligator area, Northern Territory. CSIRO Australia, Land Research Series *No*.25.

25. United States Department of Energy. 1982. Plan for stabilisation and management of commingled uranium-mill tailing*s*. Volume 1. DOE/DP-00.

26. Unger,C., Armstrong,A., McQuade,C., Sinclair,G., Bywater,J., Koperski,G. 1989. Planning for rehabilitation of the tailings dam at Ranger Uranium Mines. Proceedings North Australian Mine Rehabilitation Workshop *No*.11,153-165.

27. Wasson,R.J. 1991. Modern sedimentation and Late Quaternary evolution of the Magela Creek Plain. Commonwealth of Australia. Office of the Supervising Scientist Open File Record OFR-88.

28. Westman,W.E., 1985. Ecology, impact assessment and environmental planning. J.Wiley,NY.

29. Wells,S.G. 1982. Geomorphology and surface hydrology applied to landscape reclamation in the strippable coal belts of Northwestern New Mexico. New Mexico Energy Institute and Energy and Minerals Dept Project EMD-68R-3111.

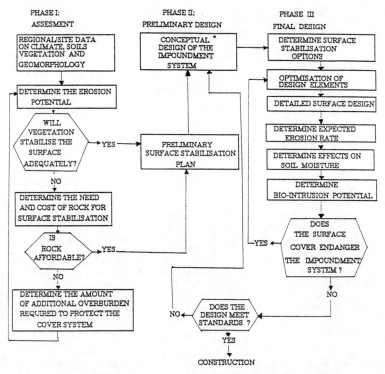

* Surface cover information contributed to an analysis of the entire impoundment system.
  In re-evaluation it may be neccessary to provide different surface stabilisation plans.

Figure 2. Decision tree for designing inactive mill tailings surface covers (modified from Beedlow et al., 1982)

212

LAND USE STRATEGIES AND THEIR

IMPACT ON SPOIL SOILS OF THE

JOS PLATEAU TIN-FIELDS OF

NIGERIA

Michael J. Alexander[1]

Commercial open cast tin mining of alluvial cassiterite ores exposed along contemporary river channels began on the Jos Plateau in 1904, (Fig. 1). Major impacts on the landscape of the Plateau did not occur however, until the introduction of dragline working in 1924. With the tin bearing alluvium occurring in narrow, sinuous channels of fossil water courses, the normal 'cut and fill' dragline operating programme could not be employed (Thomas, 1978). The end result is a disturbed landscape of linear mounds and elongated, now flooded paddocks. Although from the outset of mining, legislation enforced compensation to the indigenous peoples whose land was being used, no attempt was made to require reclamation of abandoned mine sites until the introduction of further legislation in 1947 (Alexander, 1989a).

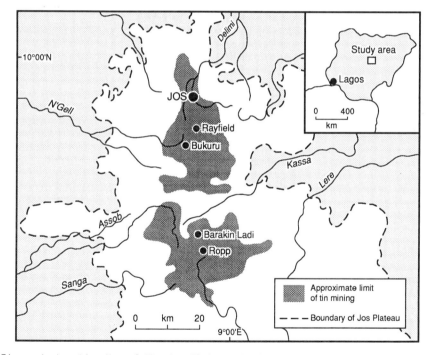

Figure 1. Location Map of the Jos Plateau tin-fields.

[1] Michael J. Alexander, Lecturer, Geography Dept., Durham University, South Road, Durham, DH1 3LE, UK.

Despite the existence of this legislation, of the 320 km^{-2} damaged by mining activities, only about 30 km^{-2} have been reclaimed, thus leaving nearly 90% of the affected area derelict to some degree. With the almost total demise of the Nigerian tin industry and the serious decline in the Nigerian economy, little reclamation has taken place on the Jos Plateau since 1982.

Of the area reclaimed since 1947, the mining companies have been responsible for no more than 1-2 km^{-2}, the remainder being carried out by either the State Government Mine Lands Reclamation Unit, or, more recently, the Federal Government Joint Consultative Committee on Mine Land Reclamation. The reclamation strategy adopted by both of these organisations has been one of crudely levelling the spoil mounds and infilling the flooded paddocks. Reclamation has been rendered more difficult because at the outset of mining, no attempt was made to adopt the normal strip-mine policy of removing and storing separately topsoil, subsoil and overburden. Consequently the spoil mounds comprise a complex mixture of these various strata, which produces extremely acid and nutrient deficient soil parent material. Following reclamation, the policy is to attempt to improve the fertility of the spoil soil by establishing plantations of Eucalypts. This policy was adopted in the early 1950's following a series of experiments in which a range of treatments involving the use of heavy applications of organic and inorganic fertilizers and the planting of nitrogen fixing crops and green crops were applied to the spoil soils in an attempt to restore them to immediate agricultural use. None of these strategies proved economically viable and thus the Eucalypt planting policy was adopted. Eucalypts appear to have been chosen as the plantation species as a result of earlier trials in which it was demonstrated that they were ideally suited to the Plateau environment, (Wimbush, 1963). They also had the added advantage that they could be couped every seven years over a thirty five year life cycle to yield up to five crops of pole or fire wood. Furthermore, being trees, it was expected that they would inevitably improve the fertility of the spoil soil. No other species appear to have been considered, nor alternative uses for the land, (Alexander, 1989a).

This paper sets out to question the effectiveness of the 'level and plant eucalypt' policy and to review possible alternative strategies.

THE EFFECT OF *EUCALYPTUS* PLANTATIONS ON THE LONG TERM FERTILITY OF SPOIL SOILS

Despite having the facilities, none of the agencies responsible for reclamation on the Jos Plateau have attempted to monitor the effect of their reclamation policies on the long term fertility of the spoil soils. In order to rectify this situation, a research project was initiated in which the effect of twenty years of *Eucalyptus* growth (mainly *E. camaldulensis*) on the tin mine spoil could be studied. Topsoil samples (0-10cm) were collected from twenty reclaimed sites and compared with raw spoil topsoils collected from twenty two unreclaimed sites. (Details of the sampling methods and laboratory procedures can be found in Alexander, 1989b; and a complete set of analyses in Alexander, 1986). Selected results of the laboratory analyses are presented in table 1.

As a result of additional input of organic matter from leaf fall etc. the reclaimed topsoil has a significantly higher content of organic carbon and nitrogen plus a significantly enhanced cation exchange capacity. Whilst exchangeable calcium and magnesium levels and available phosphate content are similarly higher, these increases are not significant. Of most interest and indeed concern however, is the significant decrease in both pH and percent base

Table 1. The long term effect of Eucalypt plantations on selected topsoil properties compared with unvegetated topsoil.

Property	Eucalypts	Unvegetated spoil	Significance
pH	4.7	5.1	p = 0.05
Organic carbon %	1.84	0.10	p = 0.001
Total nitrogen %	0.140	0.026	p = 0.001
Exchangeable bases cmol kg^{-1}			
Calcium	3.73	4.03	ns
Magnesium	1.67	1.23	ns
Potassium	0.41	0.20	ns
Cation exchange capacity cmol kg^{-1}	9.04	4.51	p = 0.001
Base saturation %	21.60	38.80	p = 0.001
Available phosphorus mg kg^{-1}	0.07	0.02	ns

(Modified from Alexander. 1989b)

saturation that has occurred beneath the Eucalypts. The cause of this decline has been explained in detail elsewhere (Alexander, 1989b). In summary however, it appears to be the result of a combination of the inherently low fertility of the spoil soil and poor management practices. The regular coupling of the trees (harvesting both timber and all slash), causes progressive reduction in the naturally low soil nutrient reserves, resulting in the inevitable decrease in both the percent base saturation and pH. The overall effect of this policy of planting Eucalypts on reclaimed sites, is thus to bring about the progressive deterioration in the quality of an already very poor soil; rather than the improvement anticipated by the Mine Lands Reclamation Unit. Buckley (1988) has emphasised the significance of this increasing acidity, arguing that it will lead to a decrease in the availability of certain nutrients, whilst increasing exchangeable aluminium levels to a point a which they will become toxic to the Eucalypts themselves. Thus, as a direct result of a misplaced policy of planting Eucalypts, the reclaimed spoil soils will have been rendered economically useless, being unable to sustain any commercially useful crops. Interestingly, this problem with Eucalypts is not confined to the Jos Plateau, similar soil deterioration beneath Eucalypts has been reported from a number of other localities eg. India, and South-west Europe (Shiva & Bandyopadhyay, 1987; Kardell et al. 1986).

Improved plantation management, in which only the timber is removed from the sites and all slash left on the ground to rot down, may improve the situation, as would regular, but economically unviable additions of fertilizer. The most effective solution however, would be to seek an alternative strategy for using the reclaimed or even unreclaimed spoil soils. A brief survey of the native tree species growing in the tin-fields and study of how local people are using these areas for productive agriculture suggested two possible alternatives (Alexander, 1986). These were:-

A) The replacement of the exotic *Eucalyptus* species with the *Faidherbia (Acacia) albida*.
B) The direct use of the land and water resources of the mined areas for irrigated agriculture.

Faidherbia albida has naturally colonised old spoil mounds and tailing cones throughout the mined area. It was selected for further study as it has a reputation across much of savanna Africa of being able to improve soil fertility, (Charreau and Vidal, 1965: CTFT, 1988). A pilot study of the effect of *F. albida* on spoil soil was therefore conducted at one site, the results of which are summarised in table 2.

Table 2. Summary of results of the pilot study comparing the long term effect of *Faidherbia albida* on selected topsoil properties with topsoil form outside the effect of the canopy zone.

Property	*Faidherbia albida*	Outside canopy	Significance
pH	5.7	5.7	ns
Organic carbon %	1.76	0.51	p = 0.05
Total nitrogen %	0.117	0.037	p = 0.01
Exchangeable bases cmol kg^{-1}			
Calcium	8.07	4.64	p = 0.01
Magnesium	2.30	1.63	p = 0.01
Potassium	0.37	0.34	ns
Cation exchange capacity cmol kg^{-1}	5.30	4.20	ns
Base saturation %	68.10	56.60	0.05
Available phosphorus mg kg^{-1}	0.09	0.07	ns

(modified from Alexander, 1989c)

The effect of the *F. albida* is to increase significantly organic carbon, total nitrogen, exchangeable calcium and magnesium and base saturation levels when compared with topsoil outwith the canopy zone. Although both exchangeable potassium and available phosphorus also show an increase, the differences are not significant. Thus the results of this pilot study clearly indicated that *F. albida* was able in the long term to improve the fertility of the spoil soils. When compared with the effect of *Eucalyptus* on spoil soil, *F. albida* appeared to increase the levels of most nutrients with the exception of nitrogen, but only exchangeable calcium, pH and percent base saturation were significantly higher than under Eucalypts, (Alexander, 1989c).

As a follow on to the pilot study, Kidd et al in 1991, carried out a larger study involving eight sites scattered throughout the mined area, the results of this more detailed study do not however substantiate the findings of the previous study, (table 3).

Whilst a marginally beneficial effect of *F. albida* can be seen in terms of increased topsoil levels of organic carbon and phosphorus, only exchangeable potassium increased significantly. These benefits are offset by a decrease in exchangeable calcium and magnesium and also base saturation and cation exchange capacity. Thus the hope that *F. albida* might prove to offer a way forward in the need to improve the fertility of the spoil soil is not supported. Nevertheless, it is apparent from both the pilot and more extensive studies, that whilst *F. albida* does not have the hoped for ameliorating effects on the soil, it does not

216

have the detrimental effects on soil fertility as shown by the Eucalypt species.

Table 3. The long term effect of *Faidherbia albida* on selected topsoil properties compared with topsoil form outside the effect of the canopy zone.

Property	*Faidherbia albida*	Outside canopy	Significance
pH	6.0	5.9	ns
Organic carbon %	0.84	0.53	ns
Total nitrogen %	0.047	0.019	ns
Exchangeable bases cmol kg^{-1}			
Calcium	2.66	3.19	ns
Magnesium	1.30	1.69	ns
Potassium	0.36	0.17	p = 0.01
Cation exchange capacity cmol kg^{-1}	8.20	0.21	ns
Base saturation %	57.00	61.80	ns
Available phosphorus mg kg^{-1}	0.09	0.07	ns

(Modified from Kidd et al, 1991)

Therefore *F. albida* could still be considered as a possible plantation species. However, when the yield and growth rate of timber of the two species are considered, then *Faidherbia* is greatly disadvantaged; it has neither the growth rate nor yield of the *Eucalyptus*. Furthermore the local farmers do not regardF. albida as an 'economic' tree and rank it low in comparison to other trees in terms of its utility, (Kidd et al ,1991). It is highly likely therefore, that they would not support extensive planting of *F. albida*. Clearly, the search for alternative tree species or different uses of the mine spoil must continue.

THE AGRICULTURAL POTENTIAL OF THE SPOIL SOILS

Despite the Mine Lands Reclamation Unit having dismissed the possibility of using reclaimed sites for agriculture on the grounds of the uneconomic levels of fertilizer input required. Since before that organisation was instituted and especially since the economic downturn of the mid-1980's, local farmers have utilised both reclaimed and non-reclaimed mine land for agriculture. The majority of this expansion has involved the use of dry season irrigation, which utilises the high quality water stored in over 200 flooded mining paddocks, together with the usual river sources. A detailed examination of two such locations by Alexander (1988) clearly demonstrated that successful agricultural activities could be established on tin mine spoil using inputs of both standard compound fertilizers and, more importantly, a range of locally available organic manures including town refuse. This latter is bought by the lorry load, burned, picked over to remove tin cans, glass and plastic, sieved and then applied liberally to the plots.

The effectiveness of traditional fertilizers in raising and maintaining the fertility of cultivated spoil soils has been the focus of two further studies at a number of sites along the Delimi river north of the town of Jos (Fig.1). Phillips-Howard and Kidd, (1990) studied the importance that local farmers attached to the different manures and fertilizers available to them. They found that the farmers were able to rank the value of such traditional manures as bird, poultry, cow, pig, town refuse ash etc., against inorganic fertilizers

(NPK, Calc-Ammonium Nitrate and superphosphate). In all cases they valued their traditional fertilizers above the modern inorganics. This study into farmers fertilizer preferences was run in parallel to a second study reported here, in which the effect of continuous cultivation on the fertility of spoil soils was investigated. In this second study, twenty three topsoil samples were collected from areas under continuous cultivation of irrigated vegetable crops for up to fifty years and from seven sites which had never been cultivated. All cultivated sites had received regular inputs of traditional organic fertilizers, plus, over the last ten years or so town refuse ash, and occasionally when available and affordable some inorganic fertilizer.

The effectiveness of the cultivation practices on the top soil properties is summarised in table 4. All the important fertility elements have been increased, with pH, calcium, potassium and available phosphorus showing

Table 4 The effect of cultivation on selected topsoil properties.

Treatment	pH	Organic Carbon %	Total Nitrogen %	Exchangeable Bases cmol kg^{-1}			Available Phosphorus mg kg^{-1}
				Ca	Mg	K	
Cultivated	7.1	1.00	0.058	6.81	0.92	0.27[a]	29.77
Control	6.3[c]	0.59	0.046	2.81[c]	0.18	0.07	2.86[c]

[a] significant difference p = 0.05
[b] significant difference p = 0.01
[c] significant difference p = 0.001

significant increases. With such a wide range of manures and fertilizers in use it is difficult to isolate the effect of any one. However, analysis of eight different manures and town refuse ash (table 5) clearly demonstrates the contribution each makes to the increased fertility of the soils.

Table 5 Nutrient composition of a selection of traditional manures and town refuse ash.

Manure/ Fertilizer	pH	Organic Carbon %	Total Nitrogen %	Exchangeable Bases cmol kg^{-1}			Available Phosphorus mg kg^{-1}
				Ca	Mg	K	
Cattle	nd	21.92	1.628	33.73	20.69	42.13	1687.67
Pig	nd	20.56	1.336	52.10	17.60	22.08	2183.00
Sheep	nd	32.09	1.946	22.35	21.84	19.28	1747.80
Poultry	nd	26.35	2.521	18.07	17.60	19.28	3197.71
Town ash	10.3	2.10	0.268	93.37	26.25	36.09	1168.50

The organic manures add a range of nutrients especially nitrogen and phosphorus and also add considerably to the organic matter of the soil. Town refuse ash, whilst also contributing phosphorus and nitrogen, is, more importantly a major source of calcium, magnesium and potassium. However, with a pH level in excess of 10, it will have an immediate and beneficial effect of raising the often very acid (pH 4.5-5) spoil soils to a more amenable pH of 6-7. Because of this important neutralizing effect, town refuse ash is applied in large quantities on land newly taken in for agriculture.

Thus, by applying their indigenous knowledge of traditional organic manures and combining this with the use of town refuse ash and occasionally normal commercial fetilizers, the local farmers have found a cheap and effective technique of converting the acid, nutrient deficient tin mine spoil soils into productive agricultural soils. The local farmers have thus succeeded where the two official reclamation bodies have failed, much of this success is attributable to the use of town refuse ash. Furthermore, such improvements take a relatively short time - usually less than twelve months, (Alexander et al, in preparation).

CONCLUSIONS

The work reported here highlights the problems encountered in any reclamation schemes whereby strategies and policies for reclamation are adopted and put into operation, without any scheme for the ongoing monitoring of the success or otherwise of the adopted procedures. From the data presented here, it is clear that the use of Eucalypts in reclamation of tin-mine spoil on the Jos Plateau has had the exact opposite effect of that intended; namely the further deterioration in the fertility of the spoil soils rather than the hoped for improvement.

On the basis of a series of studies centred on the patterns of natural colonisation of the spoils soils and agricultural practices used by local farmers, alternative strategies have been examined. The use of *Faidherbia albida* has been investigated, and whilst it would not have the same deleterious effect on the long term fertility of the spoil soils caused by Eucalypts, its low valuation by local farmers suggests it is of limited value as an alternative tree species. With this in mind, a series of experimental plots have been established, in which the suitability of a number of other species will be examined. Of more immediate significance however, are the studies made into the exploitation of the spoil and water resources of the mine-lands by the indigenous farmers. By using water from both rivers and the flooded mining paddocks, together with the use of large inputs of town refuse ash, traditional manures and some use of commercial fertilizers, they have succeeded in converting the low quality, very acid spoil soils into agriculturally very productive soils. This process can be achieved in a very short time, with distinct improvements having been recorded within twelve months of initial cultivation.

Thus 'waste' tin-mine land and 'waste' town refuse have been brought together with animal 'waste' to produce agriculturally fertile soils. This successful use of town refuse as a fertilizer offers the opportunity of greatly expanding agricultural production across the tin-field and indeed throughout the Jos Plateau. With suitable monitoring there is no reason why this cheap and widely available 'fertilizer' should not be adopted to aid agricultural output in and any other developing area.

ACKNOWLEDGEMENTS

The European Community contributed funds from the European Development Fund towards the financing of the project of which this work is a part. The grant No. 4107.002.41.21 was given under the University Linkage Programme. I am also most grateful to the following people in jos for their advice and encouragement:

C.I.B. Cox, J.D. Haruna, A.G.Musa, A.J. Kidd, K.D. Phillips-Howard and colleagues at Unijos. In Durham, Derek Coates, Joan Dorril and Brian Priestley undertook the soil analyses.

REFERENCES

1. Alexander, M.J. 1986. Soil Characteristics and the Factors Influencing Their Development on Mine Spoil of the Jos Plateau. Interim Report No. 11, Jos Plateau Environmental Resources Development Programme, University of Durham.

2. Alexander, M.J. 1988. Is agriculture a viable alternative to *Eucalyptus* plantations on reclaimed tin-mine spoil on the Jos Plateau, Nigeria? Environ. Conserv. 15:261-263.

3. Alexander, M.J. 1989a. A review of the bureaucratic, political and legislative problems encountered in the reclamation of the Plateau tin-fields of Nigeria. Landscape and Urban Planning 17:33-45.

4. Alexander, M.J. 1989b. The long term effect of *Eucalyptus* on tin mine spoil and its implication for reclamation. Landscape and Urban Planning 17:47-60.

5. Alexander, M.J. 1989c. The effect of *Acacia albida* on tin mine spoil and their possible use in reclamation. Landscape and Urban Planning 17:61-71.

6. Buckley, P. 1988. Soil factors influencing yield of *Eucalyptus camaldulensis* on former tin-mining land in the Jos Plateau region, Nigeria. For. Ecol. Manage. 23:1-17.

7. Charreau, C and P. Vidal. 1965. Influence de l'*Acacia albida* Del. sur le sol, nutrition minerale et renedments des mils *Pennisetum* au senegal. Agron. Trop. 20:600-626.

8. CTFT. 1988. Faidherbia Albida. Monograph, Centre Technique Forestier Tropical, Nogent-Sur-Marne Cedex, France.

9. Kardell, L., E. Steen and A. Fabiao. 1986. *Eucalyptus* in Portugal-a threat or a promise? Ambio 15:6-13.

10. Kidd, A.J., M.J. Alexander and K.D. Phillips-Howard. 1991. *Faidherbia albida* on mine-spoil in the tin mine region of the Jos Plateau, Nigeria. Proceedings of an International Conference, ICRAF, Niamey. (In Press).

11. Phillips-Howard K.D. and A.D. Kidd. 1991. Knowledge and management of soil fertility among dry season farmers on the Jos Plateau, Nigeria. Interim Report No. 25, Jos Plateau Environmental Resources Development Programme, University of Durham.

12. Shiva V. and J. Bandyopadhyay. 1987. Ecological Audit of *Eucalyptus* cultivation. Research Foundation for Science and Ecology, Dehra Dun, India.

13. Thomas, L.J. 1978. An Introduction to Mining. Methuen, Sydney.

14. Wimbush, S.H. 1963. Afforestation of restored tin mining land in Nigeria. Commonw. For. Rev. 42(113):255-262.

LAND USE PLANNING IN THE SOUTH AFRICAN SUGARCANE INDUSTRY

G.G. PLATFORD[1]

In the sugarcane growing areas of South Africa there are many soil, slope, elevation and climate variations, and conditions are therefore not best suited for crop growth. Rainfall is variable and storms of high intensity occur during the summer months from September to March. Soils are often granular and erodible and can also vary within farm boundaries. Better growing conditions often occur in valley bottom areas rather than on crest lines or hill sides. Sugarcane is a very good conservation crop and, despite the adverse climatic factors, grows where most annual crops cannot be grown. For optimum returns from a farm unit under these conditions, it is essential to provide protection against heavy rains before they occur and to apply the most suitable agronomic practices for the land type. The best land use practices on different parts of the farm are presented in the form of a Land Use Plan (LUP). The LUP is developed using a nomograph (Dent, 1982) and provides an overall protection plan for the farm based, on catchment units and crop management systems. Haulage and access roads of various types are then integrated into the plan. The sugarcane crop is bulky, heavy and difficult to move over steep terrain. Haulage costs are high in relation to the other production costs so the selection of correct equipment and the correct routing after harvesting are vital. Assessments of proposed field row lengths and differing transport systems are undertaken to ensure that the most suitable system with the best available equipment is used. An implementation programme is needed to ensure the estimated benefits can be achieved and included in the LUP report.

RESEARCH PROGRAMME

The programme to measure soil and water losses from sugarcane fields was started in 1975. Prior to that results of research in the United States had been used to set recommendations for cultural practices. With the local slope, soil and rainfall conditions these were seen to be ineffective. Natural runoff plots (Wischmeier and Smith, 1963) were established to measure basic soil erodibility. A catchments research project (Platford, 1985) and rainfall simulator programme were also started to obtain data on soil losses.

Results

Runoff plots: Five sets of runoff plots were established on different soil types along the coast to measure soil and water losses. The paired plots were kept in a fallow condition for seven years to calculate soil erodibility. After the fallow period the plots were planted with cane and crop management practices were measured.

Catchments: Four small sloping catchments of about four hectares each were set up at the South African Sugar Association experiment farm at La Mercy, 30 km north of Durban, to

---

1. Head, Farm Planning Department, South African Sugar Association Experiment Station

measure water runoff and soil losses from field size areas. After seven years of bare fallow sugarcane was planted using different field layouts to establish various management practices.

Rainfall simulator: The simulator programme included measuring runoff from bare fallow, mulch covered, burnt and minimum tilled plots (Haywood, 1987).

The data showed that most soil loss occurred during the replanting periods, when plots were ploughed and cultivated. It was seen that a single protection practice such as the provision of water runoff control banks in a tilled field on steep slopes would not be sufficient to prevent large scale soil losses. For the flatter areas conventional tillage and graded terrace banks with grassed waterways were effective in controlling soil erosion.

THE NOMOGRAPH

As there is a wide range of soil types, slopes, aspects and elevations throughout the sugar industry, a set of recommendations was needed to include these differences. The original recommendations for spacing of banks were modified from those designed by the Department of Agricultural Development for annual crops. A nomograph was developed to allow for the variables of soil type, slope, crop and management factors (Platford, 1987).

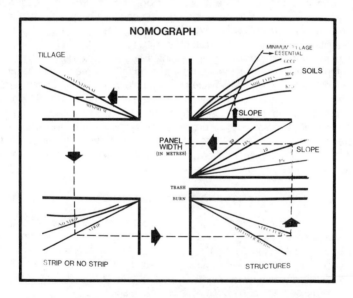

Fig 1. The SASA nomograph which is used to determine panel widths between roads in sugarcane fields.

Data from the research programme were also used in the development of the nomograph. It was designed to keep expected long term average soil losses under 20 t/ha/annum. Various slope limits were set for tillage methods because of the severe soil losses which occur on sloping ground. On highly erodible soils it was estimated from the data that unacceptable soil losses would take place on slopes of over 12%. For soils more resistant to erosion, the slope limit appeared to be 22%. Slope and soil erodibility are specific for each site and these form the starting point into the nomograph. Various combinations of soil protection options are available. The result of the different options sets a panel width between either terrace or spillover roads. One or a number of panels can be incorporated into a field depending on the management practices selected. Using this technique the grower can have some choice while still complying with the soil protection required under the Conservation of Agricultural Resources Act (1983).

MATERIALS

Land Use Planning

A number of different maps and planning aids are used to assess the resources of the farm.

Aerial photographs: Most of the sugarcane areas are regularly photographed from a height of 4 600 m. With a normal focal length of 150 mm in the camera a contact print with a scale of 1:30 000 is produced. Photograph enlargements with an approximate scale of 1:6 000 are used to identify specific field items, streams, wet spots, erosion gullies and other ground objects. Although photographs are useful for visual effects, their main function is to produce stereoscopic models for survey and topographic maps for individual growers.

Soils maps: Large areas of the sugarcane belt have soil maps or soil parent material maps (Beater, 1957). These are used to assess expected soil types on the farm being planned. Soil and slope information is vital to set protection patterns. Most soil maps have been produced at a scale of 1:6 000.

Quota maps: Individual quota maps produced from aerial photographs are at a scale of 1:6 000. They show the farm boundaries, field roads, buildings and areas where there is no sugarcane grown. Each field has a number specified by the grower and a measured area. They are used to control the position of allocated quota areas and for management decisions and cane yield analyses.

Formline maps: Developed from aerial photographs, they show topographic detail in the form of contours. The shape and spacing of the contours (lines of equal elevation on the ground) allow the planner to judge and assess the topography of the farm. Quota maps are true to scale and can be used to measure ground lengths and areas.

Ortho-photographs: These are modified aerial photographs with the form lines or contours drawn onto them using special techniques and are free of distortion. Compared with photographs they have the visual appeal of a photograph and the accuracy of a map. The expensive method of production has limited the area covered by these maps.

Databases: Field Record Service (FRS). Many growers submit records of field results to this service. The data related to field numbers on the quota map are analysed for yield trends and are available for making management decisions. Where farms to be planned have this data it can be included in the planning process.

Fertilizer Advisory Service (FAS). The results of soil and leaf sample analyses are identified by quota map field number. This information can be integrated into the database to decide on best land use.

Geographic Information System (GIS): The above types of data have been used in a GIS for the sugar industry. A Digital Terrain Model (DTM) has been included in the GIS to allow all the information to be referenced to the topography. Software modules are used to design transport routes at specific gradients, to reach set positions for loading zones requiring flat ground and for siting water control structures.

METHODS AND RESULTS

A request to prepare a Land Use Plan and assess the transport options for a group of three farms (Fig 2) in the Eston area of the Natal midlands was received from the Extension department of the Experiment Station, using the existing Specialist Advisory Service (SAR). The request covered three separate farms: "Elsinore" and "Hope Valley" which were controlled by one quota, and the recently purchased "Maxwilton" which had a different quota.

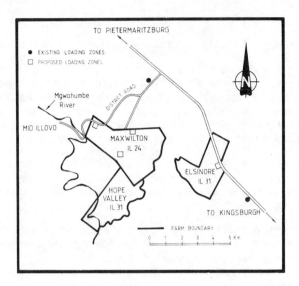

Fig 2. The relative location of the three farms planned and assessed for cane haulage efficiency.

All three farms had been planned, but the change in ownership required some re-assessment of field works, field boundaries and the cane haulage systems. The detailed planning method was the same on all farms and the plan for "Maxwilton" farm is used to show the method of planning.

Preparation of a physical plan

The detail from the soils maps and formline maps with crest and drainage lines was drawn onto an existing quota map. Catchments sizes were measured for each waterway (mostly dry) and watercourse (mostly wet). Slopes were measured along crests, down representative hill sides and along the waterways. Soil types were examined and classified into: erodible, moderately erodible and resistant to erosion. These boundaries were then marked on the same map. Field areas and crests with slopes greater than 10% were circled. Diagonal roads were marked at a 10% gradient for possible cane extraction routes, using the photograph and formline maps as a guide. Possible wet valley bottom lands were also marked. With the use of a nomograph, road spacings for each of the defined hill side blocks were established. A series of water-carrying terrace banks were designed to intercept any runoff water and carry it across the hill side to designed grassed waterways. The capacity of the banks was detailed in the specifications attached to the maps. These terrace banks were used as the basic framework for new fields and the required capacity and shape for each grassed waterway was calculated. Each of the watercourses and streams was examined on the

224

photograph, and marked where stabilization work was needed. Notes were made on the map to inspect sensitive areas such as possible wetlands. The rough drawing showed all the proposed works and the embryo LUP was ready for field checking (Fig 3).

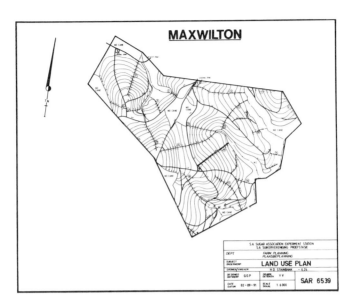

Fig 3. Terrace banks, grassed waterways and extraction roads form the framework of the Land Use Plan.

Modification by field checking

The farmer was visited to check the proposed plan on the ground. The need to modify the plan with the farmer's own preferences was discussed. The principles to be applied in the plan, such as strip planting, reduced or minimum tillage replanting, trashing or burning at harvest and watercourse, stream bank and wetland protection were outlined. Many waterways and watercourses had been repaired since they were damaged by floods that occurred before the current owner purchased the farm. Much of the repair work had been completed with material from the farm. A record was then made of crop and field details and all existing farm operations with the equipment available so that an assessment could be made and recommendations given for any changes that were needed.

Field Details: Existing field boundaries were marked clearly with a dark pen on a quota map. Many fields had terraces and waterways within the field boundary, which may be suitable for inclusion in the final plan. The current estimated replanting programme was recorded and was used as the starting point for the new programme. Where the field information was available details were noted on a copy of the quota map. Where no record was available the grower gave a subjective value to the crop in the existing field. Fields were graded into the current year's harvest with an estimated cane age or those fields which would be cut the following season. These two sets were then split into three categories: good, moderate or bad, depending on the crop condition. As most plans entail reshaping field boundaries this information is essential to ensure that any changes do not radically affect cash flows or predicted estimates. This was needed for the later stages of planning when implementation programmes were set.

Objectives and targets.

On this farm most of the production area was situated on the crest and hill sides where expected yields were similar. There was no valley bottom cane. The estimated annual crop to be cut from this section of the combined farms is about 12 000 tons. The daily ratable delivery (DRD) is close to 85 tons/day. With an estimated yield of 43 tons/ha/annum a field of five to six hectares would provide cane for harvesting for about three days. The target size for the fields was set at five hectares.

New field boundaries.

The roads and terraces of the LUP set the framework for the new fields. New field boundaries are shown on Fig 4. These fields are much longer and narrower than the existing fields and are designed to provide strips of crop at different ages across the hill sides. Diagonal extraction roads and other access roads are used to give strategic breaks to fields. The high erodibility of the soils on these farms make it necessary to apply minimum tillage replanting techniques.

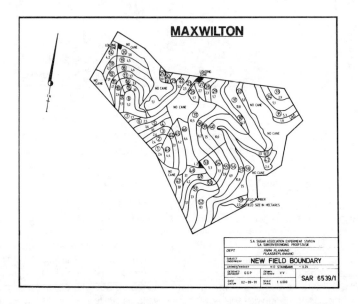

*Fig 4. After the basic Land Use Plan has been prepared horizontal panels
are combined into suitable new field shapes.*

Assessment of systems.

The new field layout system provides much greater protection for the soil. As there are more roads and terraces in the proposal, a check is needed to evaluate the efficiency of the new fields and the loss of ground due to the extra roads. Both manual and mechanical work are improved if average row lengths are increased, as most field operations follow the row. Existing and proposed row lengths in the fields are measured and compared to see if the new fields give a greater row length and hence better efficiency. The Field Machinery Index

(FMI) is a measure related to row length and shows the production time as a ratio to total time (production time plus turning time) for a specific field (Murray and Meyer, 1982). This index is adjusted by a weighting factor based on field size. The sum of these weighted values gives the FMI for the layout system in question.

Table 1. Summary of changes in field efficiency with changing row lengths.

Field Machinery Index (FMI) $= P / P + T$

P = Production time ($=$ ave row length / speed)   T = Turning time
Speed = 135 m/min   Turning time = 1.25 min

Field No.	Area (ha)	Row length (m)	FMI	FMI x Area	Field No.	Area (ha)	Row length (m)	FMI	FMI x Area
11	1.5	60	0.26	0.39	1	2.2	180	0.52	1.144
12	2.4	120	0.42	1.008	2	1.6	210	0.55	0.88
602	0.7	48	0.22	0.154	66	1.7	300	0.64	1.088
604	1.4	240	0.59	0.826	67	2.2	450	0.72	1.584

Ave row length =   156   423
Ave FMI =   0.51   0.72
Improvements % = Proposed $-$ Existing / Existing x 100 = 42%

Existing cane haulage system: Fig 1 also shows the position of the loading zones currently used. At present all cane is burnt before harvest, cut by hand and stacked into 4.5 ton bundles. Chained bundles are loaded into a contractor's road haulage vehicle by communal cranes over a 24 hour period for transport to the mill. Cane is transported from "Elsinore" and "Hope Valley" to Zone 48. "Maxwilton" cane goes to Zone 107. Both zones are outside the property boundaries. One 58kW 2WD tractor/double stack, walking beam, self loading trailer and one 45kW 2WD tractor/single stack self loading trailer are used. The routes used to transport cane to the loading zones were measured on the map and yields estimated for each field. The product of these two items is expressed as ton.kilometres or the effort required to move cane over the actual distance. The sum of all the products gives a measure of the effort needed to move cane over the existing road infrastructure.

Table 2. Existing infield cane haulage distances.

Estate	Total area (ha)	Annual tons	Zone No.	Average kms
Elsinore	157.9	6 187	48	2.48
Hope Valley	38.0	1 489	48	6.29
Maxwilton	250.7	9 824	107	3.51
Total	446.6	17 500		

Proposed cane haulage systems: After examining the topographic map additional loading sites are possible at the positions shown on Fig 2.

Option 1: Cane loads of 9.0 tons from the various farms to be transported to the nearest of four new loading zones (1, 2, 3, 4). A 58kW 2WD tractor/double stack self loading trailer combination is used. The grower's Mobemech crane is used to load contractor's road haulage vehicles over 24 hours.

Option 2: Cane from "Elsinore" is transported to Zone 4, cane from "Hope Valley" and "Maxwilton" is sent to Zone 1. One 58 kW 2WD tractor/double stack self loading trailer hauls cane to both zones. The grower's Mobamech crane loads the contractor's road vehicles over a 24 hour period.

Table 3. Field to loading zone transport efficiency.

Grower: HD Stainbank   Farms: Elsinore, Hope Valley and Maxwilton

Field No.	Size (ha)	Existing route				Option 1				Option 2			
		Zone No.	Dist (km)	Total tons	Total t/km	Zone No.	Dist (km)	Total tons	Total t/km	Zone No.	Dist (km)	Total tons	Total t/km
1	2.8	48	2.52	110	276	4	0.90	110	99	4	0.90	110	99
2	5.6	48	2.46	219	540	4	0.84	219	184	4	0.84	219	184
264	4.0	107	4.20	157	658	2	0.84	157	132	1	2.10	157	329
265	4.0	107	4.20	157	658	2	0.84	157	132	1	1.20	157	329
266	1.6	107	3.96	63	248	2	0.60	63	38	1	1.86	63	117
Totals:	447			17 500	59 167			17 500	16 192			17 500	24 114
Ave infield haul:			3.38				0.93				1.38		

The implementation of options 1 and 2 would substantially reduce cane transport cost. A reduction of around 50% of infield distance is expected by re-siting loading zones as seen in Table 3. Transloading and road haulage costs from zones to the mill will increase in both options. The increase in relation to the overall main road costs is small and is outweighed by the large saving in field to zone costs. Option 1 is slightly more favourable than option 2 (see Table 4).

Table 4. Estimated total annual haulage costs.

	Total annual cost (Rand)					
Operation	Existing		Option 1		Option 2	
Infield haulage						
9.0 ton unit	R63.15/h	51 467	R64.69/h	55 245	R59.70/h	60 416
4.5 ton unit	R49.39/h	40 895				
Transloading	R 1.60/t	28 000	R 1.97/t	34 475	R 1.97/t	34 475
Road haulage						
Zone 48	R11.14/t	85 511				
Zone 107	R11.89/t	116 807				
Zone 1			R12.30/t	54 661	R12.30/t	139 150
Zone 2			R12.54/t	65 747		
Zone 3			R12.46/t	20 260		
Zone 4			R11.43/t	70 717	R11.43/t	70 717
Total		322 680		301 105		304 758

Implementation.

Once the benefits of the plan have been assessed, the field works must be implemented to achieve any real savings. The longevity of the crop and the difficulties that arise in estimating and recording results for analysis, when existing field boundaries are changed, often results in confusion. A planned implementation programme is essential for a smooth transition to new field numbers.

Field rating: A transparent overlay of the proposed new fields is placed on top of the existing quota map with the highlighted boundaries. The state of the existing crop and the proposed replanting programme as recorded on the farm visit are used to determine where work can be started. In harvested fields, waterways and terrace roads can be marked or partly built. Diagonal extraction roads which may be needed for improvements to the haulage routes can be treated in the same way. For the areas to be replanted new works can be pegged, marked and partly built. The list of fields, ie. good, moderate and poor producers, is examined on the map and the poor yielding fields are put at the top of the list if they are to be harvested in the current season. With the target amount of replant estimated, the possible areas which can be replanted within the budget are marked. A check must be made on the amount of new cane needed to keep the cutting cycle balanced. Fields or portions of fields were selected to achieve the new boundary structure and were allocated new field numbers. In some cases it was necessary to look at the state and quality of a field adjacent to a poor field to see if portions of both could be combined to create a new field. Some fields of mixed ratoons resulted. This will be rectified at the next replant time. Although the life of individual fields is probably more than ten years there is no need to wait that long to achieve full implementation. By prudent selection of areas to be replanted and harvested the new plan can be implemented in two to three years.

CONCLUSIONS

Using a logical step-by-step approach to the preparation of a land use plan ensured that all aspects of protection and production were covered. Based on the topography and the soil type of this farm, a network of water control roads was used to develop a field layout system for best protection and optimum production. Crop management techniques were included in the selection of a suitable field layout. The layout provides long, relatively narrow fields of cane of differing age, across the hill side slopes. An analysis of the measured distances to loading sites, positioning of loading zones and diagonal extraction roads, combined with equipment requirements, showed the best haulage method and equipment for this farm. The implementation method necessitates a change in the field numbering system but the change-over period need not be longer than two to three seasons.

REFERENCES

1.   Beater, BE (1957). Soils of the sugar belt. Parts 1, 2, 3. Oxford Univ Press.

2.   Dent, MC (1982). The nomograph — an effective aid to agricultural extension. *Agric eng in SA* Vol 16: 45-49.

3.   Haywood, RW (1987). Rainfall simulator programme. *Proc S Afr Sug Technol Ass* 61: 147-149.

4.   Murray, TJ and Meyer, E (1982). Time study as a method for measuring machinery performance. *Proc S Afr Sug Technol Ass* 56: 153-156.

5.   Platford, GG (1985). The small catchment project at La Mercy. *Proc S Afr Sug Technol Ass* 59: 152-160.

6.   Platford, GG (1987). A new approach to designing widths of panels in sugarcane fields. *Proc S Afr Sug Technol Ass* 61: 150-156.

7.   Wischmeier, WH and Smith, DD (1963). Predicting rainfall losses — a guide to conservation planning. US Dept of Agric Handbook 537.

TWELVE YEARS OF ABANDONED MINELAND RECLAMATION ACTIVITIES BY THE UNITED STATES DEPARTMENT OF AGRICULTURE - SOIL CONSERVATION SERVICE IN SOUTHWEST PENNSYLVANIA

Wayne M. Bogovich, P.E.
Member ASAE

One sixth of all abandoned coal mine land in the United States is in the twelve southwestern counties of Pennsylvania. The Surface Mining Control Act of 1977 established several programs to reclaim abandoned coal mined land. One of these programs is the Rural Abandoned Mine Program (RAMP). Under the Act, a surcharge of 15¢ per ton for deep mined coal and 35¢ per ton for strip mined coal is assessed and put into a fund. The Rural Abandoned Mine Program (RAMP)is administered by the United States Department of Agriculture - Soil Conservation Service (USDA-SCS) and can receive up to twenty percent of that fund. This program is a voluntary program.

Sites reclaimed to date have all been "Priority 1 Sites". SCS defines priority 1 sites as those which present an imminent danger to life and property. These sites include but are not limited to problems such as: hazardous highwalls next to populated areas, burning spoil piles, open mine shafts, coke ovens, etc.

136 sites totaling 1137 acres (460 hectares) have been reclaimed in the twelve counties of southwestern Pennsylvania over the last 12 years. These counties are:

COUNTY	ABBREVIATION
Allegheny	ALL
Armstrong	ARM
Beaver	BEA
Bedford	BED
Cambria	CAM
Fayette	FAY
Greene	GRE
Huntingdon	HUN
Indiana	IND
Somerset	SOM
Washington	WAS
Westmoreland	WES

WAYNE M. BOGOVICH, Area Engineer, Area III, USDA-SCS, Somerset Area Office, Somerset, Pennsylvania

Figure 1 shows USDA-SCS Area III

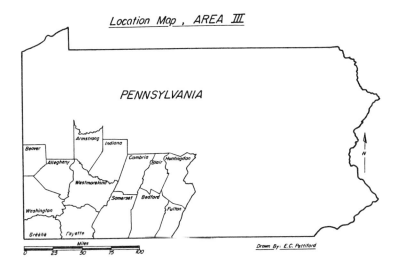

Figure 1

Figure 2 shows the distribution of area reclaimed by county.

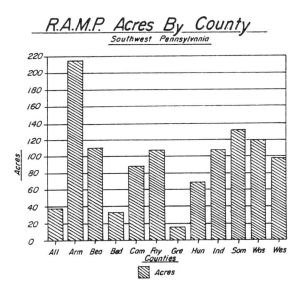

Figure 2

231

VEGETATION

One of the biggest problems associated with black gob piles
is that they are sometimes toxic to vegetation. Many
contain high concentrations of aluminum and manganese.
Agricultural limestone is incorporated to reach a pH of 7.0,
so that toxic aluminum and manganese are made insoluble.
Experience has shown two other reasons vegetation does not
grow on black piles.

First, the black surface temperature approaches 200° degrees
fahrenheit (93 degrees celsius) when the material is exposed
to the sun. These high temperatures create a micro-
environment that is hostile to seed germination and seedling
growth. The solution is 100 percent mulch cover during the
seeding operation. Hay at four tons per acre (9,000 Kg per
hectare) or straw at three tons per acre (6,700 Kg per
hectare) will accomplish this.

Mulch is anchored by: non-toxic asphalt emulsion applied at
the rate of 150 gallons per acre (1,400 liters per hectare);
by non-asphaltic emulsion of natural vegetable gum blended
with gelling and hardening agents applied at one and one
half times the manufacturer's rate; by cutting using a
straight blade disc; or by cross tracking using a track
machine.

Second is mechanical action of the surface material. Gob
piles are very steep and often exceed the angle of repose of
the material. Many piles are adjacent to streams and are
subject to erosive forces of the water causing the pile to
be undercut thus making the pile steeper. We have found
that grading the pile to a 2 to 1 slope or flatter and the
addition of surface water control practices can greatly
reduce this mechanical action. Streambank stabilization
measures such as rock riprap are used resist the erosive
forces of the water at the toe of the slope.

A soil covering has been used on only 2 of the 136 sites
reclaimed. These were all 10 acres (4 hectares) of the West
Carroll Township site in Cambria County and 1 of the 33
acres (13.4 hectares) of the Vintondale Site in Cambria
County. This soil covering material was actually subsoil
with a Unified soil classification of GM, GC, SM, SC, ML,
MH, CL or CH. Sites where soil covering was used had
excessive levels of aluminum and manganese.

All sites have soil samples taken and sent to the Merkel
Laboratory at The Pennsylvania State University. Sites have
agricultural limestone and fertilizer applied at the
recommended rates from the lab. Limestone recommendations
are for a target pH of 7.0.

During the seeding process, all the limestone and half the
fertilizer is incorporated to a specified depth of six
inches to eighteen inches (46 centimeters). Depths are
determined by the heavy metal content of the mine soil.
Aluminum and manganese are common toxic elements to plant
growth in southwestern Pennsylvania. The target pH of 7.0
makes these elements insoluble; therefore they cannot be
taken up by the plants.

Typical seeding rate per acre (hectare) is:

Mixture

Tall Fescue (Festuca Arundinacea) Variety - Kentucky 31	10 Pounds (4.5 kg)
Deertongue (Panucum Clandestinum) Variety - Tioga	15 Pounds (6.8 kg)
Birdsfoot Trefoil (Lotus Corniculatis) Variety - Empire	10 Pounds (4.5 kg)

When the post reclamation land use is pasture, orchardgrass, bromegrass and timothy are substituted in the mixture for the deertongue.

When the post reclamation land use is wildlife, fescue is limited to areas where water is concentrated because of the endophytic, seed borne, fungal infection that decreases the rate of survival, growth and development in insects, birds and mammals.

Purity, ready germination, hard seed and total germination minimums are specified in The Penn State Agronomy Guide.

Warm season grasses other than deertongue are not widely used for two reasons:

They are difficult to establish. Growth of vegetation is needed as quickly as possible for erosion and sedimentation control.

Warm season grasses have not done as well as the cool season grasses especially at elevations greater than 1000 feet (305 meters).

TREES AND SHRUBS

Black locust and arnot bristly locust have been propogated on sites from seed during the vegetation phase of reclamation. Virginia pine from seed was tried on the Coral Graceton project in 1990 and was a complete failure.

EROSION AND SEDIMENTATION PRACTICES

During construction, both temporary and permanent measures for the control of erosion and sedimentation are installed. These practices include, but are not limited to: straw bale barriers, filter fabric fence, sediment basins and rock filter dams. Additional surface water control measures are integral parts of the erosion and sedimentation system.

SURFACE WATER CONTROL PRACTICES

Prior to reclamation, many sites reclaimed had high
quantities of sediment leaving the site. It was not unusual
to have a calculated soil loss in excess of 100 tons per
acre (225,000 kg per hectare). Surface water control
practices are used on sites to stabilize the soil material
and reduce the amount of gulley erosion. The amount of
sediment leaving the site is significantly reduced.

Several practices commonly used to control surface water
include:

Diversions

A diversion is a channel with a supporting ridge on the
lower side constructed across the slope (figure 3).

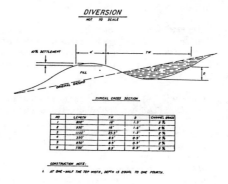

Figure 3

Vegetated Waterways

Vegetated waterways are natural or constructed channels
shaped or graded to required dimensions, including
suitable vegetation for stable conveyance of runoff
(figure 4). The most common use of this practice is as
an outlet for a diversion.

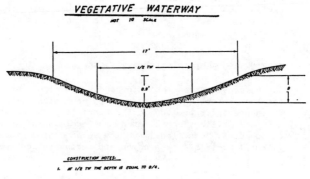

Figure 4

Rock Lined Waterways

Rock lined waterways are used when: storm flows exceed
the allowable velocity for the particular soil with
vegetation; prolonged flows are anticipated; and in wet
areas. A gravel bedding or filter fabric is commonly
used under the rock to prevent erosion of the
underlying soil (figure 5).

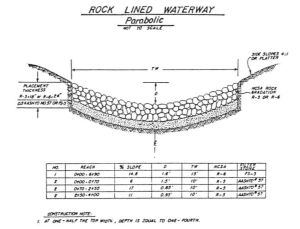

ROCK LINED WATERWAY
Parabolic
NOT TO SCALE

NO.	REACH	% SLOPE	D	TW	NCSA	FILTER STONE
1	0+00 - 6+90	14.8	1.6'	15'	R-6	FS-3
2	0+00 - 0+70	6	1.5'	10'	R-5	AASHTO #57
2	0+70 - 2+50	17	0.83'	10'	R-5	AASHTO #57
2	2+50 - 4+00	11	0.95'	10'	R-5	AASHTO #57

CONSTRUCTION NOTE:
1. AT ONE-HALF THE TOP WIDTH, DEPTH IS EQUAL TO ONE-FOURTH.

Figure 5

AIRSHAFTS AND MINE OPENINGS

Two of the biggest hazards to human life are mine openings
and airshafts. Many discharge water and some discharge air
with less than 19% free oxygen.

183 openings have been closed to prevent access. 168 of
these were mine openings and the remaining 15 were
airshafts.

Openings can be classified into four groups.

1. Horizontal - no discharge

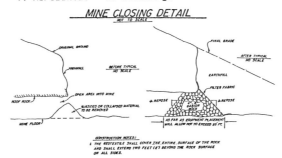

MINE CLOSING DETAIL
NOT TO SCALE

CONSTRUCTION NOTES:
1. THE GEOTEXTILE SHALL COVER THE ENTIRE SURFACE OF THE ROCK
AND SHALL EXTEND TWO FEET (2') BEYOND THE ROCK SURFACE
ON ALL SIDES.

Figure 6

2. Horizontal - discharge

P.V.C. Pipe Drain

NOT TO SCALE

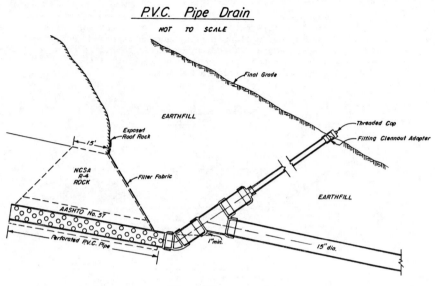

Figure 7

3. Vertical - no discharge

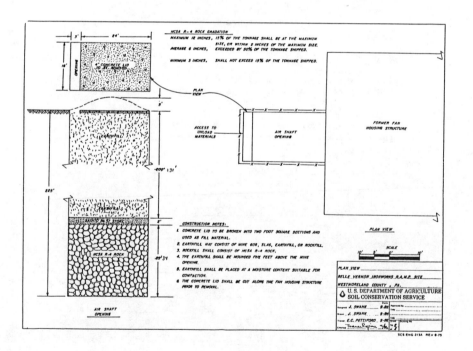

Figure 8

4. Vertical - discharge

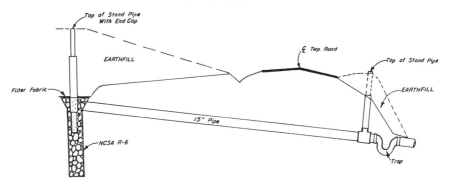

15" P.V.C. Pipe Installation

NOT TO SCALE

Figure 9

COKE OVENS

Stabilization of these would consist of collapsing the coke
oven and grading the material. The land form is graded
smooth to match the surrounding topography (figure 9).

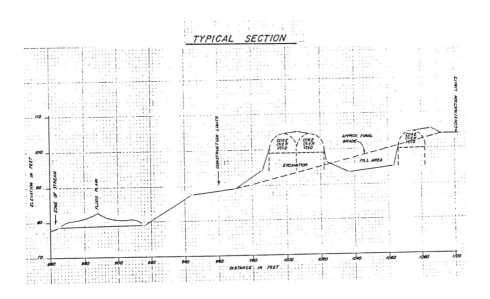

TYPICAL SECTION

Figure 10

237

TREATMENT OF ACID MINE DRAINAGE

Many sites reclaimed to date have had acid mine drainage
problems.   USDA-SCS has installed constructed wetlands on
11 sites. Monitoring and evaluation studies are being
conducted. These sites are:

1. Allegheny R. M.	Armstrong County
2. Spachtholtz	Armstrong County
3. Cottagetown	Somerset County
4. Keystone Lake	Armstrong County
5. Cedar Grove	Washington County
6. Thomas	Bedford County
7. Eichelberger	Bedford County
8. Crespo	Beaver County
9. Miner	Fayette County
10. Brooks	Indiana County
11. Zundel	Westmoreland County

The average time from initial inventory to actual
construction is approximately three years. Because of this
time delay, constructed wetland designs may not reflect the
most recent technology at the time of their construction.

In June 1989, USDA-SCS entered into an interagency agreement
with the United States Department of the Interior - Bureau
of Mines (U.S. Bureau of Mines) to develop water assessment
and design parameters for constructed wetlands.
Specifically, USDA-SCS worked with The Environmental
Technology Group of the U.S. Bureau of Mines in Pittsburgh,
Pennsylvania which provided analytical and data
interpretation services. Analysis run included: flow
measurement, pH, acidity/alkalinity, sulfate, total iron,
ferrous iron, manganese, aluminum, sodium, calcium and
magnesium. Samples were taken from inflow and outflow pipes
once a month with additional samples taken from within the
constructed wetland. The U.S. Bureau of Mines Scientists
have interpreted the data and used it in presentations and
papers that discuss the performance of constructed wetlands.

COSTS

The average total cost of reclamation is approximately
$9,500 per acre.

USDA-SCS Programs

All programs and services of the U.S. Department of
Agriculture, Soil Conservation Service, are offered on a
nondiscriminatory basis without regard to race, color,
national origin, religion, sex, age, marital status, or
handicap.

REFERENCES

1. Dove J L (1983) Reclamation of Abandoned Mines in West Virginia, ASAE 83-2032.

2. Hedin R S and Nairn R W (1990) Sizing and Performance of Constructed Wetlands: Case Studies. Preseedings, Mining and Reclamation Conference, Charlestown, WV. pp. 385-392

3. Madej C W, Clay K (1991) Avian seed preference and weight loss experiments: the effect of fungal endophyte-infected tall fescue seeds. Occologia 88:296-302.

4. Pettiford E C (1992) Standard Typical Drawings for the RAMP Program in Area III of Pennsylvania.

5. Soil and Water Conservation - Pennsylvania Technical Guide, January 1992.

6. USDA-Soil Conservation Service, Engineering Field Handbook, Third Edition with revisions, June 1975.

DEVELOPING A FLOODPLAIN SAND AND GRAVEL MINE RECLAMATION

PROGRAM IN THE AMITE RIVER BASIN OF LOUISIANA

Robert D. Vernon*   Whitney J. Autin*   Joann Mossa*
District Conservationist   Research Geologist   Assistant Professor

The impact of floodplain mining of sand and gravel has been identified as a contributing cause to modern flooding in the Amite River basin of Southeastern Louisiana (Mossa 1983, 1985). Changes in land use in areas of active sand and gravel mining coincide with basin-wide land use changes associated with urban growth, forest management, and agricultural activity. Modern land use changes have induced adverse environmental impacts to the riverine system through alteration of the natural landscape and surface water hydrology. The complexity of these changes and their effect on the basin necessitate a management approach to set priorities and direction for the assessment of present problems and to produce a plan to direct future use of the basin's resources. This paper attempts to address this issue by 1) documentation of the human influences on channel and flood plain modification in the Amite River, 2) outlining possible management alternatives for enhancement of the flood plain environment and future utilization of flood plain resources, and 3) suggesting policy recommendations for the implementation of mine reclamation and associated land use management strategies.

PHYSICAL SETTING

The Amite River basin in southeastern Louisiana and southwestern Mississippi drains about 5200 square kilometers. Its headwaters occur at an elevation of approximately 150 meters . The Amite River is about 270 kilometers long with the the Comite River and Bayou Manchac being the major tributaries. Baton Rouge and Denham Springs constitute the primary urban area in the basin (Fig. 1 Inset).

The climate of the Amite River basin is humid subtropical. Annual precipitation in the basin averages approximately 150 centimeters, but ranges from under 100 to over 200 centimeters. Flood-producing rains may occur during any month of the year and storms of large magnitude and long duration are common. During a two to three day storm, 25 centimeters or more of rainfall can be produced within 24 hours. During the winter and spring, the lack of storage potential in the soil can cause flooding to be more pronounced. Recent floods occurred in the lower basin in 1977, 1979 and 1983.

Water is supplied to the Amite River channel by numerous upland tributaries and multiple abandoned stream courses in the flood plain. Base flow constitutes only a minor portion of the hydrograph, ranging from rarely less than 6.0 m^3/s and rarely more the 56 m^3/s. The 1983 Flood of Record had a peak dishcarge of 3,171.5 m^3/s at the Denham Springs gauge. The peaks are caused by surface runoff from rainfall, which primarily occurs during thunderstorms. Discharge commonly peaks within one day following a storm and generally takes longer to crest and fall to

*ROBERT D. VERNON, District Conservationist, U.S.D.A. Soil Conservation Service, Denham Springs, Louisiana. 70727

*WHITNEY J. AUTIN, Research Geologist, Louisiana Geological Survey, Louisiana State University, Baton Rouge, Louisiana. 70893

*JOANN MOSSA, Assistant Professor, Department of Geography, University of Florida, Gainsville, Florida. 32611

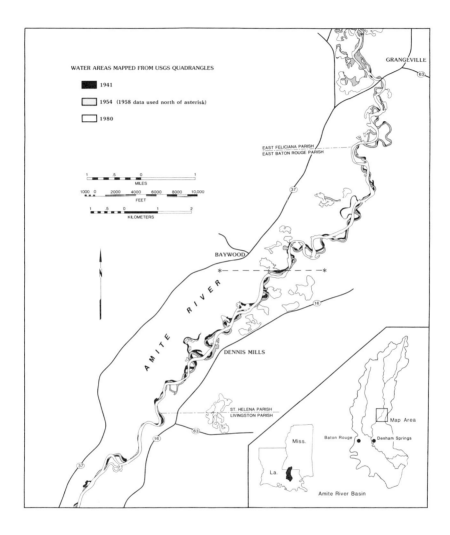

Figure 1. Historic channel positions of the middle Amite River show changes in the meander and channel geometry and an overall decrease in sinuosity through time. Inset shows location of the Amite River basin.

pre-flood levels at down stream stations. Within two to four days, discharge typically falls to pre-flood levels. Tributaries on the downstream end of the valley are sometimes affected by backwater during floods.

Land use changes and steam channelization projects have been implemented concurrent with and prior to sand and gravel mining activity. Growth in the Amite River basin has resulted in a land use pattern of mining areas, managed forests, pasture, and developed communities. A substantial part of the presently active steam channel developed since the initial period of historic European settlement in Louisiana (since ca. 1720). Prior to modern human settlement in the Amite River basin, the region consisted primarily of mixed deciduous and evergreen forests with small scattered areas of native prairie.

The Louisiana Department of Natural Resources, Office of Conservation estimates that 4,326 hectares have been disturbed within the Amite River basin, primarily by sand a gravel mining. These changes in land use have coincided with modification of channel locations, dimensions, and geometry along with the diversion of runoff. It is likely that this process has affected stormwater runoff rates, patterns, and flooding in the Amite basin (Mossa, 1983).

ECONOMICS

Sand and gravel is a major building material vital to the economic growth of the State of Louisiana. Sand and gravel producers have a substantial economic impact upon the local economy. An estimated 53 to 57 hectares are mined annually along the Amite River, providing in excess of 2,721,000 mectric tons of sand and gravel to the market. Income derived from sand and gravel production activities is estimated at $11,000,000, and is taxed at varying rates after deductions. Severance taxes are estimated to be approximately $200,000. Sales taxes on purchases to support local activities are in excess of $2,000,000 (Amite River Sand and Gravel Committe, 1992).

EEFECTS OF FLOOD PLAIN MINING ON FLOOD PROCESSES

Several mining practices affect the channel and floodplain morphology and processes. Before excavating a pit, vegetation is removed from the floodplain. The fine-grained surface sediment or overburden is scraped with a bulldozer and sold as topsoil. Generally, the coarse material beneath the overburden is saturated, causing water to slowly fill the pit. Hydraulic dredges are placed in the ponds to extract a sediment-water mixture. Some ponds are highly turbid because of stirring by dredges, failure of pit walls, and the return of fine sediment to the pond after sorting.

The sediment-water mixture is sorted into various size fractions. Gravel is generally sold and transported away. Tailings piles and fans consisting principally of sand are constructed in the sorting process. They remain unvegetated for years and are left standing on the floodplain because gravel is the more valuable commodity.

In pits on the lower floodplain, suspended sediment may be released in the channel if the levee or buffer between the turbid ponds and channel is breached. Mining activities also augment the potential for indirect modifications during floods. Part or all of the flow could be diverted during high flows because the ponds and pits on the lower floodplain become inundated during high discharge.

Hydraulic mining of floodplains has been associated with the degradation of channel pattern stability. Preliminary measurements and analysis (Mossa, 1983, 1985) suggests that the Amite River has shortened its channel length in the area of concentrated sand and gravel flood plain mining. It was theorized that channel shortening could have an adverse impact on downstream flooding (Fig.1).

In the Amite River, a stable channel pattern has mostly symmetrical bends separated by relatively short straight reaches between bends. The cross sectional geometry and channel slope should should also remain relatively constant over time. Mossa (1983, 1985) indicated that the channel section from slightly above Grangeville to the Magnolia Bridge crossing decreased in channel bend size and shortening of channel length from 1941 to 1980. Channel length decreased from 24.9 to 17.7 kilometers (30%) in the sand and gravel mining area of the Amite River.

242

Changes in channel morphology have been observed since the initiation of floodplain gravel mining in the Amite River in southeastern Louisiana. Some changes are due to indirect effects of gravel mining, after floodwaters have reworked the alluvial deposits. Removal of riparian vegetation and mining of point bars reduce the resistance of river banks to erosion during floods. Also, during high stages, breaching and channel diversion into adjacent gravel pits may occur, especially where banks are not stabilized by vegetation. This results in a local change in base level, which influences aggradation and degradation patterns. Through these processes, channel pattern and meander geometry have been altered significantly after major floods (Mossa, 1983).

A sensitivity analysis was performed by the Hydraulics Division of the U.S. Army Corps of Engineers, New Orleans District to estimate the impact of channel shortening on Amite River flood stages (Amite River Sand and Gravel Committee, 1992). The sensitivity analysis predicted flood stages based on arbitrary changes in channel length as input into a computer model. The U.S. Army Corps of Engineers had channel cross sections only for the period 1982-1985, so no analysis of changes in channel form were conducted. The sensitivity analysis suggested that a 20 per cent reduction in channel length for the Grangeville to Magnolia reach could produce a stage increase at Denham Springs of 15.2 to 24.4 centimeters without considering likely changes in channel cross section through the reach. The analysis suggested that the response outlined by Mossa (1983, 1985) can produce a measurable effect on flood stage. Although the sensitivity analysis produces generalized conclusions, an actual lowering of flood levels by 15.2 to 24.4 centimeters could produce a substantial reduction in flood damages. For a 100-year flood event, a stage reduction of 24.4 centimeters at the Denham Springs Gauge would result in a cost savings of approximately $5-million in reduced property damages (based on U.S. Army Corps of Engineers estimate). The results of the sensitivity analysis are included in table 1.

Table 1. Amite River Channel Length Change Effects on Stages at Denham Springs, Louisiana[a]

Flood Event	Exisiting Condition	20% Increase	20% Decrease
10yr	11.83	11.61	11.98
50yr	12.98	12.77	13.14
100yr	13.26	13.01	13.41

a Stages for existing conditions and changing channel lengths are in meters above mean sea level

The precise measuring techniques, boundaries of the channel reach, and time period of channel change measurement differed between Mossa's reports and the sensitivity analysis. Historic 1940 aerial photographs on file at the Louisiana State University, Department of Geography Map Library, were compared with current high altitude infrared photography (1981-1983) on file at the Soil Conservation Service office in Denham Springs. Channel length measurements from the Grangeville bridge to the Magnolia bridge showed a reduction in channel length from 43.85 kilometers in 1940 to 39.27 kilometers in 1981-83, or a reduction of 4.58 kilometers (about 10 per cent reduction). The most dramatic reductions in length occurred in the reach of intensive sand and gravel mining. Comparison of the aerial photographs suggests that the channel length decreased due to the shortening of individual meanders as floodplain mining progressed in the Amite River basin.

RECLAMATION ISSUES

Present methods of sand and gravel extraction in the the Amite River produce substantial areas of open water, mine tailing piles of barren and sterile sand, and areas sparsely vegetated by scrub and pioneer plant species. This process contributes to reduction in wildlife habitat, degradation of the stream and flood plain environment, and aggravation of existing flooding problems. Reclamation of mine lands could help to minimize these adverse impacts.

Although recognition of the adverse effects of floodplain mining is still in the early stages, practices causing the most severe environmental damage should be minimized. Removal of riparian vegetation and the mining of point bars and channel bottoms should be avoided, and buffer zones next to the channel should be established.

Implementation of a reclamation program can be costly. Estimates vary, but if extensive restoration is required, costs could exceed $800 per hectare. Low cost reclamation can be accomplished in some areas by natural vegetative succession, a process that could take long time periods (decades or longer). Actual reclamation costs depend on the procedure adopted and projected post mining land use. However, use of best management practices and wise pre-planning of mining operations can help to minimize actual reclamation costs.

Abandoned mine reclamation requires a new dimension in problem solving. Most of the land in the Amite basin was mined under lease agreements between private landowners and gravel mining companies. The resources have been extracted and the leases have expired thus leaving the abandoned mines in the hands of the private landowners. Reclamation of land mined for sand and gravel is not required and rarely practiced in Louisiana. The only mining activities that are presently regulated are those that directly affect water quality.

The cost of reclamation of future mining areas needs to be incorporated into the production and\or taxation of sand and gravel resources. However, mine reclamation legislation and the development of State rules and regulations should consider the implications of reclamation costs.

Reclamation regulations are essential to protect river channel stability in areas that have not been mined. In the Amite River basin over 4,300 hectares have been disturbed by mining with the great majority still in an unreclaimed condition. The Amite River needs an active management plan to restore previously mined land if a reduction in flood levels is ever to be realized.

Presently active and abandoned sand and gravel mines located on lands leased by mining companies require sources of funding or planning assistance from governmental programs. Abandoned mine lands typically revert back to private ownership, but most have not been converted to a planned post mining land use. Programs structured towards assisting landowners in development of future land use alternatives and application of best management practices subsequent to mine reclamation are the most optimistic alternatives.

Government agencies that may be well equipped to enforce reclamation regulations on newly mined land may be limited when it comes to implementing a program on abandoned mine lands. The participation of all agencies that can assist in the development of reclamation practices and the development of best management practices is essential.

The U.S. Department of Interior, Office of Conservation and the U.S.D.A. Soil Conservation Service have a cooperative Rural Abandoned Mine Program (RAMP) designed to fund the reclamation of abandoned coal mines. Coal mined in Louisiana is assessed a fee to fund this program,however, Louisiana has no abandoned coal mines. The program has provisions for reclaiming other types of surface mines once the coal mines have been reclaimed. The Louisiana Department of Natural Resources should coordinate with the Soil Conservation Service, and appropriate local agencies to pursue an active, Federally funded program that addresses abandoned sand and gravel mines..

Management should also encourage the sand and gravel industry to provide planning input to balance various local and regional, short - and long-term goals. Information regarding resource distribution should be provided to concentrate mining in preferable locations. Guidance and recommendations to facilitate reclamation should be given at the local and state level. The continued availability of resources depends upon the cooperation of the industry, whose input in decision-making and issues is important to balancing adverse economic and environmental interests.

Minimal environmental damage and additional land use benefits are achieved with reclamation, which is particularly important near river channels where sediments and talus piles may be reworked in subsequent floods. These efforts are most successful if they are integrated into the total mining operation from the beginning and directed toward a desired post-mining land use (Dunn, 1982). Although this has not been the case in Louisiana, remaining landscapes can be left in a stabilized, nonhazardous, and useful condition if some planning measures are taken.

Once a river has changed its channel pattern and form, problems become much more difficult to address. Whether reclamation should go beyond sculpturing and revegetating the floodplain and attempt to restore the previous channel character is a question that requires consideration. Although time will probably allow the Amite River to restore itself, little is known about how rapid or effective these changes will be. Aggravated flood conditions could persist for years and intensify if unregulated mining continues. Establishing management guidelines prior to intensive mining is the better approach to minimizing environmental impacts.

A regional land use plan has not yet been developed for the Amite River basin. A basin-wide master land use plan is needed that includes development and design standards for best management practices for reclamation and/or impact mitigation of currently and previously mined lands. Use of best management practices and wise pre-planning of mining operations can help to minimize actual reclamation costs. Regulations should be implemented that are compatible with best management practices for reclamation of lands currently and previously mined for sand, gravel, and construction fill as defined for the Amite River basin. Agencies that can define best management practices and stimulate wise use of reclaimed land are the U.S.D.A. Soil Conservation Service, the U.S. Army Corps of Engineers, the Louisiana Department of Natural Resources, the Louisiana Department of Agriculture and Forestry, and the Louisiana Department of Environmental Quality.

CONCLUSIONS AND RECOMMENDATIONS

The magnitude of the impacts of sand and gravel mining on channel and flood plain stability are poorly understood and inconclusive. The potential effects of flood plain mining, mine reclamation, and future flood control projects on stream channel behavior needs to be assessed.

Additional data is needed to determine how turbidity relates to stream discharge and sediment transport in the Amite River. The effect of mining on turbidity needs to be empirically assessed to estimate the effectiveness of reclamation and/or best management practices to minimize sediment load in the stream.

Federal, State, and Local government should coordinate to implement a pilot revegetation program in an abandoned mining area in the Amite River basin to test the potential for mitigation in the Amite River basin.

A basin-wide master land use plan is needed for the Amite River basin that includes development and design standards for best management practices for reclamation of currently and previously mined lands.

Louisiana does not have a regulatory program directed towards the reclamation of sand and gravel mines. The State should adopt legislation to establish a noncoal surface mine reclamation program. Regulations should be implemented that are compatible with best management practices for reclamation of lands currently and previously mined for sand, gravel, and construction fill as defined for the Amite River basin.

REFERENCES

Amite River Sand and Gravel Committe. Final Report to Governor's Interagency Task Force on Flood Prevention and Mitigation. 1992. p 7, 22.

Dunn, J. "COSMAR (Committee on Surface Mining and Reclamation)." Pages 9-12 in P.Y. Amimoto, Ed. Proceedings of Mined Land Reclamation Workshop. Davis, California, June 11-12, 1980. Sacramento: State of California, Department of Conservaion, Division of Mines and Geology, Special Publication 59.

Mossa, J. 1983. Morphologic changes in a segment of the Amite River. Abstracts with Programs, Geological Society of America. 96th Annual Meeting 15: 648.

Mossa, J. 1985.Management of floodplain sand and gravel mining in Flood Hazard Management in Government and the Private Sector: Association of State Floodplain Managers, Natural Hazards Research and Applications Information Center Special Publication 12, p. 321-28.

REGULATIONS VS. RECLAMATION AND RESTORATION

by
Bill F. Schwarzkoph[1]

By 1970, a potential energy shortage became a national issue. Coal was one of the answers to the energy problem. As "Big Coal" began to tie-up leases in western states, citizens became concerned about environ-mental degradation. Surface mining had historically left ugly scars on the land throughout eastern and midwestern states. At Colstrip, Montana, surface mining for coal from 1923 to 1958 left 1,000 acres of land in rows of barren spoil banks. Montana developed initial reclamation regulations in 1973 to stop the ruination of land through surface mining. The Department of State Lands (DSL) Coal Bureau was assigned the responsibility for regulatory authority. When the federal Office of Surface Mining (OSM) was developed in 1979 (Federal Register, 1979), DSL changed their regulations to conform with OSM (MT 1980).

During this same time, researchers were busy developing equipment and methods to reclaim surface mined land in an economical and environmentally compatible manner, (DePuit 1978). After a decade or more of research, good standard reclamation methods had been achieved (Munshower, 1984). Reclamation plans varied from mine to mine dependent on mining methods, location, and corporate commitment to the environment.

At Western Energy Company's (WECO) Rosebud Mine, located in Southeastern Montana, near the town of Colstrip, the major focus of reclamation was rangeland (i.e. grazing land for livestock). Rangeland encompasses a myriad of plant communities which include grasslands, shrub-grassland and pine-savanah grasslands. Interspersed among the rangeland types were small parcels of cropland.

Although one of the main objectives of rangeland reclamation was grazing for livestock, wildlife habitat was also an important consideration. Reclamation plans were developed to reclaim grassland, shrub-grassland, pine-grassland and croplands. They provide good wildlife habitat, especially when interspersed among the undisturbed environment.

In 1983, DSL approved a WECO mine permit with a stipulation to develop a plan to establish elevated and exposed, highly weathered clay (gumbo) knobs.

This type of reclamation plan may not be regarded as a "higher and better use" by some factions. Differences of opinions developed as plans were prepared as to whether a plan of this fashion was <u>reclamation</u> or <u>restoration</u>. Several reclamation rules may actually prohibit the type of work required to accomplish restoration projects. Examples are listed below:

- 26.4.501(3)(a) Backfilled material must be placed to minimize erosion and sedimentation both on and offsite.

- 26.4.501(4)(a) The permitee shall backfill to ensure stability and grade all spoil material to eliminate all spoil piles.

---

[1]Bill F. Schwarzkoph is the Reclamation Superintendent for Western Energy Company, Colstrip, MT 59323.

- 26.702(6) Soil must be redisturbed in uniform thickness.

- 26.4.721(1) When rills deeper than 9" form, the rills must be filled, graded or stabilized and reseeded.

The permit stipulation left WECO in a difficult situation. Strictly adhering to the present rules to meet the obligation would require a different interpretation of the rules mentioned above.

If the result of the project was to imitate as closely as possible, the natural features desired, rules regarding regrading, topsoiling, revegetation cover and production would require new interpretations.

HISTORY

Colstrip was founded in 1923 when coal was mined for use in Northern Pacific railroad locomotives. Mining lasted until 1955 and during this period, 1,000 acres of land was left in rows of spoil banks. WECO reopened the mine in 1968 prior to the development of reclamation rules. Slopes were left at 3:1 and soil salvage was minimal. Much time and effort was placed on surface manipulation and seed mixes consisted entirely of introduced cool season grasses. WECO began a reclamation research program that it still enjoys today. Research contracts at Montana State University in Bozeman provided information on soils, native seeding trials, fertilization, and grazing practices to name a few. Research with the University of Montana in Missoula provided much needed information on the establishment of ponderosa pine (Pinus ponderosa). These research efforts led to the reclamation program employed today.

WECO's research program and practical experience led to a consistent reclamation program which has been used since 1984. In general, the program appears successful as partial bond release has been received for regrading, topsoiling and revegetation on approximately 3,000 acres.

PRESENT RECLAMATION PROCEDURES

WECO stockpiles soil only when regraded areas are not available for direct placement. Soil is salvaged by scrapers and pushcats in a two-lift operation. Topsoil is salvaged to a depth of 6-12" and subsoil is salvaged to a depth of 1-2'. When stockpiled, the soil is piled separately and seeded to prevent loss of soil through erosional processes.

Dozers regrade the spoil ridges by pushing the material into the empty pit. Regrading is done to the approximate original contour (AOC). Prior to placement of soil, the regraded surface is ripped to a depth of 12" to provide a good interface between soil and spoil. Once a regraded area is available, stockpiling ceases and the "direct haul" soil program is enacted (i.e. all soil is salvaged and hauled directly across or around the pit to the regraded area and laid down). This method allows for all the viable native seeds to germinate and helps to diversity the plant community. Mycorrhizae and other organisms are retained, making the soil a much more suitable planting medium. It also reduces soil salvage costs, since the soil is only handled once.

After placement of the soil, the fields are ripped with a farm subsoiler to loosen soil compaction, disced and cultipacked to produce a firm seedbed in which to seed the native seed mixes.

WECO uses four different seedmixes, the uplands seed mix and supplemental seed mix, are used in the majority (90%) of WECO's reclamation. A conifer seed mix is drill seeded wherever ponderosa pine and/or skunkbush sumac are desired and a lowland seed mix is drill seeded in major drainages.

The uplands mix is drill seeded as a rate of 7 1/2 pounds per acre and immediately following, the supplemental seed mix, is broadcast seeded at a rate of 15 pounds per acre. After the grass/forb mixes have been seeded, areas designated as shrub and pine areas, silver (Artemisia cana) and big sagebrush (Artemisia tridentata), skunkbush sumac (Rhus trilobata), ponderosa pine and Rocky Mountain juniper (Juniperus scopulorum) seedlings are planted using a three point tractor-mounted tree planter. Rates vary from 100 - 500 per acre.

In addition to the native seedings, some former cropland areas are seeded back to dryland winter wheat, or spring wheat (Triticum aestivum), and alfalfa, (Medicago sativa). Seeding and harvesting is done by local farmers.

After seeding, the reclamation is monitored and managed during the responsibility period which lasts a minimum of ten years prior to Phase III final bond release. No fertilizer or irrigation is used. Management consists of mowing, burning, spraying and grazing. Most first-year growth is mowed to eliminate the residual skeletal plants such as Russian thistle (Salsola kali). Mowing also occurs in later years where grazing is not possible because of field size or lack of stock water. Mowing places litter on the ground where it can readily decompose. Burning is used on small sites where grazing is not yet practical due to field size or location. Chemical spraying is used only to control noxious weed infestations. Noxious plants only occur near roadsides and railroad lines.

Grazing is the primary management tool employed. At present, WECO grazes 500 cattle each year. Livestock from four adjacent ranches are used. WECO has 3900 acres of reclamation of which 3,000 are fenced for grazing. Using a prescribed grazing system, the cattle herds are rotated through the pastures to obtain WECO's goal of establishing an esthetic, diverse, healthy, permanent rangeland condition.

Methods used since 1984 have given WECO a consistent reclamation program that in our opinion has been to a higher and better use. The goals of the reclamation rules written by DSL and OSM are being achieved. The reclaimed land is stable, revegetated and has a good land use (i.e. livestock grazing). Revegetation efforts appear to be successful, at least in terms of stability, native species establishment and ground cover. Reclamation is not the mystery as it once was, and the reclamation methods described here appear to be a straight forward approach to successful reclamation. Webster's definition of reclamation is defined as "the process of procuring a usable substance from a waste product." WECO's primary business is mining coal and spoil banks are a waste product. Reclamation is being accomplished and the land will be useful for generations to come.

PROPOSED RESTORATION PROCEDURES

Some environmental groups contend that reclamation as done today will not address all wildlife issues. Some wildlife habitat is lost through mining (Figure 1). In southeastern Montana, draglines have a "smoothing" effect on the erosionally-formed landscape. Reclaimed surfaces are smooth and gently rolling. The rough, steep breaks and badlands are replaced by a gently rolling terrain.

WECO's permit stipulation, "to develop a reclamation plan to establish, reclaim, or more correctly "restore" elevated and exposed highly weathered clay (gumbo) knobs, habitat deemed essential to wildlife, required new methods.

In WECO's early attempts to comply with the permit stipulation, the fatal flaws were always excessive costs and contradictions with some reclamation rules. Current reclamation rules do not always apply to restoration projects, (26.4.501, 702, 721). Restoration is defined by Webster as "to bring back to a previous normal condition." There are cases when an area should be restored to its previous condition. At other times, it may be wise to reclaim to a higher and better use.

In order to comply with the permit stipulation, WECO developed a draft plan (Figure 2). Prior to developing a final plan, much debate occurred between WECO and the regulatory authorities. Decisions had to be made on whether this type of

Figure 1. Undisturbed Natural Thin-Breaks Habitat

Figure 2. Proposed Thin-Breaks Restoration Site

habitat was indeed critical to wildlife. Opinions differ greatly between various special interest groups. WECO did not believe this type of habitat warranted the expense required to reconstruct or to rebuild the necessary topography needed by using scrapers and dozers. Dragline placement of spoil seemed to be the most sensible method to obtain the natural topography that was desired.

Natural features such as gumbo knobs have parameters similar to a spoil ridge. Old spoil banks left from early mining have many of the same characteristics. Both have steep slopes (greater than 20%), sparse vegetation (70% bare ground) and barren ridges with weathered shale. WECO's latest draft plan appears acceptable to the state regulatory authorities, but several rules had to be interpreted in a new light to allow for the desired topography. For example, most natural slopes on these exposed elevated sites are steeper than 20% and the restored area should be allowed to simulate the natural features desired. Also, rills greater than 9" occur at the natural sites and at the restored site, spoil material will probably wash onto topsoiled areas. Topsoiling will only be done up to the base of the ridges. The natural sites were void of soil having only weathered shale. All of these situations contradict previously established reclamation practices. However, these methods appear to be a realistic way to "restore" the features that most closely resemble the natural habitat requested by the permit stipulation.

Revegetation will be done by hydro-seeding, hand seeding and/or aerial seeding. A new seed mix will be designed to replace vegetation similar to the natural sites. The objective of the revegetation plan, if the goal is to duplicate the natural features of this type, is to at least establish a sparse stand of trees and shrubs with only a limited stand of grasses and forbs. Trees and shrubs will be hand planted except at the base of the slopes where a tree planter will be used.

In order to approve the plan, which seems to contradict rules 26.4.501, 26.4.702 and 26.4.721, both DSL and OSM have recommended a different permitting approach. For OSM approval, the restoration must be done on an experimental basis. For DSL approval, the restoration must be submitted as an alternate reclamation plan.

In summary, this type of "restoration" should adequately address the permit stipulation without increasing reclamation costs. The resulting features will be highly similar to natural sites and wildlife, the ultimate beneficiary, should readily use the habitat. Whether it is critical to any species remains to be seen.

LITERATURE CITED

Depuit, Ed et. al. 1978. Research on Revegetation of Surface Mined Lands. Mt. Ag. Exp. Sta. MSU rept. 127. 165 pp.

Federal Register 1979. Surface Coal Mining and Reclamation Operations. Permanent Regulatory Program. Dept. of Interior. Office of Surface Mining. Vol. 44. No. 50. Book 3. pp 15311-15463.

Montana. 1980. Administrative Rules of the Montana Strip and Underground Reclamation Act. Montana Department of State Lands, Coal Bureau. pp 347-798.

Munshower, Frank, et. al. 1984. Native Species Response to Fertilizers on Surface Mined Lands. Reclamation Research Unit. Mt. Ag. Exp. Station MSU. pp 86.

REMOTE SENSING OF INFILTRATION RATES ON A RECLAIMED,
SURFACE-MINED WATERSHED

Michael D. Guebert   Thomas W. Gardner

The surface mining and reclamation process greatly increases the potential for surface runoff of mined land, making the mined site, and downstream channels, susceptible to high erosion rates. Infiltration rate controls, to a large degree, the volume of surface runoff generated from a surface mined watershed, and is, itself, controlled by surface physical properties. Accurate correlation of infiltration rate to surface physical properties detectable by remote sensing methods allows remotely sensed data to have important potential in monitoring and predicting hydrologic processes on surface mined watersheds.

One hundred and thirty-eight dripping infiltrometer tests and remotely sensed digital SPOT (Systeme Probatoire d'Observation de la Terre) data are used to explore the relationships among infiltration capacity, surface properties (surface rock type and vegetation type and percent cover), and spectral signature on four mined surfaces and surrounding nonmined land in central Pennsylvania. Infiltration capacity generally increases as surface rock type varies from sandstone to shale to siltstone and as vegetation increases on surfaces of similar rock type. Unsupervised minumum distance classification of digital SPOT data identifies seven distinct spectral classes that are related to differences in surface rock type and vegetation characteristics.

From these relationships, SPOT spectral classes developed for this section of mined and nonmined land are generalized into three classes of low infiltraton capacity for areas disturbed by surface mining and bare agricultural land, moderate infiltration capacity for areas of crop land and pasture, and high infiltration capacity for undisturbed forest and pine trees on old, shaley, mined surfaces. This scale of evaluation is useful for hydrologic studies of watersheds containing each of these land-surface types.

Development of this relationship allows the use of remotely sensed data to extrapolate point infiltration data over an entire waterhsed. On spatially complex surface mined watersheds, this more spatially extensive and detailed characterization of infiltration rates should contribute to the accuracy and ease of prediction of hydrologic processes, such as water and sediment discharge and groundwater recharge.

Michael D. Guebert, Assistant Professor, Department of Geography and Geology, Middle Tennessee State Univ., Murfreesboro, TN 37132

Thomas W. Gardner, Professor, Department of Geosciences, Penn State University, State College, PA 16802

INTRODUCTION

Surface mining for coal in central Pennsylvania dramatically alters the surface physical characteristics of the disturbed area and therefore, the surface hydrology of the disturbed watershed. Surfaces disturbed by surface mining and reclamation exhibit loss of soil structure (Indorante et al., 1981) increase in bulk density (Power et al., 1978), reduction in porosity near the surface (Silburn and Crow, 1984), and increase in porosity at depth (Ciolkosz et al., 1985) caused by the redistribution of materials and the compaction of the surface by heavy equipment. An increase in coarse fragments is caused by incorporation of non-soil materials in the minesoil (Power et al., 1978). Decreased surface roughness (Dixon and Peterson, 1971) is caused by the regrading process and removal of vegetation (Jorgensen, 1985).

In response to altered soil physical conditions, infiltration capacity of newly-reclaimed surface-mined land in central Pennsylvania is an order of magnitude lower than surrounding undisturbed forest soils (Jorgensen and Gardner, 1987). Because of reduced infiltration, surface runoff on mined land is dominated by infiltration excess overland flow (Gryta and Gardner, 1983; Jorgensen and Gardner, 1987; Lemieux, 1987), and is volumetrically increased, producing up to 50% of rainfall as surface runoff (Ritter, 1990) (compared to up to 10% on nonmined pasture land in central Pennsylvania; Rawitz, 1970). Increased runoff on mined areas often results in unstable channelized flow (Figure 1), making the mine site susceptible to high rates of erosion. The result is large erosion gullies on the disturbed land (Gryta and Gardner, 1983) that expose the buried (and potentially acid-producing) mine spoil. In addition, changes in channel geometry and clogging of the channel with sediment occur in the watershed downstream (Touysinhthiphonexay and Gardner, 1984). Where rainfall is infiltrated, groundwater recharge occurs that is often discharged as acid mine drainage seeps at the perimeter of the mined area.

Infiltration of rainfall into mine surfaces is an important process regulating the quantity of surface runoff and ground water recharge that occur on disturbed watersheds (Figure 1) (Frickel et al., 1981; Lemieux, 1987). Infiltration capacity, the capacity of a soil to infiltrate water, must be known to accurately predict the surface hydrologic response of a mined surface (Jorgensen, 1985; Lemieux, 1987). However, as a result of reclamation methods, surface mines are complex; exhibiting significant spatial variation in surface physical properites and hence in infiltration capacities both across one mine and between mines (Jorgensen and Gardner, 1987).

Land cover is an important aspect of hydrologic processes, particularly the processes of infiltration, erosion, and evapotranspiration (Engman, 1981). Accurate correlation of measured infiltration rates to the surface features controlling the spectral response allows the infiltration capacity of disturbed land surfaces to be indirectly identified from remote sensed data. Surface features that control the infiltration capacity (vegetation, soil texture and lithology, surface morphology, and antecedent moisture) also control the spectral reflectance detected by remotely sensed data (Figure 1.) (Engman, 1981).

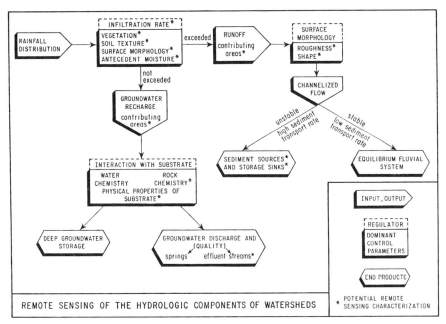

Figure 1. Flow Diagram of Water Movement Within a Watershed,
including Parameters of Potential Remote Sensing Characterization
(from Connors et al., 1986).

This research describes the relationship between infiltration
capacity (which regulates runoff) and ground surface spectral
properties, as remotely sensed by SPOT, for surface-mined
watersheds in humid, temperate climates. This relationship is
developed through three objectives. The first objective explores
the relationship between infiltration capacity and the mine
surface features controlling the spectral reflectance of the
surface, namely surface rock type and vegetation cover. This
relationship will be shown through the correlation of a dependent
infiltration variable and independent surface feature variables,
and through a trend analysis of infiltration capacity to surface
features. The second objective explores the relationship between
these mine surface features and SPOT spectral response, through
development of a contingency matrix between a SPOT unsupervised
minimum distance classification map and a ground truth map. The
third objective explores the relationship between infiltration
capacity and SPOT spectral classification by calculating, for
each spectral class, the infiltration rate and the surface
feature variables controling infiltration and spectral response.

To achieve these objectives, four reclaimed surface mines located
in northwest Centre County, Pennsylvania (Guebert and Gardner,
1989), ranging from 25 to 300 hectares in size and from 2 to 20
years in age were selected for their variation in surface
features of rock type and vegetation cover. In addition, data
from 50 previously completed infiltration tests were available
for these mines (Jorgensen, 1985). The four mines are underlain
by Pennsylvanian age rocks of the Allegheny Group, which averages
85 meters in thickness, and consists of six cyclic zones of fine
grained sandstone, siltstone, and shale as the predominant rock
types, and coals, underclays, and limestones constituting a minor
part (Dutcher et al., 1959).

INFILTRATION ON MINED WATERSHED SURFACES

Field observation of surface rock type and vegetation type and percent cover at 200 points across the surfaces of the four mines were recorded on low altitude black and white aerial photographs taken with a 70mm format Hasselblad camera. Surface rock type was recorded as a visual estimation of the percentages of sandstone, siltstone, and shale rock fragments present at the surface. Vegetation was recorded by type and visually estimated areal percentage cover of each type. The most common vegetation types are red top and fescue grasses and red pine or white pine.

In addition to the 50 previous infiltration tests, 88 infiltration tests were conducted on the surfaces of the four mines and on surrounding bare agricultural land, pasture, crop land, and forest. Sites were chosen to encompass the range of surface feature classes defined from field observations. Tests were completed with a Jorgensen-modified Alderfer-Robinson dripping infiltrometer using the procedure established by Jorgensen (1985) and Jorgensen and Gardner (1987) which gives consistent, reproducible results. Infiltration rate was calculated by subtracting runoff rate from a constant rainfall rate over a 0.4 square meter plot (Guebert and Gardner, 1989). Cumulative volume of runoff was measured approximately 50 times during each thirty minute test.

A parameter commonly used to characterize the infiltration capacity of the soil is the steady state infiltration rate (FC). The steady-state infiltration rate is the final, constant infiltration rate in the Horton (1933) curve, corresponding to the saturated hydraulic conductivity of the soil (Rubin and Steinhardt, 1963). It is calculated in this study as the average infiltration rate (cm/hr) during the 20 to 30 minute period of each thirty-minute test.

Relationships between dependent infiltration variables and independent surface feature variables were explored by use of Pearson Correlation Coefficients (Statistical Analysis System, SAS Institute, 1982) (Table 1). The correlation between FC and rainrate (RAIN) is very low (r=-0.03) because variation in rainfall intensity is limited by experimental design. The correlation between FC and Vegetation (VG) (r=0.37) is positive and strong relative to other independent variables. Vegetative growth increases soil structure, reduces bulk density, increases soil porosity, and adds surface litter and plant roots; all causing an increase in the infiltration capacity of the mine surface (Jorgensen and Gardner, 1987). The larger central portions of the mined surfaces are dominated by rock fragments of sandstone (SS), siltstone (ST) or both, with small amounts of shale (SH). The correlations between FC and SS, ST, and SS are low but statistically significant (Table 1).

Table 1. Pearson correlation coefficients for infiltration and surface feature variables.

		RAIN	VG	SS	ST	SH
	r =	-0.04	0.37	-0.36	0.24	0.18
FC	prob=	0.6575	0.0001	0.0000	0.0068	0.0481
	n=	138	135	121	121	121

Infiltration tests are divided into six groups, based on the predominance of surface rock type of the three main lithologies present on the mine (sandstone, siltstone, and shale), and four nonmined groups based on land-use practices (Figure 2). The mined groups were further subdivided by breaks in the histogram into groups of increasing percent vegetation cover of 0-25 percent, 25-45 percent, 45-65 percent, and 65-100 percent. The trend of increasing FC with increasing vegetation is clearly visible on the sandstone, sandstone-siltstone, and siltstone dominated surfaces. The general trend of FC versus rock type indicates that surfaces dominated by rock fragments of sandstone or sandstone-shale have lower FC values than surfaces dominated by rock fragments of sandstone-siltstone, siltstone, or siltstone-shale. The siltstone-shale dominated surfaces have the highest FC values. No infiltration tests were run on surfaces dominated partially or totally by shale (siltstone-shale, shale, or sandstone-shale) with greater than 25 percent vegetative cover because of their areal insignificance.

The large scatter in the infiltration data may result from inherent variation in infiltration within each subgroup, instrument error, and not subsetting the data by the age of the mined surface. During the first four years following reclamation, some mine surfaces show a significant recovery of initially low infiltration capacity toward premining levels in response to physical redistribution, chemical alteration, and vegetation growth (Jorgensen and Gardner, 1987). This explains the positive correlation between AGE and FC (r=0.40). However, infiltration data are not subset by AGE because the time since reclamation is not directly sensed by SPOT. These relationships could also possibly be improved with use of an infiltration test instrument covering a larger surface area than the 0.4 square meters covered with the instrument used here, and by including age since reclamtion as an independent variable.

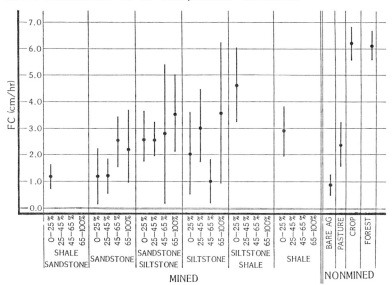

Figure 2. Plot of Infiltration Capacity (FC) of Six Mined Groups Based on the Surface Rock Type, and Four Nonmined Groups. The Mined Groups are Subdivided by Percent Vegetation Cover. The Mean and One Standard Deviation are Indicated by the Dot and Bar.

REMOTE SENSING CLASSIFICATION OF MINED WATERSHEDS

Data from SPOT was acquired for central Pennsylvania when first available on October 29, 1986 16:15 GMT. Multispectral band 2 (0.61-0.68 micrometers) and band 3 (0.79-0.89 micrometers) were coregistered to the panchromatic band (0.51-0.73 micrometers) and resampled to 10-meter pixels. Because the four mines are located up to 10km apart, the mines and a section of nommined land were subset from the SPOT data set (CUTTER and SUBSET programs, ERDAS, 1985). This subset data set (1.1 x 10**5 pixels; 11 square kilometers) contains approximately 40 percent mined land and 60 percent nonmined land. However, the fall acquisition date limits the detectable spectral differences of vegetation in the near infrared range (band 3). Also, low mean reflectance values of the four spectral bands (Guebert and Gardner, 1989) indicate that the sensors had an inappropriate gain setting for reflectance of surface mined land (Chavez, 1989), resulting in decreased ability to observe small differences in the spectral signatures of various mined surfaces.

A cubic clustering criterion (SAS, 1982) was used on the subset data to determine the number of clusters that maximize the total variance to within-group variance. The optimum number of clusters was interpreted as seven. An unsupervised minimum distance classification was performed to create a spectral class map (seven classes) for the mined and non-mined land subset data set (Figure 3), (CLUSTR program, ERDAS, 1985). The two hundred ground observations and photointerpretation of the low-altitude black and white aerial photographs were used to determine the surface properties (rock type and vegetation), boundaries, and classification accuracy of the seven spectral classes from the unsupervised minimum distance classification. Class boundaries were transferred to a contrast stretched image of the raw data used for the unsupervised classification. This step allowed digitizing the ground truth data into a raster file with the same dimensions and cell size (10 meters) as the spectral class map (DIGPOL, MAKEFIL, and GRDPOL programs, ERDAS, 1985). The ground truth data set was then registered to the spectral class map (SUBSET program). Comparison of the digitized ground truth map and the spectral class map (SUMMARY program, ERDAS, 1985) produced a summary of classification accuracy in the form of a contingency matrix (Table 2). The diagonal elements are percentages of correctly classified pixels. The weighted average of the diagonal elements represents an overall classification accuracy of 70 percent. The off-diagonal elements represent percent errors of omission and commission. For example, the element in row 2, column 1 is the percentage (14.3 percent) of ground-truth class 2 (moderate to well vegetated, mixed lithology mined surfaces) incorrectly classified as spectral class 1 (forest and pine trees on shale-dominated mined surfaces). This represents an ommision error for the well vegetated mine class and a commission error for the forest and pine tress on shale class.

These errors are not surprising, given the high spatial variability and complexity of mine surface features, and the similarity in surface properties of the confused classes. Some errors in classification also occurred because of shadows on north facing slopes. The classification accuracy could be improved with a summer instead of the late fall acquisition date, which suppresses the effect of vegetation on spectral class differentiation, and with a more appropriate sensor gain setting (Chavez, 1989)

1 FOREST; PINES ON SHALE

2 WELL VEG MIXED LITH

3 BARE SHALE

4 BARE MIXED LITH; BARE AG

5 BARE SANDSTONE

6 CROP LAND; PASTURE

7 ACTIVE MINE AREAS; COAL

Figure 3. Unsupervised minimum distance classification map for the Cherry Run mine.

Table 2 Contingency matrix for ground truth classes versus SPOT spectral classes.

					SPECTRAL CLASSES				
			1	2	3	4	5	6	7	
		% of tot	46.8	20.3	7.1	13.3	6.8	4.3	1.4	100.0
GROUND TRUTH CLASSES	1	51.9	80.4	10.3	4.0	3.1	0.3	0.5	1.4	100.0
	2	22.0	14.8	56.2	5.5	16.4	1.5	5.7	0.0	100.0
	3	5.1	7.9	2.8	48.8	32.7	6.2	0.1	1.6	100.0
	4	5.4	4.7	6.8	3.9	73.5	10.8	0.3	0.0	100.0
	5	7.4	1.1	2.9	3.2	21.6	68.9	2.4	0.1	100.0
	6	6.5	12.1	27.6	5.1	10.2	5.2	39.8	0.1	100.0
	7	1.2	5.5	0.3	33.1	6.8	4.3	0.0	50.0	100.0
		100.0	126.5	106.9	103.6	164.3	97.2	48.8	53.2	total %

Class 1--forest; pine trees on shale mine surface
Class 2--moderate to well vegetated mixed lithology mine surface
Class 3--bare shale mine surface
Class 4--bare mixed lithology and poorly vegetated sandstone mine
         surface; bare Agricultural land
Class 5--bare sandstone mine surface
Class 6--crop land; pasture
Class 7--active mine areas and coal piles

INFILTRATION RATES OF REMOTELY SENSED CLASSES

It would be useful, for hydrologic studies, to develop a relationship between SPOT spectral classification and infiltration capacity. This relationship will allow the use of remotely sensed data in extrapolation of point infiltration data over an entire watershed. To develop this relationship, each infiltration test was placed into one of the seven spectral classes by plotting its ground location on the classification map. In addition, each test was labeled according to the type of ground surface (mined, bare agricultural, pasture, crop land, or forest) on which the test was completed. Surface features (VG, SS, ST, and SH) and infiltration capacity (FC) were calculated from the infiltration tests in each spectral class (Table 3). The surface features sensed by SPOT in each spectral class are indicated by the calculated values for the surface feature variables.

However, due to the variablilty in the relationship between infiltration rate and surface features, FC values in each spectral class have large standard deviations relative to the separation of means. Because of this, the SPOT spectral classes developed for this section of mined and nonmined land are generalized into three classes of low, moderate, and high infiltration based on the measured infiltration rates associated with each class. From Table 3, the class of low infiltration capacity (FC=2.3 ±1.2 cm/hr) represents spectral class 4 (bare mixed lithology and poorly vegetated sandstone; bare agricultural land), class 5 (bare sandstone), class 2 (moderate to well vegetated mixed lithology) and class 3 (bare shale). The class of moderate infiltration capacity (FC=3.8 ±1.9 cm/hr) represents spectral class 6 (pasture; crop land). The class of high infiltration capacity (FC=5.8 ±0.7 cm/hr) represents spectral class 1 (forest; pines on shale mine surface).

Table 3. Surface features and infiltration rate of SPOT spectral classes.

SPECTRAL CLASS	n*	SURFACE FEATURE VARIABLES+				FC++
		VG	SS	ST	SH	
4	M(8)	4.7	32.0	20.0	43.8	1.7
	B(3)	± 6.1	±12.4	±20.3	±17.1	±1.1
5	M(20)	8.1	77.5	8.0	14.5	2.2
		± 4.7	±15.1	±11.2	±10.7	±1.0
2	M(32)	59.8	47.8	43.9	8.3	2.7
	P(3)	±24.5	±30.2	±32.0	± 3.4	±1.5
3	M(8)	0.0	5.0	10.0	85.0	2.5
		± 0.0	± 0.0	± 0.0	± 0.0	±0.8
6	P(5)	96.3	NA#	NA	NA	3.8
	C(3)	± 4.0				±1.9
1	M(3)	87.5	0.0	25.0	75.0	5.8
	F(3)	±12.5	± 0.0	± 0.0	± 0.0	±0.7

*   Number of infiltration tests (in parenthesis) located on surfaces of: B=bare agricultural   C=crop   F=forest
    M=mine surface   P=pasture
+   measured in percent, mean ± 1 standard deviation
++   measured in cm/hr, mean ± 1 standard deviation
#   not applicable

SUMMARY AND CONCLUSIONS

Infiltration of rainfall into spatially complex mine surfaces is an important process regulating the quantity of surface runoff and ground water recharge occurring on a disturbed watershed (Frickel et al., 1981; Lemieux, 1987). Remotely sensed data cannot sense infiltration capacity directly. However, both infiltration capacity and spectral reflectance are related to mined land surface properties of rock type and vegetation cover. Therefore, remotely sensed data have potential use in identifying mined surfaces with different infiltration rates. By developing the relationships between infiltration and mined-land surface features of rock type and vegetaton cover, and between these surface features and spectral reflectance as observed by SPOT, a third relationship can be drawn between infiltration and remote sensing classification.

This relationship will allow the use of remotely sensed data in extrapolation of point infiltration data over an entire watershed. On spatially complex surface mined watersheds, this more spatially extensive and detailed characterization of infiltration rates should contribute to the accuracy and ease of prediction of hydrologic process. This information is useful in detecting disturbed land areas of high surface runoff as potential gully erosion sites and sediment sources, detecting areas of high ground water recharge for possible acid mine drainage production, and detecting areas of changing hydrologic response through time with repeat remote sensing data sets for monitoring reclamation maintainance and for bond release.

In this geologic and climatic setting it is possible to characterize the infiltration capacities of disturbed watersheds by remotely sensed data. Using SPOT data, an unsupervised minimum distance classification was produced for seven distinct spectral classes on four reclaimed mines and surrounding nonmined land in central Pennsylvania. Because of the variablilty in the relationship between infiltration and surface features observed by SPOT, infiltration capacity for spectral classes is generalized into classes of low (FC=2.3 ±1.2 cm/hr), moderate (FC=3.8 ±1.9 cm/hr), and high (FC=5.8 ±0.7 cm/hr) infiltration capacity.

ACKNOWLEDGEMENTS

This research was supported by the United States Department of Energy through Dr. Frank Wobber, Office of Health and Environmental Research, under contract number DE-FG02-84ER60263 to Dr. Thomas W. Gardner.

REFERENCES

1. Chavez. P. S., Jr., 1989, Use of the variable gain settings on SPOT: Photogrammetric Engineering and Remote Sensing, v.55:2, p. 195-201.

2. Ciolkosz, E. J., R. C. Cronce, R. L. Cunningham, and G. W. Petersen, 1985. Characteristics. genesis. and classification of Pennsylvania minesoils: Soil Science, v. 139:3, p. 232-238

3. Connors, J. F., Gardner, T. W., Petersen, G. W., 1986, Digital analysis of the hydrologic components of watersheds using simulated SPOT imagery, Hydrologic Applications of Space Technology, IAHS Publ. no.160.

4. Dixon, R. M., and A. E. Peterson, 1971, Water infiltration control: a channel system concept: Soil Science Society of America Proceedings, v. 35:6, p. 968-973.

5. Dutcher, R. R., Ferm, J. C., Flint, N. K., and Williams, E. G., 1959, The Pennsylvanian of western Pennsylvania, in: Guidebook for Field Trips, Pittsburg Meeting, 1959; New York, Geological Society of Americal. p. 61-113.

6. Engman, E. T., 1981, Remote sensing application in watershed modeling, in: Applied Modeling in Catchment Hydrology (Proceedings of the International Symposium on Rainfall-Runoff Modeling): Water Resources Publications, Littleton, Colo. p. 473-494.

7. ERDAS, 1985, ERDAS PC and PC-Kit image processing system, Earth Resources Data Analysis System.

8. Frickel, D.G., Shown, L.M., Hadley, L.F., and Miller, R.F., 1981, Methodology for hydrologic evaluation of a potential surface mine; the Red Rim site, Carbon and Sweetwater Counties, Wyoming: U.S. Geological Survey Water Resource Investigations OF-81-75, 65p.

9. Gryta, J. J., and Gardner, T. W., 1983, Episodic cutting and filling within gully-fan systems in disequilibrium: Geological Society of America Abstracts with Programs, v. 15, p. 587.

10. Guebert, M. D., 1991, Macropore flow on a reclaimed surface-mined watershed in central Pennsylvania: Control on hillslope and surface hydrology: Ph.D. Dissertation, Dept. of Geosciences, Pennsylvania State University, University Park, Penn. 84 pp.

11. Guebert, M. D., and T. W. Gardner, 1989, Unsupervised SPOT classification and infiltration rates on surface mined watersheds, central Pennsylvania: Photogrammetric Engineering and Remote Sensing, v. 55:10, p. 1470-1486.

12. Horton, R. E., 1933, The role of infiltration in the hydrologic cycle: American Geophysical Union Transactions, v. 14, p. 446-460.

13. Indorante, S. J., I. J. Jansen, C. W. Boast, 1981, Surface mining and reclamation: initial changes in soil character: Journal of Soil and Water Conservation, v. 36:6, p. 347-351.

14. Jorgensen, D. W., 1985, Hydrology of surface mined land: a determination of minesoil control on infiltration capacity, and runoff modelling of disturbed watersheds: M.S. thesis, Pennsylvania State University, University Park, PA, 127 p.

15. Jorgensen, D. W., and Gardner, T. W., 1987, Infiltration capacity of disturbed soils: temporal change and lithologic control: Water Resources Bulletin, v.23(6), p. 1161-1172.

16. Lemieux, C. R., 1987, Infiltration characteristics and hydrologic modeling of disturbed land, Moshannon, PA, M.S. Thesis: Pennsylvania State University, University Park, PA, 142 p.

17. Power, J. F., R. E. Ries, and R. M. Sanduval, 1978, Reclamation of coal-mined land in the northern Great Plains: Journal of Soil and Water Conservation, v. 33:2, p. 69-74.

18. Rawitz, E., E. T. Engman and G. D. Cline, 1970, Use of the mass balance method for examining the role of soils in controlling watershed performance: Water Resources Research, v. 6:4, p. 1115-1123.

19. Ritter,J. B., 1990, Surface hydrology of drainage basins disturbed by surface mining and reclamation, Central Pennsylvania: Ph.D. Dissertation, Dept. of Geosciences, Pennsylvania State University, University Park, PA, 162 p.

20. Rubin, J., and R. Steinhardt, 1963, Soil water relations during rain infiltration: I. Theory: Soil Science Society of America Proceedings, v. 27, p. 246-251.

21. SAS (Statistical Analysis System) Institute Inc., 1982, SAS users guide; statistics, 1982 edition: North Carolina, SAS Institute Inc., 584p.

22. Silburn, D. M., and F. R. Crow, 1984, Soil properties of surface mined land: Transaction of American Society of Agricultural Engineers, v. 27:3, p. 827-832.

23. Touysinhthiphonexay, K. C., and Gardner, T. W., 1984, Threshold response of small streams to surface coal mining, bituminous coal fields, Central Pennsylvania: Earth Surface Processes and Landforms, V. 9, p. 43-58.

ERAMS- A DECISION SUPPORT SYSTEM FOR LAND

REHABILITATION IN ARID REGIONS

Victor R. Squires

Concern for the environment has emerged as a pressing issue especially as populations continue to grow. The consequences of mismanagement include deterioration of soil and water quality - features which are especially serious in the arid and semi arid regions of the world. Dryland degradation is a widespread phenomenon which affects rangelands around the world (Dixon, James and Sherman 1989). Efforts to combat degradation will depend increasingly on better systems of resource inventory. A key requirement is to use land resources within their capacity. Matching land capability with the intended use is a vital step. Methods to assess land capability which are quick, reliable, cost efficient and repeatable are a prerequisite to any plan to develop a sustainable land use regime. ERAMS (Environmental Resource Assessment and Management System) is such a methodology (Squires, Grierson and Thomas 1990, Thomas and Squires 1991).

This paper describes the application of the ERAMS methodology to assessment of land capability and land rehabilitation on county-scale areas in Algeria (north Africa),north west China and south east Australia.

STUDY AREAS

Algeria

The study site was a 850,000 ha area of semi arid steppe located approximately 500 km south of Algiers and lies between the Atlas Tellien in the north and the Atlas Saharien in the south. The climate is characterised by cool wet winters and hot dry summers. The mean annual rainfall decreases from a high of 350 mm in the north to less than 200mm in the south. The dominant vegetation is a low shrub steppe of *Artemisia*, *Stipa* and *Lygeum* (Thomas et al 1986) The steppe is used for extensive grazing by sheep and goats and for opportunistic cropping with wheat and barley. The region is badly degraded with extensive areas of bare ground. Wind and water erosion are serious.

Department of Environmental Science & Rangeland Management
Faculty of Agricultural and Natural Resource Sciences
University of Adelaide, Roseworthy, AUSTRALIA 5371

China

There are two sites, one in Xinjiang in China's far northwest corner and the other in the northern Loess Plateau. The Xinjiang site is an area of approximately 3000 km^2 and encompasses Fukang county about 70 km from Urumqi. The rainfall is low (less than 200 mm p.a.), the winters are cold and the summers hot (Squires 1989). The site lies in the Junggar Basin on the western edge of he Gobi desert. The vegetation is sparse and is dominated by salt tolerant shrubs *Tamarix*, *Haloxylon* and *Kochia* spp.

The northern Loess Plateau site is in Shenmu county located approximately 520 km west of Beijing in Shaanxi Province. It is bordered to the north by Inner Mongolia, to the south by the Yellow River. The Great Wall separates the sandy soil region of the north-west from the loess hilly country to the south-east. Shenmu county is typical of the transition belt of semi-arid land between pastoralism (animal husbandry)and cropping. It is a fragile ecosystem with pressure from grazing livestock, opportunistic cropping, and urban/industrial development associated with coal mining.

The area is at an altitude of 1000-1400 m above sea level. It is a vast undulating plateau which is dominated by sand dunes (both fixed and drifting), depressions and small ephemeral lakes. The soils range from deep, undifferentiated aeolian depositions on the sandhills and sandplains to deep saline clays in the low-lying wetlands and meadows.

Mean annual rainfall varies from 300 to 400 mm with a summer dominance. There is a wide annual variation in temperature with summer maxima about 39°C and winter minima of -28° C.

The vegetation is dominated by *Artemisia* and *Salix* species. Assorted perennial and ephemeral forbs occur on the sandy soils, with *Carex* spp. in the low-lying saline meadows.

The predominant land use in the area is grazing of semi-arid pastures by sheep and goats. Semi-arid sedentary and opportunistic cropping are practised. Land degradation, salinisation, wind and water erosion are serious problems. Encroachment of mobile sand dunes onto areas formerly used for cropping has increased dramatically over the past 30 years.

Australia

The study site is an area of about 3000 km^2 located in the western Murray plains in South Australia about 150 north east of Adelaide. The regional climate is semi arid with the mean annual rainfall varying from about 300 mm in the west to about 250mm in the east. The climate is characterised by cool wet winters and hot dry summers. The vegetation is multi-layed with a tall shrubland dominated by *Eucalyptus* (mallee form) as an overstory and an understory of *Atriplex*, *Maireana* and other low shrubs.

Thus the 4 sites represent a set of contrasting conditions with moisture shortage and widespread land degradation as common features. Two of the sites (those in China) have summer dominant rainfall patterns while the other two (Algeria and Australia) have winter rains. Other contrasts (apart from botanical composition of the vegetation) relate to vegetation structure. Structure varies from single layered to multilayered. The four sites then presented a good opportunity to validate the ERAMS methodology which was developed for use in semiarid regions where the vegetation is so sparse, overutilized and degraded that remote sensing alone cannot be used to estimate land capability.

METHODS

A reconnaissance field survey was conducted at each site. Satellite imagery LANDSAT TM was interpreted prior to the field work to classify landscape types according to the methodology of Laut et al 1977. The micro-BRIAN image processing software (Jupp et al 1985) which is based around the inexpensive IBM AT personal computer, was used. This processing is a non-hierarchical agglomerative classification allowing pixels in the image to be grouped such that the major spectral variation in the image can be represented by the means of classes. This initial classification alone was not adequate to give land capability but served to delineate land units.

Sites were sampled along transects for measurement of soil and vegetation attributes. The choice of sampling sites and their distribution within the land units was aided by airphoto interpretation and by ground survey.

a) Vegetation survey

At each of the sites, projected foliage cover (FC) and botanical composition of the vegetation were assessed at each site on an average of three transects each of at least 1 km in length.

The botanical composition and foliage cover of the vegetation was assessed by the step-point method (Cunningham, 1975). In this method about 2000 separate points are assessed on each transect. Perennials were identified to the species level but ephemerals were pooled according to the ERAMS methodology (Squires et al 1990). Bare soil and litter were also discriminated.

Vegetation on each site was classified into condition classes or states according to the method of Steeley et al (1986) which classifies vegetation on the basis of the relationship between projected foliage cover (FC) and an index of botanical composition (IBC). This index is defined as the botanical composition of the desirable (palatable, non-toxic) perennials as a proportion of all perennials. Thus where desirable perennials comprise the bulk of all perennials the index is close to unity. Where perennials are predominantly undesirable the index is close to zero.

b) Soil survey

Soil samples were taken to determine texture (hand test in field), soil depth, pH and salinity. The slope at each site was measured and expressed as a percentage.

RESULTS AND DISCUSSION

a) Land capability classes (LCC)

Using data on rainfall, slope and soil characteristics (see above) the LCC was determined at each of the sites surveyed. The information was used to extrapolate to the entire area.

In the ERAMS method, sites which have an overriding constraint e.g. soil texture (such as pure sand) are automatically assigned to the lowest LCC. Erodibility is closely related to soil characteristics such as texture and to vegetative cover (Fig 1a & b).

Similarly, those sites which receive run-off from surrounding areas are given a higher LCC because this raises the AM value (see below).

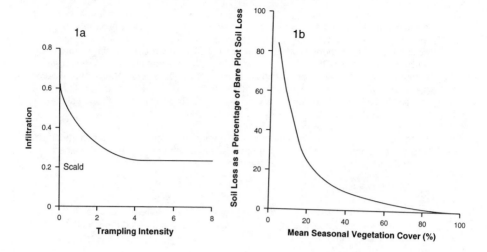

Figure 1. General relationship between soil characteristics and erodibility. 1a The
relationship between soil infiltration rate and trampling intensity (Noble and
Tongway, 1986) 1b Erosion-soil cover relationship (Stocking, 1988)

b) <u>Vegetation states</u>

From the step point data foliage cover (FC)and an index of botanical
composition(IBC) was derived. There was wide variation in FC from close to zero
to over 50%.

c) <u>Estimation of Total Annual Dry Matter</u> (TADM)

An essential step in the ERAMS method is the estimation of the total annual
increment in dry matter from each site in the current year. Each vegetation
association will have a characteristic response which is governed by factors
(called Relative Production Indices) such as rainfall, evaporation, slope, soil depth,
soil texture, and soil salinity (Thomas and Squires 1991).

Each vegetation association, indeed each community, will have a different
potential TADM production. Ideally, the TADM should be derived from sites which
are in good condition (high ground cover and near pristine botanical composition)
but sites which have enjoyed a period of protection from grazing and which
display some of the characteristics of a pristine site can be used. TADM can be
calculated with the following equation:

$$TADM = k \times 2.33^x \ AM \qquad (1)$$

where, k is a constant and x is a multiplier. AM is the available moisture of the soil
(as determined by rainfall, soil and slope characteristics and 2.33 is the water use
efficiency (kg DM/mm.)

264

The available soil moisture (AM) of a given homogeneous land unit can be parametrically related to rainfall and other parameters which together determine the water available to support plant growth (Steeley et al 1986; Thomas et al 1986).

$$AM = (k_1 \times k_2 \times k_3 ...) R \qquad (2)$$

where AM is available moisture (mm) and k_1, k_2 k_3...are relative production indices ratings ranging from 1 to 0 which give weightings for the way in which a given parameter affects the AM.

Utilizable dry matter (UDM) depends on the level of use of forage dry matter over the whole growing season. The "safe" limit of utilization varies between species and should be adjusted accordingly. The level determines the grazing capacity of a site. The utilizable rate was set, after consultation with local researchers, at 45% From a knowledge of the TADM, the UDM and the rate of forage intake it is easy to calculate carrying capacity. Where the calculated carrying capacity of a rangeland is less than the livestock population it is expected to support there are two courses of action (i) improve the rangeland to carry the extra livestock (ii) reduce the number of livestock. This latter option is not often possible.

MEASURES TO IMPROVE RANGELAND

There are several options available - reseeding, mechanical interventions to improve infiltration rate or water retention, application of fertilizer, weed control and destocking. Fig 2 shows the results of some of these rehabilitation options on semi arid steppe in Algeria. Similar responses can be expected from other rangelands.

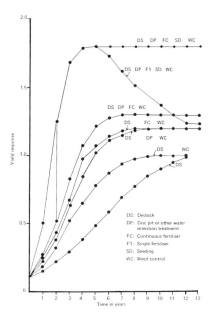

Figure 2. Effects of various rehabilitation measures on recovery rates on semi-arid rangelands (Thomas et al, 1986)

265

CONCLUSIONS

ERAMS is not as data-demanding as some land assessment methods but it does need basic information on rainfall for the site and, most importantly, data on rainfall and biomass production relationships. While techniques exist to calculate rainfall from altitude and latitude (Yevjevich 1975) there is no substitute for reliable data on rainfall use efficiency (Le Houerou 1984).

Because the actual field measurements for the ERAMS methodology is relatively simple and straightforward it lends itself to being done by over large areas by people who lack in-depth training. ERAMS is quantitative, repeatable and objective. It has relative flexibility in that parameters which are not currently included but which may be important in another environment can be readily incorporated. Knowing the land capability class of each parcel of land is a key factor in prioritising the rehabilitation treatment. Some tracts of land will hardly repay the cost and effort while others will be well worth restoration.

ACKNOWLEDGMENTS

It is a pleasure to thank Professor Xu Peng, and Professor Zhong junping of the August 1 Agricultural University, Urumqi, Professor Shen Changjiang and Associate Professor Chen Guangwei of the Commission for Integrated Survey of Natural Resources, Beijing and Ms M. Lewis of University of Adelaide for assistance with the field work in China and Australia. Dr Thomas has had involvement in the project in Algeria, China and Australia.

REFERENCES

1. Cunningham, G.1975 Modified step pointing: a rapid method for assessing vegetative cover. J. Soil Conserv. Serv. N.S.W. 31:256-65

2. Dixon, J.A., D.E. James and P.B. Sherman 1989 The economics of dryland management. Earthscan, London

3. Jupp, D.J.B., S.J. Heggen, K.K. Mayo, S.W. Kendall, J.R. Bolton, and B.A. Harrison 1985 The BRIAN Handbook CSIRO Div. of Water and Land Resources, Canberra Natural Res. Ser. No. 3

4. Laut, P., P.C. Heyligers, G. Kieg, E. Loffler, C. Margules and . Scott 1977 Environments of South Australia Handbook CSIRO Div. of Land Use Res., Canberra

5. Le Houerou, H.N. 1984 Rain use efficiency: a unifying concept in arid land ecology J. Arid Envir.7:213-247

6. Squires, V.R. 1989 Farming on the desert fringe a case study from Xinjiang, China J. Arid Envir.16: 229-33

7. Squires, V.R., Grierson, I.T. and Thomas, D.A. 1990. The use of remote sensing and environmental resource measurements to determine the present and potential grassland production in semi-arid areas. Proc. Internat. Symp. Grassld. Veg. Science Press, Beijing pp.7-20

8. Steeley, C., D.Thomas, V.Squires and W. Buddee 1986 Methodology of a range resource survey for steppe regions of the Mediterranean basin. In: P. Joss, P. Lynch and O.B. Williams (Eds) "Rangelands: a resource under siege". Australian Academy of Science, Canberra pp.538-539

9. Stocking, M.A. 1988 Assessing vegetative cover and management effects. In: R. Lal (Ed) Soil erosion research methods, Soil and Water Conservation Society, Ankeny pp. 163-185

10. Thomas, D., V. Squires, W. Buddee, and J. Turner 1986 Rangeland regeneration in steppic regions of the Mediterranean basin. In: P. Joss, P. Lynch and O.B. Williams "Rangelands: a resource under siege" Aust. Academy of Science, Canberra pp.280-287

11. Thomas, D.A. and V.R. Squires 1990. Available soil moisture as a basis for land capability assessment in semi arid regions Vegetatio 91:183-189

12. Yevjevich. V. 1975 Probability and statistics in Hydrology. Water Resource Publications, Colorado State University

COMPARISON OF PHOTOGRAPHY, VIDEOGRAPHY AND SPOT-1 HRV

DIGITAL OBSERVATIONS FOR SALINITY ASSESSMENT IN

THE SAN JOAQUIN VALLEY OF CALIFORNIA

C. L. Wiegand[1], J. D. Rhoades[2], J. H. Everitt[1]
and D. E. Escobar[1]

Information on the extent and severity of soil salinity is needed to engineer water delivery and drainage improvements, and to monitor the effectiveness of reclamation efforts. Procedures to help meet these needs were developed from soil salinity, plant height and cover measurements, and digitized color-infrared photography, narrowband videography, and SPOT-1 high resolution visible (HRV) scanner observations for four salt-affected cotton fields in the San Joaquin Valley. Unsupervised classification procedures were used to develop seven category spectral maps by field. Regression equations were developed from the salinity measurements in the surface 30 cm (EC1) and photographic spectral data at 100-200 sample sites per field for estimating the soil salinity throughout the field in that depth interval. These equations were applied to estimate the salinity of each of the approximately 100,000 pixels per field, and the salinity categories corresponding to the spectral ones were mapped. The spectral classification maps and the estimated salinity maps corresponded well, as documented by a coincidence matrix analysis that determined the fraction of pixels classified the same in both approaches. The findings demonstrate that spectral observations which sense plant growth responses can help determine the occurrence and severity of soil salinity and argue for salinity surveys during the crop, rather than the fallow season. Higher correlations were found for the photography than for the videography and HRV observations. The HRV sampling interval (20 m) was basically incompatible with the ground sampling pattern. However, any of the systems could be used to assess salinity or monitor reclamation.

INTRODUCTION

Soils are termed saline or salt-affected when the concentration of salts in the root zone exceeds 4 dS m^{-1} (Richards, 1954). Such soils comprise 19 percent of the 2.8 billion hectares of arable land worldwide (Szabolcs, 1989). Saline soils occur naturally in arid and semi-arid climates from weathering of indigenous minerals (Tanji, 1990) but are more important economically where irrigation is practiced to produce crops (Carter, 1975).

Aerial photography (Myers et al., 1966), and Apollo 9 (Wiegand et al., 1971) and Skylab (Everitt et al., 1977) 1:3,000,000-scale space photography as well as Landsat multispectral scanner (MSS) 1:250,000-scale imagery (Sharma

---

[1]USDA, ARS, Remote Sensing Research Unit, 2413 E. Highway 83, Weslaco, TX
    78596-8344

[2]USDA, ARS, U.S. Salinity Laboratory, 4500 Glenwood Dr., Riverside, CA
    92501

and Bhargava, 1988) have been used to distinguish saline from nonsaline soils and vegetation. Everitt et al. (1988) used narrowband videography to detect and estimate the area of salt-affected soil in southern Texas. Lint yield and percent ground cover of cotton (Gossypium hirsutum L.) were estimated equally well from vegetation indices (Kauth and Thomas, 1976; Richardson and Wiegand, 1977; Tucker, 1979) calculated from videography and SPOT-1 HRV scanner data (Wiegand et al. (1990, 1992).

Vegetation indices (VI) are useful because they reduce spectral observations in two or more wavelengths to a single numerical index and because there is high contrast between living plants and the soil background in certain wavelengths, particularly the near-infrared (NIR, 750 to 1350 nm) and the visible red (600 to 700 nm) wavelengths. The widely used VI include the greenness vegetation index (GVI) (Kauth and Thomas, 1976; Jackson, 1983) that is calculated from observations in 3 or more bands of observations, and the normalized difference (NDVI) (Tucker, 1979) vegetation index that is calculated from observations in a visible red and a NIR band. All the indices are highly correlated with leaf area index, plant cover, plant height, green biomass, and yield (Wiegand et al., 1979, 1991).

In this study measurements of the electrical conductivity of extracts of water-saturated soil samples from the root zone, plant height and cover measurements, and digitized color infrared photography, narrowband videography, and SPOT-1 HRV observations from 4 intensively sampled cotton fields in the San Joaquin Valley of California were obtained. The objectives were to compare (a) relationships between specific ground measurements and the spectral observations for the three individual systems by field, (b) correlations among systems for data from common sample sites, and (c) salinity maps produced by unsupervised spectral classifications with maps based on EC1 estimation equations developed from the spectral and salinity observations at the sample sites. Our hypotheses were that the spectral observations sense the plant growth responses to soil salinity and that the growth responses can help quantify soil salinity. Successful accomplishment of the objectives would provide more quantitative relations between spectral observations and soil salinity than have appeared in the literature to date and demonstrate another way to determine the extent and severity of soil salinity and/or monitor the reclamation of cropped land.

METHODS

Field Sampling. Four fields of cotton within a 4.8 x 8.0 km (39 km^2) salt-affected intensive study area near Hanford in the San Joaquin Valley of California were used for this study (Lesch et al., 1992). The field designations and the spacing between transects and sample sites along the transects are summarized in Table 1. Spacing between transects and sampling interval along transects had been preplanned to provide at least 100 sample sites per field. Although the intervals between sample sites were determined by pacing, once selected the coordinates of each sample site were determined within 0.1 m with a Zeiss[3] DME theodolite system.

Soil samples were taken from the surface 2 cm, surface 30 cm and 30 to 60 cm depths at three positions within about 0.5 m of the central sample sites using Lord tubes and composited. Electrical conductivity of the saturated-soil extracts (ECe, dS/m^{-1}), determined by the procedures of Rhoades (1982), was the measure of soil salinity used. Salinities were designated EC0, EC1 and EC2 for the surface, surface 30 cm, and 30 to 60 cm depths, respectively.

---

[3] Trade names are included for the benefit of the reader and do not infer endorsement of, nor preference for the mentioned product by the U. S. Department of Agriculture.

Plant height (PH, inches) and percent bare area (PBARE) were the plant observations recorded. If plants were missing at the sample site, the height was recorded as zero, but the range in plant height within a 10 m x 10 m area surrounding the sample site was also measured and recorded. PBARE was estimated visually as percent of 10 m lengths of row surrounding the sample site that was devoid of plants. Thus PBARE recorded as zero meant a full stand of plants was achieved.

Spectral data. The photography and videography were acquired with systems mounted in a Aero Commander aircraft on the same date as the overpass by the satellite SPOT-1 occurred, 31 July 1989. Aerial photography using Kodak Aerochrome infrared 2443 film was acquired of the entire study area from 1500 m above ground level between approximately 1100-1300 hr Pacific standard time. After acquisition of the photography, videography of the test fields was acquired from 3050 m using the system described by Everitt et al. (1991). Wavelength sensitivity intervals are as given in Table 2.

The SPOT-1 satellite scene was centered on latitude 36° 13′ 20″ N and longitude 119° 49′ 03″ W. Wavelengths of the high resolution radiometer (HRV) system of this satellite are given in Table 2.

The vegetation indices calculated were NDVI defined by
$$NDVI = (NIR - Red)/(NIR + Red) \tag{1}$$
and GVI3 obtained by the procedure of Jackson (1983) for the three bands of each system except that the greenness of the bare soil was subtracted from the greenness calculated for each pixel (Wiegand et al., 1991). The GVI3 equations for photography (p), videography (v), and SPOT-1 HRV (s), respectively, were

$$GVI3p = -0.179 \text{ Green} -0.397 \text{ Red} + 0.900 \text{ NIR} - 39.32 \tag{2a}$$
$$GVI3v = -0.076 \text{ Green} -0.383 \text{ Red} + 0.920 \text{ NIR} + 7.01 \tag{2b}$$
(fields 2C, 3C and 9E)
$$GVI3v = 0.015 \text{ Green} - 0.224 \text{ Red} + 0.975 \text{ NIR} - 46.98 \tag{2c}$$
(field 9A only)
$$GVI3s = -0.362 \text{ Green} - 0.261 \text{ Red} + 0.895 \text{ NIR} - 7.42 \tag{2d}$$

A separate equation was needed for the videography data for field 9A because its reference soil plane differed from that of the other fields.

Digital data extraction. The positive photographic transparencies were digitized using an Eikonix model EC 78/99 digital imaging camera. Red, green and blue dichroic filters from Optical Coating Laboratories, Inc. were used successively on the camera to produce 8-bit digital count (DC) readings that characterized the film's NIR, red, and green wavelength responses (Table 2). Pixel size in the digitizations ranged from 1.0 to 1.2 m^2 ground area per digital value. Averages of 3 x 3 arrays of the digital counts centered on the sample sites were also determined as possibly more representative spectral samples than the 1 m^2 samples.

The videography images for each field in each wavelength, as recorded on 400 horizontal line resolution Super-VHS recorders, were "grabbed" with a Matrox digitizing board and IMAGER software and saved. The 8-bit digital counts acquired by this procedure represented an area on the ground about 3.5 m in diameter.

The digital tapes for the SPOT-1 HRV scene were purchased from SPOT Image Corporation. The 8-bit data for the 39 km^2 test site were extracted, displayed, and electronically magnified to better locate the corner pixels of each field.

The data extracted for each field were stored on floppy disks. Then the data from all bands of all systems were registered to the NIR band of the photography for each field using PCI, Inc. EASI/PACE image processing software. The registered images were saved. The coordinates of the sample

270

sites, in meters, were converted to pixel coordinates in the NIR photographic image and overlaid on images for the other bands. The digital counts for the sample sites for each data type were then extracted.

Data analysis. The above procedures resulted in two distinct data sets. One set consisted of the plant, soil, and spectral data for the sample sites, whereas the other was the digital spectral data for all pixels in each field (the whole population) in the photography, videography and HRV images.

The sample site data were used to determine how the observations interrelated, to examine them for outliers, and to select a single depth of salinity measurements to characterize the sample sites. Scatter plots of data pairs and correlation matrices were the main procedures used. In addition, the EC1 and spectral observations for the sample sites were submitted to multiple regression analyses to produce equations for estimating EC1 for every pixel in each field from the sample site data. Those equations by field for photography were

2C: $EC1p = 2.11 - 0.031$ NIR $+ 0.131$ Red $- 0.073$ Grn $\quad R^2 = 0.68 \quad$ (3a)
3C: $\quad\quad\;\; = 6.48 - 0.056$ NIR $+ 0.038$ Red $+ 0.016$ Grn $\quad\quad = 0.64 \quad$ (3b)
9A: $\quad\quad\;\; = 2.64 - 0.020$ NIR $- 0.057$ Red $+ 0.138$ Grn $\quad\quad = 0.39 \quad$ (3c)
9E: $\quad\quad\;\; = 5.49 - 0.027$ NIR $+ 0.182$ Red $- 0.094$ Grn $\quad\quad = 0.64 \quad$ (3d)

The corresponding equations for the videography were

2C: $EC1v = -1.65 - 0.004$ NIR $+ 0.033$ Red $+ 0.029$ Grn $\quad R^2 = 0.59 \quad$ (4a)
3C: $\quad\quad\;\; = 12.08 - 0.083$ NIR $+ 0.010$ Red $+ 0.020$ Grn $\quad\quad = 0.39 \quad$ (4b)
9A: $\quad\quad\;\; = -1.71 - 0.006$ NIR $+ 0.032$ Red $+ 0.068$ Grn $\quad\quad = 0.46 \quad$ (4c)
9E: $\quad\quad\;\; = 8.15 - 0.054$ NIR $+ 0.092$ Red $+ 0.026$ Grn $\quad\quad = 0.59 \quad$ (4d)

The whole field data for the digitized photography were analyzed in two ways. First, unsupervised classifications of the digital counts into 8 spectral categories were performed for each field with PCI, Inc. software. One category was a small threshold group of outlier pixels while 7 are meaningful categories. The procedure used migrating means and 4-dimensional histograms to develop and separate spectral classes and generated mean and covariance matrices for each class (or category). Individual pixels were classified by a maximum likelihood ratio criterion using the statistics generated for each class. Outputs of the procedure provided the digital count means, for each of the three bands used, that characterized each category and the number of pixels classified into each category. These classifications were saved, color-coded, and displayed on a CRT as a color map of the classifications. To reduce the number of inclusions of individual and small "islands" of pixels in the displays, the individual pixel classifications were smoothed by the median DC of the 3 x 3 array surrounding each pixel. These smoothed classifications were saved, the report was again generated, and the results were color-coded, displayed, and photographed.

In the second analysis for each field, the multiple regression equations from the sample sites (Eqs. 3 and 4) were used to estimate the mean salinity of each spectral class from the mean digital count for each classification category. These mean EC1 values were graphed versus spectral category ordered by increasing salinity. The EC1 values at the midpoint between categories were used to set the ranges in each salinity class. The computer was then programmed to apply Eq. (3) to each of the approximately 100,000 photographic pixels per field and to assign each pixel to the salinity category that its estimated EC1 fell in. These classifications were saved and the number of pixels in each category was listed. Color codes corresponding to those for the unsupervised spectral classifications were assigned and the images were displayed and photographed.

The results from the two above procedures were submitted to a matrix coincidence analysis using the PCI, Inc. subroutine, MAT. The procedure sorts pixels by a look-up procedure into the 2-way matrix of boxes corresponding to the categories from the spectral classification (image 1) and the salinity classification (image 2). Pixels along the diagonal of the

271

matrix were classified into the same category in both images, while increasing distance from the diagonal indicated increasing disparity in category correspondence between images.

For publication purposes the spectral and salinity classifications were converted from PCI, Inc. software raster files to the personal computer version of ARC/INFO vector files. The vector files were used to create line drawing classification maps. The data were smoothed twice with a 5 x 5 pixel array mode filter before the figures were produced.

RESULTS

<u>Plant, Soil and Spectral Interrelationships</u>. Table 3 summarizes the correlation coefficients between soil salinity, expressed as electrical conductivity of the saturated-soil extracts, for each depth sampled and plant height (PH) and percent bare (PBARE) observations at the sample sites. Salinity of the surface 30 cm of soil (EC1) was more closely correlated with both the plant and spectral observations than either EC0 or EC2 and was chosen as the measurement to characterize the fields for soil salinity. Scatter diagrams between plant height and EC1 are displayed by field in Figure 1.

Table 4 summarizes the correlations between the spectral measurements (individual bands and the vegetation indices NDVI and GVI3) and both PH and EC1 by field. The magnitudes of the correlation coefficients were similar, but opposite in signs for the two variables. For field 2C, EC1 related somewhat more closely to the photographic and videographic spectral observations than did PH, but for fields 3C, 9A, and 9E the reverse was true. The negative correlation between the NIR band for photography and PH resulted from the inverse relation between plant vigor and digital counts in the digitization of the photography. The correlations for the SPOT-1 HRV data were quite poor, except for field 9A which had larger areas that were more uniform in both the salt-affected and unaffected portions of the field than did the other fields. We concluded that the 20 m ground resolution HRV data was not an even multiple of the sampling interval used in any of the test fields, which made it difficult to obtain a close correspondence between the two samplings. From Table 4 it was also decided to emphasize NDVI as the spectral characterizer of plant growth and soil salinity conditions.

<u>System Comparisons</u>. Table 5 summarizes the correlations among bands of the three systems used for two fields, 3C and 9A. For the photography the correlations are for the nominal 1 m^2 pixels at the sample site (p1) and the means of a 3 x 3 array of pixels (p3) centered on the sample sites. The latter have a ground resolution between 3 and 4 m similar to the resolution of the video, 3.5 m. The 3 x 3 pixel means for the red and green bands of photography related somewhat better to the red and green bands of video than do the central pixel data. For field 3C the NIR band of the video correlates poorly with all other bands. However, all correlations that exceed 0.21 are significant at the p = 0.01 level, and those between photographic and SPOT data are higher than those between videography and SPOT data. In contrast, the correlations among the red and green bands of SPOT-1, photography, and video were relatively high for field 9A. The video NIR and SPOT-1 NIR bands were also rather highly correlated (r = 0.76).

We learned from the sensor band and system comparisons that the red and green bands contained more information than the NIR bands and that differences in ground resolution <u>per</u> <u>se</u> were not a principal source of variation. We also deduced at this point in data analysis that videographic and photographic data sources should support very similar conclusions about plant growth and soil salinity.

<u>Spectral and salinity classifications</u>. Spectral and salinity classifications are reported for only the full resolution photographic data. Figure 2

displays the spectral classes for each field versus mean estimated EC1 from Eqs. 3a - 3d. Equation (3c) for field 9A had a coefficient of determination, R^2, of 0.39, because of disagreement between the EC1 measurements at some sample sites and the plant appearance at those sites, as verified by direct inspection of color prints of the CRT displays of the digitized photography. Equations 4a, 4b, and 4d for estimating EC1 from the videographic data had lower R^2 values than those for photography. Therefore, EC1 estimates from them would be less reliable than those for the digitized photography from Eqs. 3a, 3b, and 3d.

Table 6 summarizes the percent of the area in each field and the EC1 range for the unsupervised spectral classifications. The number of pixels in each class from the unsupervised spectral classification report was divided by the total number of pixels within the field and multiplied by 100 to get the percent of the field area in each class (classification category). The EC1 range was determined from Fig. 3. Figure 3 was obtained, in turn, by inserting the mean digital count for each spectral band by class into Eqs. 3a - 3d. Field 9A was not included in Table 6 because of uncertainty in Eq. 3c. In Table 6, the zero or threshold class consisted of pixels with erratic DC that defied classification. Those pixels often occurred at field edges. According to Table 6, 70% of the area in field 2C had EC1 <4, 78% of the area in 3C had EC1 <4.2, and 42.8% of 9E had EC1 <4.8.

Figure 3 displays the patterns of the spectral classification (SC) and the salinity classification (EC1) for field 2C in upper and lower parts of the figure, respectively. In this field three soil berms cross the field horizontally that sometimes interrupt the patterns. The cross-hatch patterns, which are the same for both parts of the figure, were chosen so that they graded from lightest (whitest) for the least saline areas to darkest (grayest) for the bare saline areas. The cross-hatch symbols corresponding to increasing (or decreasing) salinity usually occurred adjacent to each other as one proceeds from most saline to least saline, or vice versa. In Fig. 4, there are 474 polygons in the spectral classification map and 861 in the salinity map probably because of more intermingled classification categories from Eq. (3a) than in the pure spectral classifications. The data for both were smoothed twice before the maps were produced. The correspondence between the two maps is evident and is especially good between the saline areas along the top center of the maps. The least saline area in both maps also forms a generally upper left to lower right pattern.

The matrix analyses provided a more refined examination of the agreement/disagreement between the maps. That analysis for field 2C is summarized in Table 7, where pixels along the diagonal were classified into the same class by both procedures. For this field 62.7% of the classifications coincided. The matrix analysis showed that most of the confusion was with the adjacent class which was encouraging since point samples of salinity were interpolated to represent unsampled areas. Variation also existed in the photographic digitizations due to skips in the plant stands, changes in soil type (color) across fields, and film exposure variations within frames. For comparison, the percent coincidence was 37.8% for field 3C, 68.4% for field 9A, and 62.1% for field 9E. The low correspondence between spectral and salinity categories for field 3C is due to the large number of incidences of assignment of salinity to the next lower or higher category, relative to the spectral classification, for this heterogeneous field. Field 9A had fewer rapid changes in salinity and the coincidence of classification was good, even though estimates of salinity for the sample sites (Eq. 3c) were imprecise.

DISCUSSION

The salinity category classifications in this work are based on the salinity estimation equations (3) and (4). Therefore, outliers in the data sets used to produce those equations should be deleted before the equations are developed.

There was an inconsistency between the salinity observations for field 9E and plant growth. Figure 1 shows that no plants grew in fields 2C, 3C and 9A if EC1 exceeded 15 dS m^{-1}, while in 9E plants were about 50 cm (20 in.) tall at EC1 = 15 dS m^{-1}. Evidently the soil samples from field 9E did not represent the salinity of the root zone well.

The literature indicates that cotton is one of the most salt tolerant agricultural crops (Maas and Hoffman, 1977), but its response in a particular environment depends on stage of development, soils, management practices and weather (Maas, 1990). Seedlings are less salt tolerant than older plants, so in saline environments the first effort is to achieve a stand. Rains et al.(1987) reported that, provided stands were achieved, vegetative growth was suppressed much more than lint yields. Maas and Hoffman (1977) and Maas (1990) give the yield suppression threshold for cotton as 7.7 dS m^{-1} and the slope of the yield reduction at higher salinities as 5.2% per dS m^{-1}.

One reliable spectral system is adequate for measuring and monitoring salinity. We used three systems in order to intercompare them. The digitized aerial photography was better than the digitized videography. The 20 m SPOT-1 HRV data would be useful for synoptic studies of salinity but did not associate well with the sample site data for these intensively sampled fields if salinity gradients were frequent and steep. Wiegand et al. (1991) sampled a 15 ha salt-affected field of cotton on a 60 m grid and found essentially the same relationships with yield and plant cover for videography and HRV observations. For all systems the visible red and green bands related more closer to the plant and soil variables than the near-infrared band. Thus, they contained more of the scene information. For both photography and videography the range in the NIR band was rather narrow and monocolor displays of them lacked contrast.

CONCLUDING REMARKS

In this study there were moderate correlations among spectral observations (individual bands and vegetation indices) for three systems, the plant observations height and (1-cover), and the soil salinity measurements. We have also demonstrated that unsupervised spectral classifications identify the plant growth categories associated with soil salinity, and that spectral data for sites sampled for salinity can be used to estimate the salinity of all pixels in the field. Reports generated from the spectral and salinity classifications provide the percent of the field in each salinity category and the classifications can be mapped. These information forms are very practical for managing individual fields and monitoring salinity changes in them.

ACKNOWLEDGEMENTS

We have many colleagues to thank: Rene Davis for acquisition of the photography and videography; Scott Lesch for clarifying sampling procedures, preparing the sample site data sets, and performing the photographic film digitizations; Ricardo Villarreal for conducting the spectral and salinity classifications and matrix analyses; Arthur J. Richardson for deriving equations for locating sample sites, for matrix analysis interpretation, and along with Wayne Swanson for preparation of Fig. 4; Romeo Rodriguez for numerous statistical analyses and preparation of figures; and, Carol Harville and Saida Cardoza for manuscript preparation.

Table 1. Size and Designations of Fields, Sample Intervals and Number of Samples, and Range, Mean and Standard Deviation of Electrical Conductivity of Saturation Extracts EC1 from the Surface 30 cm of Soil for the Fields Studied

| Field | Size | Sample transects | Spacing Between | | Samples taken | EC1 | | |
| | | | Transects | Samples in transects | | Range | Mean | S.D. |
	(ha)	(No.)	(m)	(m)	(No.)	- - - - dS/m - - -		
2C	13.7	13	23	15 or 16	198	0-17	2.25	3.3
3C	12.5	14	24	13 to 6	149	0-25	3.07	4.0
9A	16.1	13	31	13	169	0-17	4.29	3.3
9E	12.4	6	50	17	102	0-27	7.65	5.3

Table 2. Systems Used, Wavelengths of Each System, and Nominal Pixel Size

| System | | | |
Photography a	Videography	SPOT-1 HRV	Band
- - - - - - - - - -nm - - - - - - - - - - - - -			(Name)
610 - 730	845 - 857 b	790 - 890	Near-infrared
515 - 570	644 - 656	610 - 680	Red
390 - 480	543 - 552	500 - 590	Green
	Pixel Size (m)		
1.0 - 1.2	3.5	20	

a Filters used on Eikonics camera to digitize the Kodak Aerochrome infrared film 2443.
b A 0.5 neutral density filter is also used.

Table 3. Correlations Among Electrical Conductivity (EC) of Saturated Soil Extracts by Soil Depth, Plant Height (PH) and Percent Bare Area (PBARE). ECO = Soil Surface, EC1 = 0 - 30 cm depth, EC2 = 30 - 61 cm depth.

Plant variable	C2	C3	9A	9E
			FIELD	
		- - - - - - - - - - -r - - - - - - - - - - -		
			ECO	
PH, In.	-0.62	-0.45	-0.33	No
PBARE,%	0.75	0.55	0.31	ECO
			EC1	
PH, In.	-0.72	-0.65	-0.64	-0.82
PBARE,%	0.81	0.74	0.55	0.75
			EC2	
PH, In.	-0.72	-0.56	-0.35	-0.78
PBARE,%	0.79	0.65	0.14	0.74
r for p = 0.01	0.18	0.21	0.25	0.18
r for p = 0.05	0.14	0.16	0.20	0.14

Table 4. Correlations of PH and EC1 by Field with Spectral and Other Ground Truth Variables.

Variable	2C PH (In.)	2C EC1 (dS/m)	3C PH (In.)	3C EC1 (dS/m)	9A PH (In.)	9A EC1 (dS/m)	9E PH (In.)	9E EC1 (dS/m)
				Field				
A. Photography				- - - - - - - - - r[a] - - - - - - - - - -				
NIR	-0.46	0.58	-0.33	0.10	-0.59	0.50	-0.38	0.46
Red	-0.69	0.77	-0.57	0.47	-0.70	0.60	-0.90	0.78
Grn	-0.67	0.75	-0.55	0.45	-0.71	0.62	-0.90	0.78
NDVI	0.77	-0.73	0.63	-0.53	0.72	-0.57	0.90	-0.68
GVI3	0.61	-0.57	0.52	-0.69	0.03	-0.03	0.89	-0.70
B. Videography								
NIR	0.54	-0.46	0.35	-0.41	0.43	-0.21	0.80	-0.61
Red	-0.68	0.72	-0.59	0.43	-0.73	0.62	-0.88	0.71
Grn	-0.66	0.71	-0.50	0.36	-0.69	0.64	-0.83	0.69
NDVI	0.70	-0.69	0.60	-0.46	0.74	-0.56	0.85	-0.67
GVI3	0.69	-0.68	0.59	-0.51	0.61	-0.40	0.86	-0.67
C. SPOT-1 HRV								
NIR	Data		-0.09	0.19	0.23	-0.08	-0.53	0.36
Red	not		-0.02	-0.12	-0.67	0.55	0.44	-0.25
Grn	extracted		-0.02	-0.08	-0.67	0.53	0.45	-0.25
NDVI			-0.03	0.17	0.58	-0.41	-0.51	0.33
GVI3			-0.07	0.19	0.35	-0.18	-0.53	0.36
ECO	-0.62	0.80	-0.45	0.68	-0.33	0.47	No data	
EC1	-0.72	1.00	-0.65	1.00	-0.64	1.00	-0.82	1.00
EC2	-0.72	0.91	-0.56	0.75	-0.35	0.62	-0.78	0.82
PBARE	-0.73	0.81	-0.68	0.74	-0.72	0.55	-0.85	0.75

[a]r for p = 0.05: 0.14   0.16   0.20   0.14
r for p = 0.01: 0.18   0.21   0.25   0.18

Table 5. Interband Correlations of Digital Counts (DC) for Photography Central (p1) and 3x3 Array of Pixels (p3) with Videography and SPOT-1 HRV Central Pixel DC for the Sample Sites in Fields 3C and 9A.

Field	Band	Photography (p)			Video (v)			SPOT-1 HRV (s)		
		NIRp1	Redp1	Grnp1	NIRv	Redv	Grnv	NIRs	Reds	Grns
							-(r)-			
3C	NIRp1	1.00	0.84	0.85	0.22	0.63	0.64	-0.18	0.32	0.30
	Redp1		1.00	0.99	-0.14	0.78	0.71	-0.01	0.18	0.18
	Grnp1			1.00	-0.12	0.79	0.72	-0.05	0.19	0.19
	NIRp3	0.93	0.74	0.75	0.22	0.67	0.72	-0.20	0.32	0.29
	Redp3	0.74	0.87	0.87	-0.24	0.88	0.85	-0.01	0.18	0.16
	Grnp3	0.76	0.87	0.88	-0.19	0.87	0.85	-0.06	0.19	0.17
	NIRv	0.22	-0.14	-0.12	1.00	-0.36	-0.20	-0.22	0.02	0.04
	Redv	0.63	0.78	0.79		1.00	0.87	-0.02	0.14	0.11
	Grnv	0.64	0.71	0.72			1.00	0.01	0.09	0.08
	NIRs							1.00	-0.54	-0.61
	Reds								1.00	-0.94
	Grns									1.00
9A	NIRp1	1.00	0.82	0.84	0.05	0.59	0.66	0.09	0.53	0.52
	Redp1		1.00	0.99	-0.29	0.80	0.81	-0.15	0.73	0.73
	Grnp1			1.00	-0.23	0.80	0.82	-0.10	0.75	0.74
	NIRp3	0.94	0.80	0.82	0.02	0.66	0.70	0.07	0.53	0.52
	Redp3	0.76	0.89	0.90	-0.28	0.84	0.82	-0.15	0.74	0.75
	Grnp3	0.78	0.88	0.91	-0.23	0.83	0.82	-0.10	0.76	0.76
	NIRv	0.05	-0.29	-0.23	1.00	-0.41	-0.24	0.76	-0.37	-0.45
	Redv	0.59	0.80	0.80		1.00	0.89	-0.20	0.75	0.77
	Grnv	0.66	0.81	0.82			1.00	-0.05	0.76	0.76
	NIRs							1.00	-0.28	-0.35
	Reds								1.00	0.98
	Grns									1.00

Table 6. Percent of field area and EC1 range in each spectral class for fields 2C, 3C, and 9E.

	2C		3C		9E	
Class code	Field area (%)	EC1 range (ds/m)	Field area (%)	EC1 range (ds/m)	Field area (%)	EC1 range (ds/m)
0[a]	2.3	-	3.5	-	1.2	-
1	23.6	<0.5	25.2	<0.9	42.1	<4.8
2	11.7	0.5-0.8	14.6	0.9-1.6	10.6	4.8-6.0
3	19.3	0.8-2.2	15.9	1.6-2.4	16.1	6.0-8.9
4	15.7	2.2-4.0	14.6	2.4-3.3	10.4	8.9-12.3
5	12.4	4.0-6.2	8.1	3.3-4.2	8.1	12.3-15.5
6	9.2	6.2-8.8	10.7	4.2-5.9	6.7	15.5-18.4
7	5.8	>8.8	7.4	>5.9	4.8	>18.4
Total	100		100		100	

[a] Class 0 is composed of pixels that don't fit the pattern for any of the established classes.

Table 7. Distribution of numbers and percent of pixels in salinity classification relative to total number of pixels in each spectral class.

EC1 class	Spectral Class						
	1	2	3	4	5	6	7
	- - - - - - - - - - - - - No. Pixels - - - - - - - - - - -						
	(% of class)						
1	24659	4567	5260	111	25	16	1
	(76.2)	(27.7)	(19.4)	(0.5)	(0.1)	(0.0)	(0.0)
2	4424	8681	3644	71	5	5	0
	(13.7)	(52.6)	(13.5)	(0.3)	(0.0)	(0.0)	(0.0)
3	3134	3239	13775	5129	178	33	1
	(9.8)	(19.6)	(50.9)	(24.5)	(1.0)	(0.3)	(0.0)
4	106	17	4175	11663	4857	142	1
	(0.0)	(0.0)	(15.4)	(55.8)	(28.2)	(1.1)	(0.0)
5	18	0	148	3758	9148	2751	2
	(0.0)	(0.0)	(0.5)	(18.0)	(53.2)	(21.3)	(0.0)
6	7	0	57	188	2990	8976	329
	(0.0)	(0.0)	(0.2)	(0.9)	(17.4)	(69.4)	(4.1)
7	0	0	1	0	11	1008	7671
	(0.0)	(0.0)	(0.0)	(0.0)	(0.0)	(7.8)	(95.8)
	32348	16504	27060	20919	17203	12931	8005

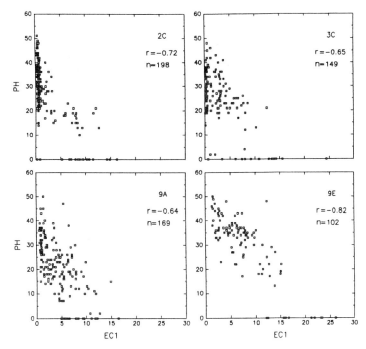

Figure 1-Plant Height (PH) Versus Salinity of the Surface 30 cm of Soil (EC1) for Four Fields (2C, 3C, 9A, 9E).

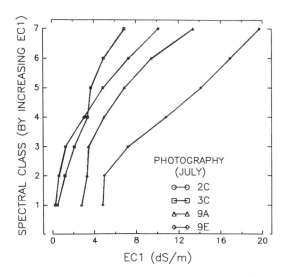

Figure 2-Spectral Class Number in Order of Increasing Salinity Versus Mean Salinity of Each Class. Class Mean Digital Counts Were Inserted into Eqs. 3a - 3d to Estimate the Mean Salinity of Each Class.

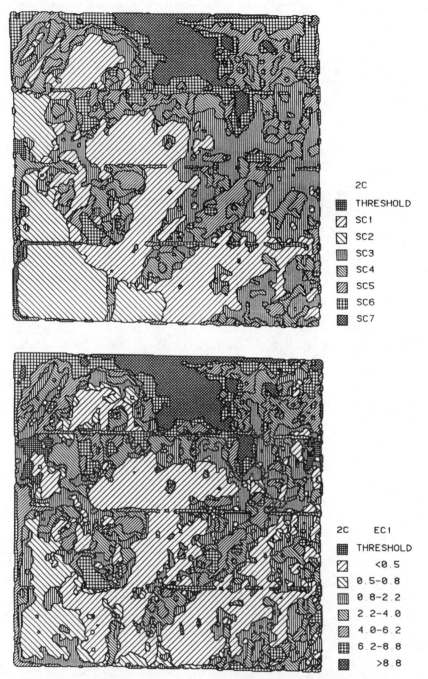

Figure 3-Spectral Classification (SC) Map (Upper) and Predicted Salinity (EC1) Map (Lower) for Field 2C.

REFERENCES

1. Carter, D.L. 1975. Problems of salinity in agriculture. In: Ecological Studies. Analysis and Synthesis, Vol. 15, Plants in Saline Environments, eds. A. Poljakoff-Mayber and J. Gale, 25-35. New York: Spranger-Verlag.

2. Everitt, J.H., A.H. Gerbermann, and J.A. Cuellar. 1977. Distinguishing saline from non-saline rangelands with SKYLAB imagery. Photogram. Eng. Remote Sens. 43:1041-1047.

3. Everitt, J.H., D.E. Escobar, A.H. Gerbermann, and M.A. Alaniz. 1988. Detecting saline soils with video imagery. Photogram. Eng. Remote Sens. 54:1283-1287.

4. Everitt, J. H., D. E. Escobar, and J. R. Noriega. 1991. A high resolution multispectral video system. Geocarto Int. 6:45-51.

5. Jackson, R.D. 1983. Spectral indices in n-space. Remote Sens. Environ. 13:409-421.

6. Kauth, R.J. and G.S. Thomas. 1976. The tasseled cap--A graphic description of the spectral temporal development of agricultural crops as seen by LANDSAT. In Proc. Sympos. Machine Proc. Remotely Sensed Data, 41-49. New York: Insti. Elect. and Electronic Eng.

7. Lesch, S.M., J.D. Rhoades, L.J. Lund, and D.L. Corwin. 1992. Mapping soil salinity using calibrated electromagnetic measurements. Soil Sci. Soc. Amer. J. 56:540-548.

8. Maas, E.V. and G.J. Hoffman. 1977. Crop salt tolerance--current assessment. J. Irrig. and Drainage Div., ASAE. 103(IR2):115-134.

9. Maas, E.V. 1990. Crop salt tolerance. In: Agricultural Salinity Assessment and Management. ASCE Manuals and Reports on Engineering Practice No. 71, ed. K.K. Tanji, 262-304. New York: Amer. Soc. Civil Eng.

10. Myers, V.I., L.R. Ussery, and W.J. Rippert. 1966. Photogrammetry for detailed detection of drainage and salinity problems. Trans. ASCE 6(4):332-334.

11. Rains, D.W., S. Goyal, R. Wayrauch, and A. Lauchli. 1987. Saline drainage water reuse in cotton rotation system. Cal. Agric. 41(9-10):24-26.

12. Rhoades, J.D. 1982. Soluble salts. In Methods of Soil Analysis, Part 2, 2nd edition, ed. A.L. Page. Agronomy 9:167-178. Madison, Wisconsin: Amer. Soc. Agronomy.

13. Richards, L.A., ed. 1954. Diagnosis and Improvement of Saline and Alkali Soils. U.S. Dept. Agric. Handbook No. 60. Washington, DC: GPO.

14. Richardson, A.J. and C.L. Wiegand. 1977. Distinguishing vegetation from soil background information. Photogramm. Eng. 43:1541-1552.

15. Sharma, R.C. and G.P. Bhargava. 1988. Landsat imagery for mapping saline soils and wetlands in north-west India. Int. J. Remote Sens. 9:39-44.

16. Szabolcs, I. 1989. Salt-affected soils. Boca Raton, Florida: The CRC Press, Inc.

17. Tanji, K.K. 1990. The nature and extent of agricultural salinity problems. In Agricultural Salinity Assessment and Management. ASCE Manuals and Reports on Engineering Practice No. 71, ed. K. K. Tanji, 1-17. New York: Amer. Soc. Civil Eng.

18. Tucker, C.J. 1979. Red and photographic infrared linear combinations for monitoring vegetation. Remote Sens. Environ. 8:127-150.

19. Wiegand, C.L., R.W. Leamer, D.A. Weber and A.H. Gerbermann. 1971. Multibase and multiemulsion space photos for crops and soils. Photogramm. Eng. XXXVII:147-156.

20. Wiegand, C.L., A.J. Richardson and E.T. Kanemasu. 1979. Leaf area index estimates for wheat from Landsat and their implications for evapotranspiration and crop modeling. Agron. J. 71:336-342.

21. Wiegand, C.L., A.J. Richardson, D.E. Escobar and A.H. Gerbermann. 1990. Vegetation indices in crop assessments. Remote Sens. Environ. 35:105-119.

22. Wiegand, C.L., J.H. Everitt and A.J. Richardson. 1992. Comparison of multispectral video and SPOT-1 HRV observations for cotton affected by soil salinity. Int. J. Remote Sens. 13:1511-1525.

A GEOGRAPHIC INFORMATION SYSTEM FOR USE IN THE SOUTH AFRICAN SUGARCANE INDUSTRY

G.G. PLATFORD[1]   J.M. DINKELE[2]

There are many proprietary Geographic Information Systems (GIS) available. The Universal GIS (UNIGIS, a product of the Aircraft Operating Company SA) was selected because of the practical requirements of the sugar industry. This market is relatively new in South Africa and the choice depends on the software support service available rather than the refinement of the product. This paper does not compare different systems but reports on the one selected.

In South Africa sugarcane is grown on the east coast, where the climatic and topographic features are not ideal. Steep slopes, variable soil types and rainfall often limit growth in this area, but sugarcane is a good conservation crop which can often tolerate harsh conditions. The crop is a perennial, propagated by vegetative means and, depending on climatic conditions, it matures and is ready to be cut at cyclic periods from twelve to twenty-four months of age. After harvest, the new crop (ratoon) grows from the root stock which has been left undisturbed in the ground. A number of ratoons are cut from the same root system before yields or plant populations decline below an economic threshold. When this happens the existing crop is removed and a new crop is planted. For most areas this means that the ground is tilled only once in ten years or longer.

It is essential to have an accurate record of ground slope, soil type, rainfall, temperature and crop management factors such as yield, applied fertilisers and herbicides, so that logical decisions can be made on the time to replant a field. Most sugarcane growers in South Africa have industry quota maps with farm and field boundaries and aerial photographs to help them associate their visual impressions of crop, soils and slopes with the actual positions on the farm. Other climatic maps (rainfall, temperature, etc.) are available to help them in reaching management decisions. To compare crop production from farms at different locations is difficult unless all the input factors are known and comparisons are often made using too few of these growth controlling factors. The use of a GIS which can allocate all the parameters to a specific site can improve any analyses of data (Berjak, 1989).

To achieve a reasonable analysis vast amounts of digital data are required, which are at present mostly in line form on maps or photographs. This needs to be converted into a digital format before it can be used in a computer system, but once that is achieved the data can be used for all conventional mapping tasks as well as for the analysis of spatial and attribute data.

OBJECTIVES

The first step in setting up the system for the sugar industry was to decide on the requirements from the system. Many different map types and scales are used and there is a constant demand for these maps for different applications. Queries about the crop and

---

1. Head, Farm Planning Department
   SASA Experiment Station

2. Director AOC Systems
   Durban

ground conditions are also frequently posed together with enquiries about meteorology, soils and slopes. Recommendations for surface water runoff control are given to growers to enable them to protect their soils from the high intensity storms which occur in the industry.

A sugar industry GIS

The GIS provides a mapping service and co-ordinates all queries from the database files for the sugarcane areas.

An integrated mapping service: many types of maps such as quota control maps, soils maps, contour maps, land use plans, climate maps and others are required at different scales and for different regions.

Cadastral and survey maps: maps are required to be legally accurate and to have updating and reporting facilities. The individual grower's allocation of sugarcane growing land is controlled by the quota map. This is constantly in need of updating as field roads change over time.

Analysis of spatial and alpha-numeric data: the system must be able to analyze the data for specific times. Crop, fertilizer, herbicide and pest and disease data require to be analysed in relation to all the other data sets allocated to each site.

Scale change facilities to interpret data on:

an industry scale (Natal and Eastern Transvaal)
mill group scale (Umzimkulu, Sezela, etc) 14 to 15 mill group areas
ward scale (ie. a number of growers or miller planter sections)
farm and field scale (ie. 500 ha to 1 ha).

Farm surface and management planning: resources need protection and must be planned according to the slopes, rainfall and soils of the site. Included in this is the requirement to plot lines at variable gradients and to design works using accepted models for soil losses.

Based on PC technology: single stand alone or in a network system. A high degree of compatibility with other languages and systems is essential. It must be able to accept data from all other sources.

Easy to operate: user friendly and fast.

GIS AND CAD

The difference between a GIS and many advanced Computer Aided Drawing (CAD) packages is that a GIS normally includes a CAD package for drawing or graphics functions. The GIS also has attached database files and data management software which gives the data some artificial intelligence. The GIS software allows drawing entities to be formed and linked to other entities at different levels or to know where line segments are shared with other polygons. The data files are distributed to specific co-ordinates and can be questioned and the answers used to make management decisions. The software selected for use in the sugar industry was a Universal Geographic Information System (UNIGIS) package supplied by a local aerial mapping company. It is built up of several modules, most of which can be operated independently.

STRUCTURE OF UNIGIS

UNIGIS is a collection of data which have a geographic connotation. Geographic information consists of all data that refer to mans' environment. It has both positional and non-positional attributes. Positional attributes include position, size and topology, while non-positional attributes include any descriptive data associated with a geographic feature, such as ownership of a property, type of vegetation, soil depth, etc.

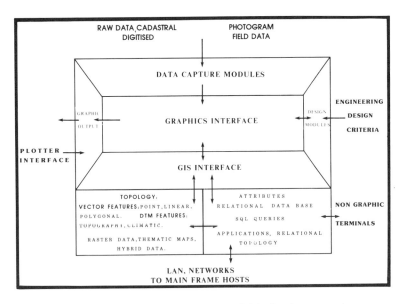

Fig 1. UNIGIS consists of a number of individual software packages which are all designed to interact.

Topology defines the position between objects in space. It is the study of those geometric relations which can be defined without reference to co-ordinates. For example, a field is inside a farm boundary. In the context of geographical information, topological relationships include adjacency, coincidence, inclusion, exclusion, containment and intersection.

The structure of UNIGIS is summarised in Fig 1. Most of the data resides in an integrated database, which consists of spatial data, and non-spatial or attribute data in a Relational Database Management System (RDMS). These data interact with a graphics interface in UNIGIS and are capable of being manipulated for non-geographic applications. The graphics interface is the core of the system for data capture, data presentation and data exchange. Modules included are:

PROCAD: this is a locally produced graphics package which uses a "head up" approach for ease of operation with minimal use of a keyboard. Instantaneous pop-up menus and simple graphic icon selections are used. All the usual CAD functions such as construction sets, symbol and text insertion, overlays and measuring facilities are included.

PROMAP: the module has been specifically designed for cadastral and related mapping requirements (Sanderson, 1987) and extends the PROCAD capability to cover topography. This design module includes surface modelling, roads design, town planning and cadastral calculations, digitizing and digital mapping functions, and data exchange modules using the SIF and DXF exchange formats (Luijendijk, 1988). The graphics interface consists of a library of graphics and CAD functions, although not requiring that the data reside in a drawing file.

PADS: this module (Photo Analytic Digitizing System) controls digitizing from single aerial photographs. Various checking and squaring functions are carried out to correct anomalies in the photograph.

DIGIPAC: this is used to convert line drawings into a form which can be read by the computer. The data can then be used by all the computer programs.

SURFACE: the module is capable of modelling any surface with options to generate contours, calculate bulk earthworks or view a site in perspective (3D). It can be used for slope and aspect analyses.

PROFILE: profiles and sections along roads or pipelines can be generated by this module with the surface DTM.

GRADE: defined gradients can be drawn between certain points on the DTM. This module is designed to allow the siting of diagonal extraction roads, terrace banks or any other line which needs a gradient.

DATA CAPTURE

The major and most expensive task in the GIS is to capture the positional elements data in a digital format. The alpha-numeric or attribute data are easily transferred as data base files.

Positional data capture

Cadastral (surveyed legal lines) data and text: Two paths were available to capture this data (Dinkele, 1989). Firstly, for legal data, the cadastral boundaries for individual ground plots were captured by entering distances and directions of lines from the legal document (surveyor's diagram or general plan). Checking was done by conventional survey techniques. Secondly, when the legal data was not required, the cadastral or field boundaries were captured either by drawing all line types or by digitizing from line drawings. At this stage, the data were a set of lines and text in a CAD drawing, with no topological structure or intelligence. The lines and text were differentiated into levels to separate the data into identifiable homogeneous groups. The data are then processed into topological data structures by batch mode line splitting and polygon processing software. The data structures allow the UNIGIS interrogation software to extract information such as adjacency, inclusion, intersection and route analysis. The data are now object orientated, the objects being polygons, which relate on one level to their topological components or entities and on the other to any number of attributes stored in a relational database.

Topographic data capture

Relief data: have been traditionally represented as contours lines. These lines join points of equal elevation. They are easily interpreted by the human eye and brain combination, quick to generate by manual techniques and easy to use on a paper map. However, in the digital environment, they take up a lot of space and are awkward for interpretive analysis. A truly digital representation of relief is the Digital Terrain Model (DTM), where a grid or triangulated network of spot heights is generated, from which all other relief information such as contours, ground heights, ground profiles, and slope analyses are interpolated.

DTMs have been generated from ground surveyed spot heights, from contours digitized from existing maps, from spot heights captured from stereo-photographs in a photogrammetric stereo plotter, or from contours captured digitally in a stereo-plotter. The data are stored in a regular grid for ease of data retrieval and to conserve the space that vector co-ordinates would use. Contours are not needed in the system and can be generated for viewing on the screen or at the map production phase.

Planimetric topographic data: consists of shapes which are formed from discreet point and line elements. These are stored as strings of co-ordinates, i.e. in vector format. Many of the features are topographically related and share common boundaries or intersect at common points. Height is used also when defining topology, but is more easily confined to the DTM and to specific points on features which protrude above or are below the terrain surface.

Shared points and line segments are stored only once and are related to their features by two-way pointers. This conserves space and preserves the topological relationships within the positional data structures. The data structures provide smooth transitions between different feature entities, i.e. from line segment to line segment, line segment to circular arc, circular arc to polynomial curve segment, and so on. Similarly, the data capture software provides a direct method to move from one such entity to another. Specialised mapping functions are included. These include automatically squaring buildings, capturing both sides of parallel features (e.g. roads), simultaneously indicating areas to be hatched or filled with symbols, or lines with symbols along their length.

Planimetric data have been captured in several ways. Firstly, they have been digitised from existing maps. Secondly, some features have been captured directly from stereo photographs in a photogrammetric stereo-plotter (Dinkele, 1990). This involves orienting the photographs relative to each other in space and then digitizing the co-ordinates from the resultant stereoscopic model. Transformations to a map projection system is then possible. A third method is to digitize co-ordinates from a single photograph enlarged to a scale of 1:10 000 using the PADS module and then to subject them to a transformation using true ground reference points. The cadastral information and planimetric topographical data are stored in the same format. The editing functions can be used for both data sets, and topological relations are set up between cadastral and topographic information, e.g. a river can be viewed both as a topographic feature and also the boundary of a farm.

Alpha-numeric data capture

Data sets in most formats have been entered into the GIS where they are attached to specific locations or centroids. Growers' field records on crop performance were extracted from the Field Record System (FRS), stored in the mainframe computer and read directly into the GIS using dBASE software. Fertiliser, crop pathology or any other data files are entered in a similar way.

Data import

The ability to communicate with other CAD and GIS packages makes UNIGIS an extremely valuable management and mapping tool.

HARDWARE

The use of two "386" high speed personal computers with large amounts of storage space and ancillary equipment enables the UNIGIS to run effectively in a small office. Databanks have been established and stored on disk and on a back-up tape streamer. The hardware used for this particular system also includes two large digitizers and an eight pen plotter.

ACCURACY AND REPETITION

When cadastral legal data are stored from co-ordinates they are exact. Thereafter the accuracy of captured data depends on the scale at which the data is captured. With existing digitizers, which have a resolution of 100 lines per inch (4 per mm), at a scale of 1:6 000 one millimetre on the map equals six metres on the ground. Digitizing from maps is accurate to within two to three metres of its ground position. For most applications at a farm or district scale this is sufficient, as these maps are captured into an accurate cadastral grid network.

Usage

Map maintenance and production: papers and other materials used to record mapping data deteriorate with time, so maps and plans are continuously replaced or need to be updated. In digital mapping systems changes are made to the digital data, and the tracing techniques with associated human errors are replaced by digital plotting machines, taking a fraction of the time required to trace or copy a map.

The production and updating of acceptable maps of different types and at varying scales is one of the major benefits of UNIGIS. As growers develop their farms according to prepared plans, or as new photography becomes available, updating of existing maps is easily accomplished. Producing new maps at different scales is just as simple, as there is a scale change facility built into the system.

The continuous digital map is often conceptualised as a single database file containing geo-referenced information. Although this is possible in a massive computer system, it is more practical to divide the data into smaller data sets stored in separate data files. These smaller data sets are often called "coverages", and are related to one another by a common map projection. Data sets are split into an interactively accessible map at any scale, which can be displayed, interrogated, edited, and plotted. Data from each individual coverage can be selectively displayed, and there is full integration of data between different coverages.

Soil parent material maps

The conversion of existing soil parent material maps to more meaningful soil maps, using the DTM to locate slope position or aspect and elevation, allow catena effects in soil development to be used. The import of data from external sources is possible and Fertilizer Advisory Service (FAS) or soil profile information can be used.

Land use plan production

The production of land use plans for individual growers has to date been completed by hand. With the terrain modelling facility now available soil protection banks at specified gradients are sited semi-automatically depending on the slope and soil type of each position. Roads at detemined gradients to be used for cane haulage routes are sited again using the module. The surface area net function together with the other topology query functions can also identify wetland positions or drainage area problems defined by the user. Estimates of areas during queries are also possible by the software and this can be presented in report or map form.

Grid and surface survey queries

By using the module for surface topology these types of surveys are completed quickly and more efficiently than when drawn by hand. The lengths and areas of features are calculated when they are entered into the system. Maps according to desired scales can be generated. The terrain model can also be used when slope analyses are required or slope aspect is requested.

Management queries

If sufficient data on crop yields, fertiliser applications, herbicide sprayed and pest or disease surveys are available, they can be used in the UNIGIS and allocated to a specific location. Once this has been completed questions can be asked about any of the other relational databases and geographic information stored in the system.

Meteorological data queries

Existing meteorological data has been entered into the databank. As each site is located by ground co-ordinates, contours of the different recorded values for rain, temperature, evaporation, sunshine and other factors can be easily generated for various times. These can be integrated with any of the other relational database values to answer specific or general questions.

TRIAL AREA

Forty-three private farms and three sections belonging to a sugarcane miller, CG Smith, Illovo Group in the Mid-Illovo district in the Natal midlands were selected as a trial area (26 000 ha). For these farms all the available quota maps, soils maps, ortho-photos, form line maps (contour), land use plans and various aerial photographs were assembled. Cadastral information from the Surveyor General's office was used to set up the frame work for the selected farms.

The databanks of crop related details were transferred from the main frame computer on to dBASE files on 5.1/4" discs. These consisted of FAS and FRS records and could also have included any pest and disease surveys or varietal records. Real long term meteorology data was entered from the Computer Centre for Water Research (CCWR) databank. The legal cadastral data of farm boundaries were entered from files to set up an accurate framework for the model. The remainder of the information from the maps was captured in digital format using the software procedures described. Only nine of the farms which were included in the trial area are currently on the FRS. However, as long as individuals keep accurate field records directly related to existing field numbers, they can be used in the databases. Similarly, for records of other parameters, the same procedures can be followed.

Exercises:

The first exercise carried out on the data was to check the mapping accuracy. The original quota maps for three quota holders were selected. The cadastral information in legal format was entered and the planimetric data was digitized using the AO digitizer. Text and other databases were added. Measurements were made of the areas digitized using the software. The resulting data was stored on a 4.5" computer disc and plotted using a standard A1 multipen plotter. The transparent original was placed on top of the plotted paper copy to check for differences. No significant differences could be seen between the original and the computer generated drawing. The same map was then produced at a scale of 1:10 000 and 1:5 000.

Some examples of queries used in the trial area:

a) Show and measure the area which is in Quota 7531053 between slopes of 15 − 23%, has a north-easterly aspect, has erodible soils less than 500mm deep, is planted with variety N12, and which has produced more than 5,6 tons cane/ha/month.

b) Show and plot the area which is in the Illovo mill group (7531), above 700 m elevation, has TMS (mistbelt) soils, had more than 500 mm rain in the past nine months, and where the mean monthly evaporation has been greater than 205 mm.

c) Draw, measure and report the areas in the Sezela mill group with less than 2% slope, less than 500 metres from a drainage line and without cane.

d) Show and plot Quota number 7531-0213, all fields cut between 10-04-1988 and 12-12-1988, variety 376, with Dwyka soils greater than 350 mm, on slopes of less than 15%, and with a north-west to north-east aspect.

e) Using the PADS module an aerial photograph of one of the farms was digitized onto the cadastral framework. The software made the necessary changes in scale required by distortion in the photograph.

f) A series of sugarcane haulage routes and a band 50 metres wide along some indicated streams were plotted using DTM. Soil boundaries were added to these areas.

g) A single farm was used to site extraction roads and possible loading sites from selected points. Terrace banks and grassed waterways for soil protection purposes were designed for different soil types with changing erosion hazard ratings.

h) Terrain models of the meteorology data were established and contours for rainfall were calculated. Areas on the north-west to north-east slopes of between 10 and 20%, and soils deeper than 500 mm which had received more than 800 mm of rain were isolated.

After the trial area was completed, data capture for the rest of the mill group area continued. Because of the high cost of obtaining legal data from the Surveyor General, cadastral farm boundaries, field and infield roads, contours and soil boundaries were digitized from existing line maps. This data was put into various drawing files before being processed in UNIGIS. Meteorological models of regional rainfall and temperatures were extracted from an external database and entered into the system.

DISCUSSION

Substantial data must be captured before any meaningful analysis can be completed. The exercise in the Natal Midlands area showed that once the database has been captured it can be used effectively, as the system is very flexible. The large amount of data which must be handled in any GIS limits the speed with which questions can be answered. With the advent of faster machines and more advanced data storage and retrieval techniques, this will become less of a problem. The use of scanning procedures to replace or supplement digitizers in the capture of data will increase the efficiency with which information is entered into the database. Although UNIGIS is a powerful mapping and information tool, it does need competent and skilled personnel to operate the system. Farm management and positional queries must be addressed to skilled operators who can then interrogate the total database. The data entered by digitizing must be edited and checked for accuracy, and this is at present time consuming. Despite this, the mapping facilities and data queries which can be answered justify the initial outlay on the system and the time taken to capture information.

The system is used on a regular basis and specific requirements for the sugar industry are incorporated into the package as needed. Specific sugarcane growth models and water balance models have been added as sub-routines, to enable predictions of yields to be made using all the accumulated data in the system. As technological advances are made the system will become useful.

REFERENCES

1. Berjak, M (1989). The development of a GIS at the Institute of Natural Resources. Paper presented at Session 10 of SAGIS 89, International Conference on Geographic Information Systems in Southern Africa, Pietermaritzburg, July 1989.

2. Dinkele, JM (1989). UNIGIS topological data base management package User Reference Manual. Aircraft Operating Company, Johannesburg, October 1989.

3. Dinkele, JM (1990). The capture and storage of topographic information in digital format from analogue stereo plotters. Masters thesis, Department of Surveying and Mapping, University of Natal, Durban.

4. Luijendijk, SJ (1988). Promap SIF input and output processors Reference Manual. Published by Promap (Pty) Ltd, P.O. Box 9107, Johannesburg.

5. Sanderson, MJ (1987). Promap interactive surface and contouring system User Reference Manual. Published by Promap (Pty) Ltd, P.O. Box 9107, Johannesburg.

A NEW TECHNOLOGY FOR ARMORING AND DEACTIVATING PYRITE

V. P. (Bill) Evangelou*   Xiao Huang**

It is estimated that each year in the United States alone, wet cleaning of coal leaves behind aqueous slurries of refuse containing at least 10 million tons of pyrite. Upon exposure to the atmosphere, pyrite oxidizes and generates acid drainage which is usually enriched with heavy metals, causing widespead pollution of surface and underground waters. Finding an effective method to prevent pyrite oxidation has been a long-term concern for mine engineers and environmental scientists. Currently, acid metallic drainages produced by pyrite oxidation are controlled by several technologies: 1) application of limestone or rock phosphate, 2) application of bacteriocides, and 3) creation of fully anoxic environments by using clay liners, plastic liners, asphalt etc. The first two acid drainage remediation technologies have a short life span, and the third, liner technologies can be cost prohibitive as well as ineffective over time due to deterioration. In our laboratory*, we developed a new acid drainage remediation technology which involves specific targeting, where pyrite crystals are coated with ferric-phosphate, a highly acid stable mineral which renders pyrite inert.

---

*Patent pending by the University of Kentucky

INTRODUCTION

It is estimated that each year in the United States alone, wet cleaning of coal leaves behind aqueous slurries of refuse containing at least 10 million tons of pyrite (Blessing et al., 1975). Upon exposure to the atmosphere, pyrite oxidizes and generates acid drainage which is usually enriched with heavy metals, causing widespead pollution of surface and groundwater.

A number of scientists have carried out research to control pyrite oxidation but no one has been fully successful. Oxidation of pyrite by an oxidizer such as hydrogen peroxide (H_2O_2) can be represented as follows:

$$FeS_2 + 7.5H_2O_2 + H_2O = Fe^{3+} + 2\ SO_4^{=} + 7H_2O \qquad [1]$$

$$FeS_2 \overset{\curvearrowright}{\underset{\searrow Fe^{2+}}{}} H_2O_2$$

According to Eq. [1], the observed pyrite oxidation rate is the sum of direct oxidation of S_2^{2-} by H_2O_2 and oxidation of S_2^{2-} by Fe^{3+}. Oxidation of Fe^{2+} by H_2O_2 is a rapid reaction and, at any time t, all Fe released from pyrite

---

*V.P. Evangelou, Professor, and Xiao Huang, Visiting Scientist, University of Kentucky, Lexington, KY   40546-0091 U.S.A.

oxidation would be expected to be in the form of Fe^{3+}. It is believed that in nature, the rate at which pyrite oxidizes is controlled by regeneration of Fe^{3+} which catalyzes oxidation of pyrite (Singer and Stumm, 1970). In nature, generation of Fe^{3+} is carried out quite rapidly microbiologically. Based on the above, pyrite oxidation can be significantly reduced by complexing Fe^{3+}, depriving the system of oxygen (O_2), and using alkaline material to neutralize any acid products produced. Examples of such technologies and their weaknesses are given below.

Acid drainage abatement technologies involve physical barriers to prohibit transfer of water and oxygen to the sulfidic minerals. The physical barriers include plastic liners, clay liners, and even asphalt. None of these techniques has proven effective due to the tendency of the liners to break (Caruccio and Geidel, 1983; Skousen et al., 1987). Additionally, use of such liners is costly and often technically unfeasible.

Another technology for controlling acid drainage generation is use of alkaline materials such as limestone, rock phosphates, and, at times, sewage sludge (Stiller et al., 1984; Stiller et al., 1986; Loomis and Hood, 1984). All these materials have one major limitation. They are difficult to apply; because of their low solubility, physical mixing with pyritic material is required. Moreover, evidence shows that addition of limestone may, in fact, enhance pyrite oxidation (Evangelou et al., 1985; Stiller et al., 1984). Alkaline earth materials are believed to control acid drainage production through neutralization of pyrite oxidation products and through precipitation of Fe^{3+}. However, a low pH could exist near pyrite surfaces even when alkaline earth materials are present. The relatively high pH near alkaline material surfaces promotes inorganic oxidation of Fe^{2+} to Fe^{3+} and consequently a large quantity of Fe^{3+} available near pyrite surfaces promotes S_2^{2-} oxidation. This is demonstrated below

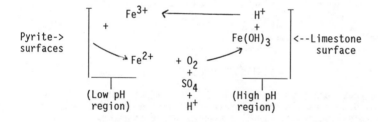

Under the conditions described in the above diagram, pyrite oxidation appears to proceed rapidly. (The primary applicant has observed pyrite refuse piles from lead ore processing plants in Greece where the chemical equivalent ratio of $CaCO_3$ to pyrite was 2:1, yet, sulfate production was widespread).

Another form of acid drainage control is through application of bacteriocides which have a suppressing effect on activity of Thiobacillus Ferro-oxidans bacteria that convert Fe^{2+} to Fe^{3+}. Kleinmann (1980) was one of the first to introduce bacteriocidal control on acid drainage. Lately, several companies, including BF-Goodrich, are producing slow release pellets of such bacteriocides (Rastogi et al., 1986; Greskovich, 1986). The major disadvantage of this technology is that acid mine drainage production is suppressed for relatively short periods; pyrite oxidation by O_2 remains unaffected.

The major goal of this study was to develop and evaluate the technology of coating pyrite particles with $FePO_4$ precipitates by oxidation in phosphate solution.

In our laboratory, we have recently developed a new acid drainage control technology by which a relatively inert ferric phosphate coating could be generated on pyrite surfaces. The coatings shut off electron transfer between pyrite and oxidizers necessary for oxidation (Huang and Evangelou, 1991a,b). There are many advantages to using this technology. We believe, the inactivation of pyrite will be permanent and the technology is expected to be highly cost effective because only the surface of pyrite must be inactivated. Currently, no available technology for treating pyrite meets these two conditions.

The mechanism of ferric-phosphate coating deposition is demonstrated below.

```
        A                        B

   |    |                   |    |
 -Fe(II)-S₂(I)            -Fe(II)··PO₄
   |    |                   |    |
 -S₂(I) -Fe(II)           -S₂(I)  Fe(III)
   |    |   +      -->      |    |
 -Fe(II)-S₂(I)            -Fe(II)··PO₄
   |    |                   |    |
 -S₂(I) -Fe(II)           -S₂(I)  Fe(III)
   |    |                   |    |
```

Figure 1.   Schematic of oxidation-proof phosphate surface coating.

Physical evidence of formation of $FePO_4$ coating are presented in the electron microscope photos shown in Fig. 2.   Photo A reveals surface appearance of coated pyrite, while photo B shows surface appearance of uncoated pyrite.

A

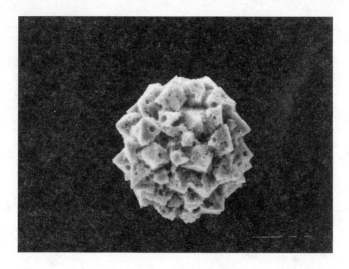

B

Figure 2. Scanning electron microscope photos showing morphology of framboidal pyrite particles with (A) or without (B) $FePO_4$ coatings (Huang and Evangelou, 1992).

In photo B crystals of pyrite in an octahedral arrangement (every Fe^{2+} is surrounded by six S_2^{2-}) can be clearly seen with holes in the middle of surfaces where oxidation had most likely taken place. The role of $FePO_4$ coating on pyrite oxidation is shown in Fig. 3. Note difference in release of SO_4^{2-} during pyrite oxidation by H_2O_2 in the absence and presence of 0.013 M ethylenediaminetetraacetic acid (EDTA) and 10^{-3} M phosphate. In the presence of EDTA, a metal-complexing ligand, Fe^{3+} produced by direct oxidation with H_2O_2 is prevented from oxidizing pyrite. This leads to a decrease in the rate of pyrite oxidation (Fig. 3) . In the presence of phosphate, Fe^{3+} is also prevented from oxidizing pyrite due to the formation of $FePO_4$ precipitates. If $FePO_4$ exists as a discrete phase rather than as coatings, the effect of phosphate on pyrite oxidation should be the same as that of EDTA. The difference in the release of SO_4 between curve II and curve III strongly indicates the formation of surface $FePO_4$ coatings. As time passes, the coating increases in thickness and the release of SO_4^{2-} diminishes.

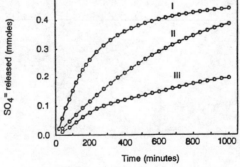

Figure. 3. Release of SO_4 during oxidation of 50 mg of pyrite under the following conditions: I) 0.5% H_2O_2; II) 0.5% H_2O_2 in the presence of 0.013 M EDTA; and III) 0.5% H_2O_2 in the presence of 10^{-3} M KH_2PO_4.

Based on the above, it can be concluded that pyrite particles can be coated with a protective coating at the expense of a certain fraction of pyrite. The data in Fig. 4 show that formation of phosphate coatings with a solution of 0.1% H_2O_2 and 10^{-3} $\underline{M}$ KH_2PO_4 consumed less than 5% of the pyrite sample. We believe that this consumed fraction of pyrite can be decreased by decreasing concentrations of H_2O_2. In order to test stability of coatings, we exposed pyrite with coatings to extremely strong oxidizing conditions (not encountered in the fields), 0.5% H_2O_2. As shown in Fig. 4 (curve B), the pyrite sample with phosphate coatings displayed a much lower oxidation rate.

Stability of phosphate coating could be increased by the addition of a small concentration of phosphate in solution or by addition of a small quantity of akalinity. The latter is under investigation.

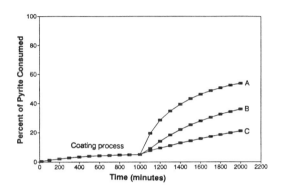

Figure 4. Pyrite oxidation as a function of time. The section of the curve before 1000 minutes represents the coating process. Curve A (1000-2000 minutes) represents oxidation of pyrite with coatings removed by leaching with 50 mL of 2 $\underline{M}$ HCl and then exposed to 0.5% H_2O_2; curve B represents oxidation of $FePO_4$-coated pyrite by 0.5% H_2O_2 (Huang and Evangelou, 1991 a,b).

At this point it is important to note that the technology of coating pyrite as described above is not to be confused with application of rock phosphate (Renton et al., 1988). Rock phosphate complexes dissolves iron (Fe^{2+}) and thus reduces potential production of Fe^{3+}. Consequently the potential for pyrite oxidation is also reduced (Stumm and Morgan, 1970). Rock phosphate does not coat pyrite, rather, it complexes released Fe^{2+} from oxidizing pyrite (Sainju, et al. 1991). This ferrous phosphate surface coating renders rock phosphate inactive. Therefore, effectiveness of rock phosphate in controlling pyrite oxidation in nature is short lived. These results are supported by field observations (Meek, 1991). Our ferric phosphate treatment controls pyrite oxidation via two mechanisms. 1) It converts Fe^{2+} to Fe^{3+} and the latter is strongly complexed by phosphate and 2) ferric phosphate precipitate forms a stable coating on the surface of pyrite and renders it inactive.

REFERENCES

1. Blessing, N.V., J.A. Lackey, and A.H. Spry. 1975. In Minerals and the Environment. (ed. M.J. JONES). pp 341. Institution of Mining, London.

2. Caruccio, F.T., and G. Geidel. 1983. The effect of plastic liner on acid loads/DLM site, W.V. In Proceedings, Fourth West Virginia Surface Mine Drainage Task Force Symposium, Clarksburg, W.V.

3. Evangelou, V.P., J.H. Grove, and F.D. Rawlings. 1985. Rates of iron sulfide oxidation in coal spoil suspension. J. Environ. Qual. 14:91-94.

4. Greskovich, J.A. 1986. Success I - A case study on improving the quality of gob pile leachate. In Proceedings, Seventh West Virginia Surface Mine Drainage Task Force Symposium. Morgantown, WV.

5. Huang, X. and V.P. Evangelou. 1992. Kinetics of pyrite oxidation as influenced by phosphate. Submitted to Geochim. Cosmochim. Acta.

6. Kleinmann, R.L.P. 1980. Bacteriocidal control of acid problems in surface mines and coal refuse. Proceedings of National Symposium of Surface Mining Hydrology, Sedimentology and Reclamation. University of Kentucky, Lexington, KY. pp. 31-38.

7. Loomis, E.C., and W.C. Hood. 1984. The effects of anaerobically digested sludge on the oxidation of pyrite and the formation of acid mine drainage. Proceedings of National Symposium of Surface Mining Hydrology, Sedimentology and Reclamation. University of Kentucky, College of Engineering. pp. 1-18.

8. Meek, A. Jr. 1991. Assessment of acid preventative techniques employed at the Island Creek Mining Company Tenmile Site. Proceedings of the twelfth annual West Virginia Surface Mine Drainage Task Force Symposium. April 3-4. Morgantown, W.V.

9. Rastogi, V., R. Krecic, and A. Sobek. 1986. ProMac systems for reclamation and control of acid production in toxic mine waste. In Proceedings, Seventh West Virginia Surface Mine Drainage Task Force Symposium. Morgantown, WV.

10. Renton John J., Stiller Alfred H. and Rymer Thomas. 1988. The use of phosphate materials as ameliotators for acid mine drainage. In Mine Drainage and Surface Mine Reclamation, Vol. 1: Mine Water and Mine wastes, 67-75.

11. Sainju, U.M., V.P. Evangelou, and Xiao Huang. 1991. Manganese adsorption by calcite dolomite and rock phosphate and infrared analysis. J. Environ. Qual. (In Review.)

12. Singer, Philip C. and Werner Stumm. 1970. Acid mine drainage: the rate-determining step. Science. 167:1121-1123.

13. Skousen, J.G., J.C. Sencindiver, and R.M. Smith. 1987. Procedures for mining and reclamation in areas with acid-producing materials. The Surface Mine Drainage Task Force and the West Virginia University Energy Research Center. p. 43.

14. Stiller, A.H., J.J. Renton, and T.E. Rymer. 1986. The use of phosphates for ameliorization. In Proceedings, Seventh West Virginia Surface Mine Drainage Task Force Symposium. Morgantown, W.V.

15. Stiller, A.H., J.J. Renton, T.E. Rymer, and B.G. McConaghy. 1984. The effect of limestone treatment on the production of acid from toxic mine waste in barrel scale weathering experiments. In Proceedings, Fifth West Virginia Surf. Mine Drain Task Force Symp. Morgantown, W.V. p. 9.

16. Stumm. W., and J.J. Morgan. 1970. Aquatic Chemistry. John Wiley and Sons, Inc., New York, NY. p. 583.

ACID MINE DRAINAGE TREATMENT ALTERNATIVES

J.G. Skousen, T.T. Phipps, and J. Fletcher[1]

Since the early 1970's, West Virginia laws and regulations have advanced mining and reclamation techniques to prevent acid mine drainage (AMD) from being formed during surface coal mining operations. Overburden analytical methods were developed and are currently used to identify rock layers which are acid-toxic, potentially acid-producing, neutral, or alkaline-producing (Skousen et al., 1987; Skousen et al., 1990; Ziemkiewicz and Skousen, 1992). Through representative sampling, accurate analysis, and proper interpretation, overburden handling and placement plans may be developed. Each operator must carefully develop the mining and reclamation plan based on each site's unique overburden characteristics and must implement the overburden handling plan with care and consistency (Larew and Skousen, 1992).

Even with the application of techniques and amendments to prevent AMD from occurring, AMD is still a persistent problem. When AMD is present during active mining operations and also after mining, treatment of this poor quality water to NPDES standards for discharge into a receiving stream is the only option. For this reason, much money and time are spent by the coal industry in utilizing the most cost effective method and chemical for treating their water. Treatment of AMD includes neutralization of acidity and also removal of metals through precipitation reactions.

Active Systems

Active systems are those AMD treatment systems which require continual addition of chemicals or other alkaline agents for neutralizing acid water. Treating AMD in this conventional fashion is expensive and requires time and manpower to keep the system operative. Alkalinity added to AMD with chemicals is effective in removing metals and raising pH, but often requires a large initial equipment investment and also subsequent, constant reagent costs.

Treatment of AMD is based on the effluent standards or limits placed on the quality of the discharge. EPA established "technology based" effluent limitations which includes standards for pH, iron, manganese, suspended solids, and settleable solids. Sometimes "technology based" standards were not stringent enough for the particular discharge water, and "water quality based" effluent limitations were established in the NPDES permit. Once the effluent limitations were established, a treatment facility with a specific chemical can be designed to meet the NPDES effluent limits. The effluent limits help determine the amount of aeration and flocculation the water requires, the pH necessary for metal precipitation, the amount of chemical needed, and provide an estimate of the costs associated with the entire treatment system.

Four chemicals are typically used in treating AMD: calcium hydroxide (hydrated lime), sodium carbonate (soda ash or briquettes), sodium hydroxide (caustic), and anhydrous ammonia. Each chemical has advantages and disadvantages which make it more appropriate for a specific treatment situation and for specific effluent limitations.

---

[1] Jeffrey G. Skousen, Associate Professor; Tim T. Phipps, Associate Professor; and Jerald Fletcher, Associate Professor; College of Agriculture and Forestry, West Virginia University, Morgantown, WV 26506-6108.

The four primary characteristics important for selection of an appropriate chemical are the rate and degree of pH increase, its solubility in water which influences the degree of mechanization, handling, and cost.

The degree of pH increase is important because metals in AMD precipitate at different pH ranges. Ferric iron (Fe^{+3}) converts to an orange precipitate as ferric hydroxide at a pH of 3.5 or greater. Ferrous iron (Fe^{+2}) reacts with hydroxides to form a bluish-green solid at a pH of 8.5 or greater. Soluble manganese changes to insoluble manganese hydroxide at a pH of 9.0 or greater. Aluminum precipitates in water at a pH of 5.5, but resolublizes at a pH of 8.5 or greater. Aeration and oxidation improves these precipitation reactions. Therefore, depending on the composition of metals and their concentrations in AMD, selection of the most appropriate chemical can be determined.

Solubility of the chemical dictates the method of dispensing the material. Hydrated lime requires extensive mixing and a large aerator is necessary to adequately mix the chemical with the water. Aeration also helps in the oxidation of ferrous iron to ferric iron and, in the process, reduces the pH needed and the amount of chemical required for iron precipitation. Hydrated lime systems are usually large and require a large initial capital investment, so the length of time that the system will be in operation is also a critical factor in determining the annual and overall cost of the system.

Caustic is very soluble and reacts with water quickly. Caustic can be simply dripped into the water without investing large funds for equipment. Soda ash briquettes are somewhat soluble and dissolve as AMD flows through the briquettes. Ammonia, on the other hand, is extremely soluble since it is injected as a gas. The ammonia should be injected near the bottom because it rises to the surface of the water.

Handling of these chemicals is a concern. Because all of these reagents are strong alkaline agents, extreme caution should be exercised when handling them. Skin contact with hydrated lime causes a burning and itching sensation. Contact is minimized because the lime is hauled to the site by large trucks and usually hydraulically placed into large bins. Caustic causes extreme burning upon skin contact and immediate flushing is required. Caustic is dispensed into large tanks on the site so contact can be minimal. Briquettes come in 50 or 100 pound bags and one of the advantages of this chemical is its ease of handling. The bags can be easily emptied into barrels or drums for dissolution in AMD. Ammonia is extremely dangerous. It has a powerful corrosive action on human tissue. Fortunately, ammonia's pungent odor is detectable at levels lower than what is considered dangerous and, since it is easily detected, warns of its presence in the air (Faulkner and Skousen, 1991). Extreme caution should be exercised when working with ammonia.

Costs associated with each of these chemicals varies with the season, the amount being bought and delivered, and the supplier. Hydrated lime is the cheapest reagent, followed by ammonia, briquettes, and caustic. But each chemical has its unique applications and sometimes the choice of chemical is less based on cost and more on convenience and the necessity for a specific water.

Passive Systems

Passive systems treat AMD without the continual addition of chemicals or neutralizing agents, and typically require less operation and maintenance. Three principal passive technologies currently exist: aerobic wetlands, composted organic wetlands, and anoxic limestone drains (Hedin and Nairn, 1992).

Passive treatment technology is rapidly growing and evolving. Hedin and Nairn (1992) have recently presented a model to aid reclamationists in deciding the appropriate passive system to use. The model is based primarily on flow rate and raw water chemistry including pH, acidity, ferric/ferrous iron and aluminum concentrations, and dissolved oxygen content. Recent information on these passive systems can be found in Faulkner and Skousen (1991), Hedin and Nairn (1990), Kleinmann and Hedin (1989), Skousen (1991), Skousen and Faulkner (1992), and Weider (1989).

The objective of this paper is to evaluate the costs for treating AMD with several passive methods and costs associated with using four chemicals at four different acid loads.

METHODS

Costs for these systems can be divided into two broad categories: installation cost and variable cost. Each of these can be broken down into several sub-categories. For example, installation cost includes materials, equipment, and labor. Variable cost includes reagent cost, annual labor, and maintenance. Once the amount and timing of the cost components and labor requirements are determined, the alternative technologies can be compared on two primary factors: net present value and annualized cost (Phipps et al., 1991).

Passive system costs were averaged from construction and installation costs for several wetlands built by the State of West Virginia, Tennessee Valley Authority, and private mining companies. Costs for anoxic limestone drain construction were based on estimates from the State of West Virginia.

Active treatment system costs were developed for four treatment systems under four sets of flow (gpm) and acidity (mg/l) conditions. These conditions were: 50-100, 1000-100, 250-500, 1000-2500 gpm-mg/l, respectively. The conditions were chosen to represent a wide range of flows and acidity, and the systems modelled were hydrated lime, soda ash, caustic, and ammonia.

Annual chemical costs for each system for each time horizon (five and twenty years) were calculated using acid neutralization formulas (Skousen, 1988) and acid load. The prices for the reagents, equipment and labor were based on actual costs to mining operators in West Virginia in May 1991. The price of soda ash was $0.14 per pound, ammonia was $0.15 per pound, caustic was $0.11 per pound and hydrated lime $0.03 per pound. All dollar values reflect 1991 U.S. dollars. Alternatives were compared on the basis of net present value (NPV) and annualized cost. NPV was calculated by taking the present value of the system including installation cost, annual labor and repair costs, annual reagent cost, and salvage value using a discount rate of 6%. The annualized cost was obtained by converting the total system cost (NPV) to an equivalent annual or annuity cost over the anticipated life of the system. The parameters used in the analysis were entered in a spreadsheet and may be varied.

RESULTS AND DISCUSSION

Costs for constructing composted organic wetlands ranged from $8 to $56 per m^2 of wetland. The average cost was $38 per m^2 of wetland. Costs for construction of anoxic limestone drains were calculated differently and, instead of the area it covered, was based on the acid load (flow in gpm and acidity in mg/l) of the water that flowed through the drain. This value coincided to costs associated with active treatment systems. The construction costs for anoxic limestone drains ranged from $1100 to $1500 per ton of acid per year. A ton of acid per year is equivalent to 10 gpm of AMD with 50 mg/l of acidity (flow in gpm multiplied by acidity in mg/l multiplied by 0.0022).

Active treatment system costs are presented in Tables 1 and 2. Each table presents the itemized costs, net present value (NPV) and annualized cost for soda ash, ammonia, caustic soda, and hydrated lime treatment systems.

Soda ash had the highest labor requirements (10 hours per week) because the dispensers must be filled by hand and inspected frequently. Caustic soda had the highest reagent cost per mole of acid neutralizing capacity and soda ash had the second highest. Hydrated lime treatment systems showed the highest installation costs of the four technologies because of the need to construct a lime treatment plant and install a pond aerator. However, the cost of hydrated lime was very low. The combination of high installation costs and low reagent cost made hydrated lime systems particularly appropriate for long term treatment of high flow/high acidity situations.

As shown in Table 1, caustic soda had the lowest annualized costs during a five year planning horizon for the low flow/low acidity situation, even though it had the highest reagent cost. Ammonia had the next lowest annualized costs, soda ash was third because of its high labor and reagent costs, and hydrated lime was fourth because of its high installation costs. With the intermediate flow and acidity cases, ammonia became the most cost effective, with hydrated lime second. Soda ash and caustic soda were the most expensive alternatives for all but the low flow/low acidity case. In the highest flow/acidity category, hydrated lime was clearly the least costly treatment system, with an annualized cost $230,000 less than ammonia, the next best alternative.

With a 20 year planning horizon (Table 2), caustic soda and ammonia were still the least expensive choices for the low flow/low acidity situation, and hydrated lime was sill clearly the least expensive alternative for the highest flow and acidity conditions. Ammonia, as in the five year budgets, was the cheapest treatment system for the intermediate flow/acidity conditions and was second for high flow/acidity combination. Caustic and soda ash were the most expensive treatment systems for all but the low flow/low acidity situation.

Passive treatment systems have not generally been effective on flows greater than 100 gpm because of the size or area limitations necessary for a large wetland. Some systems have been built for high flows (> 500 gpm), but water quality was not severe and plenty of space was available to build the system. Unless the AMD has low levels of mineral acidity, AMD of greater than 100 gpm has not been consistently treated satisfactorily by passive systems. These systems are best suited for low flow situations (Skousen, 1991).

In many low flow cases and in the majority of high flow situations, active chemical treatment of AMD is necessary. The costs illustrate, based on an analysis of acid load calculations and installation/maintenance costs, those systems which are most cost effective. However, the AMD from each site is unique and must be evaluated to determine the most appropriate system to reach the effluent limits and to maintain cost efficiency.

ACKNOWLEDGEMENTS

Funding for this project was provided by the U.S. Bureau of Mines through the National Mine Land Reclamation Center at West Virginia University under project WV-10.

Table 1 .   Costs of Alternative Technologies to Treat Acid Mine Drainage in West Virginia, Five Year Planning Horizon.

Flow and Acidity Conditions

	Flow (gpm)	50	1000	250	1000
	Acidity (mg/l)	100	100	500	2500

Chemical

Soda Ash

	50	1000	250	1000
reagent costs	$3,248	$64,955	$81,194	$1,623,876
repair costs	0	0	0	0
annual labor	14,040	14,040	14,040	14,040
installation costs	229	229	229	229
salvage value	0	0	0	0
NPV	73,051	332,985	401,388	6,899,728
Annualized cost	$17,343	$79,049	$95,288	$1,637,971

Ammonia

	50	1000	250	1000
reagent costs	$1,116	$22,323	$27,904	$558,071
repair costs	495	495	495	495
tank rental	480	1,200	1,200	1,200
annual labor	7,020	7,020	7,020	7,020
electricity	600	600	600	600
installation costs	5,936	6,357	6,357	6,357
salvage value	0	0	0	0
NPV	46,843	139,627	163,135	2,396,392
Annualized cost	$11,120	$33,147	$38,728	$568,895

Caustic Soda

	50	1000	250	1000
reagent costs	$3,852	$77,036	$96,295	$1,925,891
repair costs	0	0	0	0
annual labor	7,020	7,020	7,020	7,020
installation costs	283	5,478	5,478	5,478
salvage value	0	0	0	0
NPV	46,079	359,551	440,676	8,147,602
Annualized cost	$10,939	$85,356	$104,615	$1,934,211

Hydrated Lime

	50	1000	250	1000
reagent costs	$526	$10,527	$13,158	$263,169
repair costs	1,000	3,100	3,500	10,500
annual labor	6,500	11,232	11,232	11,232
electricity	3,500	11,000	11,000	11,000
installation costs	38,400	102,000	106,000	204,000
salvage value	5,750	6,500	7,500	25,000
NPV	82,656	248,193	264,216	1,431,760
Annualized cost	$19,622	$58,920	$62,724	$339,895

301

Table 2 .   **Costs of Alternative Technologies to Treat Acid Mine Drainage in West Virginia, Twenty Year Planning Horizon.**

Flow and Acidity Conditions

Flow (gpm)	50	1000	250	1000
Acidity (mg/l)	100	100	500	2500

Chemical

Soda Ash

reagent costs	$3,248	$64,955	$81,194	$1,623,876
repair costs	0	0	0	0
annual labor	14,040	14,040	14,040	14,040
installation costs	229	229	229	229
salvage value	0	0	0	0
NPV	198,518	906,296	1,092,553	18,787,000
Annualized cost	**$17,308**	**$79,015**	**$95,254**	**$1,637,936**

Ammonia

reagent costs	$1,116	$22,323	$27,904	$558,071
repair costs	495	495	495	495
tank rental	480	1,200	1,200	1,200
annual labor	7,020	7,020	7,020	7,020
electricity	600	600	600	600
installation costs	5,936	6,357	6,357	6,357
salvage value	0	0	0	0
NPV	119,397	371,316	435,326	6,516,302
Annualized cost	**$10,410**	**$32,373**	**$37,954**	**$568,121**

Caustic Soda

reagent costs	$3,852	$77,036	$96,295	$1,925,891
repair costs	0	0	0	0
annual labor	7,020	7,020	7,020	7,020
installation costs	283	5,478	5,478	5,478
salvage value	0	0	0	0
NPV	124,981	969,590	1,190,488	22,175,851
Annualized cost	**$10,896**	**$84,533**	**$103,792**	**$1,933,389**

Hydrated Lime

reagent costs	$526	$10,527	$13,158	$263,169
repair costs	1,000	3,100	3,500	10,500
annual labor	6,500	11,232	11,232	11,232
electricity	3,500	11,000	11,000	11,000
installation costs	38,400	102,000	106,000	204,000
salvage value	0	0	0	0
NPV	170,606	513,297	552,070	3,597,957
Annualized cost	**$14,874**	**$44,752**	**$48,132**	**$313,686**

REFERENCES

Faulkner, B.B., and J.G. Skousen. 1991. Using ammonia to treat mine waters. Green Lands 21(1): 33-38.

Faulkner, B.B., and J.G. Skousen. 1991. Field trials in AMD treatment. In: Proceedings of the 12th West Virginia Surface Mine Drainage Task Force Symposium, Morgantown, WV.

Hedin, R.S., and R.W. Nairn. 1992. Designing and sizing passive mine drainage treatment systems. In: Proceedings of the 13th West Virginia Surface Mine Drainage Task Force Symposium, Morgantown, WV.

Hedin, R.S., and R.W. Nairn. 1990. Sizing and performance of constructed wetlands: case studies. pp. 385-392. In: Skousen et al. (eds.), Proceedings of the 1990 Mining and Reclamation Conference, Vol. 2, Charleston, WV.

Kleinmann, R.L.P., and R.S. Hedin. 1989. Biological treatment of mine water: an update. pp. 173-179. In: Chalkley et al. (eds.), Tailings and Effluent Management. Pergamon Press, New York.

Larew, G., and J. Skousen. 1992. An ounce of prevention is worth a pound of water treatment. In: Proceedings of the 13th West Virginia Surface Mine Drainage Task Force Symposium, Morgantown, WV.

Phipps, T., J. Fletcher, B. Fiske, and J. Skousen. 1991. A method for evaluating the costs of alternative AMD treatment systems. In: Proceedings of the 12th West Virginia Surface Mine Drainage Task Force Symposium, Morgantown, WV.

Skousen, J.G. 1991. Anoxic limestone drains for acid mine drainage treatment. Green Lands 21(4): 30-35.

Skousen, J. 1988. Chemicals for treating acid mine drainage. Green Lands 18(3): 36-40.

Skousen, J.G., and B.B. Faulkner. 1992. Preliminary results of anoxic limestone drains in West Virginia. In: Proceedings of the 13th West Virginia Surface Mine Drainage Task Force Symposium, Morgantown, WV.

Skousen, J.G., and J.C. Sencindiver, and R.M. Smith. 1987. A review of procedures for surface mining and reclamation in areas with acid-producing materials. EWRC 871, West Virginia University, Morgantown, WV.

Skousen, J.G., R.M. Smith, and J.C. Sencindiver. 1990. The development of the acid-base account. Green Lands 20(1): 32-37.

Weider, R.K. 1989. A survey of constructed wetlands for acid coal mine drdainage treatment in the eastern United States. Wetlands 9(2): 299-315.

Ziemkiewicz, P.F., and J.G. Skousen. 1992. Prevention of acid mine drainage by alkaline addition. Green Lands 22(2): 42-51.

EVALUATION AND QUANTIFICATION OF ARMORING MECHANISMS OF CALCITE DOLOMITE AND ROCK PHOSPHATE BY MANGANESE[1]

V.P. Evangelou*, U.M. Sainju*, and Xiao Huang

Calcite, dolomite and rock phosphate are three minerals commonly used by the surface mining industry to remove manganese from surface-mine waters. However, data on the relative effectiveness of these minerals to remove manganese from solution are not available. In this study Mn^{2+} adsorption by calcite, dolomite and rock phosphate ($Ca_{10}(PO_4)_6 \cdot F$) (Occidental Chemical Corporation) was evaluated by batch equilibria studies and infrared spectroscopy. It was determined that Mn^{2+} adsorption maxima was in the order of rock phosphate > calcite > dolomite. Additionally, it was shown that for each equivalent of Mn^{2+} adsorbed by these minerals an equivalent quantity of Ca^{2+} or Ca^{2+} plus Mg^{2+}, depending on the mineral, was desorbed. Manganese (Mn^{2+}) adsorption isotherms appeared to be independent of solid to solution ratio but highly dependent on size of mineral particles. Adsorption isotherm behavior, stability diagrams and FT-IR spectra of the mineral-Mn^{2+} complexes strongly suggested that Mn^{2+} adsorption by calcite and dolomite was facilitated through formation of surface-Mn^{2+} hydroxy complexes. On the other hand, Mn^{2+} adsorption by rock phosphate was most likely facilitated through substitution of mineral surface exposed Ca^{2+} by Mn^{2+}. Hydroxylation of Mn^{2+} adsorbed onto calcite and dolomite as opposed to nonhydroxylation of Mn^{2+} adsorbed onto rock phosphate signified that the latter formed significantly stronger complexes than the former.

Much interest has been given to manganese in water emanating from coal mining environments. In these environments, Public Law 95-87 requires that Mn concentration be controlled through treating the water and/or the geologic strata (coal-spoil) with alkaline substances, e.g alkaline earth-carbonates. The maximum allowable under Public Law 95-87 total manganese concentration in waters emanating from coal mining environments is 4 mg L^{-1} with an average daily value for 30 consecutive discharge days of 2 mg L^{-1}. Saturation extract data of various geologic strata from Kentucky showed soluble Mn varied from a few mg L^{-1} up to 250 mg L^{-1} (Evangelou, et al.,

---

[1]The research leading to this document was supported by the United States Department of the Interior, Office of Surface Mining, under Cooperative Agreement No. HQ51-GR87-10018, and by the University of Kentucky, Agronomy Department, Lexington, KY. 40546-0091. Contents of this publication do not necessarily reflect the views and policies of the Office of Surface Mining, United States Department of the Interior, nor does mention of trade names or commercial products constitute their endorsement or recommendation for use by the U.S. Goverment.

*V.P. Evangelou, Professor; U.M. Sainju, Graduate Student, and Xiao Huang, Visiting Scientist, Department of Agronomy, University of Kentucky, Lexington, KY 40546-0091.

1990). Concentration of Mn in water treatment basins was also shown to vary from near zero to 100 mg L^{-1} (Nicholas and Foree, 1979).

In various field experiments and in actual practice where alkaline earth-carbonates have been used as means of controling soluble Mn, the practice has been observed to be ineffective because of coating (armoring) the alkaline earth-carbonate particles with Fe-oxides and /or Mn-oxides (Caruccio, F., 1991, personal communication). Adsorption of Mn^{2+} onto alkaline surfaces such as those of $MgCO_3$ and $CaCO_3$ has been reported in the literature (Boischot et al., 1950; McBride, 1979; Stumm and Morgan, 1970; Garrels and Christ 1965). McBride (1979) employing calcite Mn^{2+} adsorption isotherms and electron spin resonance (ESR) spectroscopy has shown that at low Mn^{2+} levels in solution Mn^{2+} chemisorbed onto the surfaces of $CaCO_3$. However, at high levels of Mn^{2+} in solution, after saturation of surface sites, nucleation at $CaCO_3$ surfaces was followed by slow precipitation of $MnCO_3$.

McBride (1979) carried out this work by generating calcite-Mn^{2+} adsorption isotherms employing $MnCl_2$ solutions ranging in concentration from 10^{-3} to 10^{-6} M with a total number of points per adsorption isotherm of only five. We felt that this range of Mn^{2+} solution concentration was not representative of the Mn^{2+} levels encountered in coal spoil solutions and the number of points per isotherm were not adequate enough to provide conclusive evidence on the mechanisms of Mn^{2+} adsorption. Furthermore, Mn^{2+} adsorption has not been evaluated in a similar manner with dolomite and rock phosphate. The latter two minerals are widely used by the coal mining industry as acid-ameliorants.

The purpose of this study was to quantify adsorption of Mn^{2+} by calcite, dolomite and rock phosphate employing Mn^{2+} solution concentrations in the range encountered in mining environments, and furthermore, to elucidate the potential mechanisms of Mn^{2+} adsorption employing stability diagrams and FT-IR spectroscopy.

MATERIALS AND METHODS

Calcite and dolomite rock samples (Ward's Earth Science) and a rock phosphate sample (Table 1) with an average particle

Table 1. Chemical composition of rock phosphate $(Ca_{10}(PO_4)_6) \cdot F.*$

Particle size	$Ca_3(PO_4)_2$	Fe_2O_3	Al_2O_3	SiO_2	CO_2	F
mm	- - - - - - - - - - - - - % - - - - - - - - - - - - - - - -					
0.6 - 1.7	68.1	1.3	0.9	8.5	3.9	3.6

*Analysis was given by B. Bandyogadhaay, Technical Director of Occidental Chemical Corporation, Agricultural Products, Florida Operations, White Springs, Florida.

diameter range of 0.6 mm to 1.7 mm were ground and passed through various size sieves to obtain particle sizes in the range of 1.50 mm to approximately 0.025 mm. Two gram quantities of these samples, in duplicate, were mixed with 25 ml of deionized water in 100-ml air-tight polypropylene centrifuge tubes and agitated in a shaker for 24 hours at room temperature of 23$\pm$2°C to remove any soluble components and/or inpurities. The test tubes were centrifuged for 10 minutes at 2000 rpm and decanted. After discarding the supernatants, the samples were equilibrated with 25 ml of $MnCl_2$ solutions ranging in concentration from 0.5 x 10^{-3} to 7.5 x 10^{-3} $\underline{M}$ by shaking for 24 hours. The $MnCl_2$ solutions prior to their introduction to the solid phases were made CO_2 free by bubbling helium. At the end of 24 hr shaking the pH of each of the suspensions were taken and after centrifuging for 10 minutes at 2,000 rpm, the supernatants were transferred into plastic bottles and acidified with a drop of 1 $\underline{M}$ HCl. A 10-ml quantity of the supernatant was removed prior to acidification for alkalinity determination with an autotitrimeter (Copenhagen Radiotitrimeter set, TTT80, ABU 80, PHM 82). Manganese, Ca, Mg, Na and K of the solutions were determined by atomic absorption spectrophotomery. Phosphate was determined colorimetrically by a Technicon Auto Analyzer I (1965).

Stability lines for the various carbonate and hydroxide solid phases were calculated based on thermodynamic constants reported in Stumm and Morgan (1981) and Lindsay (1976). In the case of calcite and dolomite, stability lines were estimated based on low and high HCO_3^- activity thresholds. These activity thresholds were estimated from solution titration data. In the cases of phosphate minerals, stability lines were estimated based on low and high H_2PO_4 activity thresholds. These activity thresholds were estimated by speciating total dissolved phosphate which was determined experimentally. Single-ion solution activities were estimated with the PCWATEQ computer simulation model (Rollins, 1989). A redox potential of -100mv was used as PCWATEQ input to maintain all manganese in the Mn^{2+} form.

Fourier transform infrared (FT-IR) evaluation of Mn^{2+} adsorption onto the solids tested was carried out by a sample preparation procedure similar to that used by McBride (1979) for electron spin resonance (ESR) analysis. Two gram samples of calcite, dolomite and rock phosphate were mixed with 100 ml of CO_2 free 0.025$\underline{M}$ or 0.1$\underline{M}$ $MnCl_2$ in 250-ml polypropylene centrifuge bottles and agitated in a shaker at room temperature of 23$\pm$2°C. At the end of 1 day and 30 days, solid particles suspended in the solution were removed from the bottle by setting the bottle to rest for 5 minutes to allow coarse particles to settle. The suspension was then transferrend to another bottle and centrifuged for 10 minutes at 2000 rpm. The two types of solid materials (course and fine particles) so obtained were dried under vacuum and FT-IR spectra were obtained using diffuse reflectance. For comparison purposes infrared spectra of $MnCO_3$, and freshly precipitated $Mn(OH)_2$ and Mn-phosphate were also obtained.

Freshly precipitated $Mn(OH)_2$ was prepared by titrating 100 ml of 0.1$\underline{M}$ $MnCl_2$ with 104 ml of 0.2 $\underline{M}$ NaOH to pH 9.0 in the presence of the He gas using an autotitrimeter (Copenhagen Radiotitrimeter set, TTT80, ABU 80, PHM 82). After washing the precipitate several times with H_2O to remove excess chloride, the solid was dried in a desiccator under vacuum. Similarly, Mn-phosphate was prepared by titrating 100 ml of 0.1$\underline{M}$ $MnCl_2$ with 101.5 ml of 0.1 $\underline{M}$ Na_2HPO_4. Precipitationn took place at pH 4.58. After washing the precipitate ($MnHPO_4$) several times with H_2O to remove excess chloride, the solid phase was dried in a desiccator under vacuum.

RESULTS AND DISCUSSION

The data in Figure 1a show that rock phosphate exhibits the highest Mn^{2+} adsorption capacity followed by calcite and dolimite. The overall data in Figure 1 also clearly show that adsorption of Mn^{2+} by calcite dolomite and rock phosphate in the solution concentrations encountered in this study is followed by desorption of an equivalent quantity of Ca^{2+}. This latter observation is consistent with geochemistry literature (Stumm and Morgan, 1971; Garrels and Christ, 1965). They stated that Mn^{2+} can substitute for Ca^{2+} in calcite forming a solid solution. Although such a process is indirectly supported by data obtained in this study, the information does not offer direct support that indeed Ca^{2+} in calcite or dolomite or rock phosphate has been substituted by Mn^{2+}.

McBride (1979) postulated that Mn^{2+} removal from solution in the presence of calcite can be accomplished via two different mechanisms. One mechanism involves the precipitation of Mn^{2+} as $MnCO_3$ by the reaction of solution Mn^{2+}

with HCO_3^- followed by the liberation of H^+. This hydrogen is consumed by dissolution of $CaCO_3$. The net effect of this mechanism is an equivalent surface displacement of Ca^{2+} by Mn^{2+} with no change in pH. A second mechanism involves the direct surface displacement of Ca^{2+} by Mn^{2+} with also no change in pH. The major difference between these two mechanisms is that the first forms a separate $MnCO_3$ phase while the second forms a new phase on the surface of calcite (solid solution) by substituting Ca^{2+} by Mn^{2+}. It appears from the above that in order to distinguish the mechanism responsible for Mn^{2+} removal from solution one needs to examine the newly formed solid phases.

Further solution chemistry evidence on the possible mechanisms of Mn^{2+} adsorption by calcite, dolomite and rock phosphate is presented in Figure 1b, 1c and 1d. These data demonstrate that the adsorption of Mn^{2+} by all three solid phases tested was independent of solid to solution ratio. McBride (1970) reported that Mn^{2+} adsorption by calcite was dependent on solid to solution ratio. The data of our study were not in agreement with this observation. A possible reason for this dissagreement is that McBride (1970) did not exclude CO_2 from the suspensions as was done in the experiment in this research. The data in Figure 2 also demonstrate that Mn^{2+} adsorption was particle size dependent. The smaller the particle size, the greater the quantity of Mn^{2+} adsorbed. The above two observations, Mn^{2+} adsorption independency of solid to solution ratio and Mn^{2+} adsorption dependency on particle size, suggests that Mn^{2+} is not removed from solution as a discrete phase, i.e. $MnCO_3$, but rather the process is catalyzed by the mineral's surface. This is true for calcite, dolomite and rock phosphate.

Considering that the specific surface of the various size particles tested varied from 0.01 m^2 g^{-1} to 0.082 m^2 g^{-1} (determined by ethylene glycol), according to Jurinak and Bauer (1956) the amount of Mn^{2+} that would be adsorbed (on a theoretical basis) on the carbonates could not exceed 0.2 $cmol_c$ kg^{-1}. However, all samples under the various particle sizes tested exceeded that value. In order to elucidate the cause of these observations, cation activity data were introduced into stability diagrams (Figure 3). The data in Figure 3a show that Mn^{2+} concentration in solution supports a supersaturated state with respect to $MnCO_3$. However, the solution is undersaturated with respect to $Mn(OH)_2$. The latter's solubility is too high to control the equilibrium concentration of Mn^{2+}. The data of Ca^{2+} activity in Figure 3a show that the system is nearly at saturation with respect to $CaCO_3$ at the highest levels of Mn^{2+} added (low pH values on the plot) but supersaturated at the lowest levels of Mn^{2+} added (high pH values on the plot). In the case of dolomite (Figure 3b) the results show similar trends.

The solution is close to equilibrium with $MnCO_3$ but slightly undersaturated with respect to dolomite at high levels of Mn^{2+} added (low pH values on the plot) and near supersaturation at low levels of Mn^{2+} added (high pH values on the plot). A possible explanation for the above behavior is that surface adsorption of Mn^{2+} could have disrupted the stabilities of calcite and dolomite, releasing Ca^{2+} or $Ca^{2+} + Mg^{2+}$, depending on the mineral, and thus the solution is no longer in equilibrium with calcite or dolomite.

Activity data of the H_2HO_4 species in the rock phosphate system at the highest and the lowest levels of Ca^{2+} and Mn^{2+} activities followed closely the stability line of octacalcium phosphate ($Ca_4H(PO)_3 \cdot 2.5H_2O$). However, Mn^{2+} activity data show undersaturation with respect to $Mn_3(PO_4)_2$ and $Mn(OH)_2$ but superaturation with respect to $MnHPO_4$ at both high and low levels of H_2PO_4 activities (Figure 2c). Calcium activity data for the same system showed undersaturation with respect to octacalcium phosphate. The degree of undersaturation increased as Ca^{2+} activity increased (Figure 2c). Note that even through rock phosphate is known to be fluorapatite (Occidental Chemical Corporation, 1991, personal communication) the solution appears to be supersaturated with the mineral. This could be due to the fact that the

307

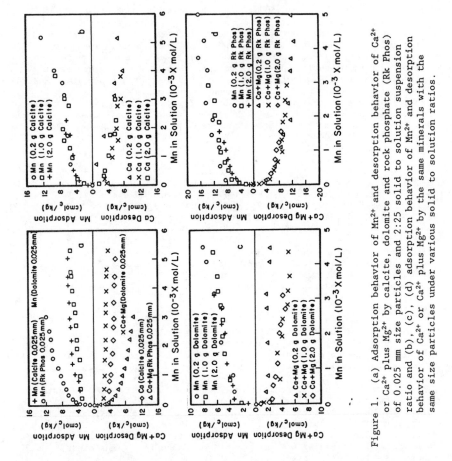

Figure 1. (a) Adsorption behavior of Mn²⁺ and desorption behavior of Ca²⁺ or Ca²⁺ plus Mg²⁺ by calcite, dolomite and rock phosphate (Rk Phos) of 0.025 mm size particles and 2:25 solid to solution suspension ratio and (b), (c), (d) adsorption behavior of Mn²⁺ and desorption behavior of Ca²⁺ or Ca²⁺ plus Mg²⁺ by the same minerals with the same size particles under various solid to solution ratios.

308

mineral's surface chemistry which controls the solution phase tends to transform itself to the most stable phase which is shown to be octacalcium phosphate (Figure 2c).

Infrared spectra of the solid phases prepared according to the procedures described in Materials and Methods are shown in Figures 4, 5, and 6. The most distinct feature of the spectra in Figure 4, which represents pure calcite and pure dolomite, is in the range of 4000 to 3300 wavenumbers. In this wavenumber range the spectra exhibit a broad adsorption band in the 3700 wavenumber. After addition of Mn^{2+} to the samples, this band has shifted to the right (Figures 4bcde) and two absorption bands (3550 and 3400 wavenumbers) have appeared. The band at 3700 cm^{-1} is assigned to OH^- of water adsorbed onto the minerals' surface (Figure 4a) (White and Roth, 1986). The shift of the 3700 cm^{-1} band to the right signifies that more energy in the mid-infrared is required to vibrate these OH^- groups. This implies that some of these OH^- groups are also coordinated by surface adsorbed Mn^{2+}. Note the two small sharp bands in the 3500 wavenumber range. These spectral information suggest that one of the mechanisms of Mn^{2+} adsorption by calcite or dolomite involves replacement of Ca^{2+} or Ca^{2+} plus Mg^{2+}, depending on the mineral, by Mn^{2+} followed by hydroxylation of adsorbed Mn^{2+}. The hydroxylation of adsorbed Mn^{2+} clearly shown by the FT-IR spectra suggest a relatively weak interaction between adsorbed Mn^{2+} and surface $-CO_3^{2-}$.

At the lower wavenumbers of the spectrum (Fig 5), in the case of dolomite an additional difference is observed with respect to $-CO_3^{2-}$ infrared vibrations. The addition of Mn^{2+} broadens the 1407 cm^{-1} band down to 1367 cm^{-1}. This shift is consistent with the vibrations of $-CO_3$ interacting with Mn^{2+} shown by the spectra of $MnCO_3$ (Figure 5(I)c). However, in the case of calcite (Figure 5(II)) the $-CO_3$ vibrational spectra in the absence and presence of adsorbed Mn^{2+} do not differ appreciably. This could be due to the fact that Ca^{2+} and Mn^{2+} affect $-CO_3$ vibrations similarly, while in the case of dolomite Mg^{2+} affects $-CO_3$ vibrations differently. Based on the above, the vibrational spectra of calcite at the lower wavenumbewrs do not exclude the possiblity of $MnCO_3$ precipitation on the calcite's surface.

In summary, FT-IR spectra data, Mn^{2+} adsorption data and stability data suggest that Mn^{2+} adsorption by calcite and dolomite is most probably facilitated via two mechanisms. One mechanism involves direct replacement of Ca^{2+} or Ca^{2+} plus Mg^{2+}, depending on the mineral, by Mn^{2+} followed by its hydroxylation; the second mechanism involves solution precipitation of Mn^{2+} as $MnCO_3$.

The FT-IR spectra of rock phosphate in the absence and presence of adsorbed Mn^{2+} are shown in Figure 6. The spectra in Figure 6 clearly show a broad absorption band in the 3,500 cm^{-1} range. This broad band was assigned to OH^- vibrations (White and Roth 1986). These OH^- vibrations remained almost intact in the presence of adsorbed Mn^{2+} in comparison to the spectra of calcite and dolomite under the same conditions. This suggests that Mn^{2+} adsorption is facilitated through replacement of Ca^{2+} by Mn^{2+} with a relatively strong interaction between Mn^{2+} and the surface $\sim PO_4$.

The FT-IR spectra of rock phosphate at the lower wavenumbers show a broad absorbance shoulder in the range of 1050-1000 cm^{-1} (Figure 6c). The spectra of Figure 8c represented the longest equilibration period (30 days) and the highest concentration of Mn^{2+} (0.1$\underline{M}$). Since the bands in this wavenumber range are representative of $-PO_4$ vibrations (White and Roth, 1986), their shift to lower wavenumbers could signify the chemical interaction of Mn^{2+} with phosphate. However, all other treatments did not alter the spectra significantly. This suggests that Mn^{2+} was most likely adsorbed via surface structural replacement of Ca^{2+}.

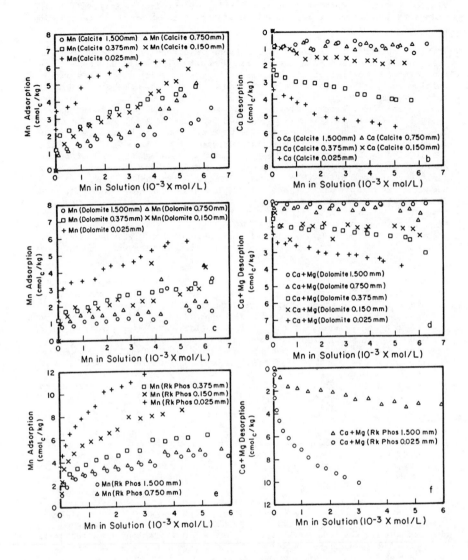

Figure 2. Adsorption of Mn²⁺ and desorption of Ca²⁺ or Ca²⁺ plus Mg²⁺, depending on the mineral by (a, b) calcite, (c, d) dolomite, and (e, f) rock phosphate (Rk Phos) of various sizes particles in 2:25 solid to solution suspensions.

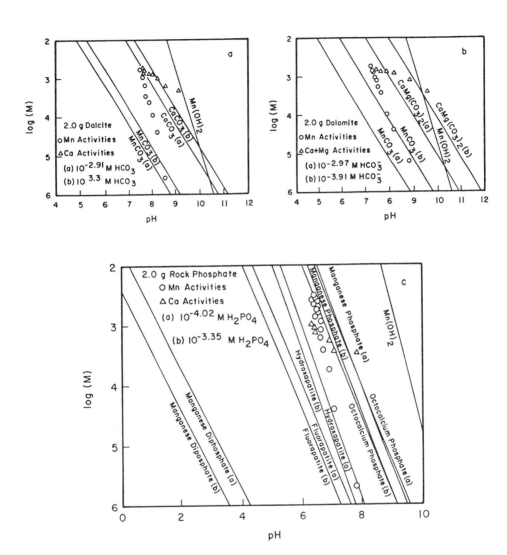

Figure 3. Values of pH and and log Ca²⁺ or log (Ca²⁺ + Mg²⁺), depending on the mineral, or log Mn²⁺ for the 0.025 mm size particles in 2:25 solid to solution suspensions in reference to: (a) calcite, Mn(OH)₂ and MnCO₃; (b) dolomite, Mn(OH)₂ and MnCO₃; (c) Mn(OH)₂, octacalcium phosphate, hydraxapatite, fluorapatite, manganese phosphate and manganese diphosphate.

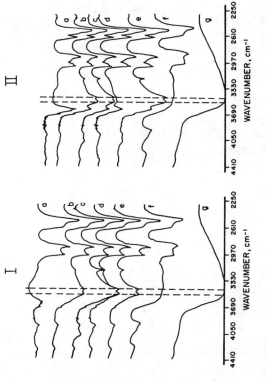

Figure 4. Infrared spectra of (I) $CaCO_3$ and (II) $CaMg(CO_3)_2$: (a) equilibrated for 30 days with distilled H_2O; (b) $CaCO_3$ equilibrated for 30 days with 0.025 $\underline{M}$ $MnCl_2$; (c) $CaCO_3$ equilibrated for 30 days with 0.1 $\underline{M}$ $MnCl_2$; (d) $CaCO_3$ equilibrated for 1 day with 0.025 $\underline{M}$ $MnCl_2$; (e) $CaCO_3$ equilibrated for 1 day with 0.1 $\underline{M}$ $MnCl_2$; (f) Ward's $MnCO_3$ as reference, and (g) laboratory synthesized $Mn(OH)_2$ as reference.

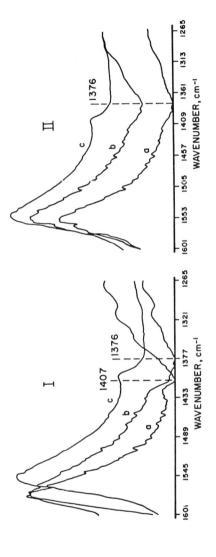

Figure 5. Infrared spectra of (I) CaMg(CO$_3$)$_2$ and (II) CaCO$_3$: (a) equilibrated for 30 days with distilled H$_2$O; (b) equilibrated for 30 days with 0.025 M MnCl$_2$, and (c) Ward's MnCO$_3$ as reference.

313

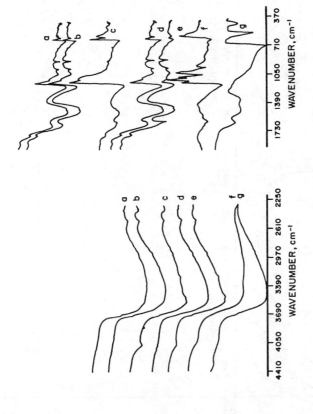

Figure 6. Infrared spectra of: (a) rock phosphate equilibrated for 30 days with distilled H_2O; (b) rock phosphate equilibrated for 30 days with 0.025 $\underline{M}$ $MnCl_2$; (c) rock phosphate equilibrated for 30 days with 0.1 $\underline{M}$ $MnCl_2$; (d) rock phosphate equilibrated for 1 day with 0.025 $\underline{M}$ $MnCl_2$; (e) rock phosphate equilibrated for 1 day with 0.1 $\underline{M}$ $MnCl_2$; (f) $MnHPO_4$, and g) $Mn(OH)_2$.

CONCLUSIONS

The results of this study demonstrate that calcite, dolomite and rock phosphate when introduced to solutions high in Mn^{2+} adsorb the latter by surface replacement of Ca^{2+} or Ca^{2+} plus Mg^{2+}, depending on the mineral. Infrared spectroscopy showed that in the case of calcite and dolomite the surface adsorbed Mn^{2+} undergoes hydroxoylation. It suggests weak $Mn-CO_3$, interactions. It is postulated that hydroxylation of adsorbed Mn^{2+} serves as a precusor to Mn-oxide formation, when O_2 is available, leading to limestone armoring.

The data also show that total quantity of Mn^{2+} needed to coat limestone particles is in the range of 4 to 8 $cmol_c$ kg^{-1}. Infrared spectroscopy suggests that hydroxylation of adsorbed Mn^{2+} by rock phosphate is not that apparent. This implies that Mn^{2+} adsorption reduces the capacity of rock phosphate to neutralize acidic drainages but it may not induce coating of the rock phosphate.

REFERENCES

1. Boischot, P., M. Durroux, G. Sylvestre. 1950. Etude sur la fixation du fer et du manganese dans les sols calcaires. Ann. Inst. Natl. Recherche Agron., Ann. Agron. [A], 1:307-315.

2. Evangelou, V. P., K. L. Wells, K. S. Sajwan, U. M. Sainju, and B. Creech. 1990. Development of rapid, cost effective laboratory tests for use in identifying potential water quality problems and quantifying control measures. Office of Surface Mining, United States Department of the Interior. No. HQ51-GR87-10018. Pittsburg, PA.

3. Garrels, R. M., and C. L. Christ. 1965. Solutions, minerals and equilibria. Harper and Row, New York.

4. Jurinak, J. J., and N. Bauer. 1956. Thermodynamics of zinc adsorption on calcite, dolomite and magnesite-type minerals. Soil Science Society America Proceedings. 20:466-471.

5. Lindsay, W. L. 1979. Chemical equilibria in soils. John Wiley & Sons, New York.

6. McBride, M. B. 1979. Chemisorption and precipitation of Mn^{2+} at $CaCO_3$ surfaces. Soil Science Society America Journal. 43:693-698.

7. Nicholas, G. D., and E. G. Foree. Reducing iron and manganese to permissible levels in coal mine sedimentation ponds." In D. H. Graves (ed.) Proceeding Symposium on Surface Mining Hydrology, Sedimentology and Reclamation, December 4-7, 1979, University of Kentucky, Lexington, Kentucky. p. 181-187.

8. Rollins, L. 1989. User's guide to DATAGEN/PCWATEQ. Shadoware, Woodland, CA.

9. Stumm, W., J. J. and Morgan. 1970. Aquatic chemistry. Wiley-Interscience, New York, NY.

10. Technicon Auto Analyzer I. 1965. Inorganic phosphate. Industrial Method 348R-6-31-5.

11. White, J. E., and C. B. Roth. 1986. Infrared spectrometry. In:
     Methods of soil analysis. Part 1. Physical and mineralogical
     methods. Agronomy Monograph No. 9. Soil Science Society of America,
     Madison, Wisconsin. pp 291-330.

RAPID ECOLOGICAL RESTORATION OF MINE LAND USING MUNICIPAL SEWAGE SLUDGE

William E. Sopper[*]

It is estimated that more than 7.7 million dry metric tons of municipal sludge are currently produced each year by the 15,300 public-owned treatment works in the U.S. Approximately 25% of this is being land applied for its fertilizer and organic matter value. One of the most efficient uses for sludge is for the reclamation of disturbed lands, like those abandoned after coal mining which are acidic, droughty, and devoid of organic matter. Sludge has been shown to improve spoil structure, water holding capacity, and bulk density in addition to adding N, P, K, and other plant nutrients (Sopper et al., 1982).

Coal is both surface-mined and deep-mined in Pennsylvania. Mining of both anthracite and bituminous coal continues to bring to the surface enormous amounts of black, shaley, acidic refuse material which requires grading and revegetation. Thousands of hectares of such material, produced by over a century of mining were left unreclaimed prior to the federal Surface Mining Control and Reclamation Act of 1977. These sites have persisted for years due to the difficulty of establishing and maintaining vegetation on the highly acidic material.

In 1977, a project was initiated in Pennsylvania for the purpose of introducing the concept of using municipal sludge for revegetation of mined land to the general public in order to gain public acceptance and support. The specific objective of the project was to demonstrate that municipal sludge can be used to reclaim mined land and return it to potential agricultural use or wildlife habitat in an environmentally acceptable manner, without adverse effects on the quality of the vegetation, soil, or water.

Three sites, 4.0 ha in area, were selected for the demonstration projects, each representing a different reclamation challenge. After sludge application, vegetation, soil, and groundwater samples were collected on each site over a 5-year period.

A question which often arises is what is the long-term effect when single large applications of sludge are applied to revegetate mine land? What happens after all the sludge has been mineralized and all the nutrients and trace metals have been released to the soil and are potentially available for plant uptake and leaching. Will the vegetative cover persist or deteriorate?

To provide some insight on long-term effects of sludge applications on mine land, two of the demonstration projects were resampled 12 years after the sludge applications. Results of those analyses are reported here.

ABANDONED STRIP MINE SPOIL BANK

One of the sites used in the 1977 project was an abandoned strip mine bank located in Venango County that had been backfilled and recontoured after mining

[*] WILLIAM E. SOPPER, Professor of Forest Hydrology, School of Forest Resources, Penn State University, University Park, PA

without top soil replacement. Several revegetation attempts were unsuccessful.
Dewatered digested sludge was applied in May 1977 to a 4.0 ha plot. In August,
1989, 12 years after sludge application, the site was revisited and samples of
vegetation, soils, and groundwater were collected to evaluate the long-term
effects.

The surface soil was compacted, stony, and extremely acid (pH 3.8). The plot
was scarified with a chisel plow to loosen the surface spoil material and
agricultural lime was applied at 12.3 Mg/ha to raise the spoil pH to 7.0.
Sludge for the project was obtained from three local wastewater treatment
plants. The sludge was applied at 184 Mg/ha with a manure spreader. The
average concentrations of nutrients and trace metals and amounts applied in the
sludge are given in Table 1. The amounts of nutrients applied was equivalent
to applying an 11 (N) -9 (P_2O_5) -0 (K_2O) chemical fertilizer at 22,400 kg/ha.

The amounts of trace metals applied are given in Table 2 along with the U.S.
Environmental Protection Agency (EPA) and Pennsylvnaia Department of
Environmental Resources (PDER) interim guideline recommendations (U.S.
Environmental Protection Agency, 1977; Pennsylvnia Department of Environmental
Resources, 1977). It is quite obvious that the amounts of trace metals applied
were well below the recommended lifetime limits except for copper, which
slightly exceeded the Pennsylvania guidelines.

Table 1
Chemical Analysis of Dewatered Sludge
Applied and Amounts of Elements Applied
at 184 Mg/ha Rate (Dwt Basis)

Element	Average concentration	Amount applied
	Mg/kg	kg/ha
Total P	4624	918
Total N	12188	2388
K	93	18
Ca	9970	1834
Mg	2082	383
Zn	811	147
Cu	661	129
Pb	349	55
Ni	69	12
Cd	3.2	0.6
Cr	413	74
Hg	0.6	0.09
pH	7.9	

Table 2
Trace Metal Loadings of the Sludge
Application

Element	Sludge application 184 Mg/ha	EPA	PDER
	---------kg/ha-------------		
Cu	129	280	112
Zn	147	560	224
Cr	74	--	112
Pb	55	800	112
Ni	12	280	22
Cd	0.6	11	3
Hg	0.09	--	0.6

Immediately after sludge application and incorporation, the site was broadcast seeded with a mixture of two grasses and two legumes, including Kentucky-31 tall fescue (_Festuca arundinacea_ Schreb.) (22 kg/ha), Pennlate orchardgrass (_Dactylis glomerata_ L.) (22 kg/ha), penngift crownvetch (_Coronilla varia_ L.) (11 kg/ha), and Empire Birdsfoot trefoil (_Lotus corniculatus_ L.) (11 kg/ha), then mulched with straw and hay at the rate of 3.8 Mg/ha.

A complete monitoring system was installed on the plot to evaluate the effects of the sludge applications on water quality, vegetation, and soil. Two groundwater wells were drilled (up-gradient and down-gradient) to sample the effects of the sludge application on groundwater quality. After sludge application, groundwater samples were collected bi-weekly for the first two months and monthly thereafter. Samples were analyzed for pH, nitrate-N by ion-selective electrode (Ellis, 1976); dissolved Cu, Zn, Cr, Pb, Co, Cd, and Ni by atomic absorption spectrophotometry (U.S. Environmental Protection Agency, 1974).

Spoil samples were collected at the 0-15, and 15-30 cm depth, passed through a 2 mm sieve, and analyzed for pH; Kjeldahl-N; Bray-P; exchangeable K, Ca, and Mg by ammonia acetate extraction; and dilute hydrochloric acid extractable Cu, Zn, Cr, Pb, Cd, and Ni (Jackson, 1958). Exchangeable cation and extractable metal concentrations were determined by atomic absorption.

At the end of each growing season vegetation growth responses were determined by measurements of percentage areal cover, and dry matter production. No crops were harvested over the 12-year period. Individual samples of tall fescue, orchardgrass, crownvetch, and birdsfoot trefoil from each plot were collected for foliar analyses. Plant samples were analyzed for N, P, K, Ca, Mg, by plasma emission spectrometry (Baker et al., 1964), and Cu, Zn, Cr, Pb, Co, Cd, and Ni by atomic adsorption (Jackson, 1958), after dry ashing and digestion.

RESULTS

Vegetation

The site was completely vegetated by August 1977, three months after sludge application, which has persisted throughout the 12-year period. Average dry matter production for the first five years (1977-81) and in 1989 were 6.0, 9.3, 11.3, 31.2, 22.6, and 15.5 Mg/ha, respectively. Average hay yield on undisturbed farmland in the County is 4.0 Mg/ha. Dry matter production increased significantly during the first four years, leveling off in 1981. In 1989 it was slightly lower but still well above the County average hay yield. During the first two years the two grass species dominated the site, but by the third growing season, the two legume species predominated and persisted through the fifth year (1981). However, by 1989 the birdsfoot trefoil had almost disappeared and the dominating vegetative cover consists mostly of crownvetch and orchardgrass.

Foliar concentrations of macronutrients are given in Table 3. No plants were available for sampling in 1977. Nutrients (N and P) were all generally higher in the sludge-grown plants. Potassium and Ca were higher in the sludge-grown orchardgrass than in control plants. Potassium and Ca were only slightly lower in the sludge-grown birdsfoot trefoil plants than in the control plants. Foliar Mg concentrations were similar in both sludge-grown and control plants. Nutrients levels in the sludge-grown plants in 1989 were about the same level as the first year when sludge was applied. There appears to be little depletion of nutrients from the site over the 12 year period. Birdsfoot trefoil data are given in Table 3 because no crownvetch plants were present on the control plot for comparison. Macronutrient concentrations in crownvetch on the sludge-amended plot are given in Table 4. Concentrations were quite similar to that of birdsfoot trefoil.

Table 3
Mean Foliar Concentrations of Macronutrient Elements in Orchardgrass and
Birdsfoot Trefoil Collected From the Control and Sludge-Amended Plots

Sludge appli-cation	Year	Orchardgrass					Birdsfoot trefoil				
		N	P	K	Ca	Mg	N	P	K	Ca	Mg
Mg/ha		------------- % -------------					------------- % -------------				
0	1977	--	--	--	--	--	--	--	--	--	--
	1978	0.92	0.18	1.51	0.36	0.23	1.03	0.24	1.93	0.61	0.26
	1979	1.17	0.22	2.41	0.30	0.22	2.59	0.14	1.74	1.82	0.40
	1980	1.11	0.24	1.86	0.32	0.20	2.11	0.17	1.92	1.02	0.23
	1981	1.22	0.18	1.62	0.68	0.22	3.32	0.17	1.89	1.52	0.29
	1989	1.67	0.17	1.82	0.42	0.30	2.31	0.17	1.71	0.92	0.22
184	1977	2.62	0.40	2.84	0.84	0.31	3.64	0.27	1.46	1.99	0.28
	1978	1.26	0.37	2.01	0.49	0.28	1.27	0.36	2.30	0.59	0.25
	1979	1.33	0.51	2.53	0.47	0.23	3.57	0.25	1.56	0.54	0.20
	1980	1.70	0.42	2.65	0.45	0.23	2.93	0.25	4.62	1.27	0.18
	1981	2.57	0.37	2.38	0.53	0.26	4.03	0.26	1.69	1.14	0.23
	1989	2.36	0.37	2.24	0.45	0.22	2.38	0.16	1.01	0.65	0.23

Table 4
Mean Foliar Concentrations of Macronutrient Elements in Crownvetch on
the Sludge-Amended Plot

Year	Crownvetch				
	N	P	K	Ca	Mg
	------------- % -------------				
1977	3.36	0.34	1.64	2.63	0.42
1978	2.35	0.37	3.14	0.96	0.45
1979	3.35	0.22	1.29	1.68	0.25
1980	3.00	0.27	1.89	1.72	0.29
1981	3.78	0.31	1.89	1.25	0.23
1989	2.62	0.21	2.20	0.91	0.26

Foliar samples were analyzed for Zn, Cu, Pb, Ni, and Cd. Foliar concentrations
of Pb, Zn, Cu, and Cd in orchardgrass and crownvetch are shown in Fig. 1.
Concentrations of Zn and Ni tended to be higher in crownvetch than in
orchardgrass; whereas, concentrations of Cu tended to be higher in
orchardgrass. Concentration of Cd and Pb were variable and showed no distinct
trends. In general, trace metal foliar concentrations tended to be highest the
first year and then decrease over time. Foliar concentrations of trace metals
in the sludge-grown orchardgrass plants were higher than in control plants.
The 1989 values for Cu and Cd were quite similar to those of 1981. Foliar
concentrations of Zn show a slight increase from 1981 to 1989 as did foliar
concentrations of Pb and Ni. Although sludge application did increase some
trace metal concentrations in the foliage, these increases were minimal and
well below the suggested tolerance levels, for agronomic crops (Melsted, 1973).
No phytotoxicity symptoms were ever observed. The suggested tolerance levels
are not phytotoxic levels but suggest foliar concentration levels at which
decreases in growth may be expected.

Spoil Chemical Status

Changes in spoil pH over time are shown in Table 5. Spoil pH tended to
increase from 1977 to 1979. Since then there appears to be a slight decline.
This may be the explanation why some of the foliar trace metal concentrations
show an increase in 1989. The nutrient status of the spoil shows a general
increase in concentrations of Kjeldahl-N up to 1981 and up to 1984 for Bray-
phosphorus, K and Ca (Table 6). The application of lime and sludge initially
resulted in a decrease in the concentration of Mg; however, since 1978 there
has been a steady increase. The 1989 values are lower but still quite adequate
to support plant growth.

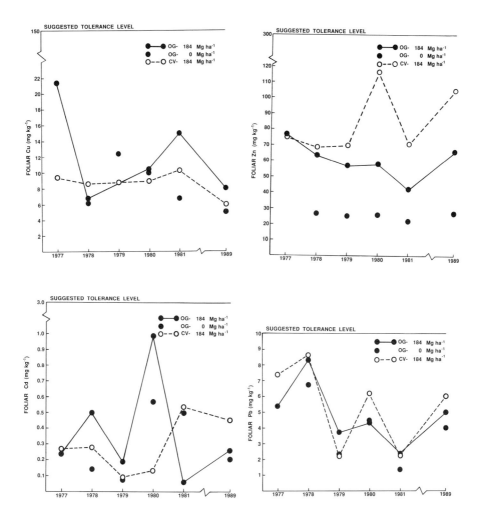

Figure 1. Mean Foliar Concentrations of Pb, Zn, Cu, and Cd in Orchardgrass and
Crownvetch Collected from Control and Sludge-Amended Plots.

Concentrations of extractable trace metals in the 0-15 cm spoil depth are given
in Table 7 and for the 15-30 cm spoil depth in Table 8. Concentrations of Cu,
Zn, Cr, Pb, Cd, and Ni all show a steady increase for the first five years
(1977-81). By this time, all the sludge organic matter was probably
mineralized and all trace metals released to the surface spoil. Results of
spoil analyses in 1984 and 1989 show a gradual decrease in concentrations of
all trace metals. Although the sludge application did increase the
concentrations of extractable trace metals in the 0-15 cm spoil depth, these
higher concentrations are still within the normal ranges for these elements in
U.S. soils (Allaway, 1968).

321

Table 5
Changes in Spoil pH Over the Twelve Year Period

Depth	Soil pH					
	May 1977[a]	Sept 1977	Nov 1978	Oct 1979	May 1981	Aug 1989
cm						
0-15	3.8	6.2	6.7	7.3	5.8	5.4
15-30	3.8	4.2	4.6	5.1	3.4	5.6

[a] Pre-sludge samples

Table 6.
Changes in Concentrations of Kjeldahl-Nitrogen, Bray-Phosphorus and Exchangeable Cations in the Spoil Collected at the 0-15 cm Depth

Year	Kjeldahl nitrogen	Bray phosphorus	K	Ca	Mg
	%	---------------------mg/kg----------------------			
May 1977[a]	0.04	2	12	541	452
Sept 1977	0.05	11	19	1222	32
1978	0.09	9	23	2600	40
1979	0.16	38	46	3873	53
1981	0.34	79	45	1298	99
1984	---	91	74	1440	108
1989	0.12	83	30	733	84

[a] Pre-sludge samples

Table 7.
Changes in Concentrations of Extractable Trace Metals from Spoil Collected at the 0-15 cm Depth Following Sludge Application

Sampling date	Cu	Zn	Cr	Pb	Cd	Ni
	----------------------------mg/kg-------------------------					
May 1977[a]	2.5	2.9	0.2	0.5	0.02	1.1
Sept 1977	10.8	7.7	0.4	3.5	0.04	0.9
1978	8.8	7.7	0.2	2.3	0.02	1.2
1979	58.7	56.9	1.7	13.0	0.27	1.5
1981	87.3	74.6	3.5	22.7	0.95	2.8
1984	57.6	59.6	---	14.8	0.56	2.8
1989	51.9	37.8	---	13.5	0.42	2.0
Normal range for U.S. soils (Allaway, 1968)	2-100	10-300	5-3000	2-200	0.01-7.00	5-500

[a] May 1977 values represent pretreatment conditions

Groundwater Quality

Results of the analyses of groundwater well samples are given in Table 8. The values for Well 1 (control) reflect quality of groundwater for the disturbed mine site. Well 2 reflects the effects of the sludge application on water quality. Results indicate that the sludge application did not have any significant effect on groundwater concentrations of nitrate-N. Average monthly concentrations of NO_3-N were below 10 mg/1 (maximum concentration for potable water) for all months sampled during the five-year period (1977-81). The highest monthly values were 3.0 mg/1 for the control well and 2.4 mg/1 for Well 2.

The application of lime and sludge and subsequent revegetation appears to have had a positive effect on groundwater pH. Groundwater pH increased from 4.6 (1977) to 6.0 by 1981. Results of the 1989 sampling indicates a pH of 6.6. There has also been a gradual increase in pH in the control well from pH 4.4 to pH 5.8. Since 1980, attempts were being made to reclaim the control area by conventional methods using lime and fertilizer. The amounts of lime and fertilizer applied and frequency of application are not known as the coal

Table 8.
Mean Annual Concentrations of Nitrate-N and Trace Metals in Groundwater

Site	Year[a]	pH	NO_3-N	Cu	Zn	Cr	Pb	Cd	Ni
						mg/l			
Well 1	1977	4.4	1.4	0.22	4.13	0.02	0.14	0.006	3.67
(control)	1978	4.3	<0.5	0.23	2.02	0.01	0.19	0.002	0.98
	1979	4.6	<0.5	0.17	1.48	0.03	0.13	0.001	0.50
	1980	5.5	0.6	0.05	0.89	0.05	0.09	0.001	0.50
	1981	5.7	0.7	0.06	0.83	0.03	0.04	0.003	0.31
	1989[b]	5.8	0.02	0.01	0.09	<0.001	0.01	0.001	0.06
Well 2	1977	4.6	1.1	0.10	3.39	0.03	0.09	0.001	2.67
(sludge)	1978	4.5	<0.5	0.14	3.29	0.01	0.20	0.002	1.26
	1979	4.4	<0.5	0.18	1.49	0.03	0.13	0.001	0.97
	1980	5.7	0.6	0.05	1.05	0.04	0.11	0.001	0.76
	1981	6.0	0.6	0.05	0.57	0.02	0.05	0.001	0.31
	1989[b]	6.6	0.06	0.01	0.07	<0.001	0.01	0.001	0.04
EPA drinking water standard			10	1	5	0.05	0.05	0.010	---

[a] Values are annual means of monthly samples
[b] Average of three samples collected in August 1989

company is no longer in business. However, these applications and vegetation growth probably contributed to the increase in groundwater pH in the control well.

There appears to be no significant increase in any of the trace metal concentrations over the initial five-year period (1977-1981) in the groundwater samples from Well 2 compared to the control well. From 1977 to 1981 most of the monthly concentrations were within the U.S. Environmental Protection Agency drinking water standards. The only exception was Pb which exceeded the limit of 0.05 mg/l for both the control well and Well 2, probably resulting from increased release of the element from the soil material due to mining. The highest monthly Pb values were 0.28 mg/l in the control well and 0.33 mg/l in Well 2 in 1978, and the mean annual Pb concentrations were 0.19 and 0.20 mg/l for control well and Well 2, respectively. By 1981, however, the mean annual Pb concentrations had decreased to 0.04 and 0.05 mg/l for the two wells. Results of analyses of the groundwater samples collected in 1989 had extremely low concentrations of all trace metals in both wells in comparison to values for the initial 5 years (1977-81.

MICROBIAL COMMUNITIES

Although the immediate goal of reclamation is to establish a vegetative cover that will prevent soil erosion, the long-term goal is soil ecosystem development and stability. Minespoils lack microbial activity and organic matter. Microbial processes such as humification, soil aggregation, and N cycling are essential in establishing productivity in minespoils, and productivity should be evaluated not only on aboveground biomass, but also on the degree of development of functional microbial populations resembling those of an undisturbed soil. Microbial processes are so important to ecosystem recovery that the activity of microorganisms may be used as an index of the progress of soil genesis in minespoils.

A recent study reported by Seaker and Sopper (1988) sheds some light on the value of sludge applications on mined land on the rejuvenation of microbial populations and activity. A field study was conducted on five strip mine sites

Table 9.
Site Descriptions for Pennsylvania Microbial Community Study

Site	Age (yr)	Amend- ment	Application rate (Mg/ha)	Date of application	Lime application (Mg/ha)	pH (1985)
1	1	Sludge	120	Sept. 1984	18	6.9
2	2	Sludge	128	June 1983	18	7.0
3	3	Sludge	128	May 1982	12	6.8
4	4	Sludge	134	July 1981	18	6.7
5	5	Sludge	134	July 1980	11	7.3
Fertilizer- amended	5	Fertilizer (23-10-20, N-P-K)	0.5	Aug. 1980	11	6.3

reclaimed with sewage sludge and one site reclaimed by conventional methods
(chemical fertilizer and lime) to assess the effects of sludge amendments and
time on populations of bacteria, fungi, and actinomycetes. The sludge-amended
sites ranged in age from 1 to 5 years following sludge applications at rates of
120 to 134 Mg/ha (Table 9). The sludge amendment was from Philadelphia and
consisted of a mixture of composted sludge (with wood chips) and digested
dewatered sludge cake. Six spoil samples (0-5 cm) were collected from each
site for analyses.

Aerobic Heterotrophic Bacteria

Bacterial populations on the sludge-amended sites ranged from 4 to 63 x 10^6/g
(Table 10). Bacterial counts were 5 to 15 times higher on Site 1 than on the
older sites, and were dramatically increased on all sludge-amended sites
compared to the fertilizer-amended site. The first-year peak and subsequent
stabilization of bacterial populations is a typical response following organic
matter additions to minespoils. Considering the extremely low initial pH of
the minespoils in this study, commonly ranging from 3.0 to 5.0 prior to lime
additions, the microbial populations achieved with lime and sludge amendments
after only 1 yr are remarkably high. They compare favorably with estimates of
1 to 34 x 10^6/g reported for undisturbed soils (Alexander, 1977; Visser, 1985;
and Segal and Mancinelli, 1987).

Table 10.
Microbial Populations on Stripmine Sites 1 to 5 yr Following Sludge
Application, and on the Fertilizer-Amended Site

Site	Aerobic hetero- trophic bacteria (10^6/g)	Fungi (10^5/g)	Actinomycetes (10^4/g)
1	63.67 ± 16.93a[a]	18.14 ± 5.45a	1.48 ± 1.04b
2	7.07 ± 1.32a[a]	5.80 ± 2.35b	9.75 ± 5.48b
3	4.09 ± 0.77b	5.54 ± 1.32b	56.21 ± 26.71ab
4	11.37 ± 3.64b	3.98 ± 0.46b	140.23 ± 59.57a
5	13.74 ± 3.58b	4.03 ± 1.05b	40.89 ± 22.68b
F value	***	**	*
Fertilizer amended	3.06 ± 1.17	0.16 ± 0.04	6.94 ± 4.01

*,**,*** Significant effect at $P < 0.05$, 0.01, and 0.001, respectively.
[a]Means followed by different letters are significantly different at the
0.05 level of probability by the Waller-Duncan k-ratio t-test.

Fungi

Sludge application resulted in fungal populations in the range of 4 to 18 x 10^5/g (Table 10). These compare favorably with fungal populations in undisturbed soils which have been reported to range from 0.05 to 9 x 10^5/g (Alexander, 1977; Segal and Mancinelli, 1987; and Miller and Cameron, 1978). Fungal numbers were three to four times higher on Site 1 than on the older sites, and were greatly increased on all sludge-amended sites compared to the fertilizer-amended site.

Actinomycetes

Sludge applications resulted in actinomycete populations ranging from 1.48 to 140.23 x 10^4/g (Table 10) compared to actinomycete populations for undisturbed soils, reported in the range of 1 to 436 x 10^4/g (Alexander, 1977; Visser, 1985, Segal and Mancinelli, 1987; and Miller and Cameron, 1978). Actinomycetes exhibited a different pattern of development than the bacteria and fungi. These microbes are less competitive than the other groups and their populations were significantly lower on Sites 1 and 2 than on the older sites. The pattern follows that described by Alexander (1972), whereby the bacteria and fungi proliferate initially upon the addition of organic matter to the soil, and the actinomycete responses do not occur until later stages of decay, when competition has decreased. Actinomycete populations on Sites 3, 4, and 5 were considerably higher than on the fertilizer-amended site.

Although minespoils can eventually recover "soil" characteristics through intensive reclamation and management techniques, annual fertilizer additions are usually required for several years. Such methods are rarely practical on vast acreages of nonagricultural land. Without annual maintenance, vegetation cover often deteriorates because microbial development is slow and nutrient cycling never becomes fully operative. The use of sludge as a spoil amendment eliminated the initial lag period that characterizes conventionally reclaimed sites, during which plant growth and microbial activity are at a low level, each one insufficient for maximum functioning of the other. Sludge amendments quickly increased the numbers and activity of microorganisms, whose activities enhance the development of a soil environment conducive to continued plant growth. Development of an indigenous microbial community was achieved on all the Pennsylvania sites, which is a key factor in providing long-term site stability through biogeochemical cycling of energy and nutrients. Recovery of normal soil populations and processes in the surface 5 cm appeared to occur within 2 yrs, and did not show a tendency to deteriorate.

SUMMARY

The use of municipal sewage sludge for the reclamation and revegetation of drastically disturbed mine land has been extensively investigated. The results to date have been encouraging and show that stabilized municipal sludges, if applied properly according to present state and federal guidelines, can be used to rapidly restore a functioning ecosystem on surface-mined land in an environmentally safe manner with no major adverse effects on the vegetation, soil, or groundwater quality.

REFERENCES

1. Alexander, M. 1977. Introduction to soil microbiology. John Wiley & Sons, New York.

2. Allaway, W.H. 1968. Agronomic controls over the environmental cycling of trace metals. Adv. In Agron. 20:235-271.

3. Baker, D.E., G.W. Gorsline, C.B. Smith, W.I. Thomas, W.E. Grube, and R.L. Ragland. 1964. Technique of rapid analyses of corn leaves for eleven elements. Agron. J. 56:133-136.

4. Ellis, B.G. 1976. Analyses and their interpretation for wastewater application on agricultural land. North Central Regional Research Publication 235-Sec. 6.

5. Jackson, M.L. 1958. Soil Chemical Analysis. Prentice-Hall, Inc., Englewood Cliffs, NJ.

6. Melsted, S.W. 1973. Soil-plant relationships. p. 121-128. In: Recycling Municipal Sludges and Effluents on Land, Nat. Assoc. of State Universities and Land Grant Colleges, Washington, DC.

7. Miller, R.M., and R.E. Cameron. 1978. Microbial ecology studies at two coal mine refuse sites in Illinois. Argonne National Laboratory Rep. ANL/LRP-3. Natl. Technical Information Serv., U.S. Dep. of Commerce, Springfield, VA.

8. Pennsylvania Department of Environmental Resources. 1977. Interim guidelines for sewage sludge use for land reclamation. In: The Rules and Regulations of the Department of Environmental Resources, Commonwealth of Pennsylvania, Chapt. 75, Subchapt. C, Sec. 75.32.

9. Seaker, E.M., and W.E. Sopper. 1988. Municipal sludge for minespoil reclamation: I. Effects on microbial populations and activity, J. Environ. Qual. 17:591-597.

10. Segal, W., and R.L. Mancinelli. 1987. Extent of regeneration of the microbial community in reclaimed spent oil shale land. J. Environ. Qual. 16:44-48.

11. Sopper, W. E., E. M. Seaker, and R. K. Bastian (Editors). 1982. Land Reclamation and Biomass Production with Municipal Wastewater and Sludge. The Pennsylvania State University Press, University Park, PA 16802.

12. United States Environmental Protection Agency 1974. Methods for Chemical Analysis of Water and Wastes. Washington, DC.

13. United States Environmental Protection Agency. 1977. Municipal Sludge Management: Environmental Factors. Tech. Bull. EPA 430/9-76-004, MCD-28.

14. Visser, S. 1985. Management of microbial processes in surface mined land reclamation in western Canada. In R.L. Tate III and D.A. Klein (Ed.) Soil Reclamation Processes. p. 203-341. Marcel Dekker, New York.

EFFICIENCY OF BIOLOGICAL AND CHEMICAL RECLAIMANTS

IN THE RECLAMATION OF SALINE SODIC SOILS

Muhammad Ramzan Chaudhry[*]   Muhammad Sadiq Rafique[**]
Director (Soils)   Junior Agri. Officer

ABSTRACT

The study was carried out in 0.5-ha saline-sodic non-gypsiferous silty-clay soil from Rice (Summer) 1988 to Rice 1990. The ECe and SAR of upper 15-cm soil were between 10.32 to 17.95 dSm^{-1} and 40.26 to 103.14 $(mmol\ L^{-1})^{1/2}$, respectively. The six treatments were:- control (T1); deep ploughing upto 45 cm (T2); gypsum @ 50% GR (T3); gypsum @ 25% GR + 20 tons/ha FYM (T4); kallar grass (Leptochloa fusca) green manured (T5); and Jantar (Sesbania aculeata) green manured (T6). Rice-wheat crop rotation was followed with 134:57:31 kg/ha NPK to each crop. Total 375-cm canal water was used in addition to 125-cm rainfall during 2½ years period.

The infiltration rate of soil was considerably increased and maximum increase of 102% was found in treatment 4. The ECe and SAR of soil were significantly affected by different treatments upto 90-cm depth except the SAR of 60-90cm where treatments effect was insignificant. The maximum and minimum reduction comparing with S6 over S1 within about 2½ years in ECe of upper 15-cm soil was observed in treatments 3 and 1, respectively. Treatment 4 seems more effective in reducing SAR upto 90-cm soil. However, on percentage, there was 90, 83, 58 and 78% reduction in sampling 6 over 1 in 0-15, 15-30, 30-60 and 60-90-cm soil in same treatment (T4). Contrarily ECe was increased in 15-30 cm in T1 and in 30-60 and 60-90cm in T1 and T2 and SAR in T1 in 60-90-cm soil indicating the accumulation of leached salts from the upper layers. The crop yield was also affected significantly. On an average maximum increase of 64 and 57% in paddy and wheat grains yield was found in treatment 3 over control. Crop yield also increased with the passage of time. Efficiency of different treatments was in the order of T3 > T4 > T6 > T5 > T2 > T1.

Pakistan is basically an agricultural country, therefore, the fate and prosperity of the farming community and nation as a whole will depend upon how efficiently the soil and water resources are utilized. But unfortunately the productive land is going out of cultivation due to salinity/sodicity which is affecting agricultural production very badly (Branson and Fireman, 1960). To bring back these saline-sodic/sodic soils to their full production level chemical (Kausar and Muhammad, 1972; Dubey et al., 1987; Chaudhry and Abaidullah, 1988a; Chaudhry et al., 1987, 1988; Chaudhry and Hameed, 1992, and Prather et al., 1978)

---

[*]   International Waterlogging & Salinity Research Institute (IWASRI), Lahore, Pakistan.

[**]   Mona Project, WAPDA, Bhalwal District Sargodha, Pakistan

and biological (Sandhu and Malik, 1975; Chaudhry and Abaidullah, 1988b; Chaudhry and Rafique, 1990; Ahmed et al., 1990) reclamation techniques and proper management practices are vital. However, these techniques will depend upon the nature and problem of soil, quantity and quality of irrigation water, depth and quality of groundwater, pervious or impervious nature of sub-soil, calcareousness and gypsum contents of soil and availability and economics of reclaimants. This study was carried out with the objectives:

- To evaluate efficiency of chemical and biological reclaimants in the reclamation of saline-sodic soil.

- To evaluate the efficiency of chemical and biological reclaimants on biomass production.

- To evaluate the economics of these reclaimants.

MATERIAL AND METHODS

The study was carried out in 0.5 ha saline-sodic non- gypsiferous silty clay barren soil having ECe and SAR of upper 15cm between 10.32 to 17.95 (dSm^{-1}) and 40.26 to 103.14 (mmolL^{-1})$^{1/2}$ in Mona Reclamation Experimental Project (Pakistan) since Rice (summer) 1988 to Rice 1990. Canal water (375-cm) was used for irrigation and rainfall received (125- cm) was also counted for meeting the crop water requirements. The treatments were:

T1. Control (No amendments).
T2. Deep ploughing (upto 45cm soil depth).
T3. Gypsum @ 50% gypsum requirements (GR) of soil.
T4. Gypsum @ 25% GR of soil + 20 tons farmyard manure (FYM)/ha.
T5. Kallar grass (Leptochloa fusca, green manuring first crop).
T6. Jantar (Sesbania aculeata, green manuring first crop).

The treatments were randomly allocated in a randomized block design. The calculated quantity of gypsum was applied before the initiation of the experiment.

Soil samples were collected from 0-15, 15-30, 30-60 and 60-90 cm soil depth before initiation of the experiment and subsequent post-harvest of each crop. The soil samples were sun-dried, sieved through 2mm sieve and assayed for ECe and SAR (U.S. Salinity Laboratory Staff, 1954) and mechanical analysis (Bouyoucos, 1951). The infiltration rate was measured by Standard Ring Method (Aronovici, 1955) after harvesting wheat (winter) crop. Rice-wheat crop rotation was followed with 134:57:31 kg/ha NPK to each crop. Crop yield was estimated on whole plot basis.

RESULTS AND DISCUSSION

Electrical Conductivity (ECe, dSm^{-1})

0-15-cm Depth; The electrical conductivity of soil was significantly higher in control as compared with other treatments which varied insignificantly among themselves (Fig.1). Although the latter five treatments varied insignificantly yet on percentage basis the

328

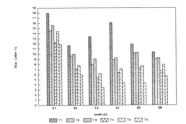

Trts	Means	% Decr./Incr.[*] in S6 Over S1
T1	14.45(a)	34
T2	8.68(b)	49
T3	7.58(b)	74
T4	8.66(b)	73
T5	8.58(b)	64
T6	8.15(b)	45

T1 Ctrl, T2 Deep plowing (45 cm), T3 50% GR,
T4 25% GR+20 tons/ha FYM, T5 Kallar grass, T6 Jantar

LSD(T) 1% = 1.73
LSD(S) 1% = 1.73

Figure 1. Effect of Different Treatments on ECe of Soil (0-15 cm)

maximum reduction of 74% in sampling 6 over 1 (within about 2½ years) was found in treatment 3 and minimum of 34% in treatment 1 during same period. The ECe was reduced below safe limits (< 4 dSm^{-1}) only in treatment 3 within about two and half years manifesting that salts were moved down beyond this depth with irrigation and rain water.

The ECe was also significantly affected during different sampling periods and was significantly higher in sampling 1 compared with the ECe of later samplings. The ECe after sampling 2 was generally increased after wheat and decreased after rice over the preceding sampling which is possibly due to difference in delta of water applied and sampling time after crop harvesting.

15-30-cm Depth; In this soil depth the ECe was again significantly higher in control whereas insignificant differences existed among the ECe of other treatments (Fig.2). However, after

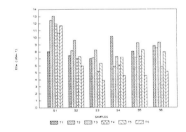

Trts	Means	% Decr./Incr.[*] in S6 Over S1
T1	11.32(a)	45[*]
T2	7.61(b)	20
T3	6.29(b)	45
T4	6.76(b)	55
T5	7.44(b)	43
T6	7.60(b)	42

T1 Ctrl, T2 Deep plowing (45 cm), T3 50% GR,
T4 25% GR+20 tons/ha FYM, T5 Kallar grass, T6 Jantar

LSD(T) 1% = 2.034
LSD(S) 1% = 2.034

Figure 2. Effect of Different Treatments on ECe of Soil (15-30 cm)

about two and a half years period differences were observed in different treatments in the

ECe of soil. The maximum reduction of 55% in sampling 6 over 1 was found in treatment 4. Contrary to the upper 15-cm depth, here the ECe in control was increased (45%) depicting the accumulation of some salts leached from the upper layer.

The ECe of soil was significantly higher in sampling 3 compared with later samplings which is possibly due to accumulation of some of the leached salts which could not pass beyond this depth.

30-60-cm Depth; The data presented in Fig.3 revealed the significant effect of different treatments on the ECe of soil and it was significantly higher in control as compared with treatments 3, 4, 5 and 6 which varied insignificantly among themselves. The ECe remained above safe limits in all the treatments except in treatment 3 where it was reduced below safe limits (< 4 dSm^{-1}) during Rice 1990. This may be due to the effectiveness of reclaimant applied and lower initial ECe of soil. On percentage basis maximum reduction of 37% in sampling 6 over 1 was found in treatment 3 and was followed by treatments 6, 4 and 5, respectively. Contrarily it was increased in treatments 1 and 2 and this increase was 119% and 20%, respectively during same period of time. On average, the ECe increased upto sampling 3 but decreased during Rice 1989 (S4) depicting movement of salts from the upper layers to lower layers and their deposition.

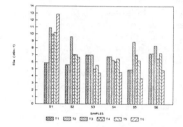

Trts	Means	% Decr./Incr.[*] in S6 Over S1
T1	9.66(a)	119[*]
T2	7.31(ab)	20[*]
T3	6.16(b)	37
T4	6.33(b)	32
T5	6.57(b)	24
T6	7.19(b)	33

T1 Ctrl, T2 Deep plowing (45 cm), T3 50% GR, LSD(T) 1% = 2.40
T4 25% GR+20 tons/ha FYM, T5 Kallar grass, T6 Jantar

Figure 3. Effect of Different Treatments on ECe of Soil (30-60 cm)

60-90-cm Depth; At the end of the experiment the ECe was significantly higher in treatment 1 compared with treatments 3, 4, 5 and 6 (Fig.4). The maximum reduction of 41% in sampling 6 over 1 was found in treatment 4 within about two and a half years but during same period of time an increase of 156% and 26% was observed in treatments 1 and 2, respectively manifesting the treatments effect on salts movement and their deposition in different layers.

The ECe was also significantly affected during different soil samplings. On average it was increased with the passage of time but decreased during Rice 1990 which was significantly lower than the ECe of soil in samplings 1, 2 and 3. Results are in conformity with those as reported by Kausar and Muhammad, (1972) and Chaudhry and Hameed, (1992).

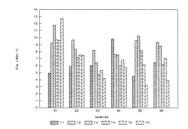

Trts	Means	% Decr./Incr.[*] in S6 Over S1
T1	9.69(a)	156[*]
T2	7.72(ab)	26[*]
T3	5.85(b)	30
T4	7.28(b)	41
T5	6.99(b)	30
T6	6.98(b)	39

T1 Ctrl, T2 Deep plowing (45 cm), T3 50% GR,   LSD(T) 5% = 2.15
T4 25% GR+20 tons/ha FYM, T5 Kallar grass, T6 Jantar   LSD(S) 5% = 2.15

Figure 4. Effect of Different Treatments on ECe of Soil (60-90 cm)

Sodium Adsorption Ratio (SAR)

0-15-cm Depth; The SAR (mmol L^{-1})$^{1/2}$ of soil in treatment 1 differed significantly compared with other treatments where differences were insignificant (Fig.5). However, differences were

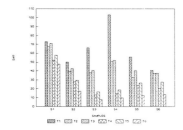

Trts	Means	% Decr./Incr.[*] in S6 Over S1
T1	61.62(a)	35
T2	34.54(b)	65
T3	30.42(b)	88
T4	41.49(b)	90
T5	32.10(b)	77
T6	29.46(b)	66

T1 Ctrl, T2 Deep plowing (45 cm), T3 50% GR,   LSD(T) 1% = 17.03
T4 25% GR+20 tons/ha FYM, T5 Kallar grass, T6 Jantar   LSD(S) 1% = 17.03

Figure 5. Effect of Different Treatments on SAR of Soil (0-15 cm)

there and on percentage, there was 35, 65, 88, 90, 77 and 66% reduction in SAR in sampling 6 over 1 in treatments 1, 2, 3, 4, 5 and 6, respectively showing the varying degree of effectiveness of treatments. The higher reduction in treatment 4 was possibly due to improvement in the physical properties of soil on account of addition of farm yard manure. The SAR was reduced below safe limits (< 13) only in treatments 3, 4 and 5 within two and a half year.

The SAR in different soil samplings also varied significantly and after sampling 2 it was slightly increased during wheat and decreased during rice depending upon the delta of water applied and soil sampling time.

15-30-cm Depth; In about two and a half years period the maximum reduction of 83% in sampling 6 over 1 was found in treatment 4 and was followed by 80, 62, 59, 47 and 28% reduction in treatments 3, 6, 5, 4 and 1, respectively (Fig.6). The SAR in treatment 1 was

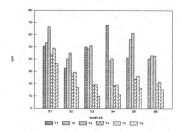

Trts	Means	% Decr./Incr.[*] in S6 Over S1
T1	50.01(a)	28
T2	32.11(b)	47
T3	33.10(b)	80
T4	32.59(b)	83
T5	37.64(ab)	59
T6	30.50(b)	62

T1 Ctrl, T2 Deep plowing (45 cm), T3 50% GR,   LSD(T) 1% = 12.65
T4 25% GR+20 tons/ha FYM, T5 Kallar grass, T6 Jantar   LSD(S) 1% = 12.65

Figure 6. Effect of Different Treatments on SAR of Soil (15-30 cm)

significantly higher as compared with the SAR in treatments 2, 3, 4 and 6 but varied insignificantly with treatment 5. It was brought below safe limits during Rice 1990 only in treatments 3 and 4 depicting that Ca^{++} applied through amendments played its role in replacing the Na^+ from the soil exchange complex which leached below this depth with water. However this status could not be achieved in other treatments.

The SAR increased during the first year and was maximum in sampling 3 and again reduced in the later samplings. Significantly higher SAR, on average, in sampling 3 is possibly due to accumulation of some of the Na^+ salts leached down from the upper 15cm layer.

30-60-cm Depth; The treatments from 2 to 6 varied insignificantly among themselves and the SAR in these was significantly lower as compared with treatment 1 (Fig.7). On percentage basis maximum reduction of 66% in sampling 6 over 1 was observed in treatment 3 and minimum of only 2% in treatment 1 indicating the effectiveness of biological and chemical amendments on the replacement of Na^+ from the soil exchange complex resulting in low SAR. Only in treatment 3 SAR was reduced below safe limits.

The SAR was also significantly higher in samplings 2 and 3 as compared with the SAR of other samplings but varied insignificantly between themselves. Data also show a sharp reduction during Rice 1989 (S4) but later on this process was slowed down.

60-90-cm Depth; The treatments effect on the SAR of this soil depth was insignificant, however, differences existed in the SAR of soil due to treatments (Fig.8) showing their efficiency in reducing the SAR. Maximum reduction of 78% in sampling 6 over 1 was observed in treatment 4 followed by 58, 56, 43, 39% in treatments 3, 6, 5 and 2, respectively whereas an increase of 29% was found in treatment 1 during same period. This increase is possibly due to leaching down of the Na^+ salts from the upper layers with irrigation water which could not pass beyond this depth due to insufficient leaching or hard soil pan.

The SAR in samplings 4, 5 and 6 was significantly lower as compared with the SAR of preceding ones. Maximum SAR was found in sampling 2 revealing the accumulation of Na⁺ salts leached down from upper layers. Very rapid reduction was observed during Rice 1989 which slowed down during later period. Similar results were reported by Kausar and Muhammad, (1972), Ahmed et al., (1990) and Chaudhry and Hameed, (1992).

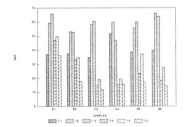

Trts	Means	% Decr./Incr.* in S6 Over S1
T1	49.22(a)	2
T2	38.23(b)	32
T3	33.28(b)	66
T4	34.87(b)	58
T5	38.66(b)	55
T6	38.47(b)	66

T1 Ctrl, T2 Deep plowing (45 cm), T3 50% GR,   LSD(T) 5% = 9.11
T4 25% GR+20 tons/ha FYM, T5 Kallar grass, T6 Jantar   LSD(S) 1% = 12.32

Figure 7. Effect of Different Treatments on SAR of Soil (30-60 cm)

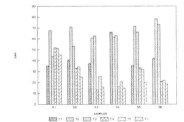

Trts	Means	% Decr./Incr.* in S6 Over S1
T1	45.47	29*
T2	24.90	39
T3	15.82	58
T4	14.75	78
T5	20.12	43
T6	18.30	56

T1 Ctrl, T2 Deep plowing (45 cm), T3 50% GR   LSD(S) 1% = 18.21
T4 25% GR+20 tons/ha FYM, T5 Kallar grass, T6 Jantar

Figure 8. Effect of Different Treatments on SAR of Soil (60-90 cm)

Infiltration Rate

The infiltration rate of soil was not significantly affected by different treatments (Fig.9) however, differences were observed. On percentage, there was 31, 65, 96, 102, 86 and 82% increase in the infiltration rate in 1988-89 in treatments 1, 2, 3, 4, 5 and 6, respectively over initial i.e. pre-rice 1988 manifesting the treatments effect. The maximum increase of 102% was found in treatment 4 which may be possibly due to addition of organic matter in the form of farm yard manure which improved the physical conditions of the soil resulting in higher intake of water. The infiltration rate was significantly higher in 1988-89 and 1989-90 as compared with the initial one (pre-rice 1988). On average there was 39 and 77% increase in the infiltration rate during 1988-89 and 1989-90 over initial, respectively. Results are in conformity with those of Chaudhry and Hameed, (1992).

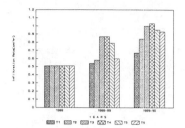

Trts	Pre-rice 1988 (Initial)	Post-wheat 89-90	% Incr. in 1989-90 over 1988
T1	0.51	0.67	31
T2	0.51	0.84	65
T3	0.51	1.00	96
T4	0.51	1.03	102
T5	0.51	0.95	86
T6	0.51	0.93	82

T1 Ctrl, T2 Deep plowing (45 cm), T3 50% GR,   LSD(Y) 1% = 0.16
T4 25% GR+20 tons/ha FYM, T5 Kallar grass, T6 Jantar

Figure 9. Effect of Different Treatments on the Infiltration Rate (cm/hr) of Soil

Crops Yield

Paddy; Impressive increase in paddy yield was observed by applying amendments. Yield was significantly higher and lower in treatment 3 and 1 compared with other treatments (Fig.10). On average, there was 32%, 64%, 47%, 54% and 47% yield increase in treatments 2, 3, 4, 5 and 6 over 1, respectively. This was expected as physical and chemical properties of soil were improved in these treatments. Yield also increased statistically with the passage of time and this increase was 47% and 64% in 1989 and 1990 over 1988, respectively.

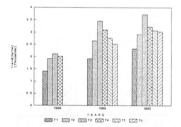

Trts	Means	% Incr. over T1
T1	1886(d)	-
T2	2492(c)	32
T3	3099(a)	64
T4	2778(b)	47
T5	2908(b)	54
T6	2771(b)	47

T1 Ctrl, T2 Deep plowing (45 cm), T3 50% GR,   LSD(T) 1% = 224.39
T4 25% GR+20 tons/ha FYM, T5 Kallar grass, T6 Jantar   LSD(Y) 1% = 158.67

Figure 10. Effect of Different Treatments on Paddy Yield (kg/ha)

Wheat Grains: Like paddy, wheat grains yield was also significantly affected by different treatments and the yield obtained in treatment 3 was significantly higher as compared with the yield in treatments 1, 2, 5 and 6 (Fig.11). On average, the yield increase in treatments 2, 3, 4, 5 and 6 over 1 was 31%, 67%, 42%, 32% and 19%, respectively confirming that reclamation technology has contributed towards increasing the wheat grains yield. Likely

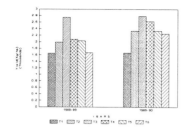

Trts	Means	%Incr. Over T1
T1	1658(c)	-
T2	2164(b)	31
T3	2765(a)	67
T4	2356(ab)	42
T5	2185(b)	32
T6	1964(bc)	19

T1 Ctrl, T2 Deep plowing (45 cm), T3 50% GR,   LSD(Y) 5% = 254.90
T4 25% GR+20 tons/ha FYM, T5 Kallar grass, T6 Jantar

Figure 11. Effect of Different Treatments on Wheat Grains Yield (kg/ha)

Chaudhry et al., (1987, 1988), Chaudhry and Hameed, (1992) and Ahmed et al., (1990) have also reported an increase in yield on reclamation of saline-sodic soils.

Economic Analysis:

Total present worth benefits for treatments 1, 2, 3, 4, 5 and 6 were Rupees 41782, 53923, 65699, 59270, 44847 and 41300 and cost Rupees 40479, 41809, 45673, 44469, 40703 and 39513 (1 US$ = Rs.25.00), respectively. Benefit cost ratio of treatments 1, 2, 3, 4, 5 and 6 was 1.03, 1.29, 1.44, 1.33, 1.10 and 1.05, respectively depicting that treatment 3 is more economical.

CONCLUSIONS

- The ECe and SAR of soil was significantly affected by different treatments.

- Gypsum @ 50% GR and gypsum @ 25% GR + 20 tons/ha FYM seems equally effective in reducing ECe and SAR of soil but were certainly superior over other treatments.

- Application of biological and chemical reclaimants improved the infiltration rate of soil considerably.

- Gypsum @ 50% GR of soil produced significantly higher paddy and wheat grains yield.

- Based on the present data gypsum application @ 50% GR is more profitable with 1.44 benefit-cost ratio.

RECOMMENDATION

Further experiments should be carried out in semi-dense to dense saline-sodic soils to evaluate the efficiency of different reclaimants in varying doses and combinations under different soil and climatic conditions.

REFERENCES

1. Ahmed, N; R. H. Qureshi and M. Qadir. 1990. Comparative effectiveness of gypsum and forage plant species in reclamation of a calcareous saline-sodic soil. Pak. J. Agri. Sci. 27 (2): 168-173.

2. Aronovici, V. S. 1955. Model study of infiltrometer performance under low initial soil moisture. Soil Sci. Soc. Amer. Proc. 18:1-6.

3. Bouyoucos, G. J. 1951. A recalibration of the hydrometer for making mechanical analysis of soil. Agron.J.43: 434- 438.

4. Branson, Roy L., and M. Fireman. 1960. Reclamation of an "impossible" alkali soil. Int. Congr. Soil Sci. Trans. 7th (Madison, Wis.) VI:543-551.

5. Chaudhry, M. R. and Abaidullah. 1988a. Efficiency of reclaimants in reclaiming saline-sodic soil. Proc Ist. National Congr. of Soil Sci. (Lahore Oct. 1985): 415-422.

6. Chaudhary, M. R. and M. Abaidullah. 1988b. Economics and effectiveness of biological and chemical methods in soil reclamation. Pak. J. Soil Sci. 2 (1-4):11-16.

7. Chaudhry, M. R., B. Ahmed and M. S. Rafique. 1988. Efficiency of chemical amendments in reclamation of saline-sodic soil. Presented at 2nd National Congress of Soil Sci. "Soil for Agri. Development" held from Dec. 20- 22 at Faisalabad.

8. Chaudhry, M. R., Ihsanullah and B. Ahmed. 1987. Comparative effect of sulphuric acid and gypsum on the reclamation of moderately salt affected soil and crop production. Mona Recl. Expt. Project, Wapda, Publication No.164, pp-10-16.

9. Chaudhry, M. R. and A. Hameed. 1992. Infiltration rate, salinity/sodicity and crop yield as affected during reclamation process. Proc. 5th Int. Drainage Workshop Vol.III Session 6: 35-45.

10. Chaudhry, M. R. and M. S. Rafique. 1990. Comparative efficiency of sulphuric acid and gypsum alone and in combination with farm yard manure on reclamation and crop yield. Mona Recl. Expt. Project, Wapda, Publication No.179.

11. Dubey, S. K., R. C. Mondal and A. Swarup. 1987. Effect of gypsum and pyrite with different moisture regimes on sodic soil improvement and rice yield. International Rice Research newsletter 12 (6): 35.

12. Kausar, M. A. and S. Muhammad. 1972. Comparison of biological and chemical methods for reclaiming saline-sodic soils. Pak. J. Scientific Res. XXIV:252-261.

13. Prather, R.J., J.O. Boertzen, J.D. Rhoades and H. Frenkel. 1978. Efficient amendment use in sodic soil reclamation. Soil. Sci. Soc. Amer. J. 42 (5): 782-786.

14. Sandhu, G. R. and K. A. Malik. 1975. Plant succession, A key to the utilization of saline soils. Nucleus 12: 35- 38.

15. U.S. Salinity Lab. Staff. 1954. Diagnosis and improvement of saline and alkali soils. USDA Hand book No.60 Washington, D.C.

ALLELOPATHIC INFLUENCES OF HERBACEOUS SPECIES AFFECT EARLY GROWTH

OF TREE SEEDLINGS IN MINESOIL

M. M. Larson* and S. H. Patel*

ABSTRACT

Dried foliage (litter) of several herbaceous species was mixed with either
vermiculite or two minesoils (topsoil and spoil) in containers planted with
black locust (Robinia pseudoacacia), white ash (Fraxinus americana) and
sweetgum (Liquidambar styraciflua) seedlings in a greenhouse. Also,
germinated seed of northern red oak (Quercus rubra) was planted in containers
previously seeded with herbaceous species. In vermiculite, black locust
growth was inhibited by 12 g litter additions of alfalfa (Medicago sativa),
birdsfoot trefoil (Lotus corniculatus), tall fescue (Festuca arundinacea), and
bluegrass (Poa pratensis), but stimulated by red clover (Trifolium pratense)
litter. White ash growth was strongly inhibited by alfalfa and trefoil added
to vermiculite at 12 and 18 g levels. In topsoil, sweetgum was strongly
inhibited by alfalfa litter. Both sweetgum and red oak grew poorly in spoil,
but seeded ryegrass (Lolium perenne), orchardgrass (Dactylis glomerata) and
fescue grew well. Some aspects of red oak growth were inhibited if grown in
containers seeded with alfalfa, ryegrass, orchardgrass, red clover and fescue.
These results demonstrate that there may be important allelopathic
interactions between herbaceous species and trees planted on minelands.

Several tree planting projects have been started on surface mined lands in the
Appalachian Region in recent years. A mixture of several herbaceous species
is almost always established on reclaimed areas before trees are planted. One
grass species, tall fescue, has been reported to be allelopathic as well as a
severe competitor for water and nutrients (Walters and Gilmore 1976). Several
herbaceous species appear to be allelopathic to tree seedlings under certain
conditions, but not all tree species are equally affected (Hollis et al. 1982,
Larson and Schwarz 1980). Little information is available regarding the
allelopathic interactions between herbaceous and woody species used on
minelands.

Reported here are the results of three greenhouse studies on allelopathic
relationships between herbaceous species and hardwood tree seedlings commonly
used in reclamation projects. These studies are part of a larger cooperative
project between the School of Natural Resources, Ohio State University and the
American Electric Power Service Corporation (AEP) to investigate the
reclamation of calcareous coal spoils with trees, shrubs, and forages.

----
* M. M. Larson, Professor and S. H. Patel, Graduate Student, School of Natural
Resources, Ohio Agricultural Research and Development Center, The Ohio State
University, Wooster, OH 44691

EXPERIMENT 1. ALLELOPATHIC EFFECTS OF EIGHT HERBACEOUS SPECIES ON BLACK
LOCUST AND WHITE ASH SEEDLINGS.

Methods and Materials.

Mature foliage of eight herbaceous species, Orchardgrass, Timothy (Phleum
pratense), Perennial Ryegrass, Ranger Alfalfa, Birdsfoot Trefoil, Mammoth Red
Clover, Kentucky Bluegrass, and Kentucky Tall Fescue was collected in the
field, air-dried in the greenhouse, ground separately by species in a Wiley
mill using a 20 mesh screen and stored at -18°C until used. One-year-old
seedlings of black locust and white ash were obtained from the State Nursery
at Zanesville, Ohio and root pruned at 15 cm from the root collar to
facilitate planting and measurement of new root growth at harvest. Green
weight of each tree was recorded just prior to planting and used as a
covariate in the analysis of new growth.

Trees were planted in coarse vermiculite in 1 L milk cartons lined with a
plastic bag. Prior to filling, one of the bottom corners of the carton was
removed leaving an opening about 2 cm in diameter. About 3 cm of the plastic
liner was pulled through the opening and the lower end clipped off to allow
the soil leachate to drain through and collect in a 0.28 L styrofoam cup. One
of two levels (6 and 12 g) of ground foliage (litter) of each herbaceous
species was mixed with vermiculite in cartons at time of planting black
locust. For white ash, three litter levels (6, 12, and 18 g) were used. The
control treatment was vermiculite plus 6 g of air dried sphagnum per carton.

Trees in cartons were randomly placed on a wooden frame elevated 15 cm above
the bench to allow drainage from the cartons into the styrofoam cup. The soil
leachate (plus sufficient deionized water to fill the cup) was recycled
through the vermiculite twice daily. Recycling was necessary to reduce
excessive loss of soluble organic compounds from the soil. Greenhouse
temperatures were maintained at 24±4°C.

Black locust trees were harvested at 6 weeks, white ash at 8 weeks. Number of
stems, leaves, and lengths of new roots and stems was recorded. The new
leaves, stems and roots of each tree were oven dried at 75°C and weighed.

Seedling growth data were analyzed using a two factor analysis of covariance,
and multiple comparisons of means made by using the least significant
differences method.

Results and Discussion.

Black locust grown without litter added to vermiculite grew poorly and could
not be used as a control treatment. The reason for the unusually poor growth
of control trees was not apparent although these were the only trees with
sphagnum in the soil medium. Black locust grew very well in vermiculite in
earlier studies (Larson and Schwarz 1980). Within each litter type, growth of
black locust at the 6 g level was used as a standard to determine effects of
12 g litter additions.

Increasing the amount of litter of alfalfa and trefoil in potting media from 6
g to 12 g reduced new growth of stems and roots of black locust seedlings
(Table 1). Tall fescue and bluegrass litter at 12 g also reduced root dry
weight. The difference between mean root dry weights at 6 g and 12 g litter
levels, when expressed as a percentage of the 6 g level, ranged from -38 to
-53% for the above four species. Only trefoil litter significantly decreased
stem length of locust at the 12 g level (Table 1).

In contrast, increasing red clover litter from 6 g to 12 g stimulated dry
weights of leaves and roots by 40% (Table 1). Growth of stems and leaves was
either stimulated or unaffected in all 12 g litters except alfalfa and
trefoil.

Table 1. Length of New Stems and Dry Weight of New Growth (Stems, Leaves, and Roots) of 1-0 Black Locust Seedlings Grown in Vermiculite Soil with Litter of Various Herbaceous Species Added at 6 g and 12 g Levels.

	Black Locust Seedlings							
	Stems, ln*		Stems, dw*		Leaves, dw*		Roots, dw*	
Litter added =	6g	12g	6g	12g	6g	12g	6g	12g
	-----cm-----		-----g-----		-----g-----		-----g-----	
R. Alfalfa	51.3	41.6	0.63	0.38#	3.24	1.89#	1.05	0.49#
B. Trefoil	55.8	34.6#	0.67	0.30#	3.78	2.01#	0.90	0.48#
K. Tall Fescue	51.0	39.3	0.61	0.48	2.96	2.85	1.04	0.63#
K. Bluegrass	53.9	52.3	0.81	0.65	3.41	3.56	1.09	0.66#
Timothy	49.5	54.2	0.63	0.65	3.38	3.27	1.08	0.80
Orchardgrass	40.1	45.1	0.42	0.49	2.60	3.08	0.83	0.91
P. Ryegrass	33.9	42.6	0.44	0.46	2.31	2.55	0.60	0.86
Red Clover	51.0	61.0	0.63	0.90	3.23	4.39#	0.95	1.33#

* Least significant difference values at P=0.05 level: stem length = 15.0 cm, stem dw = 0.25 g, leaf dw = 0.96 g, and root dw = 0.38g.
# Indicates mean for 12 g litter differs from mean for 6 g litter at P=0.05.

The tendency for reduced stem length in four litter types at the 12 g level suggested that this result was due to osmotic effects of recycled soil leachate. The osmotic potential determined by freezing point depression of leachates (6 and 12 g of litter soaked in 0.28 L water for 24 hours and filtered) of seven herbaceous species ranged from -0.09 to -0.18 MPa. However, stem lengths were not correlated with these osmotic potentials ($r^2 = 0.068$).

Growth of new stems of white ash was stimulated by 6 g of trefoil litter. However, stems were strongly reduced in both trefoil and alfalfa at 18 g level (Table 2). Dry weights of leaves and roots were also lowest at the 18 g

Table 2. Length of New Stems and Dry Weights of Leaves and New Roots of White Ash Seedlings Grown in Vermiculite Soil with Litter of Herbaceous Species Added at 6 g, 12 g and 18 g Levels, and without Litter (Control).

	White Ash Seedlings								
	Stems, ln*			Leaves, dw*			Roots, dw*		
Litter added =	6g	12g	18g	6g	12g	18g	6g	12g	18g
	------- cm -------			------- g --------			-------- g -------		
R. Alfalfa	26.0	15.4	4.4#	2.26	1.20	0.39#	0.72	0.31#	0.05#
B. Trefoil	30.5#	11.8	5.9#	2.04	1.00#	0.53#	0.80	0.24#	0.09#
K. T. Fescue	18.6	26.3	21.9	2.36	2.09	1.91	0.78	0.64	0.59
K. Bluegrass	17.8	16.7	17.2	1.76	1.74	1.53	0.74	0.58	0.46
Timothy	18.9	18.8	15.0	2.21	1.81	1.30	0.82	0.63	0.50
Orchardgrass	15.5	16.9	21.8	1.45	1.76	1.64	0.51	0.74	0.71
P. Ryegrass	23.9	21.0	19.1	2.06	2.02	1.66	0.76	0.68	0.54
Red Clover	19.2	21.2	21.9	1.89	2.04	1.74	0.79	0.65	0.50
Control		19.1			1.82			0.62	

* Least significant difference between means at P=0.05 level: stems = 9.9 cm, leaves = 0.71 g, and roots = 0.31 g.
# Mean differs from control at P=0.05.

level. Timothy litter tended to reduce leaf and root dry weight of ash trees but only at the 18 g level (Table 2). However, the two most toxic litters were alfalfa and birdsfoot trefoil which, at the 18 g level, reduced all aspects of ash growth to only 8 to 31 percent of that of control trees.

In general, the lowest level (6 g) of all litter types tended to stimulate dry weight growth of ash trees or was without significant effect (Table 2). Previous research also found that low levels of litter of several species (including fescue and timothy) slightly stimulated growth of black locust and red clover (Larson and Schwarz 1980). Other measures of growth (time in days from planting to budbreak and numbers of leaves and stems) were not affected by litter treatments, and therefore these data are not shown.

EXPERIMENT 2. EFFECTS OF MINESOIL TYPE AND HERBACEOUS LITTER ON GROWTH OF SWEETGUM SEEDLINGS.

Methods and Materials

Gray cast overburden, hereafter referred to as spoil, and topsoil were obtained from an active mine site in southeastern Ohio. The two soils were stored under cover near the greenhouse until used. Seven different potting mixtures, some with perlite added to separate possible effects of poor drainage from other soil effects, were used as soil media as follows: (1) Topsoil, (2) Topsoil and perlite, 1:1, (3) Spoil, (4) Spoil and perlite, 1:1, (5) Topsoil and spoil, 1:1, (6) Topsoil, spoil and perlite, 1:1:2, and (7) Vermiculite and peat, 1:1. (Note: all soil mixture ratios are on a vol:vol basis.)

Litter of three herbaceous species, orchardgrass, perennial ryegrass and ranger alfalfa, was collected as described above, and added to soil media in pots at 0-, 6- and 12-gram levels.

Sweetgum seedlings, 1-0 stock, were obtained from the Zanesville Nursery, root pruned at 15 cm from the root collar and planted in 1 L milk cartons containing one of the above soil materials. Plastic bag liners to facilitate collection and recycling of soil leachate were used as described earlier. Green weight of each tree was used as a covariate in the statistical analysis of growth. Two trees were planted in each carton and replicated eight times for each soil/litter treatment. The experiment was a completely randomized design. Greenhouse temperatures were maintained at approximately 24°C without artificial light.

Seedlings were harvested at 6 weeks and growth measurements taken as described in Experiment 1. Data were analyzed using a two-way analysis of covariance, and mean separation by least significant difference at P=0.05 level.

Results and Discussion

When planted in seven different soil media without litter, sweetgum seedlings grew best in topsoil+perlite mixture (TS+PER) and poorly in pure spoil (SP) (Table 3). Trees in topsoil (TS) benefitted from the addition of perlite. Root dry weight increased 3-fold, and dry weight of leaves was significantly greater when perlite was added. Since perlite is relatively inert, the benefit was probably the result of improved drainage.

In topsoil+perlite, addition of any herbaceous litter inhibited growth, with alfalfa at 6 and 12 g levels showing significantly stronger inhibition than other litter types (Table 3). In fact, alfalfa at 6 g was as effective as 12 g level in reducing growth. Also, addition of ryegrass and alfalfa litter at both 6 g and 12 g levels strongly inhibited growth of sweetgum in vermiculite+ peat. Tree growth in pure spoil was already suppressed (see below) and not further inhibited by litter.

Table 3. Dry Weight of Leaves and New Roots of Sweetgum Grown in Various Soil Media and with Added Herbaceous Litter at 6 g and 12 g Levels.

Soil medium@	Measured variable	Control 0g	Orchardgrass 6g	12g	Ryegrass 6g	12g	Alfalfa 6g	12g
					Sweetgum growth* in: ─────────── g ───────────			
TS	Leaves	1.04	1.09	1.13	0.86	0.49#	0.38#	0.42#
	Roots	0.09	0.16	0.24	0.06	0.06	0.02	0.04
TS+PER	Leaves	1.94	1.10#	1.34#	0.98#	1.29#	0.33#	0.23#
	Roots	0.28	0.14#	0.20#	0.16#	0.20#	0.02#	0.03#
SP	Leaves	<0.01	<0.01	0.01	<0.01	0.01	0.03	0.06
	Roots	<0.01	<0.01	<0.01	0.01	0.02	0.02	<0.01
SP+PER	Leaves	0.29	0.35	0.28	0.42	0.23	0.18	0.05
	Roots	0.02	0.06	0.03	0.05	0.03	0.03	0.01
SP+TS	Leaves	0.41	0.44	0.12	0.15	0.04#	0.10	0.12
	Roots	0.04	0.03	0.01	0.02	0.02	0.02	0.02
SP+TS+PER	Leaves	0.72	0.61	0.42	0.67	0.57	0.39	0.07#
	Roots	0.08	0.10	0.07	0.14	0.08	0.07	0.01
VERM+PEAT	Leaves	1.28	1.31	0.94	0.91#	0.49#	0.42#	0.66#
	Roots	0.21	0.22	0.17	0.16	0.05#	0.04#	0.09#
Total Mean	Leaves	0.81	0.70	0.60#	0.57#	0.45#	0.26#	0.23#
	Roots	0.10	0.10	0.10	0.09	0.08	0.03#	0.03#

@ Codes for soil media are as follows: TS=topsoil, PER=perlite, SP=spoil, VERM+PEAT=vermiculite+peatmoss; see Methods for mixture ratios.
* Least significant difference values at P=0.05 for soil/litter treatments are 0.36 g (leaves) and 0.08 g (roots), and for total means are 0.20 g. (leaves) and 0.03 g (roots).
# For each soil medium, litter treatment differs from control (0 g) at P=0.05.

In spoil, dry weights of leaves and new roots were less than 1% of that of trees in topsoil (Table 3). When perlite or topsoil was added to spoil, leaf dry weight increased 28% and 40%, respectively, of that of trees in topsoil alone. When both perlite and topsoil were added to spoil (SP+TS+PER), leaf dry weight was 70% of trees in topsoil alone. Trees in pure spoil were stunted, and several exhibited symptoms of root rot when harvested.

Spoil samples had a mean pH of 7.7 and a salinity of 968 ug/ml extractable Na+ (compared to pH 6.4 and 22 ug/ml extractable Na+ for topsoil). These spoil characteristics may have contributed to poor growth of trees. Sweetgum will tolerate acid minesoils as low as pH 4.0 (Vogel 1981). Clearly, spoil alone was not a suitable medium for growth of sweetgum seedlings.

EXPERIMENT 3. GROWTH OF NORTHERN RED OAK SEEDLINGS PLANTED IN TWO MINESOILS SEEDED WITH HERBACEOUS SPECIES

One gallon (3.78 L) plastic pots were filled with either topsoil or spoil (described above) plus 1.0 g of NPK (8-32-16) fertilizer and 0.6 g of ammonium nitrate. These correspond to the fertilizer levels used by Central Ohio Coal Company in reclaiming mineland.

Each of 8 herbaceous species listed in Experiment 1 was seeded in the pots. Once the herbaceous cover was well established (about 3 weeks), a newly

germinated northern red oak seedling was planted in the center and watered
daily in an attempt to keep plant moisture stress at a low level. Tree
heights were recorded every 7 to 10 days and the herbaceous growth was clipped
twice to a height of about 5 cm during the study. Trees were harvested at 9
weeks.

Eight replications of each soil type by herbaceous species plus control (soil
without herbaceous species) were randomly located in the greenhouse. Leaves,
stems and roots were oven dried at 75°C and weighed. Root dry weights of
herbaceous species in pots were also determined when the trees were harvested.

Data were analyzed by analysis of variance and regression analysis for tree
height data. Mean separation was by method of least significant difference at
P=0.05 level.

Results and Discussion.

Northern red oak seedlings in spoil grew poorly when compared to trees in
topsoil (Table 4). Oak trees in spoil averaged only 31% of the mean dry
weight of trees in topsoil, and effects of herbaceous cover types on growth
were suppressed. For instance, leaf dry weight among cover types in spoil
ranged from 0.10 to 0.70 g (a difference of 0.60 g) compared to 0.91 to 2.82 g
(a difference of 1.91 g) in topsoil (Table 4).

Table 4. New Growth of Northern Red Oak Seedlings in Containers with either
Spoil or Topsoil that had been Seeded with One of Eight Herbaceous Species or
Unseeded, and Total Root Dry Weight of Herbaceous Species in Containers.

	Northern Red Oak			Herbaceous Sp.
	Height Growth*	Leaves, dw*	Roots, dw*	Roots, dw**
	Topsoil:Spoil	Topsoil:Spoil	Topsoil:Spoil	Topsoil:Spoil
	---- cm ----	---- g ----	---- g ----	---- g ----
R. Alfalfa	16.9# 7.6	0.96# 0.40	1.74# 1.06	5.08a 3.75b
P. Ryegrass	11.4# 9.7	0.91# 0.64	1.50# 1.29	4.70a 6.71a
K. T. Fescue	12.2# 9.1	1.24# 0.32	2.16 0.85	4.60a 4.44b
Orchardgrass	15.3# 11.3	1.66# 0.70	2.59 1.20	2.75b 4.86b
Red Clover	15.7# 8.0	1.46# 0.63	2.43 0.89	2.20bc 1.58c
K. Bluegrass	23.9 8.8	2.82 0.40	3.12 0.75	1.87bc 1.10c
B. Trefoil	24.8 3.8	2.13 0.10	3.28 0.52	1.01c 0.34c
Timothy	23.9 8.5	2.70 0.61	2.78 1.08	0.84c 1.17c
Unseeded	23.0 4.2	2.46 0.32	2.68 0.66	

* Least sigificant difference at P=0.05 for n. red oak are: height = 6.3 cm,
   leaves dw = 0.60 g, roots dw = 0.76 g.
** Within each soil, means followed by a similar letter not significant, least
   significant difference at P=0.05 for herbaceous root dw = 1.56 g.
Lower value than that of corresponding unseeded mean at P=0.05.

In topsoil, height growth was similar for trees in unseeded, timothy, trefoil
and bluegrass cover types, ranging from 23.0 to 24.9 cm (Table 4). Height
growth was reduced about 50% in both ryegrass and fescue covers. In spoil,
seedling height in unseeded cover averaged only 4.2 cm. Although height of
trees in several spoil/herbaceous cover types was greater than that of trees
in unseeded spoil, only trees in orchardgrass cover had a significantly
greater mean height (11.3 cm)(Table 4).

342

Trends in leaf dry weight of trees, as influenced by soil media and herbaceous cover types, were nearly identical to those described above for height except that inhibition by alfalfa was even stronger (Table 4). Root dry weight of trees in topsoil was more than 3.10 g in trefoil and bluegrass covers but less than 1.75 g in ryegrass and alfalfa covers (Table 4). Mean root dry weight of all trees in spoil was only 0.92 g.

Root growth of the eight herbaceous species was strikingly different in the two soil types. For instance, ryegrass and orchardgrass grew better in spoil than in topsoil (Table 4). Tall fescue and alfalfa also grew quite well in spoil, although alfalfa growth was best in topsoil. Red clover and bluegrass growth was greatest in topsoil, while trefoil and timothy did not grow particularly well in either soil type.

When height data of red oak trees in topsoil was compared to root dry weight of herbaceous species (Table 4), an inverse relationship was found ($r^2 = 0.687**$). An even closer relationship ($r^2 = 0.756**$) is found if one substitutes leaf dry weight for height growth. Trees grown in the three cover types with >4.50 g dry weight of herbaceous roots averaged 13.5 cm in height compared to 24.2 cm for trees in three cover types with <2.00 g of herbaceous roots. The sig-nificant negative correlation between growth of oak seedlings and amount of herbaceous roots in containers, regardless of species, suggests competition for moisture was also a factor even though plants were watered daily.

In spoil the correlation between tree growth variables and amount of herbaceous roots in pots was not significant. Instead, seedlings tended to grow slightly better in orchardgrass and ryegrass than in unseeded cover.

GENERAL DISCUSSION AND CONCLUSIONS

Ranger alfalfa was clearly the "winner" of the eight herbaceous species in inhibiting growth of tree seedlings. Growth of all tested tree species was inhibited when alfalfa litter was added to the soil medium (indicating presence of allelopathic toxins). Only 12 g of litter was needed to reduce growth of black locust and white ash. Sweetgum may be even more sensitive to alfalfa as evidenced by strong inhibition in 6 g litter. Also, seeded alfalfa grew rapidly in topsoil, a result that supports its reputation as a strong competitor for soil moisture and nutrients.

Birdsfoot trefoil litter also exhibited allelopathic characteristics, but vegetative growth of trefoil seeded in containers was among the lowest of the herbaceous species, and red oak trees grew well with trefoil. In the field, the trait of slow early development of trefoil indicates that allelopathic effects on tree seedling establishment is unlikely if seeded when trees are planted. Inhibition of seedling growth at a later date remains a possibility, however.

A similar case can be made with regard to competition between trees and herbaceous species for soil moisture in that use of slow-developing herbaceous species such as trefoil, bluegrass and timothy on newly-planted areas would be less detrimental to tree establishment than alfalfa, fescue or ryegrass.

Strong allelopathic effects of alfalfa and trefoil have been noted by others. Grant and Sallens (1964) tested aqueous extracts of alfalfa, birdsfoot trefoil, red clover, ladino clover (T. repens forma lodigense), timothy, bromegrass (Bromus inermis), orchardgrass, and reed canarygrass (Phalaris arundinacea). Each species was tested against all others with respect to seed germination and growth. The species were ranked according to decreasing inhibition in the following order: alfalfa, trefoil, ladino clover, red clover, reed canarygrass, bromegrass, timothy, and orchardgrass. Grant and Sallens (1964) also noted that timothy and red clover were quite compatible.

The mechanism by which alfalfa, trefoil, and other species reduce growth may be through inhibition of mineral uptake by altering the electric potential of cell membranes or activity of ATPases, or decreasing membrane permeability (Blake 1985). Bosisio (1989) reported that D. L. Dornbos identified "medicarpin" as one of the toxins in roots and shoots of alfalfa. In the field, alfalfa yields begin to decline after 4 or 5 years due to autotoxicity (Miller 1982).

Spoil alone was a poor medium for growth of both sweetgum and red oak trees. Sweetgum growth improved when spoil was amended with perlite and/or topsoil (Experiment 2), and oak tended to grow better in containers seeded with orchardgrass and ryegrass than in unseeded spoil (Experiment 3). Poor drainage of spoil in containers was apparent during the study. In the field, heavy, wet soils accumulate phenolic inhibitors that affect growth, whereas light, well-drained soils do not (Fisher 1976, Patrick 1971). Also, the quantity of phenolic compounds in soils tends to increase as the pH increases (Whitehead et al. 1981)

Growth of sweetgum in spoil was lower than expected. In the field, green ash (F. pennsylvanica) seedlings planted on the mined area where spoil material for this study was obtained have 98% survival after 2 years (Olah, 1990). Apparently, green ash is more tolerant than sweetgum of the high pH and salinity of this soil type.

Ryegrass, fescue, and orchardgrass grew equally well or better in spoil than topsoil. Alfalfa also performed well in spoil. However, alfalfa is not recommended as it is both allelopathic and a severe competitor to trees.

Results of this study, together with those of companion field studies (Larson and Vimmerstedt 1990, Olah 1990), demonstrate that spoil without topsoil can be successfully reclaimed with trees if: 1) the spoil is not compacted, 2) the tree species chosen are suited for establishment and growth on spoil, and 3) the herbaceous species selected will provide protection against erosion, but not overly interfere with tree establishment and growth.

Some of the more aggressive herbaceous species, such as orchardgrass and ryegrass, could be used if seeding is delayed until after the trees are planted. This has been successfully demonstrated in other studies (Ashby et al. 1988, Vogel 1980). Also, the amount of seed could be reduced if an area must be seeded before tree planting, and the more slowly developing species such as bluegrass, timothy and red clover are used.

REFERENCES

1. Ashby, W.C., M.R. Norland, and D.A. Kost,. 1988. Establishment of trees in herbaceous cover on graded Lenzburg minesoil. In: Mine Drainage and Surface Mine Reclamation. Vol.II. Mine Reclamation, Abandoned Mine Lands and Policy Issues. pp. 48-53. USDI Bureau of Mines Information Circular 9184.

2. Blake, N.E. 1985. Effects of allelochemicals on mineral uptake and associated physiological processes. In: The Chemistry of Allelopathy. A.C. Thompson, ed., American Chemical Society, pp. 161-177.

3. Bosisio, M. 1989. Self-destructing alfalfa? USDA Agric. Res. 37(2):18.

4. Fisher, R.F. 1976. Juglone inhibits pine growth under certain moisture conditions. Am. J. Soil Sci. Proc. 42:801-803.

5. Grant, E.A. and W.G. Sallens. 1964. Influence of plant extracts on germination and growth of eight forage species. J. Br. Grass Soc. 19:191-197.

6. Hollis, C.A., J.E. Smith, and R.F. Fisher. 1982. Allelopathic effects of common understory species on germination and growth of southern pines. For. Sci. 28:509-515.

7. Larson, M.M. and E.L. Schwarz. 1980. Allelopathic inhibition of black locust, red clover and black alder by six common herbaceous species. For. Sci. 26:511-520.

8. Larson, M.M. and J.P. Vimmerstedt. 1990. Effects of minesoil and seeded herbaceous species on survival of planted trees. Int. J. of Surface Mining and Reclamation 4:53-56.

9. Miller, D.A. 1982. Allelopathic effects of alfalfa. North Am. Symp. on Allelopathy, Nov. 14-17, 1982. Urbana-Champaign, IL. (abstr.)

10. Olah, P. 1990. Analysis of tree establishment on stripmined land in southeastern Ohio. MS. Thesis, School of Natural Resources, The Ohio State University.

11. Patrick, Z.A. 1971. Phytotoxic substances associated with decomposition in soil plant residues. Soil Sci. 3:13-18.

12. Vogel, W.G. 1981. A guide for revegetating coal minesoils in the eastern United States. USDA Forest Service Gen. Tech. Rept. NE-68, 190 p.

13. Vogel, W.G. 1980. Revegetating surface mined lands with herbaceous and woody species together. USDA Forest Service Gen. Tech. Rept. NE-61.

14. Walters, D.T. and A.R. Gilmore. 1976. Allelopathic effects of fescue on the growth of sweetgum. J. Chem. Ecol. 2:469-479.

15. Whitehead, D.C., H. Dibb, and R.D. Hartley. 1981. Extractant pH and the release of phenolic compounds from soils, plant roots and leaf litter. Soil Biochem. 13:343-348.

RECLAIMING LAND TO MAXIMISE CONSERVATION BENEFITS

A.D. Kendle*

The awarding of grant aid, and the conditions imposed, represent the main tools by which the UK government directs where derelict land reclamation is carried out and the type of afteruse that is encouraged. The traditional targets of land reclamation have usually been 'productive' land use such as agricultural grazing or timber production. Recently studies have highlighted the potential economic and social benefits of 'nature conservation' end uses for land reclamation (Land Capability Consultants, 1989). The cost effectiveness of different reclamation end points showed average investment in the order of £20000/Ha for agriculture, £13000/Ha for woodland and £5000/Ha for 'nature conservation'. Major reclamation costs are clearance of spoil, regrading, drainage and capping if necessary. (Because of inefficiencies of scale and restricted access urban reclamation schemes are often much more expensive, up to approximately £70000/Ha for public open space). Woodland establishment can be cheaper because regrading and soil quality improvements need not be carried out to as high a standard. 'Nature conservation' is cheapest because on many sites more extreme topography can be retained (within the limitations of safety), poor soil quality or poor drainage may not be a disadvantage and there may even be existing vegetation that can be retained. Agriculture therefore represents an average additional cost input of £15000/Ha and often the results are of marginal productivity. The value of the crops that result may never justify the additional restoration investment.

These findings also need to be set against the background of agricultural surpluses and the growth in interest in 'environmental issues' which helped to defuse the political pressure for agricultural afteruse of restored land. Also wildlife pressure groups have been aware for a long time that many officially 'derelict' sites were developing a spontaneous vegetation that was in itself interesting and valued by the local communities. Even where agricultural afteruse is clearly appropriate, such as in the restoration of open cast coal land, an improved understanding of the multiple social benefits of countryside has lead to an appreciation that some percentage of the reclaimed land is treated, or preserved, in a way that will allow it to develop into semi-natural habitat rather than productive land.

Although conservation afteruse clearly has attractions, it is still necessary to develop a sound methodology for achieving this goal in a politically and socially acceptable way. It is relatively easy to allow reclamation sites to 'go wild'; to develop rank vegetation. This is cheap but may be of limited value to conservation and in the long term would simply undermine the concept of this form of afteruse. Certainly there are situations where conservation afteruse is proposed by developers as mitigation for extraction proposals which may cause habitat destruction. In such cases a credible criteria for assessment of proposals should be developed. Although it is possible to identify areas where natural colonisation has lead to 'interesting wildlife' on derelict land; it is far harder to develop this recognition into a predictive tool suitable

* Dr Tony Kendle, Lecturer in Landscape Management, University of Reading, Department of Horticulture, PO BOX 221, Whiteknights, Reading RG6 2AS, U.K.

for guiding planning decisions. Research is needed to determine what environmental qualities would be necessary to support the development of a species-rich environment, and to establish what the reclamation programme should do to encourage and direct this. These new approaches should focus on overcoming the limitations to natural colonisation and on speeding the development of the natural site vegetation.

It is possible to identify certain sites which contain rare or unusual species precisely because the habitat is hostile and has not long been in existence. The colonisation of waste spoils by uncommon plants is well documented and is attributed to the low nutrient status and lack of competition from more aggressive species. Gemmell (1982) points out that in the Greater Manchester area there are more sites containing populations of terrestrial orchids (especially *Dactylorhiza spp.*) on derelict industrial land than in more traditional rural habitats. There can be as many as 100 plants per m2 and as many as 20 000 plants in a population, which contrasts with their uncommon status across much of the established countryside. One strategy is therefore to identify such 'early succession' communities of conservation interest and to maintain those, in other words to encourage a flora characteristic of the waste spoil habitat. Gilbert (1989) has done much to awaken interest in the unusual communities of urban and industrial habitats in the UK.

After a period of time many such 'disturbance' habitats gradually become less hostile and are invaded by scrub which in turn leads to a loss of the orchids. They are therefore essentially ephemeral communities. Management options for spoil tip habitats include re-creating the disturbance of the land using heavy earth moving equipment to destroy the scrub and to exploit the hostility of the soil to control succession.

In contrast, most habitat creation schemes focus on traditional biome models and attempt to create habitats which are much closer to those valued in traditional countryside (Hopkins, 1989). The problem with semi-natural rural communities is that they have often developed over a very long time and their complexity reflects this. To claim to be able to create one anew is arguably overambitious if not exactly fraudulent. It is particularly frustrating to think of derelict sites being reclaimed to a 'conservation afteruse' in order to produce what may be poor emulations of rural communities without consideration first being given to the way that the site may develop its own unique habitat types. Of course some traditional habitat types are easier to emulate than others - the least feasible are those ecosystems which are most natural and least influenced by man, such as ancient woodland. On the other hand, simple scrub communities are relatively easy to produce. Wetlands of some form are amongst the simplest habitats to create as the environmental effects of the water are so dominant on the ecosystem. Many wetland species are also adapted to withstand the risk that their habitat may be temporary and prone to drying out; they therefore tend to have good dispersal characteristics.

RECLAMATION METHODOLOGY

In biological terms 'nature conservation' should not be seen as simply another form of soft afteruse to rank alongside agriculture, forestry or even some forms of recreation. The methodology of revegetation of land that has developed over the last forty years has been implicitly targeted towards the goals that would be set by agronomists, with the resulting soil types judged against an agricultural norm. The principle objectives of vegetation management in traditional agronomy include limiting adversity and controlling competition that may harm the desired species. We control competition in direct ways. We clean the soil before planting. We space the plants in ways which we may now take for granted but which reflect years of experience of how they compete with each other. We maintain the community by weeding or using herbicides. We often separate out the most ecologically vulnerable stage of seedling germination and transfer this to the protected and controlled environment of the plant nursery. These exercises are matched by those aimed at overcoming environmental limitations to growth and ensuring maximum productivity and uniformity. We minimise stress by fertilising, irrigating and so on. Nearly all plants, including wild species, will benefit from these inputs in controlled conditions. Low biodiversity in the resulting vegetation is not a problem, it is characteristic of agronomic situations.

However ecological theories on the functioning of natural habitats shows that these are exactly the wrong criteria for developing conservation interest (Grime, 1979). In complex and competing plant communities stress is one of the factors which limits the growth of dominant, competitive, species and which leads to the development of diversity. For conservation ends it is important not to make conditions too favourable. Environmental variability and low productivity, the very factors that we try to overcome when establishing and managing most crops, are the criteria that promote the development of biodiversity. The fundamental difference in approach was succinctly summarised by Green (1986): *if the amenity land manager is ever in doubt as to his best course of action, he has merely to think of what a modern farmer or forester would do, and do the opposite. His objective is to make one blade of grass grow where two grew before.*

Traditional land reclamation has been orientated towards the recreation of productive soils and the temptation is always to equate the most fertile soil with the best soil. Nature, of course, does not agree - vegetation can adapt to a very wide range of soil types and often some of the most diverse and distinctive communities are found on the most extreme soils. Nature conservation goals in reclamation can also be complex as the interests of different species may conflict. In the absence of other criteria managers often aim to maximise species richness. Even this nebulous target implies greater than usual complexity of management and application of ecological principles. To improve methodology requires a basic understanding of how diverse communities develop. This is the next great challenge in reclamation work.

The Need for Plant Introduction

As discussed above, many derelict sites spontaneously develop an interesting flora. As well as having their own character, these colonisation patterns are also informative and can teach us more about ecological succession. Many workers therefore argue that natural plant colonisation should be left to progress at its own speed (Londo, in press).

A natural community assembly is controlled by the prevailing environment, including the management, which creates a framework within which certain species/communities are favoured and are able to establish. However the full expression of the potential community depends on the effectiveness of species dispersal. Traditional ecology theory holds that diversity increases as succession progresses, due to the diversification of niches but because the process of colonisation takes time, there is often a decrease in species richness associated with a change from one biome to another, e.g. the move from grass to scrub woodland that follows a decline in grazing. Reclamation has been likened to accelerated succession, and rapid biome change is going to be the least diverse of all.

Initial communities on derelict land may be slow to develop, but are characterised by the presence of many niches which can be filled by wind dispersed plants with low competitive ability. There is a medium term stage, when a grass and scrub community becomes established, that is characterised by a dramatic drop in diversity and a reduction in opportunities for new colonisers. Other colonisation constraints may also exist on industrial sites. Loss of habitat increases fragmentation and dispersal distances, making it less likely that the same processes of species invasion that created existing semi-natural communities would be able to progress on new sites. Transplanting and seed dispersal therefore have important rôles to play.

Transplanting can also overcome constraints to the establishment of seedlings or vegetative propagules. Weins' (1977) theory of the 'ecological crunch' suggests that many natural communities are constrained by competition operating at certain vulnerable stages in the development of different species. The seedling stage is often the most vulnerable, and we know from the experience of horticulturists and foresters, that once established many plants have wide physiological tolerances. The danger is that establishment may create communities which appear to be successful but that have no long term viability or ability to reproduce. On the other hand, the species introduced may gradually become to dominate the community, particularly if the management inhibits new colonisation. Some of these issues cut right to the heart of our understanding of natural community build-up and succession (Gilpin, 1989; Connell & Slatyer, 1977). (For a broader discussion of some issues of what may be called 'transplant ecology' see Kendle, 1992.)

Identifying Sites with Conservation Potential

Criteria used for the assessment of sites of conservation value are often inadequate to cope with skeletal ecosystems. For example newly colonised reclamation sites are rarely species-rich even when they contain some uncommon species. Above all, because the development of conservation interest involves the passage of time, it is essential that criteria are developed for assessing the validity and potential of restoration proposals as well as evaluating the results as seen on the ground. The goals are to allow planners to identify viable projects, and also to educate them in the methodology requirements that would suit both long and short term objectives. The following factors should be taken into account when considering which sites are worth devoting to conservation afteruse.

pH: High pH is usually a significant advantage in soils intended for habitat creation. Some of the most fascinating 'industrial habitats' have arisen on moisture retentive and highly alkaline wastes such as pulverised fuel ash from coal fired power stations. A high pH tends to encourage diversity in vegetation by limiting nutrient availability which in turn limits the invasion of competitive species. In the UK, limestone or chalk grassland habitats may have up to 40 species of plants per square metre. Low pH, below 5, may also reduce the vigour of aggressive species but there are relatively few species in the UK flora which can tolerate acidic conditions and species richness does not usually result. Of course species-richness is not the only measure that can be of importance. Habitats on acidic soils may support only a few, highly tolerant, species but these species may still be valuable or attractive.

Low Fertility: Nutrients and soil fertility are major factors which control plant community development. In particular the negative effects of over-fertility on conservation land are well understood. The management of nutrition will therefore be one of the greatest problems in successful habitat creation (Marrs & Gough, 1990). When discussing fertility it is necessary to take account of the habitat type to be created and the timescale that the project is planned for. Londo (in press) points out that the slower a spoil or subsoil is to revegetate, the more likely it will be to develop an interesting grassland flora. In reclamation work it is not usual to take such a long term view.

In long-term habitat creation schemes successional processes may also come into play. Ecology theory holds that as succession progresses, leading to woodland dominated by large forest tree species, there is an accumulation of living and dead biomass in the ecosystem. Increasingly nutrients are taken from the soil and become locked up in this biomass (Green, 1990). A succession that begins on a soil that is too fertile for species-rich grass may still end up as a woodland with a diverse species complement, although the process may take decades or centuries. On the other hand, succession which starts from a more infertile soil supporting species-rich grass may finish with a very stressed, and hence species poor, woodland.

Diversity in Topography and Soil Type: Ecologists recognise two types of environmental diversity which are termed alpha & beta. Á diversity is where there are high numbers of species present within any one community. ß diversity is where the environment is very patchy so that many different communities co-exist near each other in a complex mosaic. ß diversity will arise naturally where there is diversity in the landform and the substrate. Differences in moisture retention, fertility, and texture will all lead to the development of the different communities. These effects can be quite subtle. In a classic ecological experiment Harper et al (1969) showed that very minor alterations in soil surface treatment was enough to control the germination of different plant species. The value of environmental gradients also needs to be appreciated. Broad transition zones between different habitats (ecotones) are preferable to abrupt changes (Londo, in press).

Landform will affect the aspect of soil, the drainage patterns and the depth to the ground water table. All of these will interact with the soil type in order to encourage slightly different communities. Ideally some areas of a restoration site will be made poorly draining in order to encourage wetland communities. Inevitably a diverse topography may not be tolerable on all sites. In some cases it would still be possible to consider producing complex subsurface landforms which are then covered to an even grade by the top layer of the soil profile. This will be particularly effective where a subsoil is used with extreme drainage characteristics, such as a clay or a sand. Sowing a seed mix over such a diversity of soil types and treatments will lead to the development of very different vegetation communities. Alternatively a complex mosaic of plant community types, such as woodland, scrub, grassland etc., can be superimposed. This will increase the likelihood that some valuable communities will find a niche somewhere.

Niche Maintenance: Even in good examples of habitat creation it is likely that the initial species complement will only be a small subset of what would naturally be found in similar, long established, ecosystems. Ideally the habitats should gradually improve over time as additional plants and animals colonise. It is therefore important that the habitat should be kept 'open' so that new species are encouraged to invade. This can be done through disturbance introduced as part of the management. Traditional agricultural soil management has concentrated on ways of developing a good 'tilth' for sowing seed. A tilth is a uniform surface which ensures good contact between the soil and seed and encourages rapid and uniform germination. Once more, this may be exactly the wrong technique for habitat development. It may actually be better to have a soil which produces erratic germination.

Other criteria obviously need to be considered. The site should be safe and not present an environmental hazard in the absence of more fundamental treatment. Ideally it should be in close proximity to source of appropriate colonising species, although there is also social value from encouraging conservation afteruse in areas deficient in natural habitats. Finally there should be scope for adequate management where necessary. Many semi-natural habitats in the UK have developed as the result of management, and rely upon management to maintain their interest. The changes in farming practice which lead to farmers becoming destroyers rather than creators of habitats has produced a problem that conservationists still have not resolved. Lack of appropriate and adequate management is arguably a greater threat to protected habitats than any overt development disturbance. It is clearly pointless to create new habitats unless the necessary management is allowed for. Management may not need to be prolonged or recurrent, but may take the form of certain critical inputs to guide the succession.

Management Inputs

In the majority of reclamation schemes management, whilst accepted as important, has been seen as a largely routine and one-dimensional operation by which a target community is preserved once created. The possible rôle of management as the primary tool for habitat creation is rarely considered, yet many semi-natural habitats have been created by management patterns working over time. There needs to be more research into the effect of maintenance techniques as the major determinant of species colonisation and community development, so that processes such as cutting and gap formation can be used in a less empirical way.

The management of a new habitat is likely to differ from the management of a superficially similar but long established community. In new habitats the manager may be trying to encourage the movement towards a plagioclimax which has not yet been reached. There may therefore be a need to deal with species which belong to earlier successional stages or which are relicts from a previous land use. The community dynamics and resilience of a man-made community will also differ from an established semi-natural community. The large storage organs and extensive root mat found in old grasslands withstands disturbances such as poaching and is likely to be more resistant to weed invasion (Hopkins, 1989). Depending on the previous land use the soil in a new habitat may contain a large reservoir of buried seed or propagules of persistent and vegetatively spreading weeds, such as *Urtica spp.* or *Rumex spp.* Another characteristic of man made sites is that there is likely to have been a substantial degree of soil disturbance during preparation work. This will influence water relations in summer and winter, patterns of nutrient mineralisation and temperature fluctuations which in turn will encourage a ruderal flora (Londo, in press).

Minimal Restoration

Natural colonisation may take too long to meet the political and social objectives of a reclamation programme and it is likely that some inputs will be required. It is essential that any activities undertaken to encourage early results do not compromise the long term development of natural communities. The ideal is to rapidly reach the stage where communities of nature conservation interest can develop, shortening the stages of colonisation, succession and soil formation, but without raising productivity too much.

The management of nutrition is one of the greatest problems in successful habitat creation. Soil nutrient content is a major factor controlling plant community development and diversity and the negative effects of over-fertility on conservation land have been well documented (Green, 1990). On derelict land initial fertility is often chronically low and reclamation has nearly always been targeted towards increasing nutrient capital, yet it is obviously important not to destroy conservation potential in the process. Early vegetation establishment requirements may mean that some initial nutrient inputs are necessary, even where the target vegetation, such as *Calluna* heathland, may be very tolerant of infertility as an established community (EAU, 1989). Fertilisation may also allow rapid greening in order to reduce erosion, which would otherwise be a constraint on vegetation development. The desirable necessary size and likely fate of such inputs must be determined, given that it is often easier to raise fertility than it is to lower it. The use of nitrogen fixing plants in order to give early cover and to raise soil fertility is another common reclamation technique and again the manager needs to know how long these should be encouraged to remain as dominant parts of the community. New techniques need to be determined to meet conservation rather than agricultural targets, but this presupposes an understanding of the minimum nutrient capitals required by different ecosystems.

CASE STUDY - WOODLAND ESTABLISHMENT ON CHINA CLAY WASTE

The most intensively mined deposits of china clay in the UK stretch over 80km^2 to the north of St. Austell in Cornwall, with smaller workings on the southern edge of the Dartmoor National Park. The deposits are effectively bottomless and are never backfilled. Each tonne of kaolin generates eight of waste, tens of millions of tonnes of which are dumped each year in surrounding heaps that rise up in a series of terraces, individually up to 30m tall. Most reclamation carried out so far has produced low productivity grazing land. China clay waste consists of 66% gravel, 28% sand, 1% silt, less than 1% clay (Roberts et al, 1981). It is structureless and lacks binding organic matter and therefore is prone to water and wind erosion, aggravated by steep topography and exposure. Water retention is one third of a normal soil but water availability is high and in the moist climate of Cornwall water deficits usually only prove a problem for young plants. The sands have low ionic exchange properties and almost no organic matter. There are low stores of available nutrients. The waste is slow to weather, limiting the release of mineral nutrients and the development of a fine soil fraction. There are notable deficiencies of phosphorus, potassium, magnesium and calcium relative to normal healthy soils. However these are relatively easily corrected by fertilising and lime requirements are low. Factorial fertiliser experiments demonstrate, almost without exception, that nitrogen addition is fundamental to grass growth before any response to other fertilisers is achieved (Handley et al, 1978). Unlike other nutrients nitrogen can only be stored in soils in the long term as complex organic matter, hence total levels are only high in soils that have already supported plants or have had organic matter additions. Initial total nitrogen content on the waste is something like 1/300th to 1/1000th of that of a normal soil. Nitrogen build up is the critical factor in determining the development of a functioning ecosystem on these sites. However determining the necessary levels of nitrogen required to support a woodland can be difficult.

How Much Nitrogen is Necessary for Tree Growth?

Typical annual woodland nitrogen uptake rates can be found in the literature. Duvigneaud & Denaeyer De Smet (1970) quote the following figures: for conifers 56, 62, 60, 34 kg ha^{-1}; for broadleaves 99, 123, 123, 74, 91, 92, 104, 92, and 45 kg ha^{-1}. The lowest recorded annual uptake found in the literature was 2.6 kg ha^{-1} yr^{-1} for black spruce Picea mariana (Cole, 1981). These figures do not necessarily represent the required minimum, as this will also depend on the intended afteruse. Cole (1981) reports that ideal conifer growth for timber production requires net uptake in the order of 70-80 kg ha^{-1} yr^{-1}. If the end use is amenity/conservation then canopy closure may be all that is required, which could perhaps be provided by a value of about 10kg ha^{-1} yr^{-1}, with the proviso that low fertility may lower disease or pest resistance.

An alternative measure of fertility can be found from figures of total soil nitrogen beneath woodland. Carlyle (1986) found that over twenty sites, the minimum total soil N in conifer systems was 1753 kg ha^{-1}, the maximum was 7110 kg ha^{-1} and the mean 4117 kg ha^{-1}. In deciduous systems the minimum found was lower, 1380 kg ha^{-1}, the maximum 13800 kg ha^{-1} and the mean 6142 kg ha^{-1}. Again it is uncertain whether any of these figures represent true minima, which may be more accurately determined from studies of ecosystem development on primary habitats. Some studies have suggested that 1000 kg ha^{-1} may be needed in a primary soil to support colonisation by non-nitrogen fixing trees (Crocker & Major, 1955). Dancer et al (1977a) also found that on china clay waste natural broadleaved scrub species only form a notable part of the biomass at a soil level of 700 kg N ha^{-1}, and a mature broadleaf woodland seems to require a store of 1000 kg N ha^{-1}. Some woody plants were found at 350-500 kg N ha^{-1} but these were not a significant part of the biomass. If an annual mineralisation rate on these sites of 1/10-1/16 is assumed (Bradshaw, 1983), this would suggest uptake by the vegetation of approximately 50-100 kg N ha^{-1} yr^{-1}. Such figures are plausible as they are at the low end of the range suggested by Duvigneaud and Denaeyer De Smet (1970).

Although the values cannot be defined precisely, an order of magnitude can be determined. It would appear that about 100 kg N ha^{-1} yr^{-1} is required to provide for the needs of annual uptake and satisfactory woodland growth, and that this can be achieved in temperate conditions by release from a soil capital of 1000 kg N ha^{-1}.

Options for Nutrient Build-up.

Adding inorganic nitrogen fertilisers is at best a temporary solution to major nutrient deficiencies. To avoid toxicity on the skeletal, buffer deficient, china clay waste, the maximum addition of fast release fertiliser (in one application) should be roughly 50kg ha^{-1} of nitrogen. This is approximately equivalent to the annual mineralisation from a store of 800kg. Leaching losses can be huge but if there is a standing crop of vegetation, and climatic conditions are favourable, a large proportion of the nitrogen may be quickly utilised and converted into an organic form within the plants. The efficiency of the recycling of this organic nitrogen will depend on many factors. If the nitrogen levels added to the soil pool remain too low the organic matter produced will also tend to have a high carbon:nitrogen ratio and be slow to decompose. The annual mineralisation from an addition to the ecosystem of 50kg ha^{-1} may be only 1-3 kg ha^{-1}.

An alternative approach for reclamation is to boost the organic matter levels in the soil directly by adding a nutrient rich source such as sewage sludge. As a guide for calculation, if an organic material has 1% nitrogen content, applications of 10 tonnes Ha^{-1} should prove adequate.

The third option is to make use of nitrogen fixers which can survive and grow on deficient sites. These in turn build up the organic pool of nitrogen to a level where other plants can colonise and grow. The organic matter these produce has a low carbon:nitrogen ratio and hence begins to decompose and cycle rapidly. Depending on the substrate and climatic conditions annual nitrogen fixation rates can on china clay waste can vary between 26 kg ha^{-1} under Ulex to 185 kg ha^{-1} under Lupinus arboreus (Palaniappan et al, 1979; Skeffington & Bradshaw, 1981). The latter is equivalent to the release of nitrogen from an organic store of well over the critical 1000 kg ha^{-1}. However as a result of erosion, immobilisation in biomass, grazing and other losses, net annual soil N accumulation for the first 100 years may be as little as 10 kg ha^{-1} (Skeffington & Bradshaw, 1981). Eventually the colony is invaded by woody scrub and trees, particularly if Ca and P levels are low which keeps the sward open (Dancer et al, 1977a). A parallel example of the role of nitrogen fixers as precursors for other vegetation is given by Crocker and Major (1955) who quote that on average 40 kg N ha^{-1} yr^{-1} accumulates under Alnus on glacial moraines.

Obviously the most important consideration in the soil build up process is the actual rate of N fixation in the field as the target level of 1000 kg ha^{-1} could be reached within 10 years or take 100 or more. Small additions of P and Ca may have critical effects on performance (Roberts et al, 1981). Nitrogen is therefore only part of the story. A major determinant of plant productivity is often the phosphorus level of the soil. Unlike nitrogen, it is fairly easy to raise phosphorus levels on reclamation sites by fertilisation. However P additions must be carefully judged and it is essential not to add too much to the soil. This nutrient is highly immobile so that once the productivity of a system is raised it can be centuries before the effect wears off; in some cases the effect may be permanent. The levels of phosphorus also tend to control the activity and competitiveness of nitrogen fixers and can indirectly lead to a build up of this nutrient as well. On the other hand, adding nitrogen without phosphorus can lead to a short term improvement in productivity but the N may gradually be lost from the system. This prevents long term dominance by nutrient demanding species.

Where early impact is needed there is the possibility of using very localised phosphorus additions. For example plug-grown wildflowers can have some phosphate fertiliser already in the compost. If these are planted at a low density into a sward which has been sown onto an infertile soil the visual effect can be quite considerable, particularly as these individuals will have limited competition. However the net input of P into the site will still be very low and the chances of developing a species-rich sward in the long term will still be good.

CONCLUSIONS

Adapting restoration methodology to maximise conservation benefits is not a simple option; it requires a fundamental re-evaluation of methodology and also of preconceptions and assumptions of reclamation philosophy. If opportunities are not to be wasted, and if credible restoration proposals are to be forwarded in mitigation of mineral extraction, the technology needs to be as sophisticated as for the highest quality agricultural end use. Certain environmental conditions can be identified which are likely to lead to maximum biological diversity, although the timescale of the habitat development also needs to be taken into account. For political and social reasons it is essential to develop techniques for rapid greening of reclamation sites without compromising the long term conservation potential. Constraints to natural colonisation are likely to mean that plant introduction will be required, but there is the risk of creating artificial communities which will not succeed in the long term. This is a problem for evaluation of the quality of restoration proposals. Above all, the management of nutrient cycles, which has often been the key to land reclamation, will need to be adjusted to meet nature conservation rather than agronomic goals.

REFERENCES

1. Bradshaw, A.D. (1983) The Reconstruction of ecosystems. J. Appl. Ecol. 20: 1-17. Part Two.

2. Carlyle, J.C. (1986) Nitrogen cycling in forested ecosystems. Forestry Abstracts 47(5):307-336.

3. Cole, D.W. (1981) Nitrogen uptake and translocation by forest ecosystems. In: Clark, F.E. & Rosswall, T. (Eds). Terrestrial Nitrogen Cycles. Processes, Ecosystem Strategies and Management Impacts. Ecol. Bull. (Stockholm) 33:219-31.

4. Connell J.H. & Slatyer R.O. (1977) Mechanisms of succession in natural communities and their role in community stability and organisation. American Naturalist 122: 661-696.

5. Crocker, R.L. and Major, J. (1955) Soil development in relation to vegetation and surface age at Glacier Bay, Alaska. J. Ecol. 43:427-48.

6. Dancer, W.S., Handley, J.F. & Bradshaw, A.D. (1977) Nitrogen accumulation in kaolin mining wastes I. Natural communities. Plant and Soil 48:153-167.

7. Duvigneaud, P. & Denaeyer de Smet, S. (1970) Biological cycling of minerals in temperate deciduous forest. In: Reichle, D.F. (Ed) Ecological Studies 1. Temperate Forests. pp Springer Verlag, Berlin.

8. Environmental Advisory Unit (1988) Heathland Restoration. British Gas, Southampton.

9. Gemmell (1982) The origin and importance of industrial habitats. In: Urban Ecology. Bornkomm, R.; Lee, J.A. and Seaward, M.R.D. (Eds) Blackwells, Oxford. pp 33-39.

10. Gilbert O.L. (1989) The Ecology of Urban Habitats. Chapman & Hall.

11. Gilpin M.E. (1987) Experimental community assembly: competition, community structure and the order of species introductions. In: Jordan W.R. Gilpin M.E. & Aber J.D. (Eds) Restoration Ecology. Cambridge University Press. pp 151-162

12. Green, B.H. (1986) Controlling Ecosystems for Amenity. In: Bradshaw, A.D., Goode, D.A. and Thorp, E. (eds) Ecology and Design in Landscape. The 24th symposium of the British Ecological Society. Blackwells, Oxford. 195-210

13. Green, B.H. (1990) Countryside Conservation. 2nd Ed. Allen & Unwin, London.

14. Grime, J.P. (1979) Plant Strategies and Vegetation Processes. John Wiley, Chichester.

15. Handley, J.F., Dancer, W.S., Sheldon J.S. & Bradshaw A.D. (1978) The nitrogen problem in derelict land reclamation. In: Goodman, G.T. & Chadwick, M.J. (Eds) Environmental Management of Mineral Wastes, 215-235. Sijthoff & Nordhoff, Alphen, Netherlands.

16. Harper J.L., Williams J.T. & Sagar G.R. (1969) The Behavior of Seeds in Soil. In: Contemporary Readings In Ecology. A.S. Boughey (ed). Dickenson, California.

17. Hopkins J. (1989) Prospects for Habitat Creation. Landscape Design (179) 19-23.

18. Kendle A.D. (1992) The management of man-made habitats. Aspects of Applied Biology 29: The Management of Vegetation in Forestry, Amenity and Conservation Areas. Association of Applied Biologists, Wellesbourne. pp 25-32

19. Kendle A.D. & Bradshaw A.D. (1992) The Role of Nitrogen in Tree Establishment and Growth on Derelict Land. Arboricultural Journal.

20. Land Capability Consultants (1989) Cost Effective Management of Reclaimed Derelict Sites. DOE HMSO, London.

21. Londo G. (In press) Planting for Nature Gardens & Parks. Packard Publishing, Chichester.

22. Marrs R.H. & Gough M.W. (1990) Soil fertility - a problem for habitat restoration. In: Biological Habitat Reconstruction. G.P. Buckley (Ed). Belhaven, London. pp 29-44

23. Palaniappan, V.M., Marrs, R.H. & Bradshaw A.D. (1979) The effect of Lupinus arboreus on nitrogen status of china clay wastes. J. Appl. Ecol. 16:825-831.

24. Roberts, R.D., Marrs, R.H., Skeffington, R.A. & Bradshaw, A.D. (1981) Ecosystem development on naturally colonised china clay wastes, I. Vegetation changes and overall accumulation of organic matter and nutrients. J. Ecol 69:153-161.

25. Skeffington, R.A. & Bradshaw, A.D. (1981) Nitrogen accumulation in kaolin wastes in Cornwall, IV. Sward quality and the development of a nitrogen cycle. Plant and Soil 62:439-451.

26. Weins J.A. (1977) On competition and variable environments. American Scientist (68) 590-7.

USE OF NON-WOVEN GEOTEXTILE REINFORCED VEGETATED CHUTES AS COST
EFFECTIVE GRADE STABILIZATION STRUCTURES

Jeffrey P. Porter[1]   Fred Gasper[2]   James C. Dickie[3]   James R. Vosburgh[4]
Member ASAE

Grass is commonly used as a low-cost means of protecting the soil surface
against the erosive forces of flowing water. The major drawback of using
vegetation as the sole protection medium is that high flow velocities tend to
dislodge both soil and vegetative growth. By incorporating a non-woven
geotextile as a reinforcing material, soil erosion and vegetative detachment
are greatly reduced. The geotextile provides added shear and tensile strength
to the vegetative structure allowing relatively high flow rates. The concept
of using geotextiles as a soil-vegetative reinforcement has been used in the
past on grassed waterways (Hewlett, H.W.M. et al., 1987).

The geotextile reinforced vegetative chutes (GVC), as described in this paper,
provide a more aesthetically pleasing appearance than traditional mechanical
structures. Once adequate vegetative cover is established, it becomes
difficult to distinguish the GVC from the surrounding natural conditions.

Installation costs of GVC's are one-fourth to one-half that of pipe structures.
Cost savings are due to short installation time (1.5 hours) and low material
costs ($75).

SITE DESCRIPTION

The initial test sites for studying the effectiveness of using GVC's are
located in Section 8 of Hazelton Township along the Coon Creek Drain in
Shiawassee County, Michigan. The watershed is in conventionally tilled row
crops on agricultural land. A total of eight GVC's were installed at locations
of concentrated flow into the drain.

The soils are predominantly Berville loam on flat slopes (<0.5 percent).
Drainage area for each GVC is approximately 3.2 hectares (8.0 acres). Average
vertical drop from field level to ditch bottom is 1.2 meters (4.0 feet). Peak
discharge for each GVC, based on a 10-year frequency 24-hour storm duration
(USDA-SCS, 1977), was determined to be 0.2 cubic meters per second (cms) or 7.0
cubic feet per second (cfs).

DESIGN CRITERIA

Velocity design was obtained from the sod chute criteria (USDA-SCS, 1984). The
maximum allowable velocity is eight feet per second (2.4 meters per second).

---

1 Jeffrey P. Porter, Area Engineer, USDA-SCS, Burton, Michigan.
2 Fred Gasper, Assistant State Conservation Engineer, USDA-SCS, East Lansing,
Michigan.
3 James C. Dickie, District Conservationist, USDA-SCS, Owosso, Michigan.
4 James R. Vosburgh, District Conservationist, USDA-SCS, Lapeer, Michigan.

For calculating capacities of various GVC slopes, the energy equation (1) was used (USDA-SCS, 1956). The hydraulic radius was assumed to equal the mean flow depth. By incorporating the friction slope (2) into Eq.1, acceptable GVC slopes were determined. Manning's roughness coefficient was derived from the velocity-hydraulic radius curves with a "D" retardance (USDA-SCS, 1954). This assumes a short vegetative cover, and vegetation bending from the effects of high velocities. Flow depths do not exceed 0.15 meters (0.5 feet) so that the "D" retardance criteria is maintained.

$$v_1^2/2g + d_1 + s_0 l = v_2^2/2g + d_2 + s_f l \tag{1}$$

where:

v = mean velocity
d = depth of flow
s_o = slope of channel
s_f = friction slope
l = length of reach

$$s_f = (n^2 \, v_m^2)/(2.2082 \, r_m^{1.33}) \tag{2}$$

where:

v_m = mean velocity in a reach
n = Manning's roughness coefficient
r_m = mean hydraulic radius in a reach

Based on this criteria, maximum GVC capacity is 0.06 cms per meter (2.0 cfs per foot) bottom width for slopes less than 33 percent. On steeper GVC slopes, between 33 and 50 percent, capacity is limited to 0.04 cms per meter (1.5 cfs per foot) bottom width.

The GVC is reinforced with a non-woven geotextile. This geotextile serves a threefold purpose. First, it provides an erosion resistant barrier until the vegetation becomes established. In the initial stages of grass growth, an unprotected soil surface would be highly susceptible to the erosive nature of any runoff event. Second, the interwoven nature of the soil, geotextile and vegetation work together to provide a more stable channel than vegetation alone. Non-reinforced vegetated areas are more likely to have individual plants dislodged due to flowing water than reinforced vegetated water courses such as GVC's (Hewlett, 1987). As the fibrous root systems grow through the geotextile into the soil, an interwoven vegetative mat is created. The vegetation in conjunction with the geotextile function as a single unit instead of individual plants. Finally, the geotextile acts as a filter to limit soil movement from under the geotextile.

The non-woven geotextile is required to meet the subsurface drainage criteria under the Michigan Geotextile Construction Specification (USDA-SCS, 1990). Heat bonding is allowed on one side of the material. Heat bonding on both sides may lower the geotextile porosity and hinder root penetration. The smoother fabric surface created by heat bonding also increases the likelihood of the seed mixture rolling or sliding off the geotextile material. As a result, any heat bonded face is placed in direct contact with the soil.

The geotextile is to weigh from 99 to 156 grams per square meter (3.5 to 5.5 ounces per square yard). This weight criteria is an indirect indication of the geotextile thickness. The thickness limits are set to meet geotextile strength and root penetration requirements.

Work by Hewlett, 1987, has shown that root penetration through the geotextile layer reduces as the thickness of overlying soil is increased. For these GVC's, the grass mixture was sown directly on the geotextile material. No soil was placed over the seed.

357

Two different seed mixtures with varying combinations of perennial ryegrass, smooth bromegrass, tall fescue and creeping red fescue were used on the trial GVC's. Further GVC installations have used the following seed mixtures in kilograms per 100 square meters (pounds per 100 square feet): 1.2 (0.25) perennial ryegrass, 2.4 (0.5) smooth bromegrass, 2.4 (0.5) tall fescue and 2.4 (0.5) creeping red fescue.

Either an erosion control blanket (ECB) or straw mulch with erosion control netting (ECN) is placed over the geotextile after the seed is sown. This mulch assists in keeping the seed from rolling off the geotextile. It also helps to maintain moisture around the seed to enhance germination.

INSTALLATION PROCEDURE

The most critical element of installing these GVC's is to insure good soil-geotextile contact for adequate seed germination and root penetration. Air pockets between the two surfaces prevent root contact with the soil, and as a result poor vegetative cover.

Following initial excavation for the GVC, hand shaping is necessary to reduce soil irregularities. If the soil has herbicide contamination, it should be removed and be replaced with an uncontaminated soil. Rocks and soil clods larger than 13 millimeters (0.5 inches) must also be removed. Upstream and downstream trenches are dug to anchor the geotextile.

Once the seedbed and trenches are prepared, fertilizer is applied to the soil surface. Next, the geotextile material is placed directly over the soil. The upper edge of the geotextile is secured to the soil with staples. Grass seed is then evenly distributed over the geotextile. It is also necessary to seed all other disturbed areas. The mulching material whether ECB or mulch with ECN is placed over the seed and geotextile. Staple through the mulch and geotextile to secure the GVC to the soil surface. Spacing of staples is on a 0.3 to 0.6 meters (1.0 to 2.0 feet) grid. Any areas with the geotextile not in contact with the soil must also be stapled. The upstream trench is filled with on-site soil material. Use of granular material, such as sand or gravel, may encourage water to flow under the structure. The lower trench is filled with rock riprap. Average rock diameter is four inches (102 millimeters). A final inspection is made to ensure soil to geotextile contact. Staple non-contact areas as necessary.

If multiple geotextile sheets are required, a lapping procedure is to be followed. Two different techniques have been used. The first method shingles the geotextile perpendicular to the slope. Minimum overlap of geotextile sheets is 75 millimeters (3.0 inches). The second approach uses a trench to anchor the sheets together. Ends of two geotextile sheets are placed in the trench and both are draped downstream. The trench is backfilled, and the upper section of geotextile is turned upstream. Anchor the geotextile to the soil as described above.

MAINTENANCE

Periodic inspection should be performed to ensure adequate vegetative growth. Over time, the geotextile tends to shrink and pulls away from the soil. These areas must be restapled and reseeded. A limited number of GVC's have incurred rodent damage. If significant damage is encountered, the GVC may need to be replaced.

Since these GVC's are generally installed along agricultural land, chemical applications must be monitored. Some herbicides prevent vegetative growth. Some of the GVC's have shown evidence of sedimentation at both the upstream and downstream edges. This sediment may need to be removed if the vegetation becomes buried. If the accumulated sediment does not interfere with the performance of the GVC, it may be left in place as it blocks ultraviolet light. This helps maintain the long term integrity of the geotextile. Adequate upstream protection from high sediment laden runoff is recommended.

PERFORMANCE

Over a year and one-half since the trial GVC's were installed, no evidence of erosion was found. Even if the vegetation does not germinate or small patches of vegetation are dislodged, the geotextile protects the underlying soil from erosion.

Vegetative cover for each GVC exceeded 90 percent. The trial GVC's did not reveal any significant difference in vegetative growth between the two seeding mixtures. Roots below the geotextile were discovered to a depth of 152 millimeters (6.0 inches).

Much of the vegetation was laid down during runoff events. This provided better ground cover than standing vegetation alone. Bare areas were covered during these runoff periods. This vegetation bending reduces the effect of surface irregularities which could result in higher drag forces during flow events (Hewlett, 1987).

No appreciable degradation of the geotextile was evident. As the percentage of cover increases, the geotextile is provided additional protection against ultraviolet light.

Limited data is available as to the most appropriate lapping procedure. Due to the additional thickness, shingling of the geotextile may reduce root penetration.

FUTURE APPLICATIONS

Studies are continuing on the use and application of GVC's. Areas to be considered are lighter (sandier) soils, higher flow velocities and wider chute bottom widths.

SUMMARY

The installation of GVC's in Michigan have proven successful. These GVC's have shown that vegetation used in conjunction with geotextiles serve as an effective grade stabilization structure alternative. Major advantages of the GVC's are low installation costs and aesthetically pleasing appearance.

359

REFERENCES

1. Hewlett, H.W.M., Boorman, L.A. and Bramley, M.A., "Design of Reinforced Grass Waterways", Construction Industry Research and Information Association - Report 116, 1987.

2. USDA-SCS, Engineering Field Manual Chapter 6 - Structures, 1984.

3. USDA-SCS, Handbook of Channel Design for Soil and Water Conservation - Technical Paper 61, 1954.

4. USDA-SCS, Michigan Construction Specification MI-165, Geotextiles, 1990.

5. USDA-SCS, Michigan Technical Guide Section IV, Grade Stabilization Structure, 1977.

6. USDA-SCS, National Engineering Handbook Section 5 - Hydraulics, 1956.

SITE PREPARATION USING GOATS

Peter R. Mount

In this day of increasing environmental sensitivity by the general public, it is essential that the search for acceptable alternatives to offensive management tools be accelerated. In Alabama there is a growing emphasis on goats--both Angora goats for mohair production and Spanish goats or brush goats for meat production. At Tuskegee University there is a four point approach to utilizing goats for forest management purposes:

(1) Eradication of unwanted species--a demonstration project on the Tuskegee Nation Forest is designed to eliminate Kudzu without the use of chemicals. Basic findings are that eight to ten goats per acre grazed from mid-July to frost for elimination of edible vegetation for three consecutive years will be effective.

(2) Control of unwanted species in pine plantations--a demonstration project has shown that goats like pine and they can not be used until the pine are at least ten feet tall.

(3) Site preparation prior to timber harvest--A research project has been designed and grant applied for; however, even though this shows the most promise it has the least work. Observation of goats in mature timber stands reinforces the idea that this may be an alternative to mechanical or chemical site preparation.

(4) Site preparation on clearcut areas--This paper provides preliminary results of a goat-site preparation project in Southwest Alabama.

The problem is to find an alternative to mechanical site preparation which causes excessive soil loss on highly errodible soils in hilly terrain, to find a substitute for the growing use of herbicides and the perception by the general public that this is polluting the environment, and to find something to replace fire with its attendant smoke problems.

The suggested solution is to utilized browsing as opposed to grazing animals to eliminate the vegetation on recent clearcut areas. A project on an 80 acre tract in Marengo County, Alabama is testing the effectiveness of Angora and Spanish goats to do the site clearing. The 80 acre block has been broken into ten compartments each utilizing portable electric fencing. Five different types of fencing are being compared--each capable of carrying 3600 volts for one mile without a voltage drop.

In each compartment a transect line three feet wide and between 520 and 700 feet long was used to determine the species association, biomass availability and dietary preference. Monthly samples of leaves from the thirty most abundant species were analyzed for seasonal changes in nutrient composition. Monthly water samples were collected to determine if any change in water quality occurred because of the grazing. Animal health--weights, parasite problems, predator control and hair quality are monitored weekly by the project veterinarian.

Jokingly, it is hoped that the project will demonstrate that it is profitable for local people to enter the "Rent-A-Goat" business to do site preparation work to convert low productive hardwood areas into highly profitable pine plantations. Dr. Rod Bushey, an economist with the Southern Forest Experiment Station in New Orleans, is monitoring all cost and return items to determine what it would cost for a company to use goats to do the site prep job.

Preliminary results are favorable. The vegetation analysis showed a range in early spring from a half ton of edible biomass per acre to a late season high of almost four tons per acre. Biomass determinations were made by utilizing

---

Peter R. Mount, Professor, Extension Forester, Tuskegee University, Tuskegee, Alabama

field weights and comparing to height, crown spread, crown length, stem diameter, origin and species. The only factor necessary to explain the greatest degree of variability was height. The addition of other factors did not significantly improve the biomass determination.

When the goats were introduced to the study area, twice a month measurements were made to determine dietary preference. The first species eaten were:

Bicolar Lespedeza
Sumac
Devils Walking Stick
Greenbrier
American Beauty Bush

those which were next eaten were:

Cucumber
Sassafras
Muscadine (Wild Grape)
Yellow Poplar
Blackberry

lower on the the preference scale were:

Hickory
Elm

the lowest on the menu were:

Sweet Gum
Redbud
Beech
Holly
Dogwood

It is unfortunate that sweet gum which is the most prevalent species is also one of the least desired in goat diets-regardless of the species of goat.

The vegetation began to appear thin after two weeks and trails from the shelter to the grazing sites developed. After four weeks even some of the least desired species began to show signs of browsing. At first the goats ate to the height they could reach without standing on their hind legs but as favored foods became scare they began to ride down small trees, chew the bark off, and to stand on their hind legs to reach available browse. As this is being written, the grazing is only one month old and total effectiveness has not yet been determined. It does appear promising,

DRILLING WASTE DISPOSAL IN ALBERTA

A FIELD MANUAL

DAVID A. LLOYD*

ABSTRACT

Oil and gas drilling wastes are physically and chemically complex. The land surface, which is impacted by these waste materials, is equally as complex. The waste materials are generally made of even sand, silt and clay texture proportions. The wastes often have high concentrations of salt and excessive amounts of oils in them. Land spreading or land farming these materials can be done successfully if careful planning and analyses of the waste components and the receiving land are completed before disposal occurs. Components of a drilling waste disposal manual are described to illustrate office and field procedures required to successfully dispose of drilling wastes on the land surface. Equations are presented to deal with waste, soil and volume constituents and the land area required to determine appropriate spread rates.

DRILLING WASTE DISPOSAL MANUAL IN ALBERTA

Oil and gas drilling wastes are complex and varied. They have unique physical and chemical properties. The receiving environment for disposal of these wastes is also complex and varied. To minimize environmental damage, the physical and chemical parameters of the waste materials, as well as those of the receiving environment, need to be determined. The environmental impact of land-based drilling waste disposal (i.e., surface spreading) can be minimized following a prescribed set of procedures which are outlined below. These procedures are taken from a "DRAFT" manual entitled "A Field Manual for the Management and disposal of Drilling Wastes" (Macyk et al., 1990). This is a revision of an existing manual that was produced by the Reclamation Research Technical Advisory Committee (RRTAC 81-1). The objectives for the revised manual are as follows:

* D.A. Lloyd, Section Head, Industrial Land Management, Land Management Branch, Public Lands Division, Department of Forestry, Lands and Wildlife, Government, Province of Alberta, Edmonton, Alberta, Canada.

a) develop a more definitive drilling waste disposal decision flow chart;
b) develop a glossary and simplify terminology used in the manual;
c) indicate what soil and waste parameters could be tested in the field, why they should be tested, and the appropriate procedures to be used;
d) refine the calculations used to determine sump contents;
e) provide critical levels for parameters;
f) condense and clarify the checklist for fieldmen;
g) expand on the guidelines for obtaining representative samples;
h) develop a computer program that will allow users to do the calculations prescribed in the manual.

THE OVERVIEW

There are four phases associated with the disposal of oil and gas drilling waste that must be considered before drilling has commenced. Consideration of all phases at the same time allows for proper planning, acquisition of information and consideration of disposal needs. The four phases are shown in Figure 1.

Sump Location Evaluation

At least two major steps are involved in properly assessing the location for the sump before the final location is determined and excavation begins.

Office Information Gathering

All existing information should be examined and evaluated before making a field visit so that the most logical site for a sump can be determined. Reports, air photos, maps, bore hole logs and survey data must be reviewed for information on groundwater, land use, soils, surface water, surficial geology, topography and vegetation. Assimilation of this information will allow for a good understanding of the conditions (wellsite field) before a sump site is selected.

Field Inspection

Field inspection may be cursory or detailed, depending on the quality of information reviewed in the office and the size of the sump being planned. If the sump is large, a hydrological investigation may be required. Soils in the area should always be classified to the Canadian Soil Classification designated Great Group if possible. The surficial geology should be assessed so that problems from contaminant migration can be mitigated. Vegetation species and land use activity can be checked against the office information and documented where information is lacking. Topography considerations such as degree and length of slope and proximity of the proposed sump to water channels must be determined. The site will be rated based on its limitations or potential problems which can be mitigated by good management. The ability of a site to accommodate sump disposal will depend on the site parameters and the mud type being disposed.

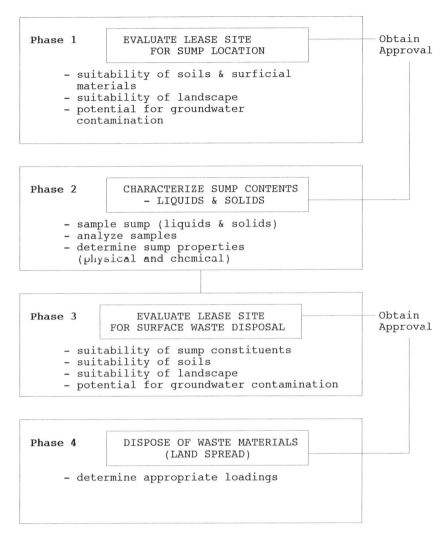

Figure 1. Phases in the management and land-based disposal of drilling wastes

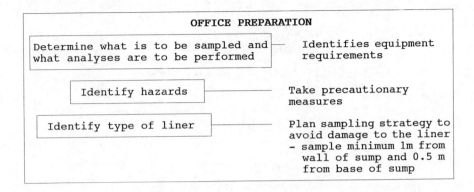

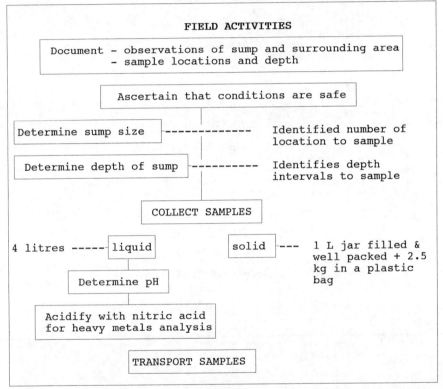

Figure 2. Outline of activities related to the sampling of drilling wastes.

Waste Characterization - Sampling

Figure 2 outlines the activities related to sampling of drilling
wastes. There are four main components that must be covered in
this process.

Office Preparation

As much information about the waste material should be obtained as
possible before physical sampling begins. The mud type and
estimated volume, hole depth, special additives, mud separation
techniques, presence or absence of sump liners, weather problems
(excess rain) start-up, disposal date and required sampling
analyses can all be obtained before the sump is sampled. A
sampling strategy should be developed prior to actual sampling.

Safety Precaution

There is a certain amount of risk involved in sampling a sump.
These risks can be lowered by using precautions, such as:

- never work alone;
- wear eye protection, protective clothing and good
  rubberized hand protection;
- keep away from sump edge;
- use proper equipment such as boats secured by a line to
  the top of the sump pit bank;
- ensure that ice coverage is sufficiently thick on liquid
  sumps during winter conditions; and
- avoid working directly on the surface of solid waste
  sumps.

Equipment

For safety and to facilitate proper sampling, appropriate sampling
equipment must be used. Table 1 outlines equipment that has been
used effectively.

Field Procedures

Both the solid and liquid components must be sampled since each
component has unique characteristics. Sump size dictates the
number of samples that must be taken. For example, if the sump
area is less than or equal to 500 m^2, then a maximum of 5 locations
should be sampled to be combined into one composite sample. For
sumps >500m^2, one location for each 100m^2 should be sampled to a
maximum of 10 samples prior to preparing the composite. For the
liquid phase, the entire liquid depth should be sampled at 5
location and equal amounts from each of the samples combined to
make one composite sampled.

For laboratory analysis, one litre of sample should be placed in an
acid washed glass jar with a teflon lid and 4L of sample should be
placed in a clear plastic container.

For the solid phase the entire depth is also colleted at 5 or more
locations (depending upon sump area) to combine into one composite
sample. Again a 1L acid washed glass jar well packed with waste
and capped with a teflon lid and 2.5 kg in a clear plastic bag is
required. To minimize puncture, material should be double or
triple bagged.

Table 1. Equipment requirements for sampling drilling waste material

LIQUID	SOLID

LIQUID

- boat or dinghy, and safety equipment
- ice auger (frozen sites)
- discrete sampler or pump device
- surgical or thicker rubber gloves
- dilute 5% nitric acid, for rinsing containers
- distilled water
- towels
- permanent markers
- labels - identification
      - transportation
- sample containers
  -    heavy metal analyses, plastic bottles and lids
  -    organics analyses, glass bottles with non-plastic lids
  -    biological tests, glass bottles with Teflon lids

SOLID

- shovels, augers, spatulas
- backhoe or suspension device (non-trafficable sites)
- surgical or thicker rubber gloves
- distilled water
- towels
- permanent markers
- labels - identification
      - transportation
- sample containers
  -    heavy metal analyses, plastic bags or plastic pails lined with clear plastic, with lids
  -    organics analyses, 1 litre glass jars with non-plastic lids

368

Waste Characterization – Analysis

A full characterization of the liquid and solid phase waste material would include the analyses listed in Table 2. These parameters are necessary to clearly evaluate the characteristics of the waste material.

Surface Waste Disposal Evaluation

The information used to determine the optimum location for a sump on a lease site can also be used to evaluate the suitability of an area for surface disposal of drilling wastes. The office information, field inspection and environmental considerations, such as soil characteristics, vegetation and landscape relative to the mud type, must all be considered when evaluating a surface disposal option. Coarse textured soils may be more appropriate for disposal of muds than fine and extremely fine textures. Acid soils may be more acceptable for salt muds and freshwater muds, whereas alkaline soils are poor for any mud.

Topography, proximity to surface and groundwater and vegetation types make the selection of a disposal site more complex. A more complete discussion of the interactive factors is presented in the manual.

Computer Program

A computer program has been developed to help determine the optimum surface disposal rate required for muds based on the most limiting factor. The program is currently being tested to refine the calculations that need to be done. Some basic calculations that are completed by computer are as follows:

369

Table 2. Analyses required for characterization of drilling wastes

LIQUID	SOLID
pH	Water content
Electrical Conductivity (EC)	pH
Calcium (Ca)	<u>Saturated paste and paste extract</u>
Magnesium (Mg)	pH
Sodium (Na)	Electrical Conductivity (EC)
Potassium (K)	Calcium (Ca)
Chloride (Cl)	Magnesium (Mg)
Sulfate (SO$_4$)	Sodium (Na)
Carbonate (CO$_3$)	Potassium (K)
Bicarbonate (HCO$_3$)	Chloride (Cl)
Nitrate (NO$_3$)	Sulfate (SO$_4$)
Ammonium (NH$_4$)	Nitrate (NO$_3$)
	Ammonium (NH$_4$)
Total dissolved solids (TDS)	Sodium Adsorption Ratio (SAR)
	(calculated)
Sodium Adsorption Ratio (SAR)	Elemental Constituents
(calculated)	(Al, Cr, Fe, V, Ti, Cd, Cu, Pb,
	Zn, Mn, Li, Sr, Ba, S, Mo, Ni,
Total suspended solids (TSS)	Se, As, Co, Si)
Total organic carbon (TOC)	Total carbon
Elemental Constituents	CaCO$_3$ equivalent
(Al, Cr, Fe, V, Ti, Cd,	
Cu, Pb, Zn, Mn, Li, Sr,	Acid neutralizing capacity
Ba, S, Mo, Ni, Se, As,	
Co, Si)	Bulk Density
Microtox bioassay	Particle size
Trout bioassay	Cation exchange capacity, exchangeable cations,
	Base Saturation percentage (calculated)
	Total elemental analysis
	Mineralogy
	Plant available elements
	Oil content
	Oil fractionation (acid, base, neutral fractions)
	- followed by GC-MS
	Microtrox bioassay
	Trout bioassay

1) Waste Content of Sump liquid

$$Total_{(Li)} = C_{Li} \bullet V_L \bullet 0.001$$

where C_{Li} in the concentration of element i in the liquid phase, mg/L;
V_L is the volume of sump liquid phase, m³; and
0.001 is a conversion factor for units.

2) Waste content of sump solid phase

$$Total_{(si)} = V_s \bullet C_{si} \bullet \frac{D_{bw}}{1 + \frac{P_w}{100}} \bullet 0.001$$

where C_{si} is the concentration of element i in the solid phase as determined by total elemental analysis, mg/kg;
V_s is the volume of sump solid phase, m³;
D_{bw} is the wet bulk density of the solid phase, g/cm³;
P_w is the water content of the solid phase, %; and
0.001 is a conversion factor for units.

3) Disposal Area determination

a) Total area

$$A_{(total)} = A_s + A_L$$

where A_s is the area required for surface spreading by the solid phase, ha; and
A_L is the area required for surface spreading by the liquid phase, ha.

b) Liquid phase spread area

$$A_L = max(A_{Li,}) \text{ where } A_{Li} = \frac{Total_{(Li)}}{L_L}$$

where A_{Li} is the area required to spread the liquid phase of the waste based on the amount of element i in the liquid phase, ha;
$Total_{(Li)}$ is the total amount of element i in the liquid phase of the waste, kg; and
L_L is the regulatory limit on element i, kg/ha.

c) Solid phase spread area

$$A_s = max(A_{si,}) \text{ where } A_{si} = \frac{Total_{(si)}}{L_s}$$

where A_{si} is the area required to spread the liquid phase of the waste based on the amount of element i in the liquid phase, ha;
$Total_{(si)}$ is the total amount of element i in the liquid phase of the waste, kg; and
L_s is the regulatory limit on element i, kg/ha.

d) Spread Rate

$$Spread\ Rate_{(L)} = \frac{V_L}{A_L}; \quad Spread\ Rate_{(s)} = \frac{V_s}{A_s}$$

where all terms have been defined previously.

371

CONCLUSION

The material presented above is a brief description of the steps described in the much more detailed disposal manual that is being produced by the Alberta Research Council in Alberta. Information in the manual must still be field-tested to determine its completeness and usability. The manual should be finalized at the end of 1992.

Alberta regulatory limits on drilling waste disposal are still in the preparation stage. The methods and procedures outlined above are guidelines only; waste disposal in Alberta does not necessarily occur according to these procedures.

REFERENCES

1. Macyk, T.M., S.A. Abboud, D.B. Cheel, <u>A Field Manual for the Management and Disposal of Drilling Wastes</u> 1990, Unpublished report prepared for the Alberta Land Conservation and Reclamation Council, Reclamation Research Technical Advisory Committee, 69 pp.

2. Leskiw, L.A., T.L. Dabrowshi, B.J. Rutherford, D. Hamilton, <u>Disposal of Drilling Wastes</u> 1987, Alberta Land Conservation and Reclamation Report RRTAC 87-1, 188 pp.

DESIGN OF THICKENING PONDS OPERATING IN THE ZONE SETTLING REGIME

P. Diplas[*]   A. Papanicolaou[*]

INTRODUCTION

Results of laboratory settling tests on slurries are frequently used in the design of settling ponds and slurry thickeners that operate in a continuous mode. Under static conditions, slurry thickening occurs as a result of the submerged weight of the slurry particles, which compacts the particles and exudes pore water from the slurry. Figure 1 presents a typical settling curve obtained from a laboratory-cylinder settling test with a mixture of intermediate solids concentration. In these tests, a homogeneous slurry is introduced into a graduated cylinder, and the distance from the bottom of the cylinder to the interface between the slurry and the overlying clear supernatant water(the so-called mudline height) is measured at subsequent times. Three different types, or regimes, of thickening, generally are distinguished during the settling process, as shown in Fig.1. In the zone - settling regime, slurry thickening results principally from the hindered (by the proximity of the adjacent particles) settling of the sediment particles through the water. A distinct interface -the mudline- rapidly forms between the slurry and the overlying supernatant. In the zone - settling regime, the mudline settles at a nearly constant velocity. At the other extreme of the settling curve, in the compression regime, the slurry has reached such a high solids concentration that interparticle bridging forms. Consolidation in this regime involves seepage expulsion of pore water from the slurry. Consequently, the rate of consolidation and the velocity of the mudline are strongly dependent on the solids concentration of the slurry and the particle-size distribution. In the transition regime the mudline velocity is regulated by both the hindered settling and the rate of pore-water expulsion from the slurry.

---

[*] P.Diplas, Assistant Professor, and A. Papanicolaou, Research Assistant, Civil Engineering Dept., Virginia Polytechnic Institute and State University, Blacksburg, VA 24061.

The present work reports the results of laboratory tests on the settling rates of slurries with intermediate to high initial solids concentration. More specifically, the influence of the slurry height and initial concentration on the zone settling velocity are examined. The significance of these results on the approach commonly employed for the design of slurry thickeners is also mentioned.

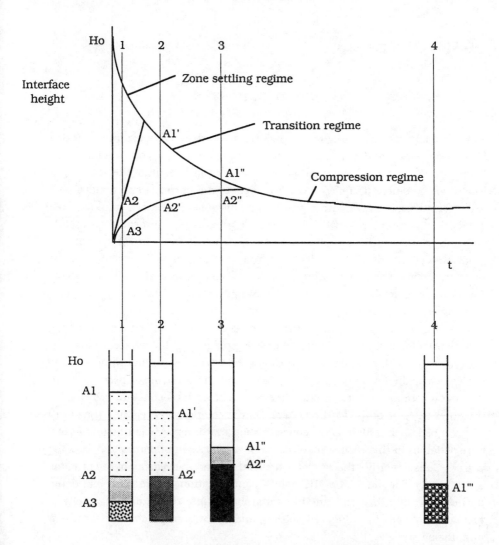

Figure 1. Typical cylinder-test settling curve.

RESULTS OF LABORATORY SETTLING TESTS

Tests in graduated cylinders were performed in the laboratory to examine the effect of slurry depth on the settling of a suspension of intermediate solids concentration. Glacial till, with particles finer than 2mm, was used for the solids in the mixture. The result of a grain - size analysis of this material is shown in Fig.2. Pychnometer tests yielded a specific gravity of 2.65 for the glacial till.

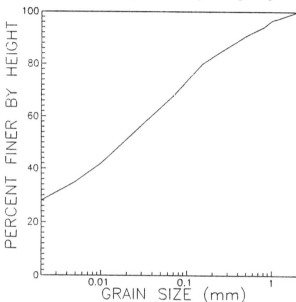

Figure 2. Grain - size distribution of the glacial till used in the settling tests.

Three graduated glass cylinders were utilized in the tests. All cylinders had the same internal diameter of 7.0 cm, and heights of 26 cm, 52 cm, and 274 cm respectively. The corresponding slurry volumes tested in these cylinders were 1lt, 2lt, and 10.5lt. Settling tests were made at initial solids contents of 15%, 20%, 25%, 30%, and 40% by weight. A three - minute stirring time was used in the preparation of the slurry. All tests were carried out at a slurry temperature of 22 °C. The duration of each test ranged from 26 hrs to 100 hrs. Table 1 presents the zone-settling regime mudline velocities, u, obtained from the tests, the duration of each test, and the slurry solids content at the

TABLE 1

Sample height	15 *			20 *			25 *			30 *			40 *	
	U	T1	C1	U	T1	C1	U	T1	C1	U	T1	C1	U **	T1	C1
26 cm	12.42	46	47	7.08	39	48	5.42	46	51	3.63	50	54		96	56
26 cm	10.92	46	47	6.56	39	48	5.03	46	51	3.69	50	54		96	55
52 cm	10.08	46	45	6.24	40	47	4.58	46	49	3.62	50	51		96	50
52 cm	9.52	46	45	5.7	40	47	4.58	46	49	3.55	50	51		96	49
274 cm	6.95	40	40	4.35	82	43	4.25	98	44	3.64	504	61		95	53

The above results are obtained from the cylinder settling tests with 3min stirring time.

* The initial solids content % by weight.
** For initial solids content there was no zone-settling regime present; thus no constant velocity values exist for these tests.

U = zone-settling -regime velocity in cm/hr.

T1 = test duration in hr.

C1 = final solids content in % by weight.

end of the test. To investigate the reliability of the results, four settling tests were repeated from new material. A comparison of the settling tests under identical conditions revealed a variation of less than + 10 % or -10% in the measured settling velocity. It is quite clear from the data presented in Table 1, that the two most important factors affecting the magnitude of the zone settling velocity are the initial solids content and the height of the column. For slurries with initial solids concentration up to 30% by weight, the zone settling velocity decreases with increasing initial solids content. The suspensions with 40% initial solids concentration did not exhibit a zone settling regime. An increase in the column height resulted in a decrease in the zone settling velocity for a given solids concentration. However, the influence of the column height declined with increasing initial solids content, and disappeared for an initial concentration of 30%. It is therefore evident from the above, that the common practice of using settling rates for the design of slurry thickeners that are based on tests carried out in 1lt cylinders, will inevitably lead to erroneous results.

The final (at the end tests) solids content of the slurry varied from about 40% to 56% solids by weight. Typically, it increased with duration of test, and with initial concentration. A special test than ran for three weeks yielded a concentration in excess of 60%. Depending on the particular application, the desirable solids content at the bottom of the container will dictate whether gravity thickening is appropriate or not. For example, typical solids content required for grouting operations is close to 55% by weight. The present results suggest that careful design and operation of setting ponds can provide thickened slurry of sufficiently high solids concentration for use as grout.

CONCLUSIONS

The height of a slurry, as well as its initial solids content, strongly influence the velocity of the mudline during the zone settling regime. It is therefore suggested that the settling rates used for the design of a thickening pond should be obtained from laboratory tests performed on graduated cylinders with a height identical to that of the pond. These tests should be carried out with slurries of various initial solids concentrations that represent the whole range of slurries expected to enter the settling pond. The results of these tests should identify the most critical settling rate for the design of the pond.

Author Index